John Kirby

The Suffolk Traveller

Second Edition

John Kirby

The Suffolk Traveller
Second Edition

ISBN/EAN: 9783337211707

Printed in Europe, USA, Canada, Australia, Japan

Cover: Foto ©Andreas Hilbeck / pixelio.de

More available books at **www.hansebooks.com**

THE SUFFOLK TRAVELLER.

First Published

By Mr. JOHN KIRBY,

Of WICKHAM-MARKET,

Who took an actual Survey of the whole County,
In the Years 1732, 1733, and 1734.

The SECOND EDITION,

With many Alterations and large Additions,

By SEVERAL HANDS.

LONDON:

Printed for J. SHAVE, at the *Stationer's Arms* in the Butter-Market, *Ipswich*; and sold by T. LONGMAN, in *Pater-noster Row*, London.

M,DCC,LXIV.

[iii]

A LIST of SUBSCRIBERS.

SIR Joseph Ayloffe, Baronet.
Sir Thomas Allen, Baronet.
Nathaniel Acton, of Bramford, Esq;
William Adair, of Flixton, Esq;
Mr. Robert Adams, of Woodbridge, Merchant.
The Rev. Mr. Lancaster Adkin.
John Affleck, of Dalham, Esq;
Jonathan Aldham, of Manningtree, Esq;
The Rev. Mr. Aldrich, of Stowmarket.
The Rev. Mr. Allen, of Blunderston.
Gilbert Alex, of Camberwell, Esq;
Mr. Jeremiah Alrich, of Woodbridge.
Mr. Robert Ansell, of Milden.
Sampson Arnold, of Beccles, Esq;
Mr. William Arnold, of Newport, Isle of Wight.
The Rev. Mr. Arrow, of Lowestoft.
Thomas Arrowsmith, of Bungay, Gent.
Mr. Joshua Arthy, of Groton.
George Ashby, of Thornham, Esq;
Thomas Ashhurst, of Castle-Hedingham, Esq;
The Rev. Mr. Aspin, of Hartest.
Samuel Atkinson, Esq; two Copies.
Mr. John Ayton, of Metfield.
Mr. John Ayton, of Ipswich.

Sir John Barker of Sproughton, Bart.
Sir John Blois, Bart. High Sheriff of this County.
Sir Thomas Charles Bunbury, Bart. of Barton, one of the Knights of this Shire, two Copies.
The Rev. Mr. Nicholas, of Baylham.
Mr. Bacon, of Bricet.
Mr. Samuel Bacon, of Ipswich.
Mr. William Bacon, of Thelnetham.
Mr. Thomas Baker, of Wickham-Market.

A List of Subscribers.

Mr. Andrew Baldry, of Ipswich, Painter.
Mr. Robert Barber, of Freffingfield.
Mr. William Barnard, of Ipswich, Ship-builder.
The Rev. Mr. Barnwell, of Lawshall.
Mr. Richard Battley, of Ipswich.
The Rev. Mr. Baynes, of Stonham-Aspall.
The Rev. Mr. William Baynes.
Mr. William Beals of Melford.
William Beckford, of Baliol College, Oxford, Esq;
The Rev. Mr. Bening.
William Berners, of Woolverstone, Esq;
The Rev. Mr. Beuet, of Albro.
The Rev. Mr. Beynon, of Boxford.
The Rev. Mr. Bishop, of Ipswich.
Mr. Robert Bishop, of Wrentham.
Wr. William Black, of Felixstow.
Patrick Blake, of Langham, Esq;
Mr. William Blakely, of Ipswich.
Mr. James Blyth, of Ipswich.
Mr. James Boatwright, of Wrentham.
Mr. Boby, jun. of Stow-upland.
Edward Bodham, Gent.
Mr. Bohun, of Beccles.
Mr. Booty, of Ingham.
Mr. John Borrett, of Benacre.
The Rev. Mr. Bosworth.
Mr. Thomas Bowel, of Ipswich.
James Boyce of Little Stonham, Esq;
William Beal Brand, of Belstead, Esq;
Mr. James Brewer, of Saxmundham.
Philip Brewster, of Wrentham, Esq;
Mr. Isaac Brereton, of Benacre.
Mr. Thomas Bridgman, of Woodbridge.
Mr. William Brinck, of Kensington-Gore.
William Brocket, Esq;
The Rev. Mr. Broke, of Nacton.
Francis Brook of Ufford, Esq;
George Brooke, of Halstead, Esq;
Mr. William Brook, of Capel.
Mr. John Brook, of Ipswich.
The Rev. Mr. Broome, of Ipswich.
The Rev. Mr. James Brown, of Ipswich.
John Brown, of Peckham, Esq;
Mr. Richard Brown, of Benhall.

Mr

A List of SUBSCRIBERS.

Mr. John Brown, of Hinderclay.
Mr. Henry Brunwin, of Nayland.
Mr. Seth Bull, of Sudbury.
Mr. Daniel Bull, of Framlingham,
Mr. Jonathan Bullen, of Bury.
Mr. Thomas Bumsted, of Boxford, Surgeon.
Mr. John Burch, of Lavenham, Surgeon.
Mr. John Burkitt, jun. of Sudbury.
The Rev. Mr. Burton, of Elvedon.
Jonathan Burward, of Woodbridge, Esq;
Mr. Thomas Burwell, of Ipswich.
The Rev. Mr. Robert Buxton, of Darsham.

Sir John Hind Cotton, Bart.
Turner Calvert, of Brundish Lodge, Esq;
—— Campbell, Fellow-Commoner, Esq; of Pembroke College.
John Canham, Esq;
The Rev. Mr. Canning.
The Rev. Mr. Richard Canning, jun,
Mr. Thomas Card, of Stradbrook.
The Rev. Mr. Carter, of Tunstal.
The Rev. Samuel Carter, Rector, of Fersfield, A. M.
Messrs. Carter and Mendham, Attornies, of Ballingdon,
Mrs. Catherine Catchpool, of Ipswich, Millener.
The Rev. Mr. Carthew, of Woodbridge-Priory.
William Chambers, Esq; Architect to his Majesty.
Mr. John Chandler, of Felixtow.
Mr. William Chase, Bookseller, of Norwich, 6 Copies.
Mr. Benjamin Chenery, of Ipswich.
Mr. John Chenery, of Ipswich.
The Rev. Mr. Chilton, of Ufford.
The Rev. Mr. Richard Chilton, of Mendlesham, 2 Copies.
Mr. John Chinery, of Chilton-Hall, near Sudbury.
The Rev. Mr. Church, of Boxford.
Mr. Peter Clarke, of Ipswich, Attorney at Law,
Mr. Stockdale Clarke, of Sudbury, Attorney at Law,
Mr. William Clarke, of Ipswich.
Mr. Rix Clarke, of Ipswich, Hosier.
Mr. John Clarke, of Bungay.
Mr. Osmund Clarke, of Struston.
Mr. Joseph Clarke, of Ipswich, Merchant.
Mr. Thomas Clements, of Norwich.

The

The Rev. Mr. Clubbe, of Whatfield.
Mr. John Clubbe, of Ipswich, Surgeon.
The Rev. Mr. Cocksedge, of Bury.
Mr. William Colchester, of Dedham.
The Rev. Mr. William Cole, late of King's College,
    Cambridge, 2 Copies.
Mr. Thomas Cole, of Charsfield.
Richard Colville, of Hemingstone, Esq;
Anthony Collett, of Eyke, Esq;
Mr. Henry Collet, of Ipswich, Attorney at Law.
—————— Cooch, of Malden, Esq;
The Rev. Mr. Thomas Cooke, of Seymer.
John Cooper, of Burgh-Castle, Esq;
Mr. John Cooper, of Sternfield.
The Rev. Mr. Cornwallis, of Ipswich.
The Rev Mr. Couperthwaite, of Clopton.
The Rev. Mr. Coyte, of Ipswich.
Joseph Cradock, Fellow Commoner, Esq; of Emanuel
    College, Cambridge.
Mr. Craddock, of Stowmarket, Surgeon.
The Rev. Mr. Crask, of Bury.
Messrs. Craighton and Jackson, of Ipswich, Printers.
The Rev. Mr. Crosman, of Sudbury.
Mr. John Crouse, Bookseller, of Norwich, 6 Copies.
Philip Champion Crespigny, of Broughton-Hall, Suf-
    folk, Esq; 3 Copies.
Claude Crespigny, of South-Sea-House, Esq;
P. Claude Crespigny, of Trinity Hall, Cambridge,
    L. L. D.
Philip Crespigny, jun. of Doctors-Commons, Esq;
Mr. Thomas Gery Cullum, Surgeon.
Mr. Jonah Cunningham, of Bungay.

The Rev. Sir Hadley D'Oyley, of Ipswich, Bart.
John Dade, of Tannington, Esq;
Isham Dalton, of Bury, Gent.
Mr. Darby, of Mutford.
Henry Dashwood, Esq;
The Rev. Mr. Davers, Rector of Little Welnetham.
Mr. Samuel Davie, of Debenham.
Griffith Davis, of Harwich, Esq;
John Dawson, of Groton, Esq;
The Rev. Mr. Dawson, of Diss.
Mr. George Death, of Ipswich, Merchant.

                           Mr.

A List of SUBSCRIBERS.

Mr. Thomas Denny, of Eye.
Mr. Dent, of Ipswich.
The Rev. Mr. Thomas D'Eye.
Nathaniel D'Eye, of Bungay, Gent.
Ambrose Dickens, Esq;
Mr. John Dobson, of Ipswich, Merchant.
The Rev. Mr. Dormer.
Mr. George Doughty, of Martlesham.
The Rev. Mr. Fyn Dove.
Peregrine D'Oyly, of Layham, Esq;
Mr. Thomas Thorowgood D'Oyley.
Mr. Francis Drew, of Chetburgh.
Mr. John May Dring, of Ipswich.
The Rev. Mr. Drury, of Claydon.
Andrew Coltee Ducarel, of Doctors-Commons, L.L.D.
John D'Urban, of Halesworth, M. D.
Mr. John Dines Willisham.
Mr. Francis Eagle.
Mr. John Easterson, of Woodbridge.
Mr. William Eaton, of Yarmouth, Bookseller.
Mileson Edgar, Esq;
Robert Edgar, Esq;
Miss Katherine Edgar, of Ipswich.
The Rev. Mr. Edge.
Mr. John Edwards, of Baddingham.
The Rev. Mr. William Ellison, A. M. Master of Sidney Sussex College, and Vice-Chancellor of the University of Cambridge,
Mr. Robert Elliston, sen. of Monks-Illeigh.
Mr. Robert Elliston, jun. of Monks-Illeigh.
Mr. John Elsden, of Ipswich.
Mr. Thomas Emmerson, of Coddenham.
The Rev. Mr. Evans, Wortham.

Capt. Fauquier.
Mr. Thomas Feltwell, of Thetford.
Thomas Fenn, of Sudbury, Esq;
John Fishe, of Great Bromley, Essex, Gent.
Mr. John Field, of Kettleburgh.
Capt. William Fielding,
Mr. Robert Flamwell, of Southwold.
Thomas Fonnereau, of Ipswich, Esq; Member of Parment for Sudbury,
Zach. Phil. Fonnereau, Esq; Member of Parliament for Aldeburgh.

Philip

Philip Fonnereau, Esq; Member of Parliament for Aldeburgh.
Martin Fonnereau, of London, Esq;
The Rev. Mr. Benjamin Forster.
The Rev. Mr. Thomas Forster, of Halefworth.
The Rev. Mr. Fowler, of Framlingham, Curate.
Mr. John Freeman, of Rickinghall Superior.
Mr. Henry Freeman, of Rickinghall Superior.
The Rev. Mr. French, of Bury.
Mr. Robert French, of Little Wenham.
Shepard Frere, of Bacton, Esq;
Mr. Thomas Fulcher, of Shottisham, Norf. Surgeon.
Mr. Nathaniel Fuller, of Woodbridge.

Mr. Henry Gallant, of Ipswich.
The Rev. John Cole Gallaway, Master of the Free School at Botesdale.
Mr. Charles Garneys, of Kenton.
Mr. Warren Garnham, of Badwell-Ash.
Mr. John Garnham, of ditto.
Mr. Thomas Garrard, of Ipswich.
The Rev. Mr. Garrod, jun.
Mr. John Gaudy, of Ipswich.
Mr. Thomas Gill, of Durham.
Mr. Simon Girling, of Stradbrook.
Mr. John Girling, of ditto.
Mr. John Girling, of Bramford.
R. G. Glanville, of Elmset, Esq;
Edward Goat, of Brent-Illeigh, Esq;
The Rev. Mr. Godfrey, of Brinkley, Cambridgeshire.
Mr. Robert Goldsbury, of Ipswich.
Mr. Bez. Gooch, of Homersfield.
Mr. Thomas Goodwyn, of Earl Soham.
Mr. John Goodwyn, of Dennington.
The Rev. Mr. Gordon, of Ipswich.
The Rev. Mr. Grant, of Foxearth.
Mr. John Gravenor, of Ipswich.
Mr. William Green, of Combs.
Mr. John Green, of Bury.
Mr. Roger Green, of Pentloe.
Mr. William Green, of Bury, Bookseller, 6 Copies.
Joshua Grigby, of Horningsheath, Esq;
The Rev. Mr. Grimwood, of Dedham.
Mr. Walter Gullifer, of Witham, Attorney at Law.

A List of Subscribers.

The Right Hon. Lord Spencer Hamilton.
The Hon. Nicholas Herbert, of Great Glemham.
The Rev. Mr. Haddick, of Brandon.
Mr. John Hall, of Hadleigh, Attorney at Law.
Mr. Thomas Halstead, of Harwich.
Walden Hanmer, of Waldingfield, Esq;
Mr. Hannah, of Norwich.
Mr. Thomas Harbur, of Barton-Mills.
Robert Harland, of Sproughton, Esq;
Mr. William Harrington, of Melford, Draper.
Mr. Canham Hart.
Mr. Hasell, of Ipswich.
Mr. Roger Hasted, of Bury.
Thomas Havers, Esq;
Mr. Richard Hawes, of Cavendish, Surgeon.
Mr. John Hawkins, of Stowmarket, Surgeon.
The Rev. Mr. Haynes, of Ipswich.
John Hayward, of Mettingham-Castle, Gent.
The Rev. Mr. Heigham, of Walsham.
Arthur Heigham, of Hunston, Esq;
Pell Heigham, of Bury, Esq;
The Rev. Mr. Hewett, of Nacton.
Mr. Edward Highmore, of Ufford, Attorney at Law.
The Rev. Dr. Hill, of Buxhall.
Mr. William Hines, of Beccles.
The Rev. Mr. Charles Hingeston.
Mr. John Hingeston.
Mr. Ezekiel Hitchcock, of Lavenham.
Thomas Hodges, of Ipswich, Esq;
Captain Holingsworth.
Mr. Thomas Holman, jun. of Rickinghall.
The Rev. Mr. Holmes, of Emanuel Coll. Cambridge.
Mr. Holmes, of Stratford.
John Holmes of Bungay, Gent.
Rowland Holt, Esq; one of the Knights of this Shire.
Thomas Holt, Esq;
Mr. Edmund Horrox, of London.
Mr. Tho. Hovell, of Mendlesham, Attorney at Law.
Mr. William Hovell, jun. of Badwell-Ash.
Mr. John Howell, of Walsham-le-Willows.
Mr. Nathaniel Howlett, of Blaxhall.
The Rev. Mr. Hubbard, of Emanuel College, Cambridge
The Rev. Mr. Hudson, of Ipswich.
Mr. Benjamin Hugman, of Halesworth.

Mr.

Mr. Jacob, of Stow-upland.
The Rev. Mr. Christopher Jeffreason, of Melton.
Edmund Jenney, of Bredfield, Esq;
Mr. Edmund Jenney, of Bungay, Attorney at Law.
The Rev. Mr. William Johnson, of Stradbrook.
The Rev. Mr. Tho. Johnson, of Wickham-market.
Mr. Cha. Johnson, of Saxmundham, Attorney at Law.
Mr. Johnson, of Ellingham, Norfolk.

Mr. Ralph Keable, of Beccles.
William Keddington, Esq;
Mr. William Keeble.
Mr. Jonathan Keer, of Framlingham.
Mr. Keller, of Bury, Surgeon.
Mr. Benjamin Keningale, of Chelsworth.
John Kerrich, of Harkeston, Esq;
Mr. John Kerridge, of Ipswich, Surgeon.
Mr. W. Keymer, of Colchester, Bookseller, 2 Copies.
Mr. John Keymer, of Hadleigh.
Mr. Samuel Kilderbee, of Ipswich, Attorney at Law.
Mr. John Kilderbee, of Framlingham.
Mrs. King, of Belstead.
Mr. William King, of Ipswich, Merchant.
Mr. James King, of ditto.
Joshua Kirby, Esq; Designer in Perspective to his Majesty, 50 Copies.
Mr. William Kirby, of Witnesham, 2 Copies.
Mr. John Kirby, of Ipswich, Attorney at Law.
Mr. Lott Knight, of Ipswich, Attorney at Law.

The Rev. Mr. Lathbury, of Westerfield.
Mr. C. Laurence, of Upper Grosvenor-street, London.
The Rev. Mr. Lawrence, of Akenham.
John Lawton, Esq;
The Rev. Mr. Layton, of Ipswich.
Matthew Lee, Esq;
The Rev. Mr. Leedes, of Woodbridge.
Mr. Robert Le Grice, of Beccles.
The Rev. Mr. Robert Leman, of Ellough.
The Rev. Mr. Robert Leman, of Debenham.
Mr. John Lemon, of Norwich.
The Rev. Mr. Lewin, of Debenham.
Mr. Richard Lifton, of Boxford.
Mr. Richard Lifton, jun. of Groton.
Mr. John Linstead, of Woodbridge.

Richard.

A List of SUBSCRIBERS.

Rich. Savage Lloyd, Efq; Member for Totnefs, Devon
Mrs. Sarah Lond, of Denfton-Hall, Norfolk.
Charles Long, Efq; of Saxmundham.
Mrs. Long.
Beefton Long, Efq;
Samuel Long, Efq;
Mr. Charles Long, of Saxmundham.
Mr. Dudley Long, of ditto.
Mr. Thomas Longman, of London, Bookfeller.
The Rev. Mr. Lord, of Welnetham.
Mr. Thomas Lorkin, of Aldham.
The Rev. Mr. Lumpkin, of Grundifburgh.
William Lynch, of Ipfwich, Efq;
Mr. James Lynn, of Woodbridge, Surgeon, 2 Copies.

Mr. Peter Maber, of Kefgrave.
John Major, of Savage Gardens, London, Efq;
The Rev. Mr. Charles Mandevile, of Harwick-houfe.
Mr. Thomas Mann, of Ixworth, Surgeon.
Thomas Manning of Bungay, Efq;
Mr. Richard Marchant, of Bildeftone.
Mr. Rob. Marriott, of Stow-upland, Attorney at Law.
Mr. Thomas Martin, of Palgrave.
Mrs. Ann Marven, of Cobdock.
Mr. James Mathew, of Bury.
Mr. Nicholas May, of Ramfholt.
Mr. William Mayhew, of Woodbridge.
Mr. Tho. Miller, of Bungay, Grocer and Bookfeller.
Mr. Thomas Miller, of Halefworth, Bookfeller.
The Rev. Dr. Mills, of Bury.
Mr. John Mills, of Rickinghall Superior.
Mr. Tho. More, of Stowmarket, Attorney at Law.
Richard Moore, of Long Melford, Efq;
Mr. Edward Moore, of Ipfwich.
Mr. John Moore, of Wantefden.
Mr. John Morphew, of Norwich.
Mr. Richard Mofs, of Norwich.
Mr. John Mofs, of ditto.
Mr. Richard Mott, of Carlton, Attorney at Law.
Mr. Tho. Mulliner, of Stratford, Attorney at Law.
Mr. Edward Mumford, of Chelfworth.
Mr. Shadrach Munnings, of Bilderfton.
Mr. Leonard Munnings, of Stowmarket.

Mr.

Mr. Wm. Musgrave, of Cambridge, Woollen-Draper.
The Rev. Mr. Myers, of Walton.

Mr. William Naunton, of Martlesham.
Mr. Thomas Naunton, jun. of Playford.
The Rev. Mr. Neal.
The Rev. Dr. Neden, 2 Copies.
Henry Negus, of Bungay, Gent.
The Rev. Mr. Newcomen, of Ipswich.
Mr. Newcome, of Layham.
The Rev. Mr. Samuel Newman, of Dedham.
The Rev. Mr. John Newman, of Sudbury.
Mr. Newson, of Leiston-Hall.
Richard Norton, of Ipswich, Esq;
Mr. William Norton, Bookseller.
Mr. John Notcutt, of Ipswich.
Mr. George Notcutt, of ditto.
Mr. William Notcutt, of ditto.
The Rev. Mr. Martin Nunn, of Holbrooke.
The Rev. Mr. Robert Nunn, of Pakenham.

The Rt. Hon. Lord Orwell, of Orwell-Park, Member for Ipswich.
Mrs. Ord, of Fornham.
Mr. John Ormes, of Walton.

Mr. John Page, of Woodbridge, Surgeon.
Mr. Thomas Page, of Ipswich, Bookseller.
Miss Pack of Palgrave.
Mr. Peter Packard, of Chelsworth.
Robert Parish, of Ipswich, Esq;
Mr. William Parker, of Dedham.
Mr. William Parmenter, of Playford-Hall.
Mr. George Parsons, of Hadleigh.
The Rev. Mr. Pawsey, of Sturston.
Mr. Jeffery Pearl, of Hoxne.
Mr. Robert Pettit, of Stowmarket.
George Pickard, of Colchester, Esq;
Mr. Samuel Pickering, of Ipswich.
Mr. William Pindar, of Woodbridge.
Mr. Giles Philips, of Ipswich.
Mr. Philips, of Boxford.
John Plampen, of Chadacre-Hall, Esq;
Mr. John Plumbstead
Mr. William Prescott, of London.

A List of SUBSCRIBERS.

The Rev. Mr. Preston, of Waldingfield.
Mr. Robert Pretyman, of Wingfield.
Mr. Prickle, of Bury.
The Rev. Mr. Humphry Primate, of Higham.
The Rev. Mr. Punchard, of Gazely.
Charles Wager Purvis, Rear-Admiral, Esq;
George Purvis, of Harwich, Esq;

The Right Hon. the Earl of Rochford.
Sir John Rous, of Henham, Bart.
Mr. Ralph Rackham, of Bungay, Surgeon.
Mr. John Ralling, of Bury.
Mr. William Ralph, of Woodbridge.
Mr. Nathaniel Randall, of Woodbridge.
Mr. John Ranson, of Stowmarket.
Richard Ray, of Haughley, Esq;
Mr. William Ray, of Worlingworth.
Thomas Crofts Reade, of Bardwell, Esq;
Mr. George Reade, of Orford.
Mr. Robert Reeve, of Halesworth.
Mr. Robert Reeve, of Lowestoft, Attorney at Law.
John Reilly, Esq;
John Revett, of Brandiston, Esq;
Mr. John Reynolds, of Yarmouth, Attorney at Law.
Mr. Thomas Richardson, of Melford.
Mr. George Richardson, of Stowmarket, Surgeon.
Mr. John Ridley, of Woodbridge, Bookseller.
Mr. Thomas Rix, of Gosnall-Hall.
Mr. William Robards, of Bury.
Mr. Roger Robinson, of Caterick, Yorkshire.
Mr. John Robson, of London.
Mr. John Rodbard, of Ipswich, Surgeon.
Mr. John Rogers, of Ipswich.
Mr. Thomas Rout, of Stowmarket.
Mr. John Rudland, of Woodbridge, Surgeon.
John Rush, of Benhall, Esq;
Barham Rushbrooke, Esq;
Mr. Thomas Rust, jun. of Wortham.
The Rev. Mr. Rustat, of Stutton.

John Safford, of Bungay, Gent.
James Sandcroft, of Ditchingham, Gent.
John Sanderson, of Camberwell, Esq;
Mr. Joseph Sage, jun. of Freston.
Mr. Samuel Savage, of Benacre.

Mr.

Mr. John Say, of Framlingham, Surgeon.
John Sayer, Efq;
William Schutz, Efq;
Francis Matthew Schutz, Efq;
The Rev. Mr. Scott, of Ipfwich.
Mr. Claude Scott, of London.
Mr. Stephen Searfon, of Ipfwich.
Mr. Francis Sewell, of Beccles.
The Rev. Mr. Jofeph Sharp, of Bury.
Mr. James Sharp, of Bury.
Mr. Martin Sharp, of ditto.
Mr. Marmaduke Shaw, of Woodbridge.
Mr. John Sherman, of Melton.
Mr. Thomas Sheriffe, of Bungay.
Mr. Robert Shimming, of Rendlefham.
Ifaac Pacatus Shard, Efq;
Mr. Thomas Shave, of Ipfwich.
Mr. Thomas Shave, of Bacton.
Mr. Luke Silburn, of Ipfwich.
Mr. Charles Simpfon, of Difs.
Mr. Geo. Simpfon, of Bramford.
Mr. Thomas Singleton, of Bury.
Mr. Thomas Slapp, of Botefdale, Attorney at Law.
John Smith, Fell. Com. of Magdalen College, Efq;
William Smyth, of Leifton, Efq;
Mr. William Snell, of Needham.
Mr. Spalding, of Framlingham, Surgeon.
Robert Sparrow, of Worlingham, Efq;
Mr. Charles Squire, of Lavenham, Attorney at Law.
Tho. Staunton, of Holbrook, Efq; Memb. for Ipfwich.
The Rev. Mr. Stebbing, of Tattingftone.
Mr. George Steel, of Chimney-mills.
The Rev. Mr. Stegals, of Wiverftone.
Henry Stevens, of Doctors Commons, Efq;
Mr. Steward, of Bury, Surgeon.
Thomas Stifted, of Ipfwich, Efq;
William Stone, of Bedingham, Efq;
Mr. John Stow, of Woodbridge, Merchant.
Edmund Strudwick, of Ipfwich, Efq;
Mr. James Stubbin, of Ipfwich.
Edward Sulyard, of Haughley, Efq;
Mr. Daniel Sutton, of Kenton.
The Rev. Mr. Dye Syer.
Mr. John Syer, of Lavenham.
William Symonds, Efq;

A List of Subscribers.

Sir Thomas Thorowgood, Knight.
The Rev. Dr. Tanner, of Hadleigh.
Mr. Lark Tarver of Ipswich.
Colonel Tash, of Haverhill.
Mr. Frederick Teush, of London, Merchant.
Mr. Taylor, of Diss, Attorney at Law.
Mr. Ambrose Taylor, of Woodbridge.
Mr. Thomas Taylor, of Sternfield.
George Thomas, of Kesgrave, Esq;
John Thompson, of Southwold, Gent.
Mr. John Thorndike, of Ipswich.
Messrs. Thurlbourn and Woodyer, Booksellers, Cambridge, 2 Copies.
Mr. William Toller, of Benhall.
Mr. Robert Tovell, of Ipswich.
The Rev. Mr. Trigg, of Leiston.
Mr. James Trimmer, jun.
William Trotman of Ipswich, Esq;
Mr. Abraham Trowell, of Woodbr. Attorney at Law.
Mr. Turner, of Harwich, Ship-builder.
Mr. Jonathan Turner, of Old Newton.
Mr. James Turner of Rattlesden.
Mr. John Turner, of Finningham.
Mr. Turner, of Felsham.
Mr. James Tuson, of Boxford, Surgeon.
Mr. Robert Twigger, of Hadleigh.
Thomas Tyndall, of Doctors Commons, Esq;
Mr. James Tye, of Woodbridge.
Edmund Tyrrell, of Stowmarket, Esq;
Edmund Tyrrell, of Gipping-hall, Esq;
Tho. Bokenham Tyrrell, of Stowmarket, Esq;

The Rev. Mr. Samuel Uvedale, of Barking.
Samuel Uvedale, of ditto, Esq;
Mr. Robert Upcher, of Sudbury, Surgeon.

Sir Joshua Vanneck, of Heveningham, Bart.
Dr. Venn, of Ipswich.
The Rev. Mr. Edward Ventris, of Burgate.
Mr. Thomas Vincent, of Ipswich.

Sir Armine Wodehouse, Bart.
Sir George Warren, Knt. of the Bath, 2 Copies.
Mr. Mark Wade, of Orford, 2 Copies.
Mr. Robert Wade, of Woodbridge.

Mr.

Mr. Miles Wallis, of Ipswich.
Mr. Samuel Walton, of Diss.
Capt. Thomas Ward, of Ipswich.
Mr. William Ward, of Haughley.
Mr. Samuel Ward, of Needham.
Mr. John Ward, of Ipswich.
Thomas Waring, of Groton, Esq;
Mrs. Warner, of Waldingfield.
The Rev. *Mr.* Warren, of Chattisham.
Mr. Samuel Watkinson, of Lavenham.
Mr. John Watling of Bacton.
Jonathan Watson, Esq;
Daniel Wayth, of Glemham, Esq;
Mr. Daniel Wayth, of Flowton.
Mr. Francis Wealy, of Saxmundham.
George Wegg, of Colchester, Esq;
The Rev. *Mr.* West, of Sutton in the Isle of Ely.
Mr. Thomas Whiting, of Woodbridge.
Edward Whitmore, of Bury, Esq;
The Rev. *Mr.* Whittington, Rector of Orford.
Mr. John Wilgress, at Parham.
The Rev. *Mr.* Wilkinson, of Brome.
The Rev. *Mr.* Willis of Jesus College, Cambridge.
Henry Willis, of Redlingfield, Esq;
Thomas Wilson, of Botesdale, Esq;
Mr. Henry Winson, of Woodbridge.
The Rev. *Mr.* Witaker, of Mendham.
William Wollaston, of Finborough, Esq; 4 Copies.
The Rev. *Mr.* Frederick Wollaston, of Bury.
Samuel Wollaston, Esq;
Robert Wollaston, Esq;
Mr. Richard Wood, of Melton, Attorney at Law.
Mr. Robert Woodgate, Attorney at Law.
Mr. Wooley, of Ipswich.
Mr. Wormington, of Southwold.
Thomas Wright, of Thetford, Esq;
Mr. J. Wynter, of Aldborough.

Mr. William Yallop, of Beccles, Attorney at Law.
Mr. Thomas Yeoman, of Westminster, Engineer.
The Rev. *Mr.* Young, Fellow of Caius College, Cambridge.
Mr. Edward Youngman, of Hepworth.

THE

THE
Suffolk Traveller, &c.

THE County of SUFFOLK, or the *Southern-Folk*, is so called with respect to NORFOLK, or the *Northern-Folk*. It is a Maritime County; bounded on the East, by the Ocean; on the West by *Cambridgeshire*; on the North, by the Rivers *Waveney* and *Little Ouse*, which part it from *Norfolk*; and on the South by the *Stour*, which parteth it from the County of *Essex*. The Length of it from East to West, is about 52 Miles; and its Breadth from North to South, about 28 Miles; making the Circumference 196 Miles: So that it contains near 1169 square Miles, or about 748,160 Acres. It is subdivided into Twenty-two *Hundreds*, in which are Twenty-eight Market-Towns: The whole Number of Parishes is 523, besides Hamlets.

This County may be considered, as naturally consisting of three different Sorts of Land, *viz.* the *Sand-land*, the *Wood-land*, and the *Fielding*. The *Sand-land* Part, is that Tract of Land which reaches from the River *Orwell*, by the Sea-Coast to *Yarmouth*, and is pretty nearly separated from the *Wood-lands*, by the great Road leading from *Ipswich*, thro' *Saxmundham* and *Beccles*,

Beccles, to *Yarmouth*; so that it contains the Hundred of *Colneis*, and Part of the Hundreds of *Carlford*, *Loes*, *Willford*, *Plomesgate*, *Blything*, *Mutford*, and *Lothingland*. This Part may also be subdivided into the *Marsh*, *Arable*, and *Heath-lands*. The *Marsh-land* is naturally fruitful, feeding great Numbers of Sheep and Oxen; and sometimes, when ploughed, affords greater Crops of Corn than any other Land in this County. That Part which is *Arable*, is in many Places naturally good for Tillage, and produces abundant Crops of all Sorts of Corn and Grain; and where it seems in a manner barren, it is fit for Improvement by Chalk, Clay, and Crag; which last is found by Experience to be preferable to the other two, and may be had cheaper (*a*). The Heathy Part, commonly used for Sheep-walks, might contain about one third of the Sand-lands, before the Discovery of *Crag*; but many hundred Acres of them are now converted into good Arable Land, by that excellent Manure.

The *Wood-land* Part extends from the North-east Corner of the Hundred of *Blything*, to the South-west Corner of the County at *Haverhill*; and includes Part of the Hundreds of *Carlford*, *Willford*, *Loes*, *Plomesgate*, *Blything*, *Blackbourn*, *Thedwastre*, and *Thingoe*; and all the Hundreds of *Risbridge*, *Baberg*, *Cosford*, *Samford*, *Stow*, *Bosmere*, *Claydon*, *Hartesmere*, *Hoxne*, *Thredling*, and *Wangford*. This Part is generally dirty, but very rich and fruitful. Here the *Suffolk Butter* is made, justly esteemed the pleasantest and best in *England*; but they who make good Butter, must, of course, make bad Cheese; and therefore the Generality of *Suffolk-Cheese* is well known to be as remarkably bad, as the Butter is good: But those few in these Parts who make little or no Butter, make as good Cheese, as any in *Warwickshire*, *Gloucestershire*, or any other Parts of the Kingdom;

insomuch,

(*a*) See *Levington*, in *Colneis* Hundred.

insomuch, that it sells for Ten-pence and Twelve-pence a Pound, or more; being little, if at all, inferior to that of *Stilton*.

The Fielding-Part contains all the Hundred of *Lackford*, and the remaining Parts of the Hundreds of *Blackbourn*, *Thedwastre*, and *Thingoe*; and is, most of it, in Sheep-walks; yet affords good Corn in many Places.

The Ecclesiastical Government of this County is in the Bishop of *Norwich*, assisted by the Archdeacons of *Sudbury* and *Suffolk*. But here we must except the following Parishes, they being not subject to the Jurisdiction of the Bishop of *Norwich*, viz. *Hadleigh*, *Monks-Illeigh*, and *Moulton*, which are Peculiars to the Archbishop of *Canterbury*; and *Frekenham*, which (with *Isleham* in *Cambridgeshire*) is a Peculiar to the Bishop of *Rochester*. The Diocesan had but one Archdeacon, till about *A.D.* 1126, when *Richard* Archdeacon of the whole County of *Suffolk*, being made a Bishop in *France*, *Eborard* or *Everard* then Bishop of *Norwich*, divided the County into the Archdeaconries of *Sudbury* and *Suffolk*; and made the Western Part of it (together with such Parishes in *Cambridgeshire* as belong to the Diocese of *Norwich*; on account of their having been anciently Part of the Kingdom of the *East-Angles*) subject to the Archdeacon of *Sudbury*; and the Eastern Part of it, subject to the Archdeacon of *Suffolk*. The Archdeaconry of *Sudbury* is subdivided into eight Deanries, *viz.* those of *Sudbury*, *Stow*, *Thingoe*, *Clare*, *Fordham* in *Cambridgeshire*, *Hartesmere*, *Blackbourn*, and *Thedwastre*; and the Archdeaconry of *Suffolk* into fourteen, *viz.* the Deanries of *Ipswich*, *Bosmere*, *Claydon*, *Hoxne*, *Southelmham*, *Wangford*, *Lothingland*, *Dunwich*, *Orford*, *Loes*, *Willford*, *Carlford*, *Colneis*, and *Samford*.

The Civil Government is in the High-Sheriff for the Time being; and in this respect the County is divided

vided into the *Geldable* and the *Franchises*. In the Geldable Part of it, the Issues and Forfeitures are paid to the King; in the Franchises, to the Lords of the Liberties. The Geldable Hundreds are *Samford, Bosmere* and *Claydon, Stow, Hartesmere, Hoxne, Blything, Wangford*, and the two Half-Hundreds of *Mutford*, and *Lothingland*; for these the Sessions are holden at *Beccles*, and *Ipswich*; viz. at *Beccles*, for *Wangford, Blything, Mutford*, and *Lothingland*; and at *Ipswich*, for the Hundreds of *Hartesmere, Hoxne, Stow, Bosmere, Claydon*, and *Samford*.

The Franchises are, *First*, The Franchise or Liberty of *St. Ethelred*, belonging anciently to the Prior and Convent, and now to the Dean and Chapter of *Ely*; it contains the Hundreds of *Carlford, Colneis, Willford, Plomesgate, Loes*, and *Thredling*; for which the Sessions are holden at *Woodbridge*. The Prior and Convent had this Liberty in King *Edward* the Confessor's Time, and when the Prior and Convent were changed into a Dean and Chapter, A. D. 1541. it was said to be of the Yearly Value of 20 *l*. *Secondly*, The Franchise or Liberty of *St. Edmund*, which was given to the Abbey of *Bury* by King *Edward* the Confessor; it contains the Hundreds of *Cosford, Babergh, Risbridge, Lackford, Blackbourn, Thedwestre*, and *Thingoe*, and the Half-Hundred of *Ixning*; for which the Sessions are holden at *Bury*. *Thirdly*, The Duke of *Norfolk* hath also a Liberty (by Letters Patent of King *Edward* the Fourth, dated 7th *December*, 1468,) of returning Writs, and having a Coroner; and all Fines and Amercements, &c. within his Manors of *Bungay, Kelsale, Carlton, Peasenhall*, the three *Stonhams, Dennington, Brundish*, the four *Ilketsals*, and *Cratfield*, in *Suffolk*.

There is but one Assize for the whole County; but, at every Assize, there are two Grand Juries; one for the Geldable, and the other for the Franchise of *St. Edmondsbury*.

mondsbury. *Suffolk* and *Norfolk* were formerly under the Government of one High-Sheriff, till the 17th Year of Queen *Elizabeth*; when *Robert Ashfield*, of *Netherhall* in *Pakenham*, Esq; was made the first High-Sheriff of this County, distinct from the County of *Norfolk*.

The ancient Kingdom of the *East-Angles* contained little more than the Counties of *Norfolk* and *Suffolk*, and from hence arose that close Connexion which so long subsisted between them. *William* the Conqueror granted the Earldom of *Norfolk* and *Suffolk*, to his Cousin *Roger Bigod*: It continued in that Family to the Thirty-fifth Year of King *Edward* I. when *Roger Bigod*, Earl Marshal, died without Issue; having first surrendered all his Honours, Manors, &c. to the King; from whom he received them again by a Re-grant, with a Limitation to himself and *Alice* his Wife, and the Issue of their two Bodies; and, for want of such Issue with Remainder to the King and his Heirs. But this County did never give a separate Title, till the eleventh Year of King *Edward* the Third; when that King created *Robert de Ufford*, Earl of *Suffolk*. He was succeeded by his Son *William*, who died without Issue Male, and the Title became extinct.

King *Richard* II. in the ninth Year of his Reign created *Michael de la Pole*, Earl of *Suffolk*: He was succeeded by *Michael* his Son, who was slain in the Battle of *Agincourt*. *William de la Pole*, Son of the last *Michael*, was created by King *Edward* VI. Marquis, and afterwards Duke of *Suffolk*; but was unlawfully beheaded on the Gunwale of the Boat that was carrying him to *France*. *John* the Son of *William* succeeded to his Father's Honours; having married *Elizabeth*, Sister of King *Edward* IV. He left many Children, and was succeeded in his Honours and Estate first by *John* his Son, who was killed in the Battle of *Stoke*-upon-*Trent*, in 1487; and then by *Edmond* his second Son, who being too nearly related

related to the Crown, was in 5 King *Henry* VIII. beheaded in the *Tower*, and the Title became extinct.

King *Henry* VIII. then created *Charles Brandon*, Duke of *Suffolk*: He left two Sons, and both died without Issue, under Age. But *Henry Gray* Marquis of *Dorset*, who married the Lady *Frances*, eldest Daughter of *Charles Brandon* by *Mary* the *French* Queen, was created Duke of *Suffolk* 11th *October*, 5 *Edward* VI. The Lady *Jane* his Daughter, was on the Demise of King *Edward*, proclaimed Queen; who suffered for the Rashness of her Friends; and her Father was himself beheaded 23d *February*, 2 Queen *Mary* I. and the Title was once more extinct. It continued so till 1 *James* I. when *Thomas Howard*, a younger Son of *Thomas* the second Duke of *Norfolk*, was made Earl of *Suffolk*; and in this Family the Earldom hath continued ever since.

In this Edition we have taken the Liberty of altering the Method that was observed in the other. *Ipswich* being the County-Town, we shall first give as good an Account as could be procured of that. We shall then conduct the Traveller through every Hundred in the Geldable Part of the County, without distinguishing the Liberty of *St. Etheldred*, which is included in this. After that, we shall attend him through all the several Hundreds in the Franchise of *St. Edmond*.

A Stranger coming from *London* to visit the *Eastern*, or *Geldable* Part of *Suffolk*, would probably enter the County at *Stratford* or *Cattiwade* Bridges, in the Hundred of *Samford*. We therefore shall begin with that Hundred, and then take the several Hundreds that lie in or near the Road leading from *Ipswich* to *Yarmouth*, viz. *Carlford* and *Colneis*, *Loes*, *Willford*, *Plomesgate*, *Blything*, *Mutford*, and *Lothingland*. Then returning to *Beccles*, we shall take the remaining Geldable Hundreds, viz. *Wangford*,

Wangford, Hoxne, Thredling, Hartesmere, Stow, Bosmere, and *Claydon.* The Hundreds in the Liberty of *St. Edmondsbury* will be taken in this Order, *Thingoe, Thedwastre, Blackbourn, Lackford, Risbridge, Baberg,* and *Cosford.* But, that any Place may be more easily found, the Towns and Villages in each Hundred will be placed alphabetically.

An ACCOUNT *of* IPSWICH, *with its Suburbs, Precincts, and Liberties.*

THE Spot on which *Ipswich* stands is so happily situated, that it could not fail of inviting Inhabitants to settle here, soon after this Corner of the Island was peopled. To Strangers who enter the Town, either by what is now the *London* Road, or by the *Yarmouth* Road, it seems to stand low: But when a Traveller approaches the Town by the ancient *London* Road, which was over *Cattiwade* and *Bourn* Bridges, upon *Wherstead-Hill,* he views it to more Advantage; situated, as in fact it is, *on the Side of a Hill,* with a South Aspect, declining by a gradual and easy Descent to the *Key,* where the Foot of it is washed by the *Orwell.* The Soil is most healthy; it is Sand, Crag, or Gravel. The Hills which rise above it to the North and East, contribute greatly to the Convenience of it; not only as they shelter the Town from those bleak and inclement Winds, but as they are well stored with Springs of most excellent Water. The Springs from *Caldwell*-Hills flow in such Abundance, that tho' the greater Part of the Town is supplied from them, they constantly run waste in what is called *St. Hellen*'s and *St. Margaret*'s Wash; and those that rise in or near *Christ-Church* Park, tho' they likewise supply many Houses with Water, do as constantly run waste, down *Brook-street*. These last are of still far greater Use; for the large Ponds at *Christ-Church*, continually replenished by them, thro' the Benevolence and Humanity of the Owner, are always let out on any Emergency; and therefore, may be considered, as perpetual Reservoirs, deposited there by Providence, to secure and protect the Town from the dreadful Ravages of Fire. To this happy Circumstance, (such as few Places can boast) we may in a great measure impute it, that tho' many Fires have happened here within the Memory of Persons now living, not one of them hath raged to any violent Degree.

As several other Towns upon the neighbouring Coast, *viz. Yar-mouth, Ald-borough*, and *Or-ford*, take their Names from their Situation near the Mouths of their respective Rivers; so the Town of *Ipswich* hath its Name from its being seated where the fresh River *Gippen* or *Gipping* empties itself into the *Orwell*. It is spelt in Domesday, *Gyppeswid, Gyppeswiz, Gyppewycus, Gyppewic*; afterwards, by dropping the Guttural, it was written *Yppyswyche*; and then, as our Spelling improved, by leaving out the superfluous Letters, *Ipswich* (a).

The Names of the Fresh and Salt River have lately been confounded, insomuch that Mr. *Kirby* was unwarily led to call the Fresh River the *Orwell*; but their Names are plainly distinct. The Salt River, or to speak more properly, that Branch or Arm of the Sea which flows up to *Ipswich*, is called the *Orwell*, probably from its spacious and commodious Haven or Harbour. Some think

(a) As to the idle Story of a Pagan King *Ippus*, who built the Town, and called it by his own Name; since no History mentions any such Person, and *Domesday-Book* calls it otherwise, that must be considered, as merely fabulous.

think this was the Place that the *Danes* failed up *A. D.* 1016, when they had a Defign upon the Kingdom of *Mercia*. " The *Saxon* Annals call it *Arwan*; and as " it may not be unreafonable to fuppofe the true Name " of this Harbour may be *Arwell*; fo do we find on one " Side of it *Harwich*, and on the other *Arwerton* (*b*)."

It is certain, *Henry* the Son of King *Henry* II. who was crowned in his Father's Life-time, when he confpired againft his Father, landed here with Soldiers from *Flanders*; and, taking *Hugh Bigod* with him, marched from hence to *Norwich*. Here *Ifabel*, Wife of King *Edward* II. landed from *France*, when fhe drove her Hufband into *Wales* (*c*). And in 20 *Edward* II. Sir *John Howard* had a Commiffion to raife Five Hundred Men in *Norfolk* and *Suffolk*, and conduct them to the Port of *Orwell*, from thence to go to Sea againft the *French* (*d*).

And the Earl of *Lancafter*, in 14 *Edward* III. had an Affignment of ten Ships to tranfport his Horfe from this Port of *Orwell* to *Flanders*; fo that we need not multiply Proofs to fhew that this Haven and Branch of the Sea is called the *Orwell*. As to the Frefh River *Gipping*, it has three Fountain-Heads; one rifes at or near the little Village of *Gipping* by *Mendlefham*, to which it gives Name (*e*). Another Head rifes near *Wetherden*; and the third near *Rattlefden*. Thefe two laft Rivulets unite with the other at *Stow-market*; and there the *Gipping*, thus fupplied, becomes more refpectable. It is true, the

Orwell

(*b*) Addit. to *Cambden*.
(*c*) *Lambard*'s Dict.
(*d*) *Dugd*. Bar. II. 260.
(*e*) For here you have a River, with a Village at one Head, and a large Town at the Mouth of it, and the fame Names common to all three, for *Gippefwic* is *Gippes*-Town; and as Rivers flowed before Towns or Houfes were built, it is, in the Nature of the Thing, more reafonable to fuppofe, that the River gave Name to the Town and the Village, than that either of them gave Name to the River.

Orwell is sometimes called the *Orwell* or *Gipping*, because the *Gipping* discharges itself into it at *Ipswich*; but the fresh River *Gipping*, cannot with any Propriety be called the *Orwell*, because it is no Part of the Haven *(f)*: The *Thames* may as well be called the *Swin*.

Ipswich strictly speaking, that is, within the Gates, was not of very large Extent. It was inclosed with a Rampart and Ditch, which was broken down by the *Danes*, when they pillaged the Town twice within the Space of ten Years, about the Years of our Lord 991, and 1000. But this Fortification was repaired and renewed in the fifth Year of King *John (g)*.

(f) One of our Correspondents, to whom we are much obliged, hath urged a Conjecture, that anciently there was at the Mouth of this Haven, (which he supposes to have been much farther out towards the Sea) a large Town called *Orwell*, which he thinks was long since demolished by the *Danes*, and then swallowed up by the Sea. But if there had been any such Town, the *Danes* could only burn and destroy the Buildings; the Land and Soil would remain, notwithstanding all that they could do. And tho' it is certain the Sea hath made vast Encroachments upon this Coast, those Encroachments have been made gradually and slowly; and therefore, as *Domesday* Book makes no mention of any such Town, we may be sure there was none when that was made; and if it had been destroyed so lately as the Conjecture supposes, some Notice would have been taken of the Place where it stood. And tho' the Word *Orwell* is sometimes used in such a manner, as may seem rather to denote a *Town* than a *River*, it appears by the Corporation Books, that by the *Port* of *Orwell* was meant the Town of *Ipswich*, in the Time of King *Edward* the Third. And therefore *Geoffrey Chaucer*, in the Prologue to his *Merchant's Tale*, intended *Ipswich* by that Word; who saith,

"He would the Sea were kept for any Thing
"Betwixt *Middleborough* * and *Orwell*,
"Well could he in Exchange *Sheldes* sell."

For these Reasons we cannot lay much Stress on this Conjecture.

(g) Ipswich Domesday.

* *Middleburgh* had at that Time a Staple for Wool.

There are not the least Remains of more than three of the Gates now standing; but, it is certain, there were more. For, in the ancient Partition of the Town into four *Letes* or *Wards*, as two of these were called *North-gate-Lete* and *West-gate-Lete*, so the two others were called *East-gate-Lete* and *South-gate-Lete* (*h*).

We read likewise of *Lose-gate*, which stood at the Ford thro' the Salt River, by what is now the House of Mr. *Trotman*. Tho' the Rampart hath in many Places been broken through, and in some entirely levelled, there are still considerable Remains of it; and it is easily traced from the Bowling-green Garden (or *Grey-Fryers* Walk) with a Road on each Side of it, to the West, or St. *Matthew's* Gate (*i*).

From

(*h*) *East-gate-Lete* reached from *North-gate* to the Stone-Cross in *Brook-street*, called St. *Lewis* Cross; so down *Tankard-street*, till you come to the common Ditch next the *Friers-Preachers* Wall, with *Carr-street* [Cross-Keys] *Thingsted* [or St. *Margaret's* Green, and the Lane leading to *Little Bolton*] and *Caldwell* [or St. *Hellen's*] Street. *West-gate-Lete* from *North-gate* by the Archdeacon's House, till you come to the Corner of the Street leading from *Brook-street* to the *Fish-Market*, and so by the same Market [which was at the *East* End of St. *Lawrence* Church-Yard, *i. e.* in *White-Hart* Lane] on the Right-hand to the farther Corner of *Walter Cobb's* [St. *Lawrence* Conduit-House] and so to the *Cornhill*, on the *North* Side of the Street, till you come at the *West-gate*, with the Suburbs that be without the Gate. *South-gate-Lete*, from *West-gate* on one Side of the High-street till you come at St. *Mildred's* Church [the Town-Hall] and so upon the Right-hand on one Part of the Street till you come to *Woulforms-lane*, in the Parish of St. *Peter*, almost against the *West* End of the said Church-yard. *North-gate-Lete* [contains] all the rest of the Town, with the Suburbs, beyond *Stoke* Bridge, and beside the Key with St. *Clement's* Street.— *Ipsw.* Domesday.

(*i*) This Gate was rebuilt and made a Goal in the Time of King *Henry* VI. at the voluntary Expence of *John de Caldwell*, Bailif and Portman. In the Will of *Walter Velvet*, dated 11 *Jan.* 1458, is this Bequest, *Item lego ad fabricatic-*

nem

From hence to *Bull-gate* facing *Weſtgate-ſtreet*, it is levelled, and the Ground built upon. But from this to *North-gate*, and ſo to the End of *Croſs-keys-ſtreet*, it is almoſt entire. It is alſo viſible at the Back of the Houſes on the Weſt-ſide of St. *Margaret*'s Waſh; and again, in the Yard of *Chriſt*'s Hoſpital; ſo that all the Pariſhes of St. *Auſtin*, St. *Clement*, and St. *Hellen*, and great Part of the Pariſhes of St. *Margaret* and St. *Matthew*, were not included within the Gates; and theſe are accordingly called in old Writings, the *Suburbs* of *Ipſwich*.

But if we conſider the Borough in a larger Senſe, as including not only the Town with its Suburbs, but the four Hamlets of *Stoke-Hall*, *Brooks-Hall*, *Wikes-Ufford*, and *Wikes-Biſhop*, which comprehends the whole Pre‑cincts and Liberties of the Borough, the Extent of it is very conſiderable. For it reaches from Eaſt to Weſt, that is, from the Place on *Ruſhmere* Common, where the Bounds of the Liberties running paſt *Ruſhmere-Hall-Gate*, and along the other Lane croſs the *Wood-bridge* Road oppoſite to the Gallows; to that Place in *Whitton-ſtreet*, where the Bounds come out of the Lane leading from *Bramford*, croſs the *Norwich* and *Bury* Road, and then go into the Lane leading to *Whitton* Church, the Diſtance is better than *four Miles*. In like manner, from North to South, or near it; that is, from that Place beyond *Weſterfield* Green, where the Bounds enter the Road leading from *Witneſham* to *Ipſwich*, and ſo to *Bourn* Bridge; it is about the ſame Diſtance: But if, inſtead of going on the Weſt of the *Orwell*, you go from the aforeſaid Place thro' St. *Clement*'s Street on the Eaſt-

---

tem unius Pontis inter Capellam Beatæ Mariæ et * *Domini Regis cum aliquis alius fabricari velit, aut fabricari faciat*——

* The Word here omitted was obſcure, but thought to be *Priſonam*. See the Account of St. *Mary*'s Chapel afterwards.

East-side of it to *Donham* Bridge by *John's* Nefs *(k)*, the Distance is greater.

These Bounds of the Liberties of the Borough have been often ascertained; but the last Determination concerning them was in 13 King *Henry* VIII. when a Felon Fugitive left Goods behind him at his House in *Whitton-street*, which the Bailives seized in Right of the Borough: But the Escheator for the Crown in the County of *Suffolk* hearing of it, he took away the Goods by Force, pretending they were not within the Liberties of *Ipswich*. The Bailives complained of this Violence, whereupon a Commission was directed to the Abbot of St. *Edmundsbury*, *Robert Curzon*, Knt. Lord *Curzon*, Sir *Robert Drury*, Sir *Richard Wentworth*, Sir *Philip Tilney*, *Lionel Talmage*, Esq; and *John Sulyard*, Esq; to enquire how far the Bounds of the Liberties of *Ipswich* extend. So a Jury was empannelled, and their Return filed in Chancery; who, upon their Oaths said, That the said Liberties did extend according to the Bounds in the said Return above-mentioned; and the said B. B. and C. of *Ipswich* have used to enjoy the said Liberties and *Fraunchefes without Mynde of Man*.

Besides the Precincts on Land before-mentioned, the Borough of *Ipswich* did always claim, as appendant to the Borough and Parcel thereof, a Precinct and Jurisdiction by Water on the *Orwell*; the Extent of which hath likewise, more than once, been ascertained: Particularly in 2 *Richard* II. when a Commission was issued for that Purpose, to *John de Sutton*, Knt. and *Richard Walgrave*, Knt. accordingly a Jury was summoned at *Shotley*, who said upon their Oaths, That the

Port

(k) This is the Place where His Majesty's Ship the *Hampshire* was built, not long since: It is now called commonly *John's* Nefs, but in the old Perambulation-Journals *King's* Nefs; which two Names put together make it *King John's* Nefs.

Port of the Town of *Ipswich* doth extend itself from the said Town to the *Polleshead (1)*, and had belonged Time out of Mind, and doth now belong, and is Parcel of the said Town, and of the Farm which they hold of our Lord the King, &c.

The Streets of *Ipswich*, like those of most other ancient Towns, which have not been destroyed by Fire and rebuilt, do not run in Right-lines; and therefore do not strike a Stranger's Eye, as they would if they were more regular; but they contain many good Houses, which generally are better within, than their outward Appearance gives Reason to expect. One favourable Circumstance is almost peculiar to this Place, which is, that most of the better Houses, even in the Heart of the Town, have convenient Gardens adjoining to them, which make them more airy and healthy, as well as more pleasant and delightful.

The many Walks and Rides which abound with a Variety of pleasing Views, together with the Goodness of the Roads in the *Environs* of *Ipswich*, do also contribute greatly towards making the Place agreeable. But however entertaining these Prospects on the Land may be, they are far exceeded by those that the *Orwell* affords; which, to speak cautiously, at least for the Extent of it, is *one of the most beautiful Salt Rivers in the World*. The Beauty of it arises chiefly from its being bounded with High-land on both Sides, almost the whole Way. These Hills on each Side are enriched and adorned with almost every Object that can make a Landscape agreeable; such as Churches, Mills, Gentlemen's Seats, Villages and other Buildings, Woods, noble Avenues, Parks whose Pales reach down to the Water's Edge,

(1) A Place well known to Mariners, upon the Sand called the *Andrews* in the High Sea beyond *Walton* and *Felixtow* Cliffs. *Polishead Common* is mentioned with *Langor-Commons* in the Court-Rolls of Sir *John Barker*'s Manor.

Edge, well stored with Deer and other Cattle, feeding in fine Lawns, &c. &c. all these and more are so happily disposed and diversified, as if Nature and Art had jointly contrived how they might most agreeably entertain and delight the Eye. Such are the Side-Views. As a Passenger sails from *Ipswich*, when he enters what is properly called *Orwell Haven*, the Scene terminates on the Right, with a View of *Harwich* and the high Coast of *Essex*; on the Left with *Landguard-Fort*, and the high Land of *Walton* and *Felixstow* Cliffs behind it; and with a Prospect of the main Ocean before him. As he returns to *Ipswich*, the Scene closes with a distinct View of that fair Town, displaying itself to some Advantage, and forming a Sort of Half-moon as the River winds.

Before the Conquest *(m)*, and for many Years after it, *Ipswich* was in the same Condition as all other Boroughs that

(m) As no Use is here made of Mr. *Bacon*'s Manuscript, concerning the ancient Condition of this Town and its Inhabitants; it may be expected that some Reason should be given for it. For Mr. *Bacon* was a Man of Learning, and good Abilities; he had also great Opportunities of informing himself: He was elected *Recorder*, in 1643; he afterwards accepted the Place of *Town Clerk*; in 1654, he represented the Borough at *Oliver Cromwell*'s Parliament, and continued his Service in these three Capacities to the Day of his Death, in 1659. It is likewise certain, that he did not grudge his Trouble; for, on the Sight of this Book, consisting of more than *Eight hundred* Folio Pages, written with his own Hand, one cannot but admire his Industry. Mr. *Bacon* begins his Annals of *Ipswich* from the *Saxon* Times, and brings them down to the Death of King *Charles* I. Here he seems to drop a Tear, and says, " *The last Day of* January [1648] *puts a* " *sad Period to my Pen*;" but his other Writings which were the Work of Years, published in 1649, shew how deeply he had interested himself in the Confusion of those Times, and he was accordingly made Master of Requests to *Oliver Cromwell*. And notwithstanding the Learning and Abilities of this Gentleman, it appears plainly from those Writings, as well as from his *Annals* of *Ipswich*, that he was a Person of strong Prejudices, and that his Partiality in favour of particular

that were in the ancient *Demefne* of the Crown, in *Dominio Regis*. The King fometimes held thefe Boroughs himfelf, and appointed one or more Officers who were called *Præpofiti*, or *Provofts*; whofe Bufinefs it was to govern the Borough, to fuperintend the Management

cular Notions adopted by him, led him into many Miftakes; fome of which are fo grofs, that they are not eafily to be accounted for. He had juftly conceived high Notions of the great *Antiquity* of the *Borough*, and from thence he unwarily inferred the *Antiquity* of the *Corporation*, which are two very different Things *Ipfwich* was perhaps *one of the moft ancient* Boroughs in the Kingdom, but it was a Royal Borough in *ancient Demefne*; fo that the Burgeffes were in general Vaffals of the Crown. If it be not one of the *moft ancient* Corporations, it is certainly one of the *very ancient* Corporations, for not many can claim before it; yet it was not a free incorporated Society till King *John* enfranchifed and made it fo. But Mr. *Bacon* fuppofes the *Corporation* to be prior to the Conqueft. Nay, he carries the Antiquity of the Town fo ridiculoufly far, that he fuppofes thefe prefent Churches to be the very identical Buildings that exifted in the *Saxon* Times. For, fpeaking of thofe mentioned in *Domefday* by Name, he adds, " And, doubtlefs, there were more; for divers more " there are that feem not inferior in Antiquity to any of the " former." Whereas we know fome of thefe, which feem as ancient as the reft, were built long fince the Conqueror's Time. But were it not fo, the Authority of *Domefday* Book is fo great, that it is allowed in all Courts to be decifive in all Points determinable by that; and as no more than nine Churches are therein mentioned, we may be very certain there were no more then ftanding. Upon relating the idle Story of King *Yppus*, before-mentioned, Mr. *Bacon* does not cenfure it, he contents himfelf with a *Quere* in the Margin, " If not " *Wippo*, a *Saxon* of Note for making Laws;" and refers his Reader to *Lindenbrogius*. But the moft glaring Thing of all is, his putting off the Charter of the 40 King *Henry* III. for a Charter of King *Henry* II. whereas Mr. *Bacon* muft know *Henry* II. did not reign *Thirty five* Years. And King *Edward* I. reciting this in his Charter, calls it exprefsly *his Father*'s Charter. In other Men, this might be confidered as an Overfight; but in a Perfon of Mr. *Bacon*'s Difcernment, we know not what to call it. Mr. *Bacon* is ftill more confufed in his Account of *Richard* the Fiift's Time. So that we think we have good Reafon not to regard his Account of the Town *during this very early Period*, but to rely upon other Authorities, which may, with more Satisfaction, be depended on.

ment of the *Demesne* Lands, to receive the Geld, Hanse, and all other Duties and Imposts (many of which there were) under the *Norman* Kings; these Officers were called *Ballivi*, or Bailives.

But the most usual Way was, for the King to grant these Boroughs to some *Earl*, at that Time the highest Order of *English* Nobility *(n)*, and a Title of Office, as well as Honour; and in this Case, the *Earl* appointed the Officers before-mention'd; and the Usage was, for the King to have two Thirds of the Revenues of the Borough to his own Use, or the Use of such Person as he thought fit to grant them to; and the Earl had the other third Part *(o)*, together with the *third Penny* of all Fines, Forfeitures, Amercements, *&c.* Sometimes the *Earl* lett the Revenues of the Borough to some other Persons, for a *certain annual Rent*, but still he had his *Third*.

As to the State of the *Burgesses*, at the Time we are speaking of; there might be some Inhabitants who had Possessions without the Borough, held by *Military* Service, which was the *only free Tenure*. These were lawful Men of the Realm, *sui juris*, and Free-men, properly so called. There were others, who, by particular Favour and Grant from the Crown, had changed their Tenures for an annual Payment, which was called a *Free-Rent*; as it freed them from the personal, and more servile Service, to which they were before obliged. The rest held by *Soccage-Tenure*, or something equivalent
to

(n) The first *English Duke*, in the present Sense of the Word, was *Edward* the Black Prince, Son of King *Edward* III. created by Him *Duke of Cornwal*.

(o) Thus *Norwich* paid 20 *l.* to the King, and 10 *l.* to the *Earl*. In *Lewes*, two Parts were the King's, and the third was the *Earl*'s. *Oxford* paid yearly to the King 20 *l.* and six Gallons of Honey; to *Earl Alger* 10 *l.* and he had a Mill adjoining. *Stafford* paid 9 *l.* two Parts of which were the King's, the other was the *Earl*'s. *Selden* and *Brady*.

C

to it, and were in a State of Vassalage and Servility *(p)*. They had, strictly speaking, no Property of their own; they held what they had at the Will of the Lord; could not aliene, nor could their Children inherit without his Permission. Nay, the Lord, under whose Dominion they were, was considered as having a Sort of Property in their very Persons, and accordingly they were called HIS Villains, and HIS Men. Even the Citizens of *London* thought it a great Point gained, when they obtained from the Conqueror what is called his Charter to them; tho' it consists only of four or five Lines, and contains only these two Privileges, *viz.* That the Burgesses should be *Law-worthy (q)*; and that their Children should be their *Heirs*. Such was the general Condition of Boroughs and Burgesses in ancient *Demesne*; Whether this were the Condition of *Ipswich* in particular, the Reader may judge by the following Extracts from *Domesday*

(p) Selden says, "against *Miles* and *Tenant* by *Knights-*
"*service*, were opposed, *LiberSokemannus, Burgensis, Villanus,*
"*Tenant in ancient Demesne*, and *Serviens*. *Sokemans* were but
"Tenants in *Soccage*, who held by Service of the Plough, and
"such like. Burgesses were Men of Towns, of *Personal*, not
"*Feudal* Worth. *Villain*, near the like, altho' applied af-
"terwards to Bond-slaves. *Tenants in Demesne*, altho' they
"had large Liberties of Discharge and Quiet, as now, yet
"were reckoned so far from the Worth of old Tenants by
"*Knights-Service*, that they *had not Rank as Liberi Homines*,
"or *Free-Men*." But, after the Enfranchisement, the Burgesses would not admit a *Villain* to be free of *Ipswich*; and by an Order of Court 23 *Henry* VII. each one, before Admission was to swear he was a *Free Man* of *England*.

(*q*) Dr. *Brady* remarking upon this says, there were two Ways of being *Law-worthy*, or having the Benefit of the Law. By the State and Condition of Men's Persons, so almost all *Free-men* had the free Benefit of the Law; but Men of servile Condition had not, especially such as were *in Dominio*, in *Demesne*; for they received Justice from their *Lords*, were judged by them in most Cases, and had not the true Benefit of the Law. So neither could their Children be their Heirs; for they held their Lands and Goods at the Will of the Lord, and were not sure to enjoy them longer than they pleased *Him*.

Domesday Book in the Exchequer, the Authority of which is allowed to be decisive and indisputable. It was finished in 20 *William* the Conqueror, or *A.D.* 1086.

"Half Hundred of *Gippeswid*. This *Roger Bigot* keepeth in the King's Hand. And in the Time of King *Edward* [the Confessor] Queen *Edith (r)* had two Parts of the Borough, and Earl *Guert (s)* had the third Part. And the Queen had a Grange *(t)* in Demesn, [*suo Dominio*] to which belonged in the Time of King *Edward* four Carucates of Land [or Plough-Lands], and now in like manner twelve Free-men, who dwell upon other Land of their own Property, always occupy fourscore Acres of this Land, for the Service and Custom of the King. And there are ten other Men, *Bordarii*, who have no Land of their own Property, but dwell upon fourscore and six Acres of the Land aforesaid."

"The Villains always have six Acres, and this Land pays nothing to the King's *Geld*."

"Earl *Guert*, in the Time of King *Edward*, had one Grange, &c. then valued at a Hundred Shillings, with the *Third Penny* of the Borough, and 20 *l.* was paid for it. But now, with the Third Penny of the Borough and with the Third Penny of two Hundreds, it pays only 15 *l.*"

(r) Queen *Edith*, Wife of King *Edward* the Confessor, was the Daughter of Earl *Goodwin*.

(s) Earl *Guert* was the sixth Son of Earl *Goodwin*, therefore Brother of Queen *Edith*, and also of *Harold*, who disputed the Crown with *William* the Conqueror; these two Brothers were both slain at the decisive Battle of *Hastings*.

(t) We suppose this to be at present the Property of Sir *Thomas Thorowgood*; it is now no more than a Farm-house, but it hath been larger; and having been formerly a *Royal Grange*, upon the re-building it, we think it might have the Name of *New Palace*, or *New Place*, which it retains to this Day. And why might not *Handford* Hall be the ancient Grange of Earl *Guert*, afterwards mentioned? But we acknowledge these to be no more than Conjectures.

" In the Time of King *Edward,* there were 538
" Burgesses, who paid Custom to the King, and they
" had forty Acres of Land. But now there are 110
" Burgesses who pay Custom, and *(u)* 100 poor Bur-
" gesses, who can pay no more than One Penny a Head
" to the King's *Geld.* So upon the whole, they have
" Forty Acres of Land, and Three Hundred and
" Twenty-eight Houses now empty, and which in the
" Time of King *Edward,* scotted to the King's *Geld.*
" *Roger* the *Vice-Earl,* lett the whole for 40 *l.* to be
" paid at the Feast of St. *Michael* ; afterwards he could
" not have that Rent, and he abated Sixty Shillings of
" it, now it pays 37*l.* And the Earl always hath the
" *Third* Part *(x).*"

It is not here said whether the Revenues of the Borough were lett to one or more Persons; but probably they were lett to some of the principal Burgesses. And they continued at the same Rent or near it, for above an hundred Years, as will appear presently.

The Policy of the *Norman* Princes led them to raise the Condition of the lower People, that by their Means they might the better be enabled to check the Power of the *Barons.* This was done gradually: First, by altering the Tenures of private Persons in the manner before-mentioned; and then by enfranchising whole Communities, especially the Boroughs in Royal *Demesne,* as being more immediately dependant upon the Crown. *Ipswich* did not enjoy this Benefit before the Reign of King *John*; yet some Steps were taken towards it, in the Reign of his Brother King *Richard* I. *viz.*

" The

(u) It is not easy to account for so great an Alteration in the Borough, within the Space of Twenty Years or thereabout ; but, in those Times of Confusion, there are other Instances of the like Kind.

(x) Ipswich Domesday, from that in the Exchequer.

"The Men of *Ipswich* owe *Forty Marcs*, for having
"their Liberties. The Men of *Ipswich* have accounted
"for *Sixty* Marcs for having their Town in their own
"Hands, by increasing the Farm One Hundred Shil-
"lings *per Annum*, for the Confirmation of our Lord the
"King, concerning their Liberties; they have paid it
"into the Treasury, and are acquitted *(y)* :" *i. e.* as we
understand it, They were to pay in the whole *One Hundred Marcs*, of which they had actually paid *Sixty*, and
stood indebted for the other *Forty Marcs*. We imagine
they found it difficult to raise so large a Sum, and their
not being able to pay the whole, together with the annual Rent which kept running on at the Rate of 35 *l.*
per Ann. was what prevented this Agreement with the
Crown from taking Effect. That the Farmers were in
Arrear, appears from the Entry of the next Year, 7th
Richard I. which says, " The Men of *Ipswich* owe 17*l.*
" 10*s.* for the Rent of *Ipswich* for last Year ," [*i. e.* Half
a Year's Rent,] " and 35 *l.* for the Rent of this Year."

And on the Back of the Great Roll of 10 *Richard* I.
it is said, to this Effect: The Men of *Ipswich* are
accountable,

	l. *s.* *d.*		*l.* *s.* *d.*
For several former Years	22 12 1	They have paid	21 13 5
Arrears of 9 *Ric.* I.	10 10 6	By Writs to the Bishop of *Norwich* for 4 Years and half due to the Hamlets of *Wykes*	45 0 0
For the Farm of this Year	35 0 0		

What has been now said, and these previous Steps
towards obtaining the Enfranchisement of the Borough,
will account for the early Date of King *John*'s Charter;
for King *John* came to the Crown on the 8th *April* 1199,
and his Charter to *Ipswich* bears *Test* on the 25th of the
very next Month.

C 3 By

(y) Ipswich Domesday.

By this King *John* granted to the Burgesses, 1. The Borough of *Ipswich* with all its Appurtenances, Liberties, &c. to be holden of him and his Heirs, to them and their Heirs hereditarily, by the Payment of the *right and usual* annual Farm, and *One Hundred Shillings more* at the Exchequer, by the Hands of the *Provost* of *Ipswich* (z) &c. 2. He exempted them from the Payment of all Taxes under the several Names of *Tholl, Lestage, Stallage, Passage, Pontage*, and all other Customs throughout his Land and Sea-ports (a). 3. That they should have a Merchant's *Gild* and *Hanse* of their own. 4. That no Person should be quartered upon them without their Consent, or take any thing from them by Force (b). 5. That they might hold their Lands, and recover their just Dues from whomsoever they be owing (c). 6. That they should hold their Lands and Tenures within the Borough, according to the Custom of the Borough of *Ipswich*. 7. That none of them shall be fined or amerced, but according to the Laws of the *Free-Boroughs*. 8. And, that they might choose two Bailives and four Coroners out of the *more lawful* (d) Men of the said Town (e).

Tho'

(z) It is not here said what this *right* and usual *Payment* was, but we have seen that it was 35 *l. per Ann.* to which if we add 100 Shillings or 5 *l.* it will make the annual Payment in King *John*'s Time *Sixty Mares*, or 40 *l.*

(a) This Privilege is now enjoyed to the great Benefit of such Masters of Ships as are free of the Borough, in all the Ports of this Kingdom, not excepting the City of *London*.

(b) A plain Proof that they were liable to these Oppressions before.

(c) This was making them *lawful* Men, which before they were not.

(d) That is, as we suppose, the principal Men of the Town, and such as were before the Enfranchisement by the Charter, in a Condition *nearest to that* of *a free and lawful Man*, properly so called. In Confirmation of what has been before advanced, it is to be observed, that almost Two Hundred Years after the Date of King *John*'s Charter, the whole Number of *lawful* Men in this good Town, was no more than 1085; *viz.*

In

IPSWICH *with its* SUBURBS. 23

Tho' the Burgesses had a due Sense of the Privileges conferred upon them by this Charter, they did not act in consequence of it, until the *Thursday* next after *June* 24, in the *second* Year of King *John*'s Reign, which was thirteen Months after the Date of the Charter. This Delay can only be imputed to the Difficulty they found in raising the Money for it. It being an usual thing not to deliver these Grants and Charters before all Fines, Fees, &c. are discharged and paid.

But on the Day now mentioned, being a Body newly created, and having no House or Place to meet in, they assembled in the Church-Yard of St. *Mary* at *Tower*, and held their *first Great Court*, which was continued for three Sessions by Adjournment. At this Court the Burgesses elected the *first Bailives*. And they resolved that there should be in this Borough *Twelve* Capital *Portmen*, as there were in the other Free Boroughs of *England*. At the second Session, they elected four Men out of each Parish, to act as a Committee for the whole Township; which Committee chose the *First Twelve Portmen*. At the third Session, they ordered a *Common-Seal* to be made; and chose an Alderman of the *Merchants Gild*, with four Associates to assist him.

The second Great Court was held on the *Sunday* next after *September* 8, in the same Year, and in the same Church-

In the Parish of

St. *Margaret*	214	St. *George*	26
St. *Ellen*'s	29	St. *Austin with Stoke*	26
St. *Clement*	137	St. *Nicholas*	136
St. *Mary at Key*	45	St. *Mary at Elms*	56
Brook's Hamlet	7	St. *Mary at Tower*	147
Wyke's Hamlet	15	St. *Laurens*	127
St. *Matthew*	89	St. *Stephen*	31

1085.

This was in 4 King *Richard* II. or 1381. *Bacon*'s M.S. Fol. 94.

(*e*) See what is said of *Norwich*, under the Article of *Beccles*, in *Wangford* Hundred.

Church-yard; when they re-elected the same two Persons to be Bailives for the succeeding Year. The second Session of this Court was held by Adjournment in the *Church* of St. *Mary Tower*; when the Common Seal was produced, and three Persons were appointed to keep that and the Charter, who were the *First Clavigers*. Soon after, in this Year, the Priors of *Trinity* and St. *Peter*'s Priories were admitted Free Burgesses, paying Fines, *viz.* the Prior of *Trinity Twenty Shillings*, and the Prior of St. *Peter*'s *One Marc*, in Aid of the Expence in obtaining the Charter. *Roger Bigot*, Earl of *Norfolk*, was likewise admitted a Free Burgess; and it is mentioned as a Reason, because the said Earl assisted in procuring the King's Charter, *to be delivered to the Town*.

But, even after the Enfranchisement took place, the Boroughs in *Demesne* found this farther Inconvenience, that they were obliged in all Aids made to the King in Parliament, to pay a greater Proportion than the other free Subjects did. Thus, in 22 King *Edward* I. when the Subjects in general were assessed one *Tenth* of their personal Effects, the City of *London* and the other Cities and Boroughs in *Demesne*, paid one *sixth* Part of their Personalty; and, in the next Year, when the Kingdom in general was assessed for one *eleventh* Part, the Cities and *Boroughs* in *Demesne* paid one *seventh*. And after the Citizens and Burgesses were regularly summoned to Parliament, as well as the Earls, Barons, and Knights of the Shires, it became a settled Rule, that the Cities and *Boroughs* in *Demesne*, should give about *one Third more*, than the Earls, Barons and Knights did grant. Thus in 34 *Edward* I. when the People in general paid a *Thirtieth* Part, the Citizens and Burgesses in *Demesne* paid a *Twentieth*; 1 *Edward* II. when the People in general paid one *Twentieth* Part, the *Burgesses* in *Demesne* paid one *Fifteenth*; and in 12 *Edward* II. when the rest

were

were taxed an *Eighteenth*, the *Burgesses* in *Demesne* were taxed one *Twelfth* Part. It doth farther appear from a Writ in 43 *Edward* III. that *Ipswich* was the only Borough in this County, that was in the *ancient Demesne* of the Crown. *(f)*.

King *Edward* I. in the Thirteenth Year of his Reign, for certain Excesses and Offences by the Burgesses of *Ipswich* committed (but what these were is not mentioned) seized the Borough into his own Hands, and kept it till his 19th Year; when being pleased, (as it is said,) with the Service performed by some Ships from *Ipswich*, in his Expedition against *Scotland*; he re-granted the Borough with its Liberties, *&c.* to the *Burgesses*, and confirmed the Charters of King *John* and *Henry* III. by his Charter, dated at *Berwick* 23 *June* 19 *Edward* III. or *A. D.* 1291. But he punished the Town sufficiently, by raising the Annual Rent full 50 *per Cent.* for instead of *Sixty Marcs*, he made it *Sixty Pounds*; and thus it hath continued ever since *(g)*. And perhaps a better Reason may be assigned for his restoring the Charters, than that before-mentioned; since it appears from that Part of the Sheriff of *Norfolk*'s Account which we have seen, that the King did not receive so much from the Borough during the Seizure, as the Annual Fee farm thus raised amounted to. But *Bacon*'s MS. says, *Philip Harneis*, *John Clement*, *Vivian Silvester*, and *John Briset* did in 18 *Edward* I. account for 60 *l.* Farm, during the King's Pleasure; and that this appeareth from *Rot. Mag. Norf.* in the *Exchequer*; so this Agreement might fix the Annual Rent at 60 *l.*

As

(f) Brady, p. 41.

(g) Out of the Fee-farm due annually from this Borough, the Corporation, by Queen *Elizabeth*'s School Charter, is authorized to detain 24 *l.* 6 *s.* 8 *d.* for the Master's Salary; and 14 *l.* 6 *s.* 8 *d.* for the Usher's Salary; the remaining Sum of 21 *l.* 6 *s.* 8 *d.* was sold in the Reign of K. *Charles* II. and is now the Property of *Robert Edgar*, Esq;

As soon as their Charters were restored, the Burgesses elected TWENTY-FOUR Men to act as a Committee, and to collect the ancient Usages and Customs of the Borough, and to enroll them, that they might be better known and ascertained than they had been since the Elopement of one *John Blake*, who was the *Town-Clerk*; and in the last Year of King *Henry* III. he fled from the Town, and carried away some of their Records. When the Body of *Twenty-four Men* was first instituted, doth not appear; but we think it not improbable, that it might have its Rise from this Committee; yet we do not find them mentioned as a *Body*, before the Time of *Edward* IV. but then they are mentioned as having been long in Use.

There are several ancient Usages and Customs, some of which continue to this Day. Particularly,

1. Upon an Alienation after *Seisin* of Tenements in the said Town delivered to a Purchaser, the *Wife* of the *Vender* may come into Court, and being solely examined, may acknowledge that Alienation to be done with her Consent; and that Recognizance being enrolled, is final.

2. Tenements in *Fee* may be devised by Will, and by Custom of the Town, such Wills may be proved *(h)* and enrolled, and *Seisin* shall be delivered to him to whom they are bequeathed.

3. Every Heir Male or Female is of full Age at the Age of *Fourteen* Years; and then the Friends who have received the Rents during the Minority, shall account.

4. All

(h) The Usage was to prove such Wills as devised Lands or Houses before the *Bailives*, when the Town-Clerk endorsed upon them a Memorandum of such Probat, and then such Wills were proved and lodged in the Spiritual Courts, for the Personalty. Many Wills are in the Archdeacon's Office with such Endorsements; some as late as the Time of King *Henry* VIII.

4. All Tenements in this Town are partable, as well between Heirs Male as Heirs Female *(i)*, if they be not foreclosed by Gift or Bequest of their Ancestor.

5. If a Burgess take a Wife, whether Damsel or Widow, so that he wedded no other Wife afore, and the Wife out-live her Husband; the Wife shall have all the chief Place of her Husband whereof he died seised in the said Town in his *Domain*, as of Fee, to hold in Name of *Free-bank*, while she keeps her Widowhood, without making Waste or Alienation in *Disherison* of the Heir.

6. All those that have Lands and Tenements in the Town, whether Male or Female, and can reckon and count; and have accomplished the Age of Fourteen Years, may give his Land or Freehold, or sell it, or lett it, and of his Right quit Claim for evermore, as if he had accomplished the Age of *Twenty-one* Years.

7. A Woman Covert may be compelled to answer in a Plea of Trespass, on Pain of Imprisonment, in like manner as she would were she *sole*; so that the Trespass be personal, and touch not Freehold.

The Body of Portmen were not originally created by Charter, but appointed by the Burgesses, as we said before. How long they continued, doth not certainly appear; but that they were not kept up in the Beginning of King *Edward* the Second's Reign, is clear: For about the 3d *Edward* II. or *A. D.* 1310, the Burgesses resolved to revive that Order, and elected *Twenty-seven* Men out of the several Parishes, *viz.* St. *Margaret's*, 4; St. *Mary Tower*, 4; St. *Matthew* and St. *George*, 3; St. *Laurence* and St. *Stephen*, 4; St. *Mary Elms* and St. *Nicholas*, 4;
St.

(i) This is called *Gavelkind*, and furnishes another Proof of the servile State of the ancient Burgesses: For wherever this Custom obtained, it was originally introduced by the Policy of the Chief Lord, in order to keep all their Vassals as near as might be upon an Equality with each other; that so, their own Superiority over them all, might appear the more considerable and conspicuous.

St. *Peter* and St. *Auſtin*, 4; St. *Mary Key* and St. *Clement*, 4. Theſe made a Committee, who were to chooſe *Twelve Portmen* to preſerve the Laws, Cuſtoms, &c. and to do all other Things as the *other Twelve Men* uſed to do; and, upon a Death it was agreed, the *Eleven* ſhould chooſe another in his Stead *(k)*.

About 18 King *Edward* III. *William Sharford* ſat as Judge of Aſſize here; and, being a moroſe Man, he was ſo offended with the Magiſtrates for not apprehending ſome Sailors who had behaved, as he thought, rudely towards him *(l)*, that he cauſed the King to ſeize the Liberties: So the Government of the Town was committed to the Sheriff of *Norfolk* and *Suffolk*; and *Edward Noon* was deputed by him as *Keeper* of the Town. But this did not laſt above a Year; for tho' upon the *Monday* after St. *Matthew* (*Sept.* 21.) a Court was held before *Edward Noon, Deputy-Keeper*, yet on the Lord's Day after the Aſſumption of the Virgin *Mary* (*Aug.* 15.) following, a Court was holden before *John de Preſtoun* and *William Ringold* Bailiffs, as uſual *(m)*.

Next to the Charter of King *John* that of 24 King *Henry* VI. was moſt beneficial; by this he incorporated the Town by the Name of " *The Burgeſſes of Ipſwich*." He authoriſed them in every Year to elect two *Burgeſſes* to be Bailives at the *accuſtomed Time and Place*, to exerciſe that Office for *one whole Year*. He granted to the Bailives, and Four ſuch other Burgeſſes as the ſaid Bailives ſhall be pleaſed to take to them out of the *Twelve Portmen*,

---

(k) Bacon's MS. Fol. 49.

(l) It is ſaid the Caſe was this: The Sailors thought the Judge ſtayed too long at Dinner; ſo at laſt one of them ſat upon the Bench, and cauſed another to make Proclamation, requiring *William Sharford* to come into Court, and ſave his Fine; who not appearing, the Sailor-Judge fined him. This was the Offence.

(m) Bacon's MS. Fol. 76.

Portmen (*n*), the Office of Juſtice of the Peace, &c. within the ſaid Town; granted all Fines, Forfeitures, and Amercements ariſing from the Office of Juſtice of the Peace, &c. and the Aſſize of Bread, Wine, and Ale; appointed ſuch one of the Bailives, as at the time of their Election the Burgeſſes ſhall chooſe, to be *Eſcheator*; and expreſsly granted the Admiralty, and Clerkſhip of the Market.

King *Henry* VI. being of the Houſe of *Lancaſter*, his Succeſſor *Edward* IV. recites in his Charter all the Charters of the former Kings, but takes no notice of this. From hence it has happened that the Charter of King *Henry* VI. is never mentioned. But it is certain the Burgeſſes accepted it, and acted under it; for in 26, *Henry* VI. it was ordered that all the Profits of the Offices of *Eſcheator* and *Juſtice of the Peace* ſhould be applied towards the Expence of the Building at the End of the Hall of Pleas. *Robert Wode* was the firſt Eſcheator, elected in Form 24 *Henry* VI. It is to be obſerved, that tho' the Aſſize of *Bread*, &c. and the Offices of *Admiral* and *Clerk of the Market* were firſt expreſsly granted in this Charter of *Henry* VI. the Bailives did always exerciſe thoſe Offices by the *Cuſtom of the Town*. Thus particularly, on a *Quo Warranto* for removing the Fiſh-Market in the Time of *Henry* III. they juſtified themſelves by *the Cuſtom*, and that Plea was admitted. *Bacon*'s MS.

Tho' *Edward* IV. would take no notice of the preceding Charter, he himſelf granted all the Privileges mentioned in that, with the following Alterations and Additions, *viz.*

He incorporated the Town by the Name of the *Bailiffs*, *Burgeſſes*, and *Commonalty* of the Town of *Ipſwich*. He confined the Election of Bailives expreſsly to 8 *September*, and

---

(*n*) This is the firſt mention that is made of the *Portmen* in any Charter.

and in the *Guild-Hall*, and they were to serve for one Year from *thence next following* (*o*). And he expressly exempted the Burgesses from Service on Juries.

The succeeding Kings confirmed the Charters of their Predecessors; but the most interesting Charter since those of *Henry* VI. and *Edward* IV. was that of King *Charles* II. who in his *seventeenth* Year (to rectify some Irregularities, and settle some Disputes which had arisen in the preceding Times of Confusion, particularly with regard to the Election of *Portmen*, and the *Twenty-four* chief Constables) granted his Charter, in which he confirmed the High Steward, the *Twelve Portmen*, the *Twenty-four* chief Constables, the *Recorder* and *Town-Clerk* for that Time being, by their Names; and directed that upon the Death or Removal of one or more of the *Portmen* or *Chief Constables*, all Elections of *Portmen* should be made by the *Rest* or *Residue* of the *Portmen*, and all Elections of the *Twenty-four* should be made by the Rest or Residue of them, &c. &c.

After the Example of most other Boroughs, towards the latter End of the Reign of King *Charles* II. the Burgesses of *Ipswich* surrendered their Charter; and, instead of it, in 36 *Charles* II. he gave them another, which reduced the Number of Chief Constables to *Eighteen*; and in this a Power was reserved, that the Crown might by an Order of Council, turn out any of the *Portmen* and

Eighteen

(*o*) From this Expression some have objected to the Practice of swearing the new Bailives on *Michaelmas-Day*; and the Contenders on different Sides have at different Times availed themselves of the Objection. But constant Usage hath more Weight than the Words of a Charter: And it is certain, the Custom hath *always been* to swear the Bailives on the 29th *September*, and they have constantly served their Office until the *Michaelmas-Day* following. Nay, it doth still appear upon Record, that this was the Usage within nine Years after the Grant of *Edward* the Fourth's Charter; for in the Month of *May*, 12 *Edward* IV. *William Style* was elected Bailiff in the room of *John Creyk* deceased, to execute the Office with *John Wallworth*, the other Bailiff, until *the Feast of St. Michael next following*. Gr. Court Book.

IPSWICH *with its* SUBURBS. 31

Eighteen Chief-Conſtables, when and as often as his Majeſty, or his Succeſſors, ſhould be pleaſed ſo to do.— In conſequence of this reſerved Power King *James* II. by two Orders of Council dated the 27 *April* and 25 *May*, A.D. 1688, out of the *Thirty* Portmen and Chief Conſtables, actually removed *Twenty-three*. But tho' the Burgeſſes received this Charter, and acted under it, yet the Surrender of the Town made to K. *Charles* II. was not *enrolled*; nor was any Judgment *entered upon Record*, upon the *Quo Warranto* brought againſt the Corporation in the Reign of King *Charles* II. And therefore upon the Publication of King *James's* Proclamation of 17 *October*, 1688, the *Bailives, Portmen,* and *Twenty-four Men*, who had acted under the firſt Charter of 17 *Charles* II. reſumed their Functions; they aſſembled and filled up their Bodies reſpectively, and from *theſe Portmen* and theſe *Twenty-four Men* are the preſent Portmen and Twenty-four Men, in Succeſſion derived.

The remaining Portmen in 1688, were, *John Burrough*, *Charles Wright, *Lawrence Stiſted, Richard Philips, Richard Sparrow, *William Neave, William Browne, *Edward Reynolds, and *John Blomfield. The remaining Twenty-four Men, were, *Robert Ridnal, *John Sawyer, J. Firman, *J. Camplin, *Tho. Bright, *J. Gibbon, *Rob. Cockeril, *Rob. Smith, *Rob. Manning, Truth Norris, *James Page, *Nat. Bateman, *Hen. Sparowe, *Hen. Capon, *Tho. Riches, *Wm. Tye, *Nic. Philips, and J. Reeve (p).

The Borough ſends two Members to Parliament, who are elected by the Burgeſſes at large, in Number between 600 and 700.

The

(*p*) Thoſe who have this Mark [*] were either left out of the Eighteen-Charter, or were removed by K. *James* II. This King did alſo grant the Town a Charter, in the laſt Year of his Reign; by which he increaſed the Number of Chief Conſtables to the ancient Number of Twenty-four; but it doth not appear to us, that this Charter was accepted, or that the Corporation acted under it, and therefore we take no farther Notice of it.

The principal Officers in the Corporation at present are, two Bailives, a High-Steward, a Recorder, Twelve Portmen, of whom four are Justices of the Peace; a Town-Clerk; Twenty-four Chief Constables, of whom two are Coroners; and the Twelve Seniors are Headboroughs; a Treasurer, and two Chamberlains, to collect the Revenues of the Town. The Corporation have also fifteen Livery-Servants, *viz.* five Musicians, four Serjeants at Mace, two Beadles, a Common-Cryer, a Water-Bailiff, a Goaler, and a Bridewell-Keeper.

An ACCOUNT *of the Churches, Religious Houses, and other Buildings,* &c. &c. *in* IPSWICH, *its Suburbs, and Precincts.*

THE following Churches are mentioned in Domesday-Book, as standing in the Conqueror's Time, *viz.* The *Holy Trinity,* St. *Austin,* St. *Michael,* St. *Mary,* St. *Botolph* [i. e. *Whitton* Church], St. *Laurence,* St. *Peters,* St. *Stephen,* and *Thurlweston.* Of these, the three former are down and not rebuilt.——15 *Edw.* I. or *A. D.* 1287. " On New year's Day at Night, as well through " Vehemency of the Wind as Violence of the Sea, many " Churches were overthrown and destroyed, not only at " *Yarmouth, Dunwich,* and *Ipswich,* but also in divers " other Places in *England.*" *Stowe*'s Annals.

There are at present, 1. St. *Clement:* This Church was early and wholly impropriated to the Priory of St. *Peter,* without any Vicarage created; and its being *thus* impropriated, when the last Valuation was made, occasioned its not being valued in the King's Books *(q).*

The

(q) But it pays a Fee-farm Rent of 40 *l.*

The Impropriation was granted, 7 *Edw.* VI. to *William Webb* and *William Breton*; but afterwards it came into the Hands of *Robert Broke* and *William Bloife*, who prefented a Clerk to the Rectory in *A. D.* 1606, and thereby reftored the Rector to all the Rights and Dues which he was entitled to before the Impropriation was made. This Church is now ͵confolidated with St. *Hellen's*. " K. *Richard* gave *Wykes* a Member of *Ipfwich* [and in " this Parifh] to *John Oxenford* Bifhop of *Norwich,* " which fhall anfwer to *Ipfwich* for 10 *l.* *(r)*; and the " Bifhop of *Norwich* holdeth it, but it is not known by " what Service." The Hamlet and Manor of *Wykes-Bifhop* was afterwards confirmed to *John le Gray*, Bifhop of *Norwich*, by K. *John*; and it belonged to the Bifhops of *Norwich* till it was given to K. *Henry* VIII. by Act of Parliament in 1535; who granted it *A. D.* 1545, to Sir *John Jermie*, Knt. While the Bifhops of *Norwich* had it, they ufed frequently to refide at their Houfe fituated near the South-fide of the Road, leading towards *Nacton* from *Bifhops-Hill*; where there is now a fquare Field, which feems as if formerly it had been moated round. Many Inftitutions, *&c.* are faid in the Books at *Norwich*, to have been granted at this Place. The Manor of *Wykes-Bifhop* is now vefted in the Heirs of Sir *Samuel Barnardifton*, of *Brightwell*. The Church of *Wykes* is fometimes mentioned in old Writings; but it is not known where it ftood; and poffibly it might be no more than a Chapel, for the Ufe of the Bifhop and his Family.

Within this Parifh of St. *Clement* lieth alfo Part of the Hamlet of *Wykes Ufford*, tho' the greater Part of it is in the Parifhes of *Rufhmere* and *Wefterfield*; it was fo called from

(r) Ipfwich Domefday. It appears by an Account copied into this Book, that in the Time of *Richard* I. the Town ufed to pay 10 *l. per Ann.* to the Bifhop of *Norwich*, which was allowed to them and deducted out of the Fee-Farm Rent.

from the Family of *De Uffords*, who were Earls of *Suffolk*, to whom it was formerly granted. *William de Ufford*, Earl of *Suffolk*, died seised of it 5 *Richard* II. Afterwards the *Willoughbys* had it by Descent from *Charles Brandon*, Duke of *Suffolk*. In Q. *Elizabeth*'s Time Sir *John Brewes*, then Sir *Edmund Wythipol*, and it hath gone with *Christ-Church* Estate ever since, being now vested in *Thomas Fonnereau*, Esq;

Beyond St. *Clement*'s Street, and between the two Hamlets stood St. *James*'s Chapel *(s)*, now wholly down: This did, probably, belong to St. *James*'s Hospital. And the Field near which it stood, is Glebe belonging to the Rectory of St. *Hellen*. From hence, and from the Grant of St. *James*'s Fair, it may be conjectured that there was some Connexion between St. *James*'s Hospital and the Leprous-House of St. *Mary Magdalene*, which is said to have stood some where opposite to St. *Hellen*'s Church. Certain it is, King *John*, within three Weeks after he succeeded to the Crown, granted a Fair to the Lepers of St. *Mary Magdalene* in *Ipswich*, to be held on the Day and Morrow of St. *James* the Apostle; some small Remains of which Fair still continue. When the Leprous-House of St. *Mary Magdalene* was dissolved, the Revenues

(s) St. *James*'s Chapel stood adjoining to the South-west Corner of that Piece of Ground after-mentioned, which is Glebe belonging to the Rectory of St. *Hellen*, and from the Use to which it was for many Years applied, called the Rope-Ground. For after the Site of it was built upon, it was sold by *Thomas Essington*, Lord of *Brightwell*, and of the Manor of *Wykes-Bishop* in A.D. 1655. And in the Conveyance to one *Noyse*, " he sells the Messuage called or known by the
" Name of *the Chapel* ———, and the Yard called the Cha-
" pel-yard, containing half an Acre more or less, now in-
" closed within a Pale, as the same are situated in the Ham-
" let of *Wykes-Bishop*, between the common Way leading
" from St. *Clement*'s-street to *Bixley* on the North, and the
" common Way leading from *Ipswich* to *Colneis* on the South,
" and abut upon the Rope yard towards the East, and upon
" a small Alley leading from the said common Way, &c. to
" to the common Way, &c. aforesaid, towards the West."

nues of it were annexed to the Rectory of St. *Hellen* of *Caldwell*, 9 *Henry* VIII *(t).* and with them probably the Revenues of St. *James*'s Hospital; for, beside the Piece of Glebe before-mentioned, the Rector of St. *Hellen* was entitled to some *Portion* of the Tythes arising annually from the Lands in the Hamlet of *Wykes-Bishop*; and for this Portion, a Composition was constantly paid by the Rector of St. *Clement*, before the Consolidation of the two Churches, when they were in different Hands.

2. St. *Hellen*. Altho' this Church was formerly impropriated to the Hospital of St. *James*, or St. *Mary Magdalene*, it hath been instituted into a Rectory, above two hundred Years. The Bishop of *Norwich* had the Advowson till he parted with the Manor of *Wykes*.

In a Field almost opposite to *Caldwell-Hall*, now called *Cold-Hall*, on the South of the Road leading to *Kesgrave*, stood the Church of St. *John Baptist*, in *Caldwell*; of which there are no Remains. It was impropriated to *Trinity* Priory, and granted with that to Sir *Thomas Pope.* The Church of St. *Hellen* enjoyeth at this Day a Piece of Land within the Chauntry-Lands in *Sproughton* and *Stoke*; two Pieces of which Chauntry-Lands, are thus described: " The South Head whereof abutteth upon the " Meadow pertaining to the Church of *Caldwell* in part, " &c." And then follow, " Two Meadows lying to-" gether in *Sproughton* and *Stoke*, abutting upon the Mea-" dow pertaining to the Church of St. *Hellen*'s in *Cald-* " *well,* towards the West."

St. *Edmund a Pountney*, corruptly so called for *Pontimiac* in *France*, where he was buried, had a Chapel which stood towards the South-west Corner of *Rosemarylane, Brook-street*; and which was impropriated to St.

D 2 *Peter*'s

(1) A Piece of Ground East of the upper Rope walk in St. *Clement*'s Parish; and behind, that is, *South* of the Houses opposite to the Church of St. *Hellen*, is Glebe belonging to the said Church; and probably, here this Leprous House might stand.

Peter's Priory; but being in the Gift of the Bishop of *Norwich*, as St. *Hellen*'s was, they were given to the same Incumbent till they were united. *John de Bergham* is mentioned 26 *Edward* I. as Parson of St. *Edmund*'s Chapel, in *Ipswich*. This St. *Edmund* was Archbishop of *Canterbury*, and being weary of the Pope's Exactions in *England*, became a voluntary Exile at *Pontiniac* in *France*, where he died, A. D. 1240 (*u*); with the Honour and Reputation of a Saint. The Rector of St. *Hellen* enjoys a Portion of Corn-Tithes from certain Lands in *Hoxne*, one Field of which is called *Pountney* Close; and these Tithes did, probably, belong to this Chapel.

3. St. *Laurence* is said, in Domesday, to have had twelve Acres of Land. *Norman*, the Son of *Eadnoth*, gave this Church to *Trinity* Priory, who got it impropriated to them. But there having been no Prædial Tithes belonging to it for many Years, there was no Grant of the Impropriation at the Dissolution. The present Building was begun by *John Bottold*, who died A. D. 1431 (*x*). The Chancel was built by *John Baldwyn*, Draper, who died A. D. 1449; and his Name is in the Stone-work under the East Window, now plastered over. Several Legacies were about that time given towards building the Steeple.

A. D. 1514. *Edmund Daundy*, Portman of *Ipswich*, founded a Chauntry in this Church for a Secular Priest to offer at the Altar of St. *Thomas*, in Behalf of himself and his Relations, among whom he reckoned *Thomas Wolsey*, then Dean of *Lincoln*; and his Parents *Robert* and

(*u*) Vid. Mat. Paris.

(*x*) Upon removing a Pew in this Church (*Weaver* saith, p. 750,) an ancient Monument came to Light; which is as follows:

    Subjacet hoc lapide John Bottold, *vir probus ipse*
    Istius ecclesiæ primus inceptor fuit iste;
    Cujus animæ, Domine, miserere tu bone Christe.
      Obiit MCCCCXXXI. Litera Dominicalis. G.

and *Jane Wolsey*, then deceased: And gave this Priest and his Successors, his House in St. *Lawrence* Parish, for a Mansion: And his Lands in *Sproughton, Stoke*, and *Alnesborne*, for a Maintenance. Mr. *Daundy* first built the Market-Cross, and was one of the most respectable Men of the Town, in his Time. All his Daughters married Gentlemen of good Fortune; and the Issue of one of them, was the Wife of Lord-Keeper *Bacon*. It appears then, that Cardinal *Wolsey* was *well allied*; and as we meet with nothing that gives *the least Countenance* to the common Notion of his being the Son of a *Butcher (y)*, it is very probable that his Parents were not in such mean Circumstances, as the Cardinal's Enemies have taught the World to believe. See St. *Nicholas*.

In the Church-Chest of this Parish, shuffled in among other Deeds, a Receipt was lately found, given by *Edward Grymeston* to *Lionel Talmage* and *William Foster*, Esquires, *John Holland* and *Matthew Goodyng*, Bailiffs of *Ipswich*, (Commissioners for the Sale of Church Goods within the said Town,) acknowledging the following Particulars, viz. *Thirty-eight Pounds Seven Shillings and Four-pence* in ready Money, arising from Goods already sold by them; *Four Hundred Threescore and Seventeen Ounces and a half* of Plate; *Eight* Copes of Cloth of Gold and Tissue; *Two* Vestments of Cloth of Gold and Tissue; and *Two* Tunicles of Cloth of Gold and Tissue, to be delivered over to the Use of the King's Majesty by the said *Edward Grymeston*; dated 28 *May*, 7 *Edw.* VI. or *A.D.* 1553.

(y) The vulgar Notion is, that the *Cardinal* built the Shambles, in the Market-square; but this cannot be true: For it is certain they were re-built, or at least very thoroughly repaired in 40 of *Elizabeth*; when a great Quantity of Timber was taken down for this Purpose, upon the Manors of *Ulverstone* Hall and *Sackvyles*, in *Debenham*. Had they been built by *Wolsey*, they could not in so short a Time have wanted such Repair. For we think, nothing considerable hath been done to them from that Time to this.

4. St. *Margaret.* This Church was impropriated to the Priory of the *Holy Trinity.*—*Trinity* Church, from which probably the Priory had its Name, stood near St. *Margaret*'s Church-yard; and is mentioned in *Domesday*, as being endowed in the Conqueror's Time with *Twenty-six Acres* of Land. The strong Foundation of this Steeple was, within these few Years, undermined and blown up with Gunpowder. The Priory was founded and chiefly endowed before *A.D.* 1177, by *Norman Gastrode*, for Black Canons of the Order of St. *Austin*; the Founder became one of the first Canons. King *Henry* II. granted the Prior and Convent a Fair on *Holy-Rood* Day, *Sept.* 14. to continue for three Days. Not long after the Founding of this Monastery, the Church and the Offices were burnt down; but they were rebuilt by *John* of *Oxford*, Bishop of *Norwich*; whereupon King *Richard* I. gave the Patronage of the Priory to him and his Successors. The Grant of the Fair was afterwards confirmed by K. *John*, who, moreover, gave to the Priory all the Lands and Rents *formerly belonging* to the Churches of St. *Michael*, and St. *Saviour*'s, in *Ipswich*. From this Expression, it seems as if both these Churches were even then dilapidated. No Man knows at this Day where they stood; but there is a sort of uncertain Tradition, which says, the Church of St. *Saviour* stood behind St. *Mary Elms*, somewhere in the Garden belonging to the House of *Robert Milner*, Esq; in *Westgate-street.* And that the Church of St. *Michael*, which is said in *Domesday* to have had eight Acres of Land, stood somewhere near to the Church of St. *Nicholas* (z). The Revenues of this Priory in 26 *Henry* VIII. were valued at 88*l.* 6*s.* 9*d. per Ann.* and were granted 36 *Henry* VIII. to Sir *Thomas Pope.* There is now a good Seat called *Christ-Church*, built by Sir *Edmund Whitapole*, and inclosed within a Pale. Sir *Edmund*'s only Child was married to *Leicester* Lord Viscount

(z) See St. *Nicholas* afterwards, and St *Mary Elms.*

count *Hereford*, whose Heiress married *Pryce* late Lord Viscount *Hereford*, and this Estate was sold by Him to *Claude Fonnereau*, Esq; whose eldest Son and Heir *Thomas Fonnereau*, Esq; Member of Parliament for the Borough of *Sudbury*, in this County, doth now enjoy it.

The Church of St. *Margaret* is not mentioned in Domesday, so that it was not then in being; but the Church of the *Holy Trinity* being wholly appropriated to the Use of the Prior and Convent, we think this Church might be built for the Use of the Parishioners.

The Parliamentary Visitors who acted in *Suffolk*, by virtue of a Warrant from the Earl of *Manchester* in the Year 1648, and who from their Hatred of painted Glass, may be called, *The Window-breaking Visitors*, took down from this Church the twelve Apostles in Stone, and ordered between twenty and thirty Pictures to be taken down. This appears from the Journal of *William Dowsing*, of *Stratford*, who was principally concerned and had a power of appointing Deputies to visit and deface Churches in *Suffolk*; a Part of which Journal accidentally came into our Hands.

5. St. *Mary at Elms*. This Church was given to *Trinity* Priory by *Alan* the Son of *Edgar Aleto*, and *Richard* the Son of *Alan*. But there seems to have been no Grant made of the Impropriation, since the Dissolution of that Monastery. In Domesday Book only one Church is mentioned, as dedicated to St. *Mary*; which is supposed to be St. *Mary at Tower*. From hence we may conclude, that this Church was not then built; but that it succeeded the dilapidated Church of St. *Saviour*, as St. *Hellen*'s did that of St. *John* in *Caldwell*, and as St. *Nicholas* was built instead of St. *Michael*'s Church. And if this be admitted, we will add one further Conjecture, that it might probably be built upon the very Spot where St. *Saviour*'s Church stood. See the Account of *Trinity Priory*, in the Parish of St. *Margaret* above.

D 4   Opposite

Opposite to this Church, an Alms-house has lately been erected, in pursuance of the Will of Mrs. *Ann Smyth* of *London*, Widow, who left 5000*l.* for it; but there being a Deficiency of Assets, after adjusting all Claims, the Court of Chancery appointed 4432*l.* 5*s.* 2*d.* for this Purpose, which was laid out in South-Sea Annuities; and the Ministers of St. *Peter* and St. *Mary at Elms*, in *Ipswich*, for the Time being, were appointed Trustees for it. The Reverend Mr. *Cornwallis* and Mr. *Bishop*, the present Ministers of these two Parishes, generously accepted the Trust, without having the least Consideration for their Trouble; and this Building hath been conducted by them: But, as they built with the Interest only, without breaking in upon the principal Sum, it is not yet compleated: When it is, twelve poor Women are to be maintained in it.

6. St. *Mary at Kay*. This Church was impropriated to the Priory of St. *Peter*, and all the Tithes belonging to it were granted 7 *Edward* VI. to *Webb* and *Breton*. The Church was new-built since the Year 1448, when *Richard Gowty* was a considerable Benefactor to it; for by his Will in that Year made, he ordered his Body to be buried in the Church-yard of St. *Mary at the Kay*, in *Ipswich*, and gave *Calyon-stone* for the whole new Church, which was to be built in the said Church-yard.

North of this Church but within this Parish, was a House of *Black* Friers *Dominicans*, called the *Friers Preachers*, who settled here in the latter End of the Reign of King *Henry* III. It was founded by *Henry Mansby*, *Henry Redred*, and *Henry Loudham*, granted 33 *Hen.*VIII. to *William Sabyn*, but bought by the Corporation of Mr. *Southwell*. It was of large Extent, for it reached from *Star-lane* to *Dirty-lane*, in St. *Margaret*'s Parish. It is applied to several useful Purposes. Here is an Hospital for poor Boys; a Grammar-School Room; a Publick Library; a Bridewell; and a great Part of it makes
Habitations

Habitations for the Poor of Mr. *Tooley*'s Foundation. In the Yard belonging to it stands the *Shire-House*. It is perhaps as entire, as any such House of equal Antiquity, and is well described in the Print that is published of it.

7. St. *Mary at Stoke*. "King *Eadgar* gave *Stoke*, a Mem-
"ber of *Ipswich*, to St. *Etheldred* [Domesday];" *i. e.* to the Prior and Convent of *Ely*. This Gift includes the Hamlet, (which takes in Part of the Parish of *Sproughton*) together with the Advowson of the Rectory, and the Manor of *Stoke-Hall*; by which Word we do not mean the modern House by the Church, but what is now called *Stoke-Park*. It is said in *Domesday*, to be of the yearly Value of *Ten* Pounds; and had in the Confessor's Time five Carucates of Land, and nine Villains for the Manor; then fifteen *Bordars*; one Church of forty Acres of free Land; one Mill; twenty Acres of Meadow; and a Mediety of a Loche beyond the Bridge, then of the Value of One Hundred Shillings. King *Eadgar*'s Grant was executed with great Solemnity, as appears from the Deed itself, *Ego* Eadgarus, *&c. Basileus——non clam in angulo, sed palam, sub Dio, subscripsi*; and it was attested by his Queen, St. *Dunstan* Archbishop, and many of the first Officers and Nobility of that Time. This was given about *A. D.* 970. and is now in the Dean and Chapter of *Ely*, and holden of them by *Nathanael Acton*, Esq. There was a Suit between the Prior and Convent, and *Roger de Munchensis*, about this Manor, in 14 *Henry* II. which was decided in favour of the Monks.

In this Parish is the Manor of *Godlesford*, now called *Gusford*-Hall; which Manor with its Appurtenances in *Godlesford, Belsted parva*, and *Wherestead*, in *Suffolk*, were granted as Parcel of the Possession of the Priory of *Canons-Leigh* in *Devonshire*, to Sir *John Rainesworth*, Knt. 32 *Henry* VIII. This House is described in the Perambulation of the 26 *Edward* III. by the Name of *Robert Andrews*;

Andrews; it seems that Family inhabited there many Years; for in 13 *Henry* VIII. it is called the Gate sometime of old *Robert Andrews*, now of Sir *Andrews Windsor*; which Sir *Andrews Windsor* was a considerable Man, and took his Christian Name from the last-mentioned Family of *Andrews:* He was afterwards Lord *Windsor*.

8. St. *Mary at Tower*, was given by *Norman* the Son of *Eadnoth*, to *Trinity* Priory. There was formerly a handsome Spire upon the Tower of this Church; and Mr. *William Edgar*, of *Ipswich*, by Will left Two Hundred Pounds towards erecting another. But, by some Misunderstanding amongst those entrusted with this Benefaction, and different Opinions concerning the Strength of the present Tower, nothing is yet done in it. Nay, it is doubtful, whether ever there will; for the Money is paid into Chancery, and in attempting to get it from thence, it hath already cost the Parishioners more Money than the original Legacy amounted to, and all without Effect.

About *A. D.* 1325, the Confraternity of *Corpus-Christi Gild* was instituted. This Brotherhood agreed to go in Procession every Year on the Feast of the *Holy Sacrament* (a). Their Tabernacle in which the Host was carried, their Money, &c. &c. used to be kept in the Church of St. *Mary at Tower*; and probably that hollow Place in the North Wall of the Vestry, guarded by an exceeding strong Door, very lately taken away, might be made for this Purpose. Among the Rules of this Society, one was, that *all the Parish* Priests of *Ipswich*, when certified of the Death of any of the Fraternity, by the Beadle thereof, *or otherwise*, were to say Mass for his Soul,

(a) They made their Procession in the following Order: 1. White Friers, *Carmelites*. 2. Grey Friers, *Minors*. 3. Black Friers, *Preachers*. 4. Clerks, in Surplices. 5. The Tabernacle, containing the Host. 6. Secular Priests. 7. Canons of the *Holy Trinity*. 8. Canons of St. *Peter*. 9. Bailives of *Ipswich*. 10. Portmen. 11. Aldermen of the Gild, &c. &c.

IPSWICH *with its* SUBURBS. 43

Soul, &c. From hence, as we think, the present Custom of ringing a Bell at *every Church* in the Town, on the Death of *every Portman*, might have its Rise. In upper *Brook-street*, within this Parish, and near the *Northgate*, is the House of the Archdeacon of *Suffolk*, sometimes called the Archdeacon's *Place or* Palace. It was built, or at least the outward Wall and Gates were, by *William Pykenham*, LL.D. who was Archdeacon of *Suffolk*, and principal Official or Chancellor of *Norwich*, *A. D.* 1471. The initial Letters of his Name are still upon the Gate-way. This House is now held on a Lease for Lives by *Thomas Staunton*, Esq; one of the Representatives in Parliament for this Borough.

9. St. *Matthew*. This Parish formerly included four other Churches or Chapels, long since down or disused, *viz. All-Saints*, St. *George*, St. *Mildred*, and St. *Mary*. It hath always been called a *Rectory*, and the Incumbent is instituted into it as such; but the great Tithes were impropriated to St. *Peter's* Priory, were granted to *Webb* and *Breton*, 7 *Edward* VI. and belong now to *Thomas Fonnereau*, Esq. The Crown did not get the Advowson by the Dissolution of the Priory, but always presented while the Priory was standing.

All-Saints Chapel was annexed to St. *Matthew*, before the Year 1383, when *Thomas Moonie* was instituted into the Church of St. *Matthew*, with the Chapel of *All-Saints* annexed. But where the Chapel stood we know not with any Certainty; yet we are inclined to think it most probable, that it stood in the triangular Field at the Corner near *Handford*-Bridge, where the Road from *Handford* Mill, meets the other Road from St. *Matthew's* Street, towards the Bridge: This is now Part of the Glebe belonging to the Rectory; and we think the other Pieces of Glebe are too near the other Chapels or Churches, unless you would suppose St. *George's* Chapel to have been built instead of this, and then, *All-Saints* Chapel

Chapel might have stood on that Spot, which is now in the Occupation of Mr. *King.* See St. *Nich.* p. 46.

St. *George*'s Chapel is yet almost entire in *George-lane* without the West-gate, but it is now used as a Barn. It was used as a Chapel so late as the Time of King *Henry* VIII. when Mr. *Bilney* who suffered Martyrdom, was apprehended there, as he was preaching in favour of the Reformation.

North of St. *George*'s Chapel, *viz.* on the Hills which lie near the North-west Corner of the open Field called *Great Bolton*, stood *Ipswich Castle.* These are still called *Castle-Hills*, tho' the Castle was demolished entirely by King *Henry* II. See *Walton*, in *Colneis.*

St. *Mildred*'s Church is now a Part of the Town-Hall. It was parochial, and impropriated to St. *Peter*'s Priory. The Prior and Convent of the *Holy Trinity*, A. D. 1393, granted a Piece of Ground to the *Bailives, Coroners, Chamberlains*, and *Burgesses* of *Ipswich*, &c. in the Parish of St. *Mildred* the Virgin, 24 Foot long and 18 Foot wide, between the Toll-House on the West, and a Shop late of *Thomas Rysing* on the East; one Head abuts upon the House of the said *Rysing* towards the South, and the other on the Corn-hill on the North.

St. *Mary*'s Chapel, commonly called the Chapel of our *Lady of Grace*, is said to have stood at the North-west Corner of the Lane without *West-gate*, from thence called to this Day *Lady-lane*, and is opposite to St. *George*'s Lane. Mr. *Daundy* who built the Alms-houses in *Lady-lane*, by his Will in *A. D.* 1515, gave Wood to every of his Alms-houses, *beside our Lady of Grace.* This Chapel became very famous for an Image of the Virgin, which was much resorted to in the superstitious Times; and, in old Wills, many Pilgrimages were ordered to be made to it. It is mentioned in the third Part of the Homily against Peril of Idolatry, together with our Lady of *Walsingham* and our Lady of *Wilsdon*, by the Stile of our
Lady

Eady of Ipswich. It was to this Chapel that Cardinal Wolsey ordered an annual Procession to be made by the Dean of his College, on *September* 8, being the Popish Feast of the Nativity of the Virgin *Mary*, the tutelar Saint of *Ipswich*. There is an Account of one of them in Dean *Capon*'s Letter, published by Dr. *Fiddes* and Mr. *Grove*. But this admired Image had the same Fate with other Puppets of the like Kind, for it was carried to *London*, and there publickly burnt. The Place where the Chapel stood is now built upon.

Brokes-hall is within this Parish, and the Hamlet so called takes in part of this, and part of the Parishes of *Bramford, Whitton, Thurleston*, and *Westerfield*. *Ipswich Domesday* saith, " King *Edward* gave *Brokes* a Member " of *Ipswich* to *Alric* of *Clare*, then of the yearly Value of " *Ten* Pounds; and R. *Bedile* holdeth it of the Countess " of *Clare*, by the Service of one Knight's Fee." The small Manor of *Brokes-hall* is now vested in Mr. *Alpes*; but the Manor of *Lufftofts* within this District is much more considerable, and that is vested in *George Thomas*, of *Kesgrave*, Esq. *Boss-hall* is not so called from a Family which once lived there named *Bull*, as the *Framlingham* MS. supposes; but it is a Contraction of *Bordshaw*-hall; so that House is called in the old Perambulations of *Ipswich* Bounds: And in pronouncing this hastily, from *Bordshaw*-hall to *Bosshaw*-hall, and *Boss*-hall, the Transition is easy.

10. St. *Nicholas* (*b*) was impropriated to St. *Peter*'s Priory, and the Impropriation was granted to *Webb* and *Breton*. No such Church is mentioned in *Domesday*; and probably it might be built to supply the Loss of the dilapidated Church of St. *Michael* before-mentioned; which is said in *Domesday* to have had eight Acres of Land, and is supposed

(*b*) The Visitors in 1648, broke down six Pictures, and took up three Brass Inscriptions here. We wish they had not, for these Brasen Inscriptions might have given some Account of C. *Wolsey*'s Relations.

posed to have stood not far from it. It might possibly be built upon the same Place, and with some Materials from that; and to this Conjecture, a Stone at the West-End of the South Isle, which rudely represents St. *Michael fighting with the Dragon*, may give some Colour of Probability. We cannot give any Account of the neighbouring Stone, or how it came there; but the Letters over the Bristles of the Boar seem to be, or rather to have been, IN DEDICATIONE ECCLESIE OMNIUM SANCTORUM. See St. *Matthew*, p. 43.

On the South-side of the Passage leading from St. *Nicholas-street* to this Church-yard, stood the House, where Tradition says, Cardinal *Wolsey* was born: It has been rebuilt since that, and is now occupied by Mrs. *Edwards*. The Cardinal's Father bequeathed in his Will 6s. 8d. to the High Altar of St. *Nicholas* in *Ipswich*, and *Forty Shillings* to the Painting of the Archangel there. *See p. 37.*

West of St. *Nicholas* Church, and on the Bank of the *Gippen*, stood a Convent of *Francifcan Grey* Friers *Minors*, founded by Lord *Tibtoth* of *Nettlestead*, in the Reign of King *Edward* I. who, with many of his Family, were buried in the Church belonging to this House.

Another Convent of *White Friers Carmelites*, stood partly in this Parish and partly in that of St. *Laurence*, founded by Sir *Thomas Loudham* and others, about A. D. 1279. Upon the Dissolution it was granted to *John Eger*. It was of large Extent; for it reached from St. *Nicholas*-street to St. *Stephen*'s-lane. Part of it was standing within 50 Years, and was used for a County-Gaol, before the County agreed with the Corporation for the common Use of their Gaol by the West Gate. Mr. *Clarke*'s House stands upon, or near the Spot where that Gaol stood: And from hence the Passage leading from the Butter-Market past Mr. *Clarke*'s House is called the *Gaol-lane.* This House was famous for many learned Men,

Men, who had their Education here: There are no Remains of it now, except a Piece of a Door-way.

11. St. *Peter*'s Church had in the Confessor's Time large Possessions. "It had six Carucates of Land, eight Villains, twenty Bordarii, and two Mills; of these *Earl Roger* claimed One hundred Acres, five Villains, and one Mill, in right of the King's Manor of *Bramford*. Five Villains of the said Manor witnessed for him; but the half Hundred of *Ipswich* witnessed that these belonged to the Church in the Time of the Confessor, then valued at One Hundred Shillings, now at 15*l.* (*c*)" It saith farther, "That to this Church belonged five Burgesses, and twenty Acres of Land within the Borough." But afterwards the Church was impropriated to the Priory of St. *Peter* and St. *Paul*, which was contiguous to the Church-yard, and founded by the Ancestors of *Thomas Lacy* and *Alice* his Wife, for *Black* Canons of the Order of St. *Augustine*, in the Reign of King *Henry* II. It was suppressed 6 *March*, 1527, by Car. *Wolsey*; who having obtained Bulls from the *Pope*, and Letters-Patent from the *King* for that Purpose, founded instead of it, a College; for a *Dean*, 12 *Secular Canons*, 8 *Clerks*, and 8 *Choristers*, to the Honour of the *Virgin Mary*; together with a Grammar-School, which he intended as a Nursery for his great College in *Oxford*. But this noble Foundation was scarce compleated, before the Disgrace of that Prelate; and the Site of the College containing by Estimation *six Acres*, was granted 23 *Henry* VIII. to *Tho. Alverde*; and in 9 *Jac.* I. to *Richard Percival*, and *Edmund Duffield*. The College was soon demolished, no Part of it was left standing except one Gate which yet remains. They dug up the very Foundation, insomuch that the first Stone was not long since found in two Pieces, worked into a common Wall in *Woulform*'s Lane, with a Latin Inscription to this Effect:

(*c*) *Ipswich* Domesday.

In the Year of Christ 1528, and the Twentieth of the Reign of Henry VIII. King of England, on the fifteenth of June, laid by John, *Bishop of* Lincoln. This was *John Longland*, who was also employed by the Cardinal to lay the first Stone of his College, in *Oxford (d)*. But tho' this Attempt did not succeed, the Cardinal occasioned some Good by it; for we may reasonably suppose that this put King *Henry* VIII. upon founding the Grammar-School, and endowing it with what was, at that time, a very handsome Allowance for a Master and Usher.

The Water from *Stoke* Hills was brought hither for the Use of the Convent, before the Year 1491.

There was a good Manor belonging to the Priory, which since the Dissolution seems to have been split into *three* Manors. For the Manor of St. *Peter* in *Ipswich*, is now vested in Dr. *Coyte*; the Manor of St. *Peter* in *Nacton, Bucklesham*, and *Kembroke*, is in *Philip Broke*, of *Nacton*, Esq; and there is yet another Manor of St. *Peter*, in *Cretingham*.

The

(d) John Longland, Bishop of *Lincoln*, did certainly lay the Foundation-Stone of the College at *Oxford*; and he preached a Sermon on that Occasion, from *Prov.* ix. 1. *Wisdom hath builded her House.* That Stone was laid 20 *March* 1525. As our Stone was laid little more than three Years after that, it seems not improbable, that the same Person might be employed on a like Occasion at *Ipswich*. For this Reason (and because the Word could not mean any other *English* Bishop in that Year) we suppose the last Word in the Inscription to stand for *Lincoln*. But as the Stone would not admit of more Letters, that Word consists of five only, and is plainly abbreviated in two Places; which Abbreviations have rendered the Meaning of it somewhat doubtful.

The Foundation-Stone of the College in *Oxford*, contained a pompous Enumeration of all Cardinal *Wolsey's* Titles and Offices; but here is not the least Mention of him upon this. Now, the Writer of his secret History, speaking of these Colleges, says, " They were *both most sumptuous* Buildings:" And considering the general Character of *Wolsey*, that this was the Place of his Nativity; and that he was now in the Zenith of his Power; we are inclined to suspect, that here was also some other Stone, containing an Account of the Founder; which, in future Times, may possibly be brought to Light.

IPSWICH *with its* SUBURBS. 49

The Journal of the Vifiters before-mentioned, faith, " At *Peter*'s, was on the Porch the Crown of Thorns, " the Sponge and Nails, and the Trinity in Stone, and " the Rails were there, all which I ordered to break in " pieces."

In this Parifh is the Houfe of the Lord Bifhop of *Norwich*, which was granted to the Bifhop in 4 King *Edward* VI. by the Name of the Meffuage called the Lord *Curfon's Houfe*; whofe Name is ftill to be feen in a *Rebus* on the old wooden Back-gate in *Silent-ftreet*. There was a ftrong and ftately Brick Porch to it, lately taken down; but the Houfe itfelf is in a moft ruinous Condition. By the Statute of 26 *Henry* VIII. Chap. 14. this Town was appointed for the Seat of a Suffragan Bifhop, and the common Notion is, that this Houfe was intended for his Refidence; but *Thomas Manning*, Prior of *Butley*, was the firft, and the laft Suffragan Bifhop of *Ipfwich*; and this Houfe was not granted to the Bifhop of *Norwich* till after his Deceafe, as we think. He was confecrated by Archbifhop *Cranmer*, 19 *March*, 1525.

In the Suburbs beyond the River ftood the Church of St. *Auftin*, near St. *Auftin*'s Green. It is often called a Chapel; but it had in the Conqueror's Time eleven Acres of Land, and Procurations were paid for it by the Prior of St. *Peter*'s; fo that it was parochial, and as we fuppofe, impropriated to that Priory. It was in ufe *A.D.* 1482; but has been long fince dilapidated. We fuppofe all the Houfes and Land on the South-fide of the *Orwell*, to have been St. *Auftin*'s Parifh; which are now become Part of St. *Peter*'s.

Not far from this Church, and perhaps almoft oppofite to it, ftood St. *Leonard*'s Hofpital: It is now become a Farm-houfe, belonging to *Chrift-Hofpital, Ipfwich*.

12. St. *Stephen*'s is a Rectory, and tho' the Revenues are now fo fmall that it is generally held by Sequeftration, it was conftantly inftituted into formerly; upon the Prefenta-

E tion

tion of Sir *Andrew de Bures*, in 1340; of the *Cavendish*'s, in 1400, &c. Sir *Gilbert Debenham* presented in 1487, then the Family of *Brewes*, till it came to Sir *Edmund Whytapole*, and went as well as St. *Peter*'s, with the *Christ-Church* Estate.

In this little Parish *Charles Brandon* Duke of *Suffolk*, had a Mansion, where the Coach-houses now are. And Sir *Anthony Wingfield*, Knight of the Garter, who was Vice-Chamberlain, Privy-Councellor, and one of the Executors of King *Henry* VIII. had another. This is now become the *Tankard Ale-house*, and a *Play-house*; opposite to which Sir *Anthony*. had a Chapel for the Use of his Family, where Dr. *Gwyn*'s House is built.

Here was also in *Ipswich* a Church of St. *Gregory*, which was impropriated to *Woodbridge* Priory; but this is all we know of it. And in the Abuttals of a Messuage, the antiquated Church of *Osterbolt* is mentioned in 21 King *Edward* III. By which it seems to have stood somewhere not far from St. *Clement*'s Stepples; and, as the *East-gate* formerly stood there, it might possibly have the Name of *Osterbolt* from that Circumstance: And this being allowed, as the Church of St. *Clement* is not mentioned in *Domesday*, it is not improbable this might be built, instead of that dilapidated Church.

In the Precincts are the Churches of *Thurleston*, *Whitton*, and *Westerfield*.

13. *Thurleston*, the Manor of *Barnes* here, with the Impropriation and Advowson of the Vicarage, belonged to St. *Peter*'s Priory. The Manor and Impropriation were granted to Cardinal *Wolsey*, 19 *Henry* VIII. and in 19. Queen *Elizabeth* to *Thomas Seckford*, Esq; they now belong to the Heirs of *Edmund Hammond*, Esq. The Church was in use since the Year 1500; but the Vicarage being united to the Rectory of *Whitton*, the Church was neglected after that Time, and is now used as a Barn.

14. *Whitton*

14. *Whitton* Church is sometimes called *Whitton* Chapel, but improperly: For it hath been inftituted into as a Parochial Church, upon the Prefentation of the Bifhop of *Ely*, ever fince the Year 1299; and probably long before. It is dedicated to St. *Botolph*. If any of the Churches now in being, were built in the Conqueror's Time (which may well be queftioned) we think this bids as fair to be one of them as any; and the neighbouring Church of *Thurlefton* feems to be of the like Kind.

15. *Wefterfield* Church is in the Hamlet of *Wykes-Ufford*. The Patronage of this Church and *Whitton* are faid in old Writings to belong to the Bifhop of *Ely*, in right of a Manor he then had in *Bramford*. The Manor of *Wefterfield*, A. D. 1596. belonged to *John Dameron*, who gave it by Will to his Grandfon *Anthony Collet*.

An Account of the TRADE, &c.

THE Trade of the Town did formerly confift chiefly in the Manufacture of Broad Cloth, and other Woollen Cloth, which was carried on fo largely that all the Towns and Villages for many Miles round were employed in it; and many of the beft Eftates of this County were raifed from it. But about the Middle of the laft Century the Manufactory began to decline; and then dwindled by Degrees, till at laft it totally ceafed. The Lofs of the Manufactory was attended with bad Effects. We muft fuppofe the principal Artificers would follow the Trade into the North and Weft Part of the Kingdom, where it has fettled ever fince. But vaft Numbers of the poorer Sort employed in it, were left behind; and thefe, when their Employment ceafed, became a Burden and Incumberance to the Town and Neighbourhood. This might very probably be one Reafon which prevented other Persons from settling here, in the room of those who followed the Manufactory. From hence it happened, that very many of the better Sort of Houses were for a long while empty; and *Ipswich* incurred the Censure of being *a Town without People*. But now, the Case is otherwise. The Inconvenience before-mentioned abated, and wore out in time. The Agreeableness of the Town invited New-comers to settle here; and the Number of Inhabitants is so much increased, that within fifty Years the Rents are advanced more than *Fifty per Cent.* almost every House is full, and more Houses are daily wanted. Insomuch that it is difficult to procure one that will accommodate a middling Family; all such being in a manner scrambled for.

The late Accounts all tell us of the Decrease of the *Shipping* in this Port; and with regard to those huge Colliers called *Ipswich-Cats*, this may be true. But there are now three Yards constantly employed in Ship-building; and if we reckon that at the Place called *Nova Scotia*, where the *Speaker East-Indiaman* is now building, there are four. And, we are credibly informed, there are more than *One Hundred and Fifty Sail* belonging to this Port; and, as some think, small and great, many more.

The chief Trade at present is in Corn: The Business of Malt-making, in particular, is carried on to a great degree. And indeed, if we may judge from the Increase of Malting Offices for several Years past, that Business must be overdoing, if it be not already overdone. It is so great, that the *Ipswich Maltsters* manifestly use more Corn than the neighbouring Country, improved as it is, will supply. For, of late Years, they have often been obliged to import Barley from the Coast of *Norfolk*.

Here are *five* Market-Days, *Tuesdays* and *Thursdays* for Butchers Meat, *Wednesdays* and *Fridays* for Fish; and *Saturday* is a general Market-Day for all Sorts of Provisions,

sions, Cattle, &c. The Town is well supplied with all Kinds of very good Provisions; unless, perhaps, we should except *Fish*. As to this Article the Town might be supplied with *more Variety*, and *in greater Plenty*, than it is. We have good reason to think, that the *Orwell* and the neighbouring Seas are in the proper Seasons well stored with several Sorts of Fish, which thro' the Ignorance, the Laziness, or the Folly of our Fishermen, are scarce ever, unless by great Accident caught here; particularly *Mullets*, *Turbots*, *Smelts*, and sometimes *Salmon*. And then the Practice of *Forestalling* is carried to such a Height, as would persuade us no Laws had ever been made against it. It is no unusual Thing for Peddars to attend the Tides regularly, receive and pack up the Fish at Noon-day, and on the common Key, to supply the Inland Towns, refusing to sell it to the Inhabitants of *Ipswich* at any Price.

Here are five Fairs; one on *Holy-Rood-Day*, O. S. where much Business is done in the two Articles of Butter and Cheese. One on St. *George*'s Day, O. S. for Toys and lean Cattle, chiefly Home-bred. St. *James's*, *July* 25, now not worth mentioning: And two Fairs for Cattle, on *May* 18 and 19, and *August* 22 and 23; at the last of which vast Numbers of Lambs are constantly sold, to the Amount of Eighty, Ninety, or sometimes One Hundred Thousand.

In this Town are *five* Charity Schools for poor Children.

One in *Christ's-Hospital* for Twenty Blue-coat Boys, who are found with every Thing, Clothes, Meat, Drink, Washing and Lodging, are taught to read, and made to work, and then bound out, chiefly to Sea.

Another for *Sixteen Red-sleeve* Boys, who are clothed, taught, and bound out.

Another for *Sixty* Grey-coat Boys, who are clothed, taught, and bound out to Sea, or low Trades.

Another for Twenty-four Blue-coat Girls, who are clothed, taught to read, to knit, to sew, and are fitted out for Services. And,

One other small School for Sixteen Green-sleeve Boys, who are clothed, taught, and bound out: This last School is supported by the Dissenters.

A *Translation* of the CHARTER of King HENRY VI. to the *Burgesses of* Ipswich.

*H*ENRY, D. G. King of *England* and *France*, and Lord of *Ireland*, &c. &c. Know ye, that whereas our beloved Burgesses of our Town of *Gippewich*, are very much burthened with the Payment of the Annual Farm which they and their Successors are obliged to pay to Us, and our Heirs, for the said Town, and hereby are grievously impoverished, as we have heard: Of our especial Favour, certain Knowledge, and mere Motion, and for the especial Relief of the said Town, and in Support of the Payment of the Farm aforesaid, We have granted to the said Burgesses, and their Successors, the Liberties, Franchises, Acquittances, and Immunities underwritten, *viz.* That the Town aforesaid be, for ever, a Free Borough Corporate, in Deed, and in Name of *The Burgesses* of the said Town; and that the Burgesses of the said Town for the Time being be, for ever, a *perpetual Community Corporate*, in Deed and in Name, and may have perpetual Succession, and a Common Seal to dispatch the Business of the Town aforesaid; and that, in every Year, at the *accustomed Time and Place*, they may choose out of themselves two Burgesses of the Town aforesaid to be *Bailives* thereof, who shall exercise that Office *for one entire Year*,

[und

[uno integro Anno] for the safe and wholesome Government of the same Town.

We have also granted to the said Burgesses and their Successors, that the said Bailives and their Successors, and four such other Burgesses of the same Town, as the said *Bailives* shall be pleased to take to them, out of the *Twelve Portmen* of that Town and their Successors; and to elect and nominate for that purpose, Five, Four, Three or Two of them, may be from henceforth for ever, Keepers of our Peace, and Justices of us and our Heirs, to keep the Peace within the said Town and the Liberty, Suburbs and Precinct thereof; and also to hear and determine all Felonies, Trespasses and Offences within the Town aforesaid, and the Liberty, Suburbs, and Precinct of the same; and all other Matters and Things, as well concerning all manner of Felonies, Trespasses, Misprisions, and Extortions, as concerning all manner of other Causes, Complaints, and Offences whatsoever, within the said Town and the Liberty, Suburbs and Precinct of the same, in any manner happening and arising, as fully and wholly, as the Keepers of the Peace, and Justices assigned or to be assigned to hear and determine, Felonies, Trespasses, and other Offences, and the Justices of Labourers, Artificers, and Servants in the County of *Suffolk*, have, or shall have, for the future without the Town and Liberty aforesaid, in any manner whatsoever. And the Keepers of the Peace, and Justices assigned to hear and determine Felonies, Trespasses, and other Offences, and also the Justices of Servants, Labourers, and Artificers within the County of *Suffolk*, shall by no means introduce themselves, nor shall any one of them introduce himself, within the Town aforesaid, the Liberty, Suburbs, and Precinct thereof, or without it, concerning such Felonies, Trespasses, or other Offences whatsoever, in any manner committed, or arising within the Town aforesaid, or the Liberty, Suburbs, and Precinct thereof, in what manner soever committed or perpe-

perpetrated; nor shall he, or they, in any manner enquire concerning them, within the said Town, or the Liberty, Suburbs and Precinct of the same. And if any Justices assigned to keep the Peace, other than the Justices of the Peace appointed or to be appointed by virtue of this our present Grant, within the said Town, the Liberty, &c. thereof, shall make any Inquisition concerning any such Felonies, Trespasses, and other Offences, or other Things whatsoever in the said Town, the Liberty, Suburbs and Precinct of the same, for the future, in any manner whatsoever, such Inquisition shall be deemed null and void.

Moreover, We have granted for Us, and our Heirs, unto the aforesaid Burgesses, their Heirs and Successors, Burgesses of the said Town, that they for ever may have all manner of Fines, Issues, Forfeitures and Amercements, belonging to the Justiciary [*Justiciariam*] of the Peace, within the said Town, and the Liberty, Suburbs and Precinct thereof; and from the said Justiciary [*Justiciaria*] forthcoming in any manner, to be recovered and levied by their own proper Officers, as fully and wholly, as We and our Progenitors, in any manner have had, and received such Fines, Issues, Forfeitures, and Amercements, before our Justices of the Peace in the said County of *Suffolk*, within the said Town, and the Liberty, Suburbs and Precinct of the same heretofore happening, and arising, in Aid of the Payment of the aforesaid Farm, and in support of the great Burdens daily incumbring on the said Town, or happening and arising therein: And that the said Bailives and Burgesses of the said Town of *Gippewich*, and their Heirs and Successors aforesaid, for ever may have the Forfeiture of Victuals, by the Law of *England*, in any manner to be forfeited, viz. the Assize and Correction of Bread, Wine, and Ale, and other Things which do not belong to Merchandise.

Moreover, of our more abundant Favour, We have granted to the said Burgesses and their Successors, that

either

either of those two Burgesses who shall be chosen *Bailives* of the said Town in Form aforesaid, and shall be one of the said two Bailives, and such one of the said two Bailives as the Burgesses of the Town aforesaid, for the Time being, at the Time of the Election of the said Bailives shall be pleased to elect to the Office underwritten, immediately, and as soon as he shall be elected and appointed to the Bailivewick of the said Town, shall be from that Time [*ex tunc*] our *Efchaetor*, and the Efchaetor of our Heirs and Successors in the Town aforesaid, and the Liberty, Suburbs and Precinct of the said Town, during the Time in which he shall continue Bailiff of the Town aforesaid. And that the said *Efchaetor* and his Successors shall have the same Power, Jurisdiction, Authority and Liberty, and whatever else belongeth to the Office of *Efchaetor* in the said Town, Liberty, Suburbs and Precinct, that our other *Efchaetors*, and the *Efchaetors* of our Heirs have or shall have elsewhere, within our Kingdom of *England*. And that in no Time hereafter any other *Efchaetor* shall introduce himself into the said Town, Liberty, &c. to execute any thing relating to the Office of *Efchaetor*, within the said Town &c. excepting only the said *Efchaetor* of the Town aforesaid for the Time being. And that every such Burgess hereafter to be elected Bailiff of the Town aforesaid, after such Election of him made to the Office of *Efchaetor* shall take his Oath, well and faithfully to execute the Office of *Efchaetor* within the Town aforesaid, before the Burgesses of the aforesaid Town; so that such *Efchaetor* shall by no means be obliged, or compelled, to take his Oath elsewhere within our Kingdom of *England*, or before any other than the Burgesses of the said Town, and that within the said Town only.

And further, for us and our Heirs we have granted to the said Burgesses and their Successors, that they may be Persons able and capable in Law, to purchase Lands,

Tenements,

Tenements, Rents, Services, and Possessions within the Town, Liberty, Suburbs, and Precinct aforesaid and elsewhere, to have and to hold the same, to them and their Successors, the Statute of not putting Lands and Tenements in *Mortmain* notwithstanding.

Moreover, We have granted to the aforesaid Burgesses, and their Heirs and Successors for ever, that the *Admiral of England*, or his Lieutenant, or Deputy, or the Steward, Mareschall or Clerk of the Market of our Houshold, or of our Heirs, or any one of them, or the Deputy of any one or more of them, shall not enter or sit within the Town aforesaid, nor the Liberty, Suburbs, or Precinct thereof to enquire concerning any Matters or Things relating to their aforesaid Offices, nor concerning any Things done, or hereafter to be done, or happening, and arising within the Town, or the Liberty, &c. aforesaid; nor shall he or they cause any Enquiry to be made concerning them; nor shall any one or more of them intrude him, or themselves, nor prosecute any Burgesses of our Town aforesaid, nor any Persons residing within the said Town, Liberty, Suburbs, or Precinct, on any Pretence, without the said Town, for any Things, happening or arising within the said Town, Liberty, &c. for the future in any manner.

Moreover, We have granted, and by this our Charter do confirm to the said Burgesses, and their Heirs and Successors, that they the said Burgesses their Heirs and Successors for ever, may have all Issues, Forfeitures, Fines, and Amercements whatsoever, before our said Eschaetor, so to be chosen as aforesaid, coming, happening, or arising: And also, all Goods and Chattels of Persons outlawed, within the Town and the Liberty, Suburbs and Precinct thereof, now resident and commorant, or hereafter to be resident and commorant within the said Town, Liberty, &c. found; to be received and levied by their own proper Officers, in Aid of the Payment of the Farm aforesaid,

IPSWICH *with its* SUBURBS.   59

aforesaid, and in Support of the great Burdens, daily falling on the said Town, or in the same happening, or arising, as fully and wholly, as we and our Progenitors have received and had, any such Issues, Forfeitures, Fines, and Amercements, before our Escheator in our said County, happening, or arising within the said Town, Liberty, &c. and the Goods and Chattels of any Persons outlawed, and heretofore resident or commorant within the said Town, Liberty, Suburbs or Precinct in any manner. Witness the Venerable Fathers *J.* Archbishop of *Canterbury* Primate of all *England,* our Chancellor, *A. Cicestr'* Keeper of our Privy Seal, *W.* Bishop of *Norwich,* our dearest Uncle *Humphry* of *Gloucester,* and our dearest Cousins *John* of *Exeter,* and *Humphry* of *Bucks,* Dukes; *Edmund* of *Dorset,* and *William* of *Suffolk,* Marquisses; *William* of *Arundel,* and *John* of *Salop,* Earls; our beloved and faithful *Ralph Cromwell* and *Ralph Boteler,* our Treasurer of *England,* Knights, and others. Given under our Hand at *Westminster* 28 *March,* in the Twenty-fourth Year of our Reign.

Kirkeby.

By Writ of Privy Seal, and of the aforesaid Date by Authority of Parliament.

This Charter is added at Length, because it is not in the Manuscript of the *Ipswich* Charters which is handed about, and therefore was not printed with the rest. Indeed, very few knew any thing of it till it was found, thrown into a Hole in the Treasury, within these last seven Years. We will only add an Observation or two upon the Stile of this Corporation. In ancient Times the Gentlemen of the Law were not so curious in this Matter, as they have been of later Years. It appears from Mr. *Bacon*'s MS. that in the Reign of K. *Ric.* II. or *A. D.* 1393. on an Exchange of a Piece of Ground with

with the Prior and Convent of the *Holy Trinity,* (as was mentioned before) the *Bailives, Coroners, Chamberlains,* and *Burgeſſes,* were the contracting Parties on the Behalf of the Corporation. This Charter, now recited in *A. D.* 1446, incorporates the Town by the Stile of " The " BURGESSES of IPSWICH;" and declares them to be a perpetual *Community* Corporate, by that Name. The Charter of King *Edward* IV. in *A. D.* 1464, altered the Stile and made it, " The *Bailives,* Burgeſſes, and *Com-* " *munity of the Town* of *Ipſwich.*" Or, as it is now commonly called in *Engliſh,* The Bailives, Burgeſſes, and *Commonalty* of the Town of *Ipſwich.* The Charter of 17 King *Charles* II. *A. D.* 1665, made no Alteration in the Stile; but that of 36 *Charles* II. *A. D.* in 1685, made an Addition to it, and called them, " The Bailives, " Burgeſſes, and Community [or Commonalty] of the " Town *or Borough* of IPSWICH *in the County of Suf-* " *folk.*" However, as the Corporation hath not acted under this laſt Charter ſince the Revolution in 1688, the proper Stile of the Corporation now is, " The Bailives, " Burgeſſes, and Commonalty of the Town of IPS- " WICH," without any further Addition.

SAM-

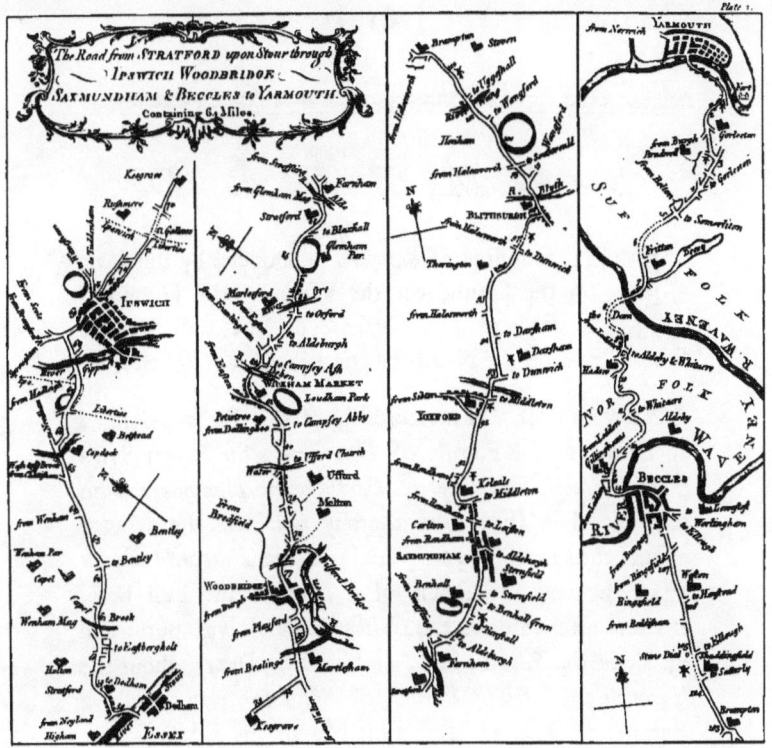

SAMFORD.

THE Hundred of *Samford* is bounded by the *Stour* on the South, on the West by the Hundreds of *Babergh* and *Cosford*, on the East by the *Orwell*, and on the North by the Liberties of *Ipswich*.

ARWERTON. The Lordship of this Place belonged anciently to the Family of *Davellers*. Sir *Robert Bacon* married *Isabel*, Daughter of *Bartholomew Danviliers*, who left no Male Issue, and thereby obtained the Manor about the Year 1330. And in 20 *Edward* III. or 1345, he had the Grant of a Market and Fair here. It came afterwards to the *Calthorpes*, and was purchased by Sir *Philip Parker*, Knt. of Sir *Drue Drury*, about the Year 1577. *Philip Parker*, of *Arwerton*, was created a Baronet 16 *July*, 1661. This Manor and Estate is now vested in the Dowager Lady of the Right Hon. the Lord *Chedworth*, who was one of the Daughters of the late Sir *Philip Parker Long*, Bart.

BELSTEAD, or *Little Belstead*. In King *John*'s Time, or that of King *Henry* III. at the latest, *William de Goldingham* paid Fines to *Ipswich*, for Freedom from Toll for himself and his Villains, in *Belstead*. This same Family continued to present to the Church till after the Year 1560; when the Manor was purchased by Mr. *Bloss*, a wealthy Clothier of *Ipswich*; and by the Heiress of that Family, it was, not long since, sold to *Robert Harland*, of *Sproughton*, Esq;

BENTLY. *Hugh Tallemache* paid a Fine to *Ipswich*, for Freedom from Toll for himself and his Villains in *Bently*, in the Reign of King *Henry* III.

This

This Church was given to the Priory of the *Holy Trinity* in *Ipswich*, by *Henry* of *Dodneis*. And the Manor of *Bently*, the Rectory and Advowson of the Vicarage, with two Woods, *Portland* Grove and *New* Grove, were granted as Part of the Possession of that Priory to *Lionel Talmage*, 36 *Henry* VIII. This Family removed from hence to *Helmingham*, in *Claydon* Hundred. See there.

At a Place called *Dodneis* in this Parish, there was a small Priory of Black Canons, which had Revenues valued at 42 *l.* 18 *s.* 8¼ *d.* It was suppressed by the first Bull of *Clement* VII. and granted to Cardinal *Wolsey*.

BRANTHAM. King *William Rufus* gave the Church of *Brantham*, with the Berewics of *Bercold, Scotlege, Meelflege*, and *Benetlege*, to the Abbey of *Battle* in *Suffex*; and the Advowson of this Rectory, as late belonging to that Abbey, was granted to *John* Earl of *Oxford*, 36 *Henry* VIII. The Church is now united with *East-Bergholt*.

Within this Parish is a Hamlet called *Cattiwade*, where was formerly a Chapel near the Bridge, which goeth over the River *Stour* into *Essex*. About the Year 1460, Sir *John Braham*, of *Braham*-Hall in *Cattiwade*, is mentioned. And afterwards *William Lancaster*, Esq; of *Cattiwade*, who married a Daughter of *Brahams*.

BURSTALL, is called a Berewic or Hamlet of *Bramford*. The Manor of *Horrolds* in *Burstall* was granted to Cardinal *Wolsey*, as Parcel of the Possession of St. *Peter*'s Priory in *Ipswich*.

CAPEL. Here are three Manors; *Churchford-Hall*, formerly *Robert Appleton*'s, now Mr. *Fielding*'s; *Boitwell*-Hall, belonging to *Queen*'s College, *Cambridge*; and another small Manor, formerly Mr. *Brewes*'s of *Little Wentham*.

ham. The Advowson of the Rectory, together with that of *Little Wenham,* is in the Rev. *Peter Hingeston,* the present Incumbent.

CHATTISHAM. The Manor, Impropriation, and Advowson of the Vicarage, belonged formerly to the Priory of *Wykes,* in *Essex* ; and were granted first to Cardinal *Wolsey,* and then to the Provost and Fellows of *Eton,* who now enjoy them.

CHELMONDISTON, commonly called *Chémton.* The Manor here is vested in the Heirs of Mr. *Lucas,* the Advowson is in the Crown.

COPDOCK. The Hall-House is the Property of *Thomas de Gray,* Esq; who is also Patron of the Church, and Lord of the Manor. This Church has been lately united with *Washbrook.*

EAST-BERGHOLT. K. *Henry* II. gave the Templars all his Lands in *Bergholt,* and a Manor here was granted to *John* Earl of *Oxford,* 36 *Henry* VIII. as lately belonging to the Præceptory at *Battisford.* Here is also another Manor, for the Relict of *John Vere* twelfth Earl of *Oxford,* held the Manors of *Chelsworth, East-Bergholt,* and *Brook-Hall,* in *Suffolk,* as her own Inheritance, *A. D.* 1472. This last Manor is now in *Nathaniel Acton,* Esq;

This is a large Village consolidated to *Brantham.* The Cloth Manufacture formerly flourished here. It is supposed to have been a Market-Town ; but the Market is disused, and the Town is greatly reduced, many Houses having lately been pulled down. About the Year 1522, many Legacies were given towards building the Church ; and in 1526 and 1527, other Legacies towards building the Steeple ; but it seems as if these were not sufficient for the Purpose, for it is not built yet. The Church is a good Structure. South from the Church is a neat Mansion, built by *Thomas Chaplin,* Esq; which by Marriage

riage came to Sir *Henry Hankey*, Knt. and the Manor first above-mentioned, and Advowson with it; where his Son Sir *Joseph Hankey*, Knt. and Alderman of *London*, now resides.

FRESTON. The Hall, Manor and Advowson of this Church, were anciently vested in a Family who took their Name from the Place. *Philip de Freston* was admitted a Free-Burgess of *Ipswich* as early as 18 *Henry* III. And the Estate continued in them for many Years till about the Time of *Henry* VIII. when it came to the *Latymers*. They continued here till about 1590, when the *Goodings* of *Ipswich* had this Estate; from whom it came to the Family of *Wright*. The last of that Family who had it, severed the Manor and Advowson of the Rectory, by selling them to *Thomas Thurston*, of *Holbrooke*, Esq; in whose Heirs they are now vested. (See *Holbrooke*.) The Hall-Farm, but much reduced from what it formerly had been, was sold to Mr. *Lark Tarver*, of *Ipswich*. The Hall-House is pleasantly situated on the Bank of the *Orwell*; but the chief Thing worth Notice here, is the *Tower*; which is a square strong Brick-Building, six Stories high, containing as many Rooms one above another, these communicate with each other by a winding Steeple Stair-case, which, for the greater Strength of the Building, is on the East-side of it next the River. It is not easy to say for what Purpose, nor is it certainly known, at what Time this Tower was built. But as there is among the Records of the Manor, a very exact and particular Account of the Manor-House, and all the Out-Buildings and Offices belonging to it in *Henry* VIIth's Time, and no mention is there made of the Tower, it is pretty certain it was not then built. So that it is reasonable to suppose it to have been the Work of one of the *Latymers*. From the Smallness of the Windows in all the other Rooms, it looks as if they were built chiefly for the Support of the uppermost Room, which, having large Windows

dows on three Sides of it, seems to have been contrived by some whimsical Man, for taking rather a better View of the River *Orwell*, than can be had on the neighbouring Hill.

Within the Manor of *Freston*-Hall, another small Manor called *Bonds* is included; this is vested in Mrs. *Beaumont*, Relict of the late Rev. *Charles Beaumont*. But the Manor of *Freston*-Hall has a Paramountship over it.

HARKSTEAD. *Odo de Campania (a)*, was Lord here at the taking of Domesday Survey. King *Edward* III. in his Charter to the Nunnery of *Dartford* in *Kent*, gives or confirms to it the Manor of *Brandiston*, in *Herkestede* in *Suffolk*. And the Manor of *Brandeston*, late belonging to that Nunnery, was granted 31 *Henry* VIII. to Sir *Percival Hart*, Knt. It came afterwards with the Advowson of the Rectory to a Family of *Cocks*, in *Worcestershire*; who had it some time, and then sold the Manor, Hall, House, &c. to *Knox Ward*, Esq; *Clarencieux* King at Arms; whose Heir lately sold them to *Thomas Staunton*, of *Holbrook*, Esq. The Advowson was sold to the Rev. *Richard Canning*, the present Incumbent. Besides the Parish Church, here was formerly a Chapel dedicated to St. *Clement*. It is now wholly down; but the Spot where it stood is still to be seen at the South-East Corner of a Field, from thence called *Chapel-Down*, belonging to a Farm late of *John Phillipson*, Esq. A Legacy was given to this Chapel of St. *Clement*, in the Year 1528. And a House was bequeathed in 1685, with the Garden and one Pightle abutting *South* upon St. *Clement's Church-yard*, and upon the *Mill-way* towards the *North*. The Site of the Chapel is now ploughed up.

HIGHAM.

(a) This *Norman* Baron was nearly related to K. *William* the Conqueror, and was made by him Earl of *Albemarle* and *Holderness*; he partook largely of his Relation's Bounty, and is said to have had fourteen Manors granted to him in this County.

HIGHAM. This was given to *Trinity* Priory in *Ipswich*, by *Maud de Munchensi*, and was impropriated thereto. But the Impropriation was purchased by Mr. *Gibbs*, or Mr. *Smith*, and given to the Minister.

HINTLESHAM, was anciently the Lordship of the *Talbots*; and for very many Years of the *Timperlys*. The Hall, &c. was bought of them by *Richard Powis*, Esq; sometime Member for *Orford*. From him it was purchased by Sir *Richard Lloyd*, Knt. one of the Barons of his Majesty's Court of Exchequer. The Church was impropriated to *Kings-Hall* (now Part of *Trinity* College) in *Cambridge*, about *A. D.* 1349, but before the Year 1400, the Impropriation was given up, and the Minister presented and instituted into the Rectory as formerly. Here was formerly a Chapel in this Parish, and there is yet a Place called *Chapel Field*, within the Farm lately in the Occupation of Mr. *Beaumont*, of *Aldham*.

Here was another Manor which belonged formerly to *Bury* Abby, and was granted to *Robert Downs*, by King *Henry* VIII. this came afterwards to the *Veseys*. Here was also another Manor or Estate, which belonged to St. *Peter*'s Priory in *Ipswich*, and was granted with that to Cardinal *Wolsey*, 19 *Henry* VIII.

HOLBROOK. This in the Time of King *Henry* III. was the Lordship of *Richard de Holbrook*, who paid Fines to *Ipswich* for himself and Villains in *Holbrook* and *Tattingston*; afterwards it was Mr. *Daundy*'s, then it was the *Clenches*; Judge *Clench*, who died in 1607, lies buried in the Church. It was lately in *Thomas Thurston*, of *Ipswich*, Esq; and is now vested in *Thomas Staunton*, Esq; one of the Representatives of the Borough of *Ipswich*, in Right of his Lady, who was the only surviving Sister and Heiress of the late Mr. *Thurston*.

HOLTON.

HOLTON. The Lordship here belonged formerly to a Family of *Faſtolf*, afterwards to the *Mannocks*, then to Sir *John Williams*, and now to Sir *William Rowley*, Knt. of the Bath.

RAYDON. *Robert de Roydon* had a Grant of a Market and Fair here, 4 *Edward* II. or *A. D.* 1310. *John Haſting* Earl of *Pembroke*, died ſeiſed of the Manors of *Ottley, Raydon*, &c. 43 *Edward* III. afterwards the Manor and chief Eſtate here came into the Hands of the ſame Owner, who had that of the next Pariſh. [See *Shelly*.]

SHELLEY. *Robert de Tatterſhall* died ſeiſed of *Shelle*, in *Suffolk*, 1 *Edward* I. The Church was impropriated to the Priory of *Battle*; and the Impropriation and two Cloſes called *Kernelſcroft* and *Wytherſeys* alias *Gerwayes*, were granted as late belonging to that Priory to *Laurence Baſkervile* and *William Blake*. The Hall in 9 *Edward* II. was the Seat of *John de Appleby*, afterwards of the *Tilneys*; it lately belonged to *Thomas Kerridge*, Eſq; and was purchaſed of his Heirs by *Samuel Ruſh*, Eſq; together with the contiguous Manor and Eſtate at *Raydon*.

SHOTLEY. Here was anciently a Hamlet, called *Kirketon:* A Market and a Fair were granted at this Place to *William Viſdelieu*, who was Lord here 31 *Edw.* I. Sir *Thomas Moſel* was Lord here afterwards: The *Feltons* had the Lordſhip for ſome Ages, and at laſt it came with the other Eſtate of that Family to the Right Hon. the Earl of *Briſtol*. [See *Playford*.]

SPROUGHTON. A good Part of this Pariſh is within the Liberties of the Borough of *Ipſwich:* But the Manor, Hall-Houſe, and Advowſon of the Rectory, &c. was Part of the *Felton's* Eſtate, and came with that of *Shotley* laſt mentioned to the Earl of *Briſtol*, in whom it is now veſted. Within this Pariſh two good Seats have been built; one called the *Chauntry*, from its being built on

Lands given by *Edmund Daundy*, for endowing a Chantry in the Church of St *Laurence*, *Ipswich*. The present House was built by the late *Edward Ventris*, Esq; Master of his Majesty's Court of King's Bench; of whose Heirs it was purchased by the late Sir *John Barker*, Bart. and is now vested in his Son Sir *John Fytch Barker*, Bart. who resides here. Near to this is the Seat of *Robert Harland*, Esq; Captain in the Royal Navy; by whom it has been partly rebuilt, and greatly improved.

STRATFORD. *William de Munchensi* died possessed of an Estate here, 14 *Edward* I. *Michael de la Pole* procured a special Charter to hold a Court-Leet in his Lordships of *Stratford* and *Heigham*, in Com. *Suff.* 7 *Ric.* II. likewise for a Market here on the *Thursday* in every Week; and a Fair on the Eve, Day and Morrow of the Translation of St. *Thomas* the Martyr, 3 *Henry* V. He died seised of the Manor of *Veseys*, in *Stratford*. *Michael* his Son died seised of the same, shortly after; and *William de la Pole* died seised of it, 28 *Henry* VI. *Thomas* Lord *Cromwell* had a Grant from the King 31 *Hen.* VIII. of the Manors of *Dedham* and *Langham*, in *Essex*, with the Manor of *Stratford* juxta *Higham* in Com. *Suff.* which three Manors the King had by the Grant of *Charles* Duke of *Suffolk*. The Advowson belonged formerly to the Dukes of *Suffolk*; but ever since the Time of *Henry* VIII. it hath been in the Crown.

The North Isle of this Church was built about *A. D.* 1500. *Edward Mors* and *Alice* his Wife, and *Thomas Mors* and *Margaret* his Wife, were so great Benefactors towards it, that their Names were expressed in the Stone-Work. In 1524, and 1526, two Legacies were given towards building the Porch.

STUTTON. The Manor of *Stutton*-Hall did belong to Mr. *Thomas May*; but it was purchased by, and is now the Estate of the Earl of *Dysert*. Another Hall in this Parish, called *Crows*-Hall, is vested in the Family of *Bowes*.

Bowes. The Manor of *Greping-*Hall in *Stutton,* was granted to *Humfry Wingfield,* 29 *Henry* VIII. and in 4 *Eliz.* to *Thomas Seckford,* as Parcel of the Poſſeſſions of the Priory of *Coln,* in *Eſſex.* A Family of the *Jermys* formerly lived here, as appears by the Monuments in the Church. The Advowſon is veſted in the Rev. *Tobias Ruſtat,* the preſent Incumbent.

TATTINGSTON. Here was a good old Seat called the Place (or Palace), which did belong to the *Beaumonts;* but it was lately purchaſed and rebuilt by *Thomas White,* Eſq; and is now enjoyed by his Son, who reſides there, and in whom the Manor is now veſted. Here was formerly a free Chapel in this Pariſh, belonging 10 *Ed.* IV. to the Earl of *Oxford;* and the Earl of *Oxford* preſented to the Rectory in the Time of *Henry* VIII. In the Years 1458 and 1459, two Legacies were given towards building the Chancel.

WASHBROOK, or *Great Belſtead.* The Manor of *Hamer-*Hall here, belonged formerly to the Abbey of *Aumerle,* or *Albemarle,* in *Normandy;* and afterwards to the Nunnery of *Dartford,* in *Kent.* At the Diſſolution it was granted to Sir *Percival Hart,* Knt. and now belongs to *Thomas de Grey,* Eſq.

Within the Bounds of this Pariſh there was formerly another Church, and perhaps a Hamlet called *Felchurch,* or *Velechurch,* which was impropriated to the Abbey of *Albemarle;* and, upon the Diſſolution of the *alien* Priories, given to the Nunnery of *Dartford;* and 31 *Hen.*VIII. granted to Sir *Percival Hart,* with the Rectory and Advowſon of the Vicarage of *Waſhbrook.* The Vicarage of *Felchurch* was inſtituted into *A.D.* 1301, 1314, and 1338. We have lately been informed that in a Field bordering on the Road leading from *Sproughton* to *Copdock* Water, about forty Rod on this Side the Water next *Sproughton,* the Ruins of the Church, if they are not now, were not long since visible. This Church has been lately consolidated to *Copdock*.

WENHAM *Magna*, or *Burnt Wenham*. Robert de *Vaux*, who was one of the Knights of *Roger Bigod*, Earl of *Norfolk*, was admitted a Freeman of *Ipswich* in the Reign of King *John*, and paid Fines for Freedom from Toll, &c. for himself and Villains in *Wenham*. The Manor and Advowson of the Rectory belong to the Heirs of Sir *Philip Parker Long*, Bart. but it did belong formerly to the Priory of *Leighs*, in *Essex*, and was granted 28 Hen. VIII. to R. *Cavendish*.

WENHAM PARVA. Little *Wenham*-Hall appears to be a fine old Building; it was formerly the Seat of the *Brews*'s, now of *Thomas Thurston*, Esq;

WHERSTEAD. *Gilbert de Reymes* had this Lordship in King *John*'s Time; for he was himself admitted a free Burgess of *Ipswich*, and compounded for an Exemption from Toll, Custom, &c. for his Villains in *Wherstead*; and *Hugh de Reymes* did the same, 5 *Ed.* I. In 1 *Ed.* IV. Sir *John Howard* had a Grant of the Manors of *Leyham* and *Wherstead*, in *Suffolk*; which were in the Crown by the Attainder of *John* Earl of *Wiltshire*. It afterwards came to the famous Lord Chief Justice *Coke*, in whose Heirs it is now vested.

The Church was early impropriated to the Prior and Convent of *Ely*; and at this Day *Nathaniel Acton*, Esq; holds the Rectory by Lease from the Dean and Chapter of *Ely*; but the Advowson of the Vicarage is in the Crown.

WOOLVERSTON. The Hall or Manor-House in this Parish stands in a most delightful Situation on the *Western* Bank of the *Orwell*, with a fine View from the Park of the

the opposite Shore of *Nacton*. This Lordship, Estate, and the Advowson of the Rectory did belong to ——— *Tyson*, Esq; but it is not easy to say whose it is now; for Mr. *Tyson* becoming a Bankrupt in the Year 1720, *John Ward*, of *Hackney*, Esq; claimed this in Right of a Mortgage that he had upon it, and the Affair hath been in Chancery ever since. It has this surprising Circumstance attending it, that the Cause doth not appear to be nearer a Conclusion now, than it was at first; for some will still find their Account in preventing the Determination of it.

Hundreds of *Carlford* and *Colneis*.

THE Hundreds of *Carlford* and *Colneis* are bounded on the South by the *Ocean*, towards the East by the Hundreds of *Loes* and *Willford*, and towards the West by the Hundreds of *Bosmere* and *Claydon*, the Franchise of *Ipswich*, and the River *Orwell*. With regard to the Maintenance and Government of the Poor, they have lately been incorporated, viz. in 29 *George* II. or 1755. Since which Time the Guardians of the Poor have built a large House on the Side of *Nacton* Common, wherein all the Poor are maintained, that require parochial Relief. For this Reason we have blended these two Hundreds together. They contain the following Villages, and Places extra-parochial.

BEALINGS, was anciently the Lordship of *Hugh Petches*, who fined to *Ipswich* for himself and his Villains in *Bealings*; then *Robert de Tuddenham* had it; afterwards it came into the Family of *Clynch*; from them to the *Webbs*; and from them it came by Purchase to *John Pitt*, Esq; who removed from *Crows-Hall* in *Debenham*, and made *Bealings*-Hall his Seat. It was bought of Mr. *Pitts*'s Heirs by *George Bridges*, Esq; who now resides here.

Seckford-Hall in this Parish, has been remarkable for a Family of that Name, who lived there about three hundred Years, viz. from the Time of *Edward* I. to that of King *Charles* I. The last *Seckford* married a Daughter of Sir *Henry North*, and gave the Estate to her about the Year 1650. It now belongs to Mr. *Atkinson*.

There

There are several Legacies in old Wills given towards building the Steeple here, about the Year 1450. And there is an Inscription of two Lines upon the Porch, shewing when and by whom that was built.

BEALINGS PARVA. The Advowson of this Church belonged to the Monks at *Thetford*; and was granted the 32 *Henry* VIII. to *Thomas* Duke of *Norfolk*, who soon sold it to the *Seckfords*; and it came with *Seckford*-Hall to Mr. *Atkinson*.

BRIGHTWELL, was anciently the Lordship of *John de Lamput*. In the Time of Queen *Elizabeth* it was Sir *Francis Jermy's*; then the *Hewetts*, who sold it to Sir *Anthony Wingfield*; from which Family it passed to *Thomas Essington*, a Merchant; who repaired the Church which was much decayed, and built a comely Steeple to it. About the Middle of the last Century it passed from the *Essingtons* to the Family of *Barnardiston*. Sir *Samuel Barnardiston* of this Place was created a Baronet 11 *May*, 1663. He rebuilt the Hall at a great Expence, and intailed his Estate upon his Heirs Male; but these failing, it is now in Sir *John Shaw*, of *Eltham*, in Right of his Mother; and in *John Williams*, Esq; and another Gentleman, in Right of their Ladies, who were Coheiresses of that Family. The Hall has been lately taken down.

BUCKLESHAM in *Colneis*. The Lordship of this Parish is in *Richard Norton*, Esq; but the Hamlet of *Kembroke*, which lies in the Road from *Kirkton* to *Newbourn*, is the Lordship of *Philip Broke*, Esq; who also hath the Advowson of the Rectory. See *Nacton*.

BURGH. *Odo de Campania* was Lord here, when Domesday-Book was made. The Lordship seems to have belonged afterwards to the *Uffords*: *Maud de Lancaster*, Relict

Relict of *William de Burgh*, gave it to the Chantry erected at *Campesse*, and removed to *Brusyard*, and it was for some time impropriated thereto, and to the Nuns of St. *Clare*, who were placed at *Brusyard*, instead of the Chantry. But the Impropriation was afterwards given up, and the Church made presentative again. The Advowson was granted 30 *Henry* VIII. to *Nicholas Hare*. It is now in Mr. *Barnes*. Besides the Parish Church, there was a Chapel here dedicated to St. *Botolph*.

CLOPTON, was likewise the Lordship of *Odo de Campania*. Sir *Robert de Sackvill* had it in the Reign of King *Henry* I. it came afterwards to the *Weylands*; for *John de Weyland* had a Grant for a Market and Fair here, 31 *Edward* I. *Bartholomew Burghersh* died seised of this Manor, 43 *Edward* III. and his Son-in-Law *Edward le Dispencer* died seised of it 49 *Edward* III. But perhaps here may be two Manors; for *Hugh* Lord *Bardolf* is said to die seised of the Manor of *Clopton* in *Suffolk*, 45 *Edw*. III. How he obtained this Manor, see *Dugd*. Bar. II. 100, 101.

CULPHO. *William de Valoines* gave this Church to the Abbey of *Leiston*; and *William Verdunx*, who married his Daughter, confirmed it. The Impropriation was granted 19 *Elizabeth* to *Edward Grimston*, and with the Manor it belongs now to Sir *John Blois*, Bart.

FALKENHAM, in *Colneis*, is a Vicarage endowed with all the Tithes, except those of *Barley*; which were appropriated to the Priory of *Dodnash* in *Bently*, in *Samford* Hundred. Some Lands in this Parish hold of Mr. *Burwood*'s Manor of *Falkenham-Dodnash*; and others hold of Sir *John Fytch Barker*'s Manors of *Walton*, and *Russels* in *Falkenham*. About the Year 1533, two Legacies were given towards making a new Isle to this Church. The Crown presents to the Vicarage. The Rectory was one of those granted to Cardinal *Wolsey*.

FELIX-

FELIXSTOW, in *Colneis*, is thought to take its Name from *Felix* the *Burgundian*, who was the first Bishop of *Dunwich*, and is supposed to have landed here at his first Arrival; *Orwell* being even at that time a noted Harbour, and much frequented. It is conjectured that he staid here some Time, before he removed to *Dunwich*; for many little mitred Images of Brass have been found here, which are thought to have been made in Honour of him. See *Walton*.

FOXHAL. *Hugo de Darnford* gave this to the Prior and Convent of the *Holy Trinity*, in *Ipswich*; and the Impropriation was granted 36 *Henry* VIII. to Sir *Thomas Pope*, Knt. The Grange and Estate called *Dernfords*, in *Foxhall*, *Nacton*, *Hallowtree*, and *Ingulveston* or *Iselton*, belonged to the Abbot and Convent of *Sibton*, and was by them granted to *Thomas* Duke of *Norfolk*; and afterwards by King *Edward* VI. to *Thomas Heneage*, and Lord *Willoughby*, A. D. 1547. The Church here was probably used in 1530, when *John Punting* gave four Marcs, towards making a new Roof for it. Perhaps it was then decayed, and for want of other Benefactions to repair it, might soon after become unfit for Divine Service. Part of it is now standing on the North-side of *Foxhal*-Hall, next the Heath; but it is used only as a Barn, or an Out-house for Cattle. *Ipswich Trinity*-Priory seems also to have had a Manor here, which was granted with the Impropriation to Sir *Thomas Pope*. All is now in the Heirs of the *Barnardiston* Family.

GRUNDISBURGH. *Hugh Peche* claimed a Market here every *Tuesday*, and a Fair during the whole *Whitsun*-Week, A. D. 1285. Sir *Robert de Tudenham* was Patron, and probably Lord in the Time of King *Edward* II. And one of his Descendants gave the Advowson about the Year 1350, to the Master and Fellows of *Michael*-House,

House, since made Part of *Trinity* College, in *Cambridge*. The Steeple of this Church falling down about the Time of the Restoration, a very handsome new one was built about thirty Years since by the Executors of Mr. *Robert Thing*, who left an Estate to be sold for that Purpose. The Hall and chief Estate have been for many Years in the Family of *Blois*, who used to reside here. *Charles Blois*, of this Place, Esq; was created a *Baronet*, 15 *April*, 1668, who removed from hence to *Cockfield*-Hall, in *Yoxford*; and dying there in 1738, was succeeded in Honour and Estate by his Grandson Sir *Charles Blois*, Bart. but he dying without Issue, the Honour went to his Uncle Sir *Thomas*; but the Chief of the Estate, by the Appointment of Sir *Charles* the first Baronet, came to his youngest Son lately, by the Death of his Brother, the Rev. Sir *Ralph Blois*, of *Cockfield*-Hall; who is succeeded by his Son Sir *John Blois*, Bart.

HASKETON. There is a small Manor belonging to the Rectory of this Parish. Another called the Manor of *Hesketon*-Hall; and another called the Manor of *Thorpe*; the Tithes of which belonged formerly to the Priory of *Letheringham*, and were granted by K. *James* I. to *Anthony Gooch* and *Thomas Parker*, and belong now to ——— ———, and not the Rector.

HELMLY, in *Colneis*. *Odo de Campania* had the Lordship of *Hemele*, in *Suffolk*, when Domesday-Book was made. The Dukes of *Norfolk* were Patrons of the Rectory from the Year 1300 to 1540, or thereabout; but the Crown hath presented ever since. In the Time of King *Henry* VI. this Parish was spelt *Olmeslee*.

KESGRAVE. This Church was impropriated to the Priory of *Butly*, and the Impropriation is now vested in the Heirs of Sir *Samuel Barnardiston*. See *Brightwell*.

KIRKTON,

KIRKTON, in *Colneis*. About the year 1520, there were several Legacies towards building the Steeple of this Church. The Dukes of *Norfolk* had the Patronage of it formerly; but the Crown hath presented to it, since the Time of *Henry* VIII.

LEVINGTON, in *Colneis*. Here is an Alms-house for six poor Persons of this Parish and *Nacton*, built and endowed by Sir *Robert Hitcham*, who was a Native of this Place. Here is a small Manor, which is in the Family of *Goodrich*, with the Manor-House. The Church is now consolidated to *Nacton*, and the Patronage of it is in the Right Hon. Lord *Orwell*. The Steeple was built by Sir *Robert Hitcham*, as appears by his Arms, and the Date upon it.

Adjoining to this Parish towards *Trimly*, the Ruins of *Stratton* Church or Chapel, now overgrown with Trees and Bushes, are still to be seen; in the Middle of the first Field going from *Levington* to *Trimly*, called *Chapel-field*. Here was formerly a Lazar-house, endowed with a Moiety of the Tithes of *Stratton*. It is now extraparochial; there is no House standing but the Hall, which, with the Lordship, is now vested in Sir *John Fytch Barker*, Bart.

In a Farmer's Yard in *Levington*, close on the Left as you enter from *Levington* into the said Chapel-Field of *Stratton*-Hall, was dug the first *Crag* or *Shell*, that has been found so useful for improving of Land in this and other Hundreds in the Neighbourhood. For though it appears from Books of Agricultute, that the like Manure has been long since used in the *West* of *England*, it was not used here till this Discovery was casually made by one *Edmund Edwards*, about the Year 1718. This Man being covering a Field with Muck out of his Yard, and wanting a Load or two to finish it, carried some of the Soil that laid near his Muck, tho' it look'd to him to be no better than *Sand*; but observing the Crop to be best where

he

he laid that, he was from thence encouraged to carry more of it the next Year; and the Succefs he had, encouraged others to do the like.

This ufeful Soil has been found in great Plenty upon the Sides of fuch Vales as may reafonably be fuppofed to have been wafhed by the Sea; towards which fuch light Shells might be naturally carried, either at *Noah*'s Flood, or by the Force of the Tides to fome Places fince forfaken by the Sea. Whoever looks into any of thefe *Cragg-Pitts* cannot but obferve how they lie Layer upon Layer in a greater or lefs Angle, according to the Variation of the Tides. But when one confiders that the Wells in *Trimly-ftreet*, about a Quarter of a Mile diftant from the Mill, are about 25 Feet deep, and that the Springs all rife in Cragg; we can no way account for this Cragg fo many Feet under Ground, but from the univerfal Deluge.

MARTLESHAM. Sir *John Verdun* was Patron, and refided here *A. D.* 1328. But before the Year 1400 it came to the *Noons*, one of whom was a Juftice of the Peace, and fevere to the Proteftants in Queen *Mary*'s Reign. It continued in that Family above 200 Years; and then it came to the *Goodwins*; who removed, as we think, from *Ipfwich* thither; and they have now their Seat at the Hall.

NACTON, in *Colneis*. The Family of *Faftolf* were Patrons, and probably Lords, from the Year 1380, till the Manor and Eftate came to the *Brokes*, by a Marriage with the *Faftolfs*. This Family is defcended from Sir *Richard Broke*, Lord Chief Baron in the Reign of *Henry* VIII. and not from Sir *Robert Brooke*, Lord Chief Juftice of the *Common-Pleas* in Queen *Mary*'s Reign, whofe Family was fettled at *Yoxford*, in *Blithing*. Sir *Richard* was poffeffed of *Alnefborn* Dairy, or the *Donham-Bridge Farm*, in the 13 King *Henry* VIII. as appears by the Return of an Inquifition taken at that Time; and it is moft probable, that he built *Cow-Hall* about the Year 1526. *Robert Broke,* of *Nacton,* was created a Baronet in 1661; but the Patent was made in the usual Way, so that he dying without Issue Male, his Brother's Son could not succeed to the Title; but he marrying Sir *Robert*'s Daughter and Heiress, enjoyed the Estate; and had by his second Lady, a Daughter of Sir *John Hewet,* Bart. *Philip Broke,* Esq; the present Possessor, and formerly one of the Representatives for the Borough of *Ipswich.* Here are two Manors, one called *Cow-Hall,* and the Stile of the other is the Manor of St. *Peter* in *Nacton* and *Kembroke.* [See *Bucklesham.*] The Tenement *Hamons* in *Nacton,* was granted as Part of the Possessions of St. *Peter*'s Priory in *Ipswich,* to *Thomas Alverde,* 26 *Henry* VIII.

The late Admiral *Vernon* made this Parish the Seat of his Residence. His Nephew, to whom he left the Bulk of his Fortune, hath, since his Death, rebuilt the House, and inclosed it within a Pale; which Inclosure he hath called from the beautiful River on which it stands, *Orwell Park.* This Gentleman hath done still further Honour to the River; for being lately created a Peer of *Ireland,* he hath taken his Title from it, and is now the Right Hon. Lord *Orwell.*

Where the Road from this Parish to *Bucklesham* crosses that other leading from *Ipswich* to *Trimly,* is a Place called the *Seven Hills* (tho' there are more) which seem to have been *Barrows*; and therefore, perhaps it may be more probable, that near this Place it was that Earl *Ulfketel* might have fought the *Danes,* and not at *Rushmere.* Unless we suppose that *Rushmere* did formerly extend so far as almost to reach the Neighbourhood of this Place. Concerning which something might be said, but too minute to be inserted here.

North of the Bounds of *Nacton,* between them and those of *Ipswich* Liberties, is a Tract of Land now become extra-parochial. Part of this abutting on the *Orwell,*

well, belonged to a little Priory of *Augustin* Monks called *Alnesbourn* Priory. The Site of the Priory is now a Farm-House belonging to *Philip Broke,* Esq; and that of the Church or Chapel to it, hath a Barn built upon it. In the Year 1452, at the Request of *William Turnour* then Prior, it was united to *Woodbridge* Priory. In a Deed among the Writings of *Woodbridge* Priory, it is called a Manor; and in 22 *Henry* VIII. it was lett by *Thomas Cooke,* Prior of *Woodbridge,* to *Thomas Alvarde* of *Ipswich,* by the Stile of *Manerium de Alvesborne et Ponds*; and among the Description of some few Fields holden of this Manor, some called *Rysing*'s Pastures, lately belonging to *Edward Grimstone,* Esq; formerly to the Chauntry of St. *Laurence, Ipswich,* are said to lie in the Hamlet of *Alvesborne* in the Parish of *Hallowtree.* Within this District there is some Account of three Churches, besides the Chapel of *Alnesbourn* Priory. *Hallowtree,* or as it was sometimes spelt *Halgehetre* now mentioned, St. *Petronille* and *Bixley.* The Church of St. *Petronille* is mentioned in *Ipswich* Domesday, where the Heath formerly belonging to the Burgesses is described as lying between the Heath of *John Rous* on the North, and the Road leading from *Ipswich* to the Church of St. *Petronille* on the *South* : The other Piece is described as lying between the said Road on the *North,* and the Road leading from *Nacton* to *Ipswich* on the *South,* the East Head abutting on the Heath of *Thomas Fastolf,* Esq; and the West Head on *Chestoyneis* Close. The Bounds of *Rushmere* include the whole of *Bixly-Farm,* and run close by the Side of *Bixly-Decoy*; and so along that Valley till they meet the Bounds of *Ipswich* Liberties, (which in the *Ipswich* Perambulation are said to go) at the End of *Bixly-Marsh.* From hence it seems probable that *Bixly* may have been united to *Rushmere*; but it doth not appear plainly where any of these Churches stood, but probably one of them near what is called *Purdis-Farm.* The most we can collect

is,

HUNDREDS of CARLFORD and COLNEIS. 81

is, that this extra-parochial Land was much fuller of Inhabitants formerly, than it is at present; for now there are not more Houses upon it, than formerly there were Churches.

NEWBOURN. The Manor of *Haspely* in *Newbourn* belonged formerly to the Priory of *Woodbridge*, and was granted 33 *Henry* VIII. to *John Wingfield* and *Dorothy* his Wife; it is now with the Advowson of the Rectory vested in —— *Western*, Esq;

OTTLEY. *John Hastings* Lord *Bergavenny*, and Earl of *Pembroke*, had the Manor here 28 and 49 *Edward* III. *Edward Nevil* Lord *Bergavenny* died seised of it 16 *Edward* IV. and *George Nevil* Lord *Abergavenny*, is now seised of it at this Day. Here is a good old House, formerly the Seat of the *Gosnolds*; and in the Church is a Monument for *John Gosnold*, who died in 1628; which sets forth that he was descended from the right ancient and worthy Families of *Naunton* and *Wingfield*, of *Letheringham*; that he was Gentleman-Usher to Queen *Elizabeth*, and King *James*; and afterwards Gentleman of the Privy Chamber to King *Charles* I. and that *Winifred* his Wife was a Grand-daughter of Sir *Richard Poole* and the Lady *Margaret* Countess of *Salisbury*, who was the Daughter of *George* Duke of *Clarence*, Brother of King *Edward* IV. This Family suffered much in the Time of the great Rebellion, insomuch that the Reverend *Lionel Gosnold*, the last of the Family, and Rector of that Parish, was obliged to sell the Estate.

PLAYFORD, is most remarkable for being the Seat of the ancient Family of *Felton*, which is said to take its Name from the Lordship of *Felton*, in *Northumberland*; and to be a younger Branch of the *Bertrams*, Barons of *Milford*, and Lords of that Manor. *Edmund Felton*, of this Family, married a Daughter of *Robert Garrard*, of

G   *Codden-*

Coddenham, in this County; whose eldest Son Sir *Thomas Felton* was Chief Justice of *Chester* in the Reign of *Edward* III. and of *Richard* II. *Richard*, the second Son, took Priest's Orders; but *John*, the youngest, turned Merchant; and with so good Success, that he was called by way of Eminence *the Chapman*. *John*, the Grandson of the *Chapman*, acquired the Lordship and Estate of *Shotly*, by marrying *Joan* Daughter and Heiress of Sir *Thomas Mosel*, of that Place, Knt. He was succeeded in that and his other Estates by his Grandson *Robert Felton*, who marrying *Margaret* the Heiress of Sir *Thomas Sampson*, of *Playford*, Knt. acquired this Lordship, with other Manors and Estates in the Neighbourhood. *Anthony*, Great Grandson of the said *Robert Felton*, was made Knight of the *Bath* at the Coronation of King *James* I. in the Year 1603; and his Son *Henry* was created a Baronet 20 *July*, 1621. Sir *Thomas Felton*, Grandson of the first Baronet, was Comptroller of the Houshold and Privy Councellor to Queen *Anne*; but dying without Issue Male, the Honour and Estate came to his Brother Sir *Compton*; and he likewise dying without Issue Male, the Honour became extinct, and the Estate reverted to the Right Hon. *John Hervey*, the first Earl of *Bristol* of this Family, in Right of his Countess *Elizabeth*, the Daughter and Heiress of the aforesaid Sir *Thomas Felton*, who was Sir *Compton*'s elder Brother.

Playford Church is said to have been built by ―― *Felbrigg*, who is therein buried. The Revenues of it were given by *Robert Mallet* to his Priory at *Eye*, and granted 28 *Henry* VIII. to *Edmund Bedingfield*; but they belong now to *Richard Norton*, Esq; whose Mother was Daughter of Sir *Compton Felton*.

RUSHMERE, was the Lordship of *William de Freney* in the Time of King *John*, for he paid Fines to *Ipswich* for himself and his Villains in *Rushmere* and *Brisete*. At this

this Place *Ulfketel* is said to have withstood the *Danes*, (but see *Nacton*) A. D. 1010. The Lordship of this Parish hath for many Years been in the *Feltons*, of *Playford* (see there); and is now vested in the Earl of *Bristol*, together with a great Part of the Parish. The Church was impropriated to the Prior and Convent of *Christ-Church*, *Ipswich*; and the Impropriation and Advowson of the Vicarage were granted 37 *Henry* VIII. to *Austin Austins*, M. D. and they were sold again by Dr. *Austins* to Sir *John Jermy*, Knt. and *Humphry Warren*, Gent. In this Deed are specified the following Particulars, *viz.* The Parsonage Barn, and the Barn-yard, the little Piece opposite to it, containing about three Roods; also two Pightles, containing by Estimation nine Acres, lying in the Parish of St. *John Baptist*, in *Caldwell*; and all other Houses, &c. late in the Occupation of *Thomas* Lord *Wentworth*, and Parcel of the Possessions of the said late Priory; but the Right of Patronage of the Vicarage is not specified as sold with the Rectory. The Rectory came thro' the *Feltons*, and is now vested in the Earl of *Bristol*; and the Advowson of the Vicarage is in the Heirs of Sir *Samuel Barnardiston*, Bart.

Catharine Cadye, Widow, A. D. 1521, left a large Legacy towards building a new Steeple of like Fashion, Bigness and Workmanship, with that at *Tuddenham*: The two Steeples do only differ in the Form of the Battlements.

TRIMLY ST. MARTIN, in *Colneis*. *Grimston-Hall* in this Parish, the Manor of *Grimston* with *Morston*, and a good Estate besides, was purchased by *John Barker*, Esq; who was created a Baronet 17 *March*, 1621. This Honour and Estate is now in Sir *John Fytch Barker*, Bart. *Grimston-Hall* was formerly the Seat of *Thomas Candish*, Esq; the second *Englishman* that sailed round the World, who was born here. There are two *Ilexes* still standing at *Grimston-Hall*, which are said to have been planted by him. This gallant Officer, fitted out three Ships, at his own Expence, against the *Spaniards*, viz. the *Desire*, Burden 120 Tons; the *Content*, of 60 Tons; and the *Hugh Gallant*, a Bark, of 40 Tons. On board these Ships he had no more than One Hundred and Twenty-three Hands, Men and Boys. With this small and inconsiderable Force, he sailed from *Plymouth*, 21 *July*, 1586. In the *February* following he passed through the Straits of *Magellan*, and entered the *South-Seas*, where he plundered and burnt the Towns of *Paita*, *Puna*, *Aquapulco*, *Natividad*, *Acatlar*, and several others on the Coasts of *Chili* and *Peru*, with great Success. After which he attacked the *St. Anna*, a large *Aquapulco* Ship of 700 Tons. Before this, he had sunk the Bark at the Island of *Puna*, for want of Hands to man her; and it does not appear that the *Content* came up, so as to have any Share in the Engagement: In his own Ship, the *Desire*, he had not, at the most, above *Sixty* Men; yet, with these he attempted to board the *St. Anna*; and tho' he was twice repulsed, at the third Attack he took her; with the Loss of only two Men killed, and five wounded. What Loss the Enemy sustained, is not said; but Capt. *Candish* set One Hundred and Ninety-one Prisoners on Shore at *Puerto Seguro*, and brought off *Seven* with him, to serve as Pilots, Linguists, &c. He took in this Prize One Hundred and Twenty-two Thousand *Pezos* of Gold, each *Pezo* being of the Value of Eight Shillings; besides a great Quantity of other rich Merchandize. After this he touched at the *Philippine* Islands, and returned Home by the Cape of *Good Hope*, and *St. Helena*. If this Expedition be duly considered, with all its Circumstances, it will be found to be by far more remarkable, than what has happened in those Seas, within our Memories. But the *Suffolk* Commodore had no Historian to celebrate his Praises; and he contented himself with sending the following short Account of his glorious Success, in a Letter to Lord *Hunsdon*,

at

at that Time Lord Chamberlain to Queen *Elizabeth*; which he dated from *Plymouth*, where he arrived safely 9 *September*, 1588. The Letter runs thus:

" *Right Honourable*,

" As your Favour heretofore hath bene moste greatly
" extended towards me, so I humbly desire a Continuance
" thereof; and though there be no Meanes in me to
" deserve the same, yet the uttermost of my Services shall
" not be wanting, whensoever it shall please your Honour
" to dispose thereof. I am humbly to desire your Honour
" to make knowen unto her Majesty the Desire I have
" had to doe her Majesty Service, in the Performance of
" this Voyage. And as it hath pleased God to give her
" the Victory over Part of her Enemies, so I trust, yet
" long to see her overthrow them all. For the Places of
" their Wealth, whereby they have maintained and made
" their Warres, are now perfectly discovered; and if it
" please her Majesty, with a very small Power, she may
" take the Spoile of them all. It hath pleased the Al-
" mighty to suffer mee to circompasse the whole Globe
" of the World, entering in at the Streight of *Magellan*,
" and returning by the Cape *de Buena Esperanza*. In
" which Voyage I have either discovered, or brought
" certeine Intelligence of all the rich Places of the World
" that ever were knowen or discovered by any Christian.
" I navigated alongst the Coast of *Chili*, *Peru*, and *Nueva*
" *Espanna*, where I made great Spoiles: I burnt and
" sunke nineteen Sailes of Ships small and great. All
" the Villages and Townes that ever I landed at, I burnt
" and spoiled; and had I not bene discovered upon the
" Coast, I had taken great Quantitie of Treasure. The
" Matter of most Profit unto me, was a great Ship of the
" King's, which I tooke at *California*; which Ship came
" from the *Philippines*, being one of the richest of Mer-
" chandise that ever passed those Seas, as the King's Re-
" gister and Merchants Accounts did shew.——Which

" Goods

"Goods (for that my Ships were not able to contein the least Part of them) I was inforced to set on Fire. From the Cape of *California*, being the uttermost Part of all *Nueva Espanna*, I navigated to the Islands of the *Philippines*, hard upon the Coast of *China*; of which Countrey I have brought such Intelligence as hath not bene heard of in these Parts. The Statelinesse and Riches of which Countrey I feare to make Report of, least I should not be credited: For if I had not knowen sufficiently the incomparable Wealth of that Countrey, I should have bene as incredulous thereof, as others will be that have not had the like Experience. I sailed along the Islands of the *Malucos*, where among some of the Heathen People I was well intreated, where our Countreymen may have Trade as freely as the *Portugals*, if they will themselves. From thence I passed by the Cape of *Buena Esperanza*, and found out by the Way homeward the Island of *St. Helena*, where the *Portugals* used to relieve themselves; and from that Island God hath suffered me to returne into *England*. All which Services with myself, I humbly prostrate at her Majesty's Feet; desiring the Almighty long to continue her Reigne among us: For at this Day she is the most famous and victorious Prince that liveth in the World.

"Thus humbly desiring Pardon of your Honour for my Tediousnesse, I leave your Lordship to the Tuition of the Almighty. *Plimmouth*, this ninth of *September*, 1588.

"Your Honour's most humble to command,

"*THOMAS CANDISH.*"

The

---

* We have taken this Account from *Hackluyt*'s Collection of Voyages, &c. where it is called, "The admirable and prosperous Voyage of the worshipful Master *Thomas Candish*, of *Trimley*, in the County of *Suffolke*, Esquire — Written by Master *Francis Pretty*, lately of *Ey* in *Suffolke*,

The Succefs of this Voyage encouraged our *Trimley* Hero to make a fecond Attempt with a larger Force. Accordingly he departed from *Plymouth*, with five Ships, 26 *Auguft* 1591, on a like Expedition. But in this he failed; for we are forry to add, that after paffing the Straits of *Magellan* a fecond Time, on 20 *May* 1592, he was parted from his Fleet in the Night, and was never heard of fince.

Mr. *Lambard*, arguing in Favour of the Opinion that formerly there were Men of moft extraordinary Stature, faith, " Since the Beginning of the Reign of Queen
" *Elizabeth*, there were found in *Suffolk*, over-againft
" *Harwich* in *Effex*, by a Gentleman called *Cavendifh*,
" the Bones of a Man whereof the Skull was able to
" contain five Pecks, and one of the Teeth remaining
" yet with Mr. Secretarie, is as big as a Man's Fift, and
" weigheth ten Ounces. Thefe Bones had fometimes
" Bodies, not of Beafts, but of Men; for the Difference
" is manifeft."—*Lambard's* Dict. p. 124. But the Numbers are in Figures, and thefe might be miftaken by the Printer, as the Book was publifhed from the Author's own Manufcript.

Altefton Rectory was confolidated to *Trimly St. Martin*, 9 *July*, 1362: No Remains of this Church are any where to be found; but from a great Number of human Bones and Skulls that were dug up at putting down the Pofts of a Cartlodge, at the Weft-end of *Altefton-*ftreet, about the Year 1720, it is probable it might ftand there over-againft the Park of *Grimfton-Hall*.

The Hamlet of *Thorp* confifted of many Houfes, (of which now are no Remains but the Memory of them, in the
" a Gentleman employed in the fame Action." To which is there added, certain rare and fpecial Notes relating to this Voyage, written by Mafter *Thomas Fuller* of *Ipfwich*, who was Mafter of the *Defire*. This Book was printed *A. D.* 1600; it is now become very fcarce, and bears a high Price, for which Reafon we the rather chofe to extract this Account from it.

the Court-Rolls only) situated in several Pightles round the common Field, still known by the Name of *Thorp Field*, in the South-west Part of this Parish towards the River.

TRIMLY ST. MARY, in *Colneis*. This Church was probably built by *Thomas* of *Brotherton*, Son of *Edward* I. for his Arms are still to be seen over the Door of the Steeple. The Earls and Dukes of *Norfolk* were formerly Patrons of it. The Crown began to present to it only in *A. D.* 1545.

TUDDENHAM. This Church was given to *Trinity* Priory in *Ipswich*, by *Anketill de Mesang*, and others; the Rectory and Advowson of the Vicarage is in *Thomas Fonnereau*, Esq; the Owner of *Christ-Church*. The last Vicar was instituted to it; but it is now held by Sequestration. The Manor here belongs to Mr. *William Minter*, in whose Family it hath been for many Years.

WALDRINGFIELD. All we have learnt of this little Parish is, that Sir *Robert Hilton*, Knt. was Patron in 1305; but the Manor and Advowson now are in the Heirs of Sir *Samuel Barnardiston*, of *Brightwell*, Bart.

WALTON and FELIXSTOW, in *Colneis*. Altho' these are now distinct Parishes, yet *Felixstow* till of late Days was always reckoned as a Part of, and to be in *Walton*. For the Lands in *Felixstow* were all anciently, and still are, except a very small Parcel which hold of *Felixstow Priory*, within the Manor of *Walton*. The constant Stile of the Court from *Richard* II. to *Henry* VII. is, the Manor of *Walton*. Then the Stile was changed to the Manor of *Walton* with *Trimly*, as it continues to this Day; but it is never called the Manor of *Walton* with *Felixstow*. And so late as *Henry* VIII. when an Inquisition was taken of the Possessions of Cardinal *Wolsey*, in *Suffolk*; he is there said to have had an annual Pension from the Church of St. *Felix* in *Walton*.

Walton, thus largely taken, was a Place of great Note, as well before, as for some Ages after the Conquest. As *Orwell* Harbour is sometimes now called *Harwich Harbour*, from *Harwich*, a Hamlet of *Dover-court*, situated on the South-side of it; so, in old Court-Rolls, it is frequently called *Wadgate-haven*, from the Hamlet of *Wadgate* in *Walton*, where now there are but three Houses remaining. Here, as *Hollingshead* informs us, the Earl of *Leicester* landed with his *Flemings* in 1173, and was received by *Hugh Bigod* Earl of *Norfolk*, then Lord of the Manor and Castle of *Walton*; and in 1176 (says the same Author) *Henry* II. caused all such Castles as had been kept against him during the Time of that Rebellion (*Walton* named among the rest) to be overthrown, and made plain with the Ground. And this was then so effectually done, that, to prevent its ever rising again, the Stones of it were carried into all Parts of *Felixstow*, *Walton*, and *Trimly*; and Foot-paths were paved with them, on both Sides of the Roads. In many Places they still remain entire, and some Fragments of them are to be met with in all. At the same time the Castle of *Ipswich* was demolished.

He that shall look for the Site of this *Castle* within the Bounds of *Walton* strictly taken, will never find it; but upon a high Cliff in *Felixstow*, at the Distance of about one Mile from the Mouth of *Woodbridge* River, and two Miles from *Orwell-Haven*, Part of the Foundation of the West-side of it, is still to be seen; being now One Hundred and Eighty-seven Yards in Length, and nine Feet thick; it is called by the Country-People, Stone-Works. How much longer it was we cannot judge, Part of the South-end being washed away; and the Sea, which is daily gaining upon this Coast, having swallowed up the Ruins.

Such was the Condition of it, about the Year 1740; but, since then, the Sea hath washed away the Remainder of the Foundation. There can be no doubt but *Walton* Caftle was a *Roman* Fortification, as appears from the great Variety of *Roman* Urns, Rings, Coins, &c. that have been found there. It is thought to have been built by *Conftantine* the Great, when he withdrew his Legions from the Frontier Towns in the Eaft of *Britain*, and built Forts or Caftles to fupply the Want of them. The Coins that have been lately taken up here, are of the *Vefpafian* and *Antonine* Families; of *Severus*, and his Succeffors to *Gordian* the Third; and from *Gallienus*, down to *Arcadius* and *Honorius*. It is certain, the Caftle had the Privilege of coining Money; for feveral Dies have been found for that Purpofe.

Roger Bigot had a Grant of a Market at *Walton*, 17 *Edward* I. or *A. D.* 1288. The Market-Crofs is ftill ftanding, tho' the Market has been long difufed.

In the Parifh of *Felixftow*, about a Quarter of a Mile North of *Felixftow* High-ftreet, and at the fame Diftance Eaft from *Walton* Bounds, are very confiderable Ruins of an ancient and magnificent Building, which goes by the Name of *Old-Hall*. This probably was erected for the Manor-Houfe foon after the *Caftle* was demolifhed, and was the Place where King *Edward* III. laid fome time at his Manor of *Walton* before his Enterprife into *France*; wherein he gained that Victory over the *French* King near *Creffey*, *A. D.* 1338; and difpatched many confiderable Things there, as appears from *Rymer*'s *Fœdera*, Vol. V. and here he confirmed the Charters granted to the Corporation of *Ipfwich*, by an *Infpeximus*, dated at *Walton* in his twelfth Year, or 1339.

In a Survey of the Manor of *Felixftow* Priory, made in 1613, we find a Clofe of Arable Land called Great *Long-dole*, in which Clofe are the Ruins of *Walton* Caftle, and the Clofe is defcribed as lying between the *Old Abbey* and the Cliff Eaft. The Clofe next mentioned is called the *Old Abbey*, lying between the Cliff, Eaft and South;
and

and Great *Long-dole*, West, containing six Acres. Also a Close of Fenn Ground, called *Old Abby-Pond*, lying open to the old Abbey, South. From these Descriptions it is plain, that the Priory dedicated to St. *Felix*, the first Bishop of the *East Angles*, was founded, and probably very early, in this Place; tho' now no Remains are to be seen, save only the Site of the *Ponds*. The *Bigots*, Earls of *Norfolk*, were great Benefactors to this House; and it is very likely, that soon after the Castle was demolished, it was by them removed into a Field abutting on *Walton* Church, North; from whence you have a delightful Sea Prospect, and may see *Orford* Church and Castle. The Monks were called Monks of *Rochester*, because *Roger Bigod* gave it as a Cell to the Monks of *Rochester*. He endowed it with the small Manor of *Felixstow* Priory, taken out of his Manor of *Walton*, and with the Churches of *Walton* and *Felixstow*. Some Ruins of this Priory are still to be seen. The Site of it, with the great Tithes of *Walton* and *Felixstow*, and the Advowson of the Vicarages, were given at the Dissolution to Cardinal *Wolsey*, 26 *Henry* VIII. But long after his Fall, in 19 Queen *Elizabeth* they were granted to *Thomas Seckford*; and are now, with the other Estates of that Family vested in Mr. *Atkinson* (see *Bealings*); but the small Manor of *Felixstow* Priory, as also the large Manor of *Walton* with *Trimley*, and *Russels* in *Falkenham*, are in Sir *John Fytch Barker*, Bart.

Langer-Fort, and not *Land-guard Fort*, as it is corruptly and vulgarly called, takes its Name from *Langer-Common* in *Felixstow* upon which it stands, on the South-east Corner of it, two Miles from the Cliff. It is not certainly known when the first Fort was built. *Cambden* takes notice of *Langer-stone* as a Place where Fishermen dried their Nets, but makes no mention of any *Fort*. The old Fort had four Bastions (with fifteen very large Guns upon each), which were called the *King's*, the *Queen's*,

Queen's, *Warwick*'s, and *Holland*'s. These Names shew that it was erected after Queen *Elizabeth*'s Time; and probably it was in the Beginning of *Charles* I. who in the Grant of his Manor of *Walton* with *Trimly*, calls it a Fort newly built, viz. *excepto toto illo solo & fundo juxta Mare prope predictum manerium de* Walton *cum* Trimly, *super quod Fortilagium pro defensione patriæ ibidem nuper ædificatum existit.* The old one was demolished by Act of Parliament, and this present Fort built in the room of it, in 1718.

The Fort being built for the Security of *Orwell*-Haven by *Harwich* in *Essex*, People at a Distance have imagined the *Fort* as well as *Harwich* to be in *Essex (a)*; and as all Letters from the Board of Ordnance, &c. to the Garrison are usually sent by the *Harwich* Bag; and directed sometimes, To ——— at *Langer-Fort*, near *Harwich* in *Essex*; and sometimes for Shortness, To ———, at *Langer-Fort*, in *Essex:* From hence many People in the Neighbourhood have been led into the same Mistake. This Mistake hath so generally prevailed, that tho' the Arm of the Sea between the Fort and *Harwich* is two Miles over, the common People in *Harwich* will tell you they have seen some old Persons that remembred the Time, when with a Board laid upon two Horses Heads they could walk over from *Harwich* to the *Fort*; and that the Sea which now runs up to *Ipswich* on the South-side of the *Fort*, did run formerly on the North of it, where now is *Langer-Common*. Whoever observes the Soil and Situation of *Langer-Common* and *Langer* Marshes, will make no difficulty in acknowledging that they have been formerly covered by the Sea; and the Sea must then have extended from the *Suffolk* Cliff to the *Essex* Cliff. How long this Common and Level of Marshes have been gained from the Sea, we cannot precisely determine.

(a) We should not take so much Notice of this vulgar Error, were it not gravely mentioned by the Right Reverend Editor of *Cambden*.

HUNDREDS *of* CARLFORD *and* COLNEIS. 93

termine. But that the Sea had not its Chanel on the North-side of the Fort, is demonstrable from the Court-Rolls of the Manor of *Walton*, which make frequent mention of *Langer-Common* in *Felixstow* for upwards of Two Hundred Years before any Fort was built there; yet so strongly are People possessed in Favour of the Marvellous, that still the Fort must be in *Essex, because it is within the Jurisdiction of the Bishop of* London. But what Jurisdiction hath the Bishop of *London* ever exercised there, except the appointing of a Chaplain? and this he may have done at *Plymouth,* or *Berwick*-upon-*Tweed*; which surely are not in *Essex.* But to put this Matter past all Dispute, it appears by the Register of the Bishop of *Norwich,* that the Chapel of the *Old Fort* was consecrated 7 *September* 1628, by the Bishop of *Norwich,* as *lying within his Jurisdiction.* By the way, this is the best Evidence we have of the Time when *Langer-Fort* was first built. The very learned Editor of *Cambden,* from the Similarity of the Words, was led to think that *Langer-Fort* was a Contraction of *Land-guard-Fort*; but it appears from what has been said concerning the Antiquity of *Langer*-Common, that the Truth is the Reverse of this; for *Land-guard-Fort* is a Corruption of *Langer-Fort.* It is true, every Fort must be supposed to guard the neighbouring Country; but the Fort we are speaking of, could never without an Irony be called *Land-guard-Fort*; for upon Sight of it every Man of common Sense must see, it could never be intended to guard *the Land*; the Use of it must be to guard the *Haven.* Even the old Fort, which was far more commodious and useful than this, could never be supposed to guard the *Land*; since any Number of Forces may evidently land at *Felixstow* Ferry, without the Knowledge, or with it, in spite of *Langer-Garrison.*

WITNESHAM. Sir *Edmund Bacon* had this Lordship about the Year 1291; Sir *Warine Latymer*, A.D. 1341; Sir

Sir *John Brewfe*, A. D. 1361; whofe Defcendants had the Advowfon till the Reign of *Henry* VIII. when the *Audleys* had it. Sir *Richard de Weyland* had a Manor here; *Bartholomew Burgherfh*, who married *Cecilie* his Daughter, had a Charter for a free Warren in his Domain Lands in ———— *Witnefham*, &c. and died 43 *Edward* III. feifed of it. And *Edward le Difpencer*, who married *Burgherfh*'s Daughter, died feifed of it 49 *Edward* III. *Bartholomew Burgherfh* had a good old Seat here, the Site of which may ftill be feen in Mrs. *Child*'s Farm, where it had a Moat round it; and that dirty Road now corruptly called *Burrage-lane*, had its Name from him. He was one of the firft Knights of the Garter, or as they are called, one of the *Founders* of that Order. The Family of *Meadows* hath had a Seat here from the Time of King *Richard* III. The Advowfon of the Rectory was bought of fome of them by the late Mr. *Beaumont*, and fold by his Son to St. *Peter*'s College in *Cambridge*. Here was formerly a free Chapel dedicated to St. *Thomas*, and mentioned in Bifhop *Tanner's Not. Mon.* the Ruins of which appeared not long fince in a Meadow called *Burgherfh*. The Rivulet *Fyn*, which empties itfelf at *Martlefham*, rifes in this Parifh, not far from the Church. From hence the Street near the Bridge is called in Domefday *Fynford*; and, in old Wills, the Bridge is called *Fynford-Bridge*.

IOES

L O E S.

THE Hundred of *Loes* lieth to the Eastward of *Carlford*, and North of the Hundred of *Willford*; and contains the following Nineteen Parishes, *viz.*

BRANDESTON, in the Conqueror's Time was the Lordship of *Odo de Campania*; his Successors granted it to the *Burwells*; and from them it came through the *Weylands*, and *Tuddenhams*, to the *Bedingfields*. *Andrew Revet*, Esq; purchased this Manor of them, and made the Hall his Seat, whose Descendants still continue there.

The Advowson of the Vicarage and the great Tithes, were appropriated to *Woodbridge* Priory by Sir *Thomas Weyland*, about A. D. 1290. After the Dissolution they came into the Hands of the *Seckford* Family; but are now vested in Feoffees, in Trust, to support some Dissenting Meeting-Houses in *London*.

BUTLEY. This Church is in *Loes* Hundred; but the Abbey in *Plomesgate.* (See that.)

CAMPSEY-*Ash*, or *Ash* by *Campsey*, was remarkable for a Nunnery of the Order of St. *Austin*, founded by *Joan* and *Agnes de Valoines*, two Sisters, who dedicated it to the Honour of God and the Virgin *Mary*. This Nunnery was seated in a fruitful and pleasant Valley on the East-side of the River *Deben*, and on the North it had a large Lake of Water; so that the Water supplied them with Fish and Wild-fowl, and the Land with the other Necessaries of Life. *Maud de Lancaster* Countess of *Ulster*,

who

who afterwards married *Ralph de Ufford*, Chief Juſtice of *Ireland*, obtained a Licence from King *Edward* III. to found a Chauntry of five Chaplains, ſecular Prieſts, to pray and ſing Maſs in the Church of this Nunnery, for the Souls of *William de Burgh* and *Ralph de Ufford*, and their Wives, *viz. Elizabeth de Burgh* and *Maud de Ufford*, her Daughters, &c. which Chauntry remained there ſome Years; and then was removed by the ſaid Lady to *Rokehall*, in *Bruiſyard*. Several curious Deeds relating to this Nunnery, are ſaid by the Authors of *Mag. Brit. nova & antiqua*, to be in the Hands of *Francis Canning*, Eſq; of *Foxcoat*, in *Warwickſhire*. In the Window of the Parlour in the Abbey-houſe, is now a Piece of Glaſs ſtained with the Arms of the *Uffords*. And in the Window of the Chamber over it, is the Figure of a Lady ſtained in Glaſs, with theſe Words GOVERNESS GRACE. The Nunnery was valued at the Diſſolution, 35 *Hen*. VIII. at 182*l*. 9*s*. 5*d. per Annum*, and granted to Sir *William Willoughby*, who ſold it to *John Lane*, Gent. It was purchaſed of the *Lanes* by *Frederick Scot*, who ſold it to Sir *Henry Wood*, of *Loudham*; and it came with the reſt of his Eſtate to *William Chapman*, now of *Loudham*, Eſq;

In this Pariſh is an old Seat, formerly the Eſtate of *Theophilus Howard*, Earl of *Suffolk*. This was purchaſed by *John Braham* or *Brame*, Grandſon of Sir *John Braham* of *Braham*-Hall, who ſettled here; but that Family failing of Iſſue Male, it is now veſted in two Maiden Ladies of that Name.

The High Houſe in *Campſey* is a good Seat, and was built by *John Glover*, Eſq; ſometime Servant to *Thomas Howard*, Earl of *Norfolk*; whoſe Succeſſor removing to *Froſtenden* in this County, ſold it to the *Shepards*, one of which Family now poſſeſſes it.

CHARSFIELD, was formerly the Lordſhip of *William de Weylond* in King *John*'s Time, who fined for his Villains in *Charsfield* and *Weſterfield*; afterwards of the *Bedingfields*, and ſold by them to Sir *John Leman*, Knt. Lord-Mayor of *London*; to him ſucceeded *William Leman*, Grandſon of *William Leman*, of *Beccles*, Eſq; who was the elder Brother of Sir *John Leman*; in whoſe Heirs it continued till it was lately ſold to *William Jennens*, Eſq; of *Acton-Place*.

The Church was impropriated to *Letheringham* Priory, and is now a Donative properly ſo called; that is, filled by the Patron, without Preſentation or Nomination to, or Licence from, the Biſhop.

CRETINGHAM. This Church was impropriated to St. *Peter*'s Priory in *Ipſwich*. The Manor of St. *Peter* in *Cretingham*, did belong to the ſaid Priory. The Manor of *Kettlebars* belonged to a Family who took their Name from it; from them it paſſed to the Family of *Mulſo*, and from them to the Family of *Cornwallis*. The Manor of *Tyes* in *Cretingham* belongeth to Mr. *Revet* of *Braudeſton*, and hath been the Eſtate of his Anceſtors about Two Hundred Years. The Pariſh was anciently divided into two Villages, one called *Great Cretingham*, the other *Little Cretingham*, near *Ottly*, which had a Chapel belonging to it; but they both now make one Pariſh.

DALLINGHOO, is Part of it in this Hundred, and the other Part in *Willford*. Here was a handſome Seat built by *William Churchill*, who ſometime reſided here. His Son-in-Law *Francis Negus*, Eſq; who was formerly one of the Repreſentatives of the Borough of *Ipſwich* to whom he gave it, rebuilt it; but it was unfortunately conſumed by Fire, A. D. 1729; the Eſtate is now in *William Negus*, Eſq; his Son.

Hundred of Loes.

One Manor in this Parish and Hundred of *Loes* belongs to the Honor of *Eye*.

The other in the Hundred of *Willford*, called for Diſtinction-ſake, *Earl-Dallinghoo* as having been in the Hands of ſeveral of the Earls of *Norfolk* and *Suffolk*, together with the Advowſon, is veſted in the Earl of *Rochford*. Before he had them they belonged to the *Wingfields*, and anciently to the *Boviles* of *Letheringham*.

EARL-SOHAM, is ſo called, becauſe it belonged to the Earls of *Norfolk*. *Roger Bigod* had a Grant of a Market as well as a Fair here, 20 *Edward* I. and *Thomas de Brotherton* Earl of *Norfolk* had it confirmed to him, 7 *Edw*. II. The Market hath been long diſuſed, but there is now a Fair yearly on *July* 12.

Soham-Lodge, is an old irregular Houſe, encompaſſed with a Brick Wall and a large Moat, ſtanding within the Park, to which the Manor of this Town belongs. It was anciently the Seat of the Family of *Cornwallis*; from one of them it was given by Will to the *Corderoys*, who ſold the Manor, Advowſon, Lodge and Park to *John Cotton*, ſecond Son of Sir *Allen Cotton*, Lord-Mayor of *London* in 1626. He dwelt here, and was Sheriff of *Suffolk* in 1644. His Son ſold this Eſtate to *Leiceſter Devereux* Lord Viſcount *Hereford*, and the Executors of his Son *Price Devereux* Lord Viſcount *Hereford*, ſold it to *John Boyfield*, Eſq;

EASTON, was formerly the Lordſhip of an ancient Family in *Kettleburgh*, ſurnamed *Charles*. Afterwards the *Wingfields* of *Letheringham*, were Proprietors of both. *Anthony Wingfield* removed from *Letheringham*, to *Godwyns* in *Hoo*; and was created a *Baronet* 17 *May*, 1627. He built the White Houſe at *Eaſton*, and removing from *Hoo* made it his Seat. To him ſucceeded Sir *Richard*, Sir *Robert*, and Sir *Henry Wingfield*, Barts. whoſe Son Sir

Henry

Henry fold this Seat and the Remainder of the *Wingfield*'s Eftate in the Neighbourhood, to the Right Hon. *William Zuileſtein*, Lord of *Zuileſtein* in the Province of *Utrecht*, Mafter of the Robes to King *William* III. and created Baron of *Enfield*, Vifcount *Tunbridge*, and Earl of *Rochford*, 10 *May*, 7 *William* III. He was fucceeded by his Son *William Henry* Earl of *Rochford*, who commanded the Left Wing of the *Engliſh* Army under General *Stanhope*, at *Lerida* in *Spain*, where he was flain 14 *July*, 1710. *Frederick*, his Brother, fucceeded him; and he dying in 1738, was fucceeded by *William Henry* the prefent Earl of *Rochford*, who fold this Eftate to the Hon. Mr. *Naſſau* his younger Brother, married to her Grace the Dutchefs Dowager of *Hamilton* and *Brandon*, who have for feveral Years made this their Refidence.

EYKE. *Roger Bigod* endowed *Alice* his fecond Wife *(inter alia)* with the Manor of *Staverton* in this Parifh, 18 *Edward* I. fo called, from a Family of the Name of *Staverton*, who had it before. *Thomas Mowbray*, firft Duke of *Norfolk*, died feifed of the Manor of *Staverton*, 1 *Henry* IV. and it was affigned to his Relict as Part of her Dowry, 3 *Henry* IV. The Pafture called *Staverton-Park*, was granted as Parcel of the Poffeffions of *Butley* Priory to *Thomas* Duke of *Norfolk*, 32 *Henry* VIII. But it now belongs to *William Chapman*, Efq; as Part of the late Mr. *Wood*'s Eftate.

At *Eyke* was a Chantry, called *Bennet*'s Chantry, of the yearly Value of 8*l*. The Lands belonging to it lying in *Eyke* and *Rendleſham* were granted 3 *Edward* VI. to Sir *Michael Stanhope* and *John Delle*.

FRAMLINGHAM, is a Parifh of large Extent, in the midft of which ftandeth the Church and Market. The Town is pleafantly feated, and pretty well built, upon a Clay Hill near the Head of the River *Ore*; which rifing in the Hills on the North paffeth through the Town, and falleth

falleth into the Sea beyond *Oreford*. The Market Weekly, on *Saturday*; and there is a Fair on *Monday* and *Tuesday* in *Whitson*-Week, procured by *Thomas* of *Brotherton*, Earl of *Norfolk*; and another Fair on *Michaelmas*-Day. The Market-place is triangular, and almost equilateral. The Church and Castle are great Ornaments to the Town. The Church is indeed a stately Edifice, built (as is supposed) by the *Mowbrays* Earls of *Norfolk*, at least great Part of the Steeple seems to have been so, as appears from their Arms at the Bottom, and on the Middle of it; but it was not completed till the latter End of *Henry* the Eighth's Reign; for there are many Wills in the Archdeacon's Office, in which Legacies are given towards building the Steeple at *Framlingham*; and in 1520 Legacies begin to be given towards the *Battlements* of the Steeple; and such Legacies occur so late as the Year 1534. In the Isles lie buried several of the Earls and Dukes of *Norfolk*. There is a curious Monument for *Thomas Howard*, the third Duke of *Norfolk*, who died in 1554; in whose Collar of SS, is this Inscription, *Gratia Dei sum quod sum*. Another Monument for *Henry Fitzroy*, Duke of *Richmond* and *Somerset*, natural Son of *Henry* VIII. who married Lady *Mary* Daughter of *Thomas Howard* Duke of *Norfolk*, and died in 1536. And another Monument to *Henry Howard* Earl of *Surry*, and *Frances* his Wife (a Daughter of *John de Vere*, Earl of *Oxford*), who was beheaded 19 *Jan.* 1546.

There are two Alms-houses in this Town; one founded in pursuance of the Will of Sir *Robert Hitcham*, for twelve of the poorest Persons in *Framlingham*, each of whom is allowed Two Shillings every Week, and Forty Shillings every Year for a Gown and Firing. These are to attend Prayers Morning and Evening at Church; and Sir *Robert* left moreover, 20 *l.* by the Year to a Clergyman to read Prayers, and 5 *l.* by the Year for the Clerk and Sexton.

The

The other Alms-house was founded by one *Thomas Mills*. This Man was a Wheel-wright by Trade; but being a gifted Brother in the Times of Diforder within the laſt Century, he turned Preacher among the *Anabaptiſts*, at *Saxſtead*, near this Town; and throve so well in this Bufinefs as to be enabled, about the Year 1703, (until which Time he lived,) to found this Houfe. Accordingly, foon after that, his Truſtees built this Alms-houfe for *Eight* poor Perſons, who are allowed Half a Crown a Week, and yearly an outward Garment, and Thirty Shillings each for Firing. But one *William Mayhew*, a Servant of this Man's, built two of the Apartments at his own Expence. Thefe eight Perſons enjoy the Benefaction for Life; unlefs, for any Mifdemeanor, they are turned out by the Truſtees.

Sir *Robert Hitcham* founded alſo a Free-School, with a Salary of 40 *l.* a Year to the Maſter, to teach Forty of the pooreſt Children of this Town, to read, write, and caſt Accounts; and when they are perfect in them, he gave each 10 *l.* to bind them Apprentice. It is faid, and with ſome Probability, that this was a Town of the *Britons*; and they ſay, conquered by the *Romans*, when they defeated *Boadicea*. The Caſtle, which is the moſt remarkable Piece of Antiquity, is ſuppoſed to have been built by ſome of the Kings of the *Eaſt-Angles*, but which of them our Hiſtories do not mention; yet it may, not improbably, be ſuppoſed to have been built by *Redwald*, the greateſt of them, who kept his Court at *Rendleſham* in this Hundred. But this is mere Conjecture. The Caſtle is a large ſtrong Building, containing in Land within the Walls, one Acre, one Rood, and eleven Perches. The Walls are 44 Feet high, and 8 Feet thick, which are now ſtanding pretty entire: There are thirteen Towers, 14 Feet higher than the Walls; two of which are Watch-Towers. It was inacceſſible on the Weſt-ſide, becauſe of the adjoining Mere; and on the other Side it was fortified with a double Ditch, &c. so that it may reasonably be supposed to have been, in those Times, a very strong Fortress. Yet it is said, that the *Danes* beat *St. Edmund* the King out of it, and kept it in their Hands for fifty Years, till they were brought under the Obedience of the *Saxons*. *William* the Conqueror gave it to *Roger Bigod*, Earl of *Norfolk*; but the *Bigods* dying without Issue, it reverted to the Crown 25 *Edward* I. And so it remained till *Edward* II. in his sixth Year gave it to his Brother *Thomas* of *Brotherton*, Earl of *Norfolk*. He left it to his two Daughters *Margaret* and *Alice*, which *Alice* marrying *Edward de Montacute*; upon the Division of the Estate, he obtained in his Part this Castle and *Demesne*. He left it to his Daughter *Joan*, who marrying *William de Ufford* Earl of *Suffolk*, carried it into that Family. From him it came to the *Mowbrays*, Dukes of *Norfolk*, who sometimes resided here. From the *Mowbrays* it descended to the *Howards*, Earls and afterwards Dukes of *Norfolk*; after them it was granted to the *De Veres*, Earls of *Oxford*; then it returned to the *Howards* again, who sold this Castle, Manor and *Demesne* to Sir *Robert Hitcham*, Attorney-General in the Reign of *Charles* I. and he gave it to *Pembroke* Hall in *Cambridge*,

HACHESTON. There is a considerable Fair held here yearly on the second and third of *November*, granted 2 *Henry* III. to the Prior and Convent of *Hickling* in *Norfolk*, who had this Church given them by *Theobald de Valeines* before the Year 1203, and got it impropriated to them.

The Manor of *Hacheston* did formerly belong to *Framlingham* Castle, until *Theophilus Howard* Earl of *Suffolk* sold it to *John Brame*, of *Ash* by *Campsey*; whose Heirs do now enjoy it.

Glevering-Hall Manor, in this Parish, did anciently belong to the Prior and Convent of *Leiston*; and was

granted

HUNDRED of LOES. 103

granted 28 *Henry* VIII. to *Charles Brandon*, Duke of *Suffolk*. Afterwards it was the Inheritance and Seat of *John Bull*, Esq; since of the Family of *Radcliff*, and now of Mr. *Thomas Whimper*.

HOO. *Hoo-Hall* did anciently belong to *Thomas* of *Brotherton*, Earl of *Norfolk :* Afterwards it came to the Earls of *Suffolk*, and was sold by one of them to Sir *Robert Naunton*.

Another considerable Estate here belonged to a Family who took their Name from this Town, by whom it was sold to one *Godin*, a Merchant of *London*; from him it came to the Family of *Wingfield*, and by them it was sold to the Earl of *Rochford*. There was formerly in this Village the Gilds of the *Holy Trinity*, *St. Mary*, *St. Peter*, *St. Andrew*, and *St. John*. The Church was presentative, till after the Year 1470; when the Advowson of it being given by *John* Duke of *Norfolk* and *Catherine* his Wife, to the Prior and Convent of *Letheringham*, they got it impropriated to them. The Impropriation was granted 7 *Edward* VI. to *Elizabeth Naunton*.

KETTLEBOROUGH, was the Lordship of the *Willoughbys*, Lords of *Eresby*, in the Reign of *Edward* IV. Afterwards of the *Mowbrays*, Dukes of *Norfolk*; and went with the Manor of *Framlingham*, till it was sold by *Thomas* or *Theophilus* Earl of *Suffolk*, to Sir *Robert Naunton* ; in whose Family it still continues, being now the Property of *William Leman*, Esq; the Heir of that Family.

King *Henry* III. *A.D.* 1265, granted a Market and Fair here; but they are both disused. In this Parish is the Seat of *Robert Sparrow*, Esq;

KENTON, belonged to the Family of that Name, who dwelt in *Kenton-Hall*; and who, besides the Manor, possessed the greatest Part of the Parish : By the Marriage of an Heir-general, this Estate descended to the Family of *Willisham*; from them thro' the *Ramseys* and *Garneys*, to the Family of *Stane*. It is now vested in *William Stane*, Esq; who is Lord of the Manor called by the Name of *Kenton* with *Suddonhall*.

The Family of *Warreyn* has a Seat in this Parish, now vested in *John Warreyn*, Esq; whose Ancestor *Robert Warreyn*, D.D. Rector of *Long-Melford*, was ejected in 1641, and treated in a very ignominious Manner. The Church was impropriated to *Butley* Abbey, and granted to *Francis Framlingham*, 34 *Henry* VIII. The Patronage of the Vicarage is now in *George Bridges*, Esq.

LETHERINGHAM, is remarkable for a little Priory of black Canons, founded by Sir *John Boynel*, or *Bovile*; it was a Cell to St. *Peter's* in *Ipswich*, valued at the Dissolution at 26*l*. 18*s*. 5*d*. and granted in 7 *Edward* VI. to Mrs. *Elizabeth Naunton*; in which Family it hath ever since continued.

The Priory was converted into a good Mansion, by Sir *Robert Naunton*; since whose Time it hath been the Seat of this very ancient Family. Sir *Robert* removed hither from *Alderton* in *Willford* Hundred, and was in the Reign of King *James* I. Secretary of State, Privy Counsellor, and Master of the Wards and Liveries. He died A.D. 1630, without Male Issue, and was succeeded at *Letheringham* by his Brother *William*, whose Son *Robert* suffered much in the great Rebellion for his Loyalty to King *Charles* I. *William Naunton*, the last Possessor, died not long since, without Issue; and left the Estate, after the Death of his Lady, to his next Heir. There is a noble Gallery in this House, adorned with several valuable Pictures. In the Chancel of *Letheringham* Church are some elegant and magnificent Monuments for the *Wingfields* and *Nauntons*, which have been ill kept for some Time.

MARLSFORD.

MARLSFORD. This Manor did anciently belong to the *Sackvills*, then to the *Rokes*, afterwards to the *Drurys*, lately to the *Devereux's*, and now to *Fynes Dove*, Clerk.

MONODEN, or MONEWDEN. *Odo de Campania* had *Mungaden*, which is said to have been the old Name of this Parish when Domesday Book was taken. It was afterwards in the Family of *Hasting*, and now belongs to ———— *Curry*, Esq;

RENDLESHAM, or RENDILISHAM, *i. e.* as *Bede* interprets it, the House of *Rendilus*. *Hugh Fitz-Otho* procured from *Edward* I. a *Market* and *Fair* at *Rendlesham*. *Cambden* tells us, "*Redwald* King of the *East-Angles*, " commonly kept his Court here; he was the first of all " that People who was baptized, and received Christia- " nity: But afterwards, being seduced by his Wife, he " had (as *Bede* expresses it) in the self-same Church, one " Altar for the Religion of Christ, and another little " Altar for the Sacrifices of Devils. *Suidhelmus* also, " King of the *East-Angles*, was afterwards baptized in " this Place, by *Cedda* the Bishop."

The Editor of *Camden* adds, "It is said, that in dig- " ging here about thirty Years since, there was found an " ancient Crown weighing about sixty Ounces, which " was thought to have belonged to *Redwald*, or some " other King of the *East-Angles*. But it was sold, and melted down." See Bishop *Gibson*'s Edition of *Cambden*, pag. 445, 446.

The Palace where *Rendulus* kept his Court, is thought to have stood in the same Place where *Rendlesham* House now stands, which was lately the Seat of the *Spencers*, and is now vested in her Grace the Duchess of *Hamilton* and *Brandon*, since married to the Hon. Mr. *Nassau*.

Here

Here were four small Manors in this Parish, *viz. Col-vyles*, to which the Advowson was formerly appendant. This belonged about the Year 1300 to a Family of *Holbrook*, afterwards to a Family of *Fastolf*, and came to the Duke of *Norfolk* about the Reformation. By his Attainder the Advowson came to the *Crown*; but the Manor, with that of *Bavents*, came to the *Corances*, and is now the Estate of ———.

The other two Manors are those of *Naunton-Hall* and *Caketons*, which in the Time of King *Henry* VIII. belonged to Mr. *Christopher Harman*; but in the latter Part of King *Edward* VIth's Reign were sold to *James Spencer*, and are now in the Duchess of *Hamilton*.

WOODBRIDGE took its Name from a *Wooden Bridge* built over a hollow Way, to make a Communication between two Parks separated by the Road which leads from *Woodbridge* Market-place towards *Ipswich*. At the Foot of the Hill from this hollow Way, about a Stone's-throw from where the Bridge might stand, is a House, which at this Day retains the Name of the *Dry-Bridge*. The River *Deben*, on which this Town is situated, discharges itself into the Sea about ten Miles below it, and is navigable up to the Town. Here are two Quays, the common Quay where the chief Imports and Exports are, and where the fine *Woodbridge* Salt is made; and above this is the Lime-kiln Quay, where formerly the *Ludlow* Man of War was built. Some Years since there was another Dock below the common Quay, where the *Kings-fisher* Man of War was built; but this is now shut from the River by a mud Wall, and almost filled up.

The Church and Steeple are beautiful Buildings, the former is said to be founded by *John* Lord *Segrave*. On the South-side of the Church stood a Priory of black Canons, founded by Sir *Hugh Reus*, or *Rufus*, as *Weaver* calls him, to which one *Hanfard* was a considerable Benefactor.

ne'actor. It was valued at 50 *l*. 3 *s*. 5¼ *d*. per *Annum*, and granted in 33 *Henry* VIII. to Sir *John Wingfield* and *Dorothy* his Wife. It is a good old Seat, now the Estate of the Rev. *Thomas Carthew*. The Town traded much in Sack-cloth; the chief Manufacture now is Salt. It has a pretty good Market on *Wednesdays*. This was granted in the Reign of King *Henry* III. There are two Fairs yearly, on *March* 25, and *Sept.* 21. In the midst of the Market-place is the Shire-Hall, where the Quarter-Sessions for the Liberty of St. *Etheldred* are holden; under which is the Corn-cross. The Market-place is clean and well-built, and so is the *Stone*-street, so called because it was the only Part of the Town which was paved. But the Street called the *Thorough-fare*, as being situated in the Road from *Ipswich* to *Yarmouth*, is now likewise well paved, and kept so clean that it will tempt the substantial Inhabitants to build and dwell there.

Here is a free Grammar-School for *Ten* Boys. The Master is elected by the chief Inhabitants of the Parish; and hath a good House, in which is a large Room for a School, and Conveniencies for Boarders: He is also entitled to the following yearly Payments, 10 *l*. out of an Estate belonging to the Parish; 5 *l*. from the *Maryotts*'s Estate, now Mr. *Negus*'s; 5 *l*. from the *Burwell*'s Estate; 5 *l*. from the *Seckford*'s Estate, now Mr. *Atkinson*'s; and to Lands given by one *Willard*, of the yearly Value of about 5 *l*.

Here is also an Alms-house for thirteen poor Men, and three Women, called *Seckford*'s; because founded *A. D.* 1587, by *Thomas Seckford*, Esq; one of the Masters of Requests to Queen *Elizabeth*. It is endowed with an Estate lying in *Clerkenwell, London*. One of the poor Men is called *Governor*; but the Governors of the Alms-house are, the *Master of the Rolls*, and the *Chief Justice of the Court of Common-Pleas* for the Time being. The three Women were appointed as Nurses, to be placed in a House called *Copt-Hall*, (now down) near the Alms-House, to attend the poor Men. The late Sir *Joseph Jekyle* and Sir *Peter* (afterwards Lord) *King*, A.D. 1718, settled the Pensions to be allowed, *viz.* to the Governor 13*l.* 13*s.* 4*d.* and to each of the twelve others 9*l.* 15*s. per Annum*, to be paid by four Quarterly, but unequal Payments. The Men are also allowed an outward Garment yearly, on which they wear a Silver Badge with the *Seckford* Arms. The three Nurses live in a House built close to the Alms-House, *A.D.* 1748, are allowed 5*l.* 6*s.* 8*d. per Annum* each, paid by equal Quarterly Payments. The poor Men are to attend Divine Service at the Parish Church on *Sundays*, Holidays, *Wednesdays* and *Fridays*.

The Manor of *Woodbridge* which belonged formerly to the Priory, was granted with that to *John Wingfield* and *Dorothy* his Wife; it was soon after *Seckford's*, since the *Norths* had it, it is now the Estate of the Rev. *Thomas Carthew*.

Here is also another, which belonged to the *Uffords*. For, 4 *Henry* V. upon the Death of *Isabel*, the Relict of *William de Ufford*, *Robert* Lord *Willoughby* as Heir to the said *William*, had Livery and Seisin of the Quay and Pool of *Woodbridge*. Sir *Robert Willoughby*, Knt. was seised the 5th *Edward* IV. of the Manor of *Woodbridge*; and in 18 *Henry* VIII. Sir *William Willoughby* assigned the Manor of *Woodbridge* (*inter alia*) for his Wife's Dower.

Adjoining to *Woodbridge* is a Manor and Hamlet, called *Kingston*, which belongs to the Dean and Chapter of *Ely*; but is leased by them to *William Negus*, Esq. The Prior and Convent of *Ely* are said to have Possessions in *Oddebruge*, in *Edward* the Confessor's Time; which we suppose to have been the same with *Woodbridge*; for in *Domesday*, this Town is written, *Udebryge*.

Hundred of Willford.

*W*ILLFORD Hundred contains eighteen Parishes, and is bounded by the Ocean on the *South*, by the Hundreds of *Loes* and *Plomesgate* on the North and *East*, and by the *Deben* on the *West*.

ALDERTON, consists of four Manors; each of which hath a Right to present to the Rectory in its Turn, *viz.* The Manor of *Naunton-Hall* or *Alderton Hall*, the first Turn; the Manor of *Bovile*'s, the second; the Manor of *Pechys*, the third; (these three are vested in the Heirs of *Thomas Bacon*, Esq;) and the Manor of *Alderton Comitis* or *Earls Alderton*, hath the fourth Turn; which Manor belongs to the Bishop of *Norwich*, and it is his Right to present the next Turn. This Manor is held by Lease from the Bishop of *Norwich*, by Sir *Robert Clarke*. The ancient Family of *Naunton*, who were formerly Lords of the first three Manors, resided here for a long time, before Sir *Robert Naunton* removed to *Letheringham*. (See *Dalinghoo*, in this Hundred.)

BAUDSEY. This Lordship belonged in the Time of *Henry* II. to *Ranulf de Glanvile*, who gave *one half* of it to his Daughter *Amabil*, married to *Ralph de Arderne*, whose Grandson *Ralph* gave this Moiety to the Prior and Convent of *Butley*; the other Moiety he gave to his Daughter *Helewise*, who married *Robert Fitz Ralph* Lord of *Middleham*, in *Yorkshire:* This Moiety came afterwards to *Robert de Ufford*, who was twice Chief Justice of *Ireland*, and obtained from King *Edward* I. in the

eleventh

eleventh Year of his Reign, a Licence for a Weekly
Market, on *Fridays* ; and a Fair on the Eve, Day, and
Morrow of the Nativity of the Virgin *Mary, September* 8,
at his Manor of *Bawdrefey.* William Lord *Willoughby*
died feifed of this Manor 11 *Henry* IV. *Robert* his Son
had Livery 4 *Henry* V. and Sir *Robert Willoughby* was
feifed of it 5 *Edward* IV. It is now vefted in the Earl
of *Dyfert.*

The Church of *Bawdfey* was given by *Ranulph Glanvile* himfelf to his Priory and Convent of *Butley*, who got
it impropriated to them. The Impropriation was granted
away after the Diffolution ; but the Advowfon of the
Vicarage remains yet in the Crown. The Steeples both
of *Alderton* and *Bawdfey* are very ufeful Sea-marks ; but
both are in a ruinous Condition.

BING, is only a fmall Hamlet of *Pettiftree*, but perhaps larger formerly; for there was a Claim made 14
Edward I. of a Right to hold a Market here every
Thurfday; *Joan* of *Huntingfield* had then the Manor ;
but it was afterwards given to *Campfey* Priory, and granted
as Parcel of the Poffeffions of that Priory, to *Anthony
Wingfield*, 30 *Henry* VIII.

BOULGE. *Odo de Campania* had *Bulges* and *Depebeck*
(probably *Boulge* and *Debach*) when Domefday-Book was
made. Sir *Thomas Hanmer* was lately Lord of this Manor and of *Debach*, and Patron of both the Churches,
as his Nephew, the Rev. Sir *William Bunbury*, Bart.
is now. As thefe Benefices are fmall, and the Churches
very near each other, Sir *William* hath lately procured the
Confolidation of them.

BOYTON. The Manor and Advowfon here were
granted as Parcel of the Poffeffions of *Butley* Priory to
William Fourthe and *Richard Moryfon*, 37 *Henry* VIII.
They

They afterwards came into the Family of *Warner*, and are now vested in the Trustees of Mrs. *Mary Warner*, who devised them together with an Estate of about 400*l.* per *Annum* to charitable Uses, *viz.* some small Part of it is appropriated to the Poor of *Parham*; another Part of it to the Endowment of a School at *Stradbrook*; the chief Part to the Endowment of an Alms-house here; and the Overplus is for the Relief of Insolvent Debtors in *Suffolk*. The first Trustees of this Charity were the late Right Hon *Pryce* Lord Viscount *Hereford*, the late Sir *John Barker*, Bart. *Dudley North*, Esq; the late *Edmund Tyrrell*, Esq; the late Rev. *Thomas Bence*, and the Rev. Mr. *Welton*. These Gentlemen, *A. D.* 1743, built the Alms-house, called from the Foundress *Warner's Alms-house*. It contains six poor Men, and six poor Women, each of whom receives *Four Shillings* every *Monday* Morning. The Men have also every Year new Coats, Waistcoats, and Breeches; and the Women every Year, new Gowns and Petticoats: They are all to attend Divine Service every Day at Church, which is very near the House; where the Reader is allowed *Forty Pounds per Annum*. The present Trustees are, *Dudley North*, Esq; the Rev. Mr. *Welton* of *Norwich*, Sir *John Rous*, Bart. *John Rush*, Esq; *John Scrivener*, Esq; the Rev. Mr. *North* of *Sternfield*, and the Rev. Mr. *John Leman*, of *Wenhaston*.

BREDFIELD. *William* Lord *Willoughby*, *Robert* his Son, and Sir *Robert Willoughby*, had this Manor as well as *Bawdsey*. It is now in the Family of *Jenney*, who have a pleasant Seat here. The Church of *Bredfield* was given to the Priory of *Butley* and *Campess*, who presented alternately to the Vicarage, and divided the Impropriation. Ever since the Dissolution the Crown hath kept the Advowson of the Vicarage.

BROMESWELL. This Lordship belongs to *William Chapman*, Esq; as Part of the Estate of the late *Charles Wood*, Esq;

CAPEL ST. ANDREW, was a distinct Parish while the Church was standing, as it was A. D. 1529; but is now accounted as a Hamlet of *Butly*. The Church was given to *Butly* Priory by *Ranulph de Glanvile*, and afterwards impropriated thereto.

DALINGHOO. Part of this Parish is in the Hundred of *Loes*. (See the Account there given.)

The Widow of *Edward* Earl of *Cornwal* had the Hamlets of *Dalinghoo*, *Alderton*, and *Thorndon* in *Suffolk*, assigned for her Dower. *John de Eltham* Earl of *Cornwal*, had a Grant of these three Hamlets 4 *Edward* III. And we take that Part of the Parish which is in this Hundred to be the Hamlet here mentioned.

DEBACH. See BOULGE.

HOLLESLY. This Manor and Advowson belonged to the Earls and Dukes of *Norfolk*, till Queen *Elizabeth*'s Time. *Roger Bigod* died possessed 25 *Edward* I. *Thomas Mowbray* died seised 1 *Henry* IV. and *Elizabeth* his Wife had it for her Dower. In A. D. 1452, several Legacies were given towards building the Steeple, and buying Bells; and about 1511 two Legacies were given towards Leading the Church. The Manor and Advowson did lately belong to *Charles Wood*, now to *William Chapman*, Esquire.

LOUDHAM, or LUDHAM, is a Hamlet of *Pettistree*, and was anciently the Seat of a Family who took their Name from it. From the *Ludhams* it descended to the *Blenherbaysetts*, who had their Seat here; and from them it came to

HUNDRED *of* WILLFORD. 113

to Sir *Henry Wood*, Knt. *Charles Wood*, Efq; rebuilt the Hall in a beautiful Manner; from him it came with the reft of the *Wood*'s Eftate to *Robert Oneby*, Efq; and from him to *William Chapman*, Efq;

MELTON. The Manor and Advowfon belongs to the Dean and Chapter of *Ely*. The Quarter-Seffions for the Liberty of St. *Etheldred*, were formerly kept in this Parifh; but were removed to *Woodbridge*, in the Beginning of Queen *Elizabeth*'s Reign. In the Will of *Richard Cook*, of *Melton*, dated the 12 *July* 1539, is a Legacy of 20*l*. towards repairing of *Willford-Bridge*, to be paid by his Executors when the County would go about it; and there were about the fame time, two other Legacies towards it. So that perhaps the prefent Bridge might be built foon after. That *Richard Cook* alfo gave his Tenement and Lands in *Melton* and *Bredfield*, called *Edgores*, to the Ufe of the Parifhioners.

PETTISTREE. This Church was impropriated to the Nuns of *Campefs*, A.D. 1413. The Family of *Wyard* long refided here, but is now extinct.

RAMSHOLT. The Ruins of a large old Building, called *Peyton-Hall*, ftill remain here, fuppofed to have been the Seat of the *Uffords*, Earls of *Suffolk*, which now belongs to Lord *St. John*. *Reginald de Peytona*, (Sewer to *Hugh Bigod*, Earl of *Norfolk*,) was Lord of *Peyton-Hall* Manors in *Boxford* and *Ramfholt*, in *Suffolk*, A.D. 1135; *i. e.* in the Time of King *Stephen*, or *Henry* I. In 53 *Henry* III. *Robert de Ufford* (a younger Son of *John de Peyton*, of *Peyton-Hall* in *Suffolk*,) affuming his Name from the Lordfhip of *Ufford* where he had then his Refidence, was made Juftice of *Ireland*. This was the firft of that Family.

I

SHOT-

SHOTTISHAM. The *Glanviles* formerly were Patrons of this Church; and the *Wingfields* were fo for a hundred Years from *A. D.* 1480.

SUTTON. The Lords of the Manor of this Parifh are, *Nicholas Bacon*, Efq; and *William Chapman*, Efq. The Manor of *Fenhal* in *Sutton*, was lately Mr. *Burwell*'s, and had been his Anceftor's from the Time of Queen *Elizabeth.* The Church was given by *Roger Wolferfton* and *John Stanton* to the Nuns of *Brufyard*, who got it impropriated to them about the Year 1390. The Impropriation and Advowfon of the Vicarage were granted 30 *Henry* VIII. to *Nicholas Hare*.

UFFORD, is no way remarkable at prefent, but was formerly, for giving Name to the noble and wealthy Family of the *Uffords*, originally defcended from the *Peytons* of *Peyton-Hall*, in *Boxford*. [See alfo *Ramfholt*.] They were a Family of vaft Poffeffions, and were at one time Proprietors of the Caftles of *Orford, Eye, Framlingham, Bungay, Mettingham*, and *Haughly*. Their Seat in this Parifh ftood about two Furlongs North of the Church, where a Farm-Houfe now ftands, appropriated to charitable Ufes in *Framlingham*.

There is in this Parifh the Ruins of a Chapel called *Sogenhoe* Chapel, and the Rector of *Ufford* pays Twenty Shillings yearly to the Crown, for the Ground on which it ftood. This Chapel was inftituted into from 1310 to 1527, upon the Prefentation of the *Uffords* and *Willoughbys*; and there is a Manor of *Sogenhoe* always mentioned with the Manors of *Bawdfey, Bredfield*, &c. among the Poffeffions of the *Uffords* and *Willoughbys*. The Manor of *Windervil* is likewife frequently mentioned among the Poffeffions of this Family, immediately after *Sogenhoe*; but we know not where it lieth. On the Weft of the Site of *Sogenhoe* Chapel is a Piece of Land in the Form of a
rectangular

rectangular Parallelogram, containing about one Acre and half: There still appears a Ditch or Moat surrounding it; on which Piece of Land, it is said, there stood a Castle; but we do not hear of any Ruins being dug up there; so this may be only Conjecture.

In this Church are good Monuments for some of the *Woods* of *Loudham*. *Weaver* saith, the Church is a very beautiful little Church. The Top of the Font has been very beautiful, as well as the Church; but they were both much defaced in the grand Rebellion. In the Journal of the Parochial Visitors, [mentioned p. 39.] they say in 27 *Jan.* 1648, "We broke thirty Pictures, and " gave Directions to take down thirty-seven more and forty " Cherubims to be taken down of Wood, and the Chancel " to be levelled; and we took up six Inscriptions in " Brass." It appears, that in *May* following they sent a Person to see, whether what they had ordered were executed, but the Churchwardens would not let him in. So, in the Month of *August* after that, they returned themselves, when they compleated what had been begun in the preceding *January*. The Journal saith, "We broke twelve " Cherubims on the Roof of the Chancel, and nigh an " hundred Jesus's and Maria's in Capital Letters, and " the Steps we levelled. And we broke down the Or- " gan-cases, and gave them to the Poor. In the Church " there was on the Roof above an hundred Jesus's and " Maria's in great Capital Letters, and a Crosier-Staff " to break down in Glass; and above twenty Stars on " the Roof. There is a glorious Cover over the Font, " like a Pope's triple Crown, with a Pelican on the Top " picking its Breast, all gilt over with Gold." Then they complain of *Brown* and *Small*, the old Churchwardens, for not obeying their Orders; and of *Sunnard* and *Strowd*, the new Churchwardens, for making them wait two Hours before they would let them have the Key of the Church; and then for abusing them, and charging them with rifling and pulling down the Church.

This Cover to the Font is still in being, tho' much impaired by Length of Time. Had the Pelican on the Top been a Dove, doubtless it would have shared a harder Fate: But as those Men, when armed with the Power of that Enthusiasm which raged in 1648, tho' they were provoked and put out of Temper by the Churchwardens, could not persuade themselves to destroy so pretty a Thing, even notwithstanding its Resemblance of the *Pope's Crown*; it is pity the Parishioners do not think it worth while to repair it; for tho' it be but a Toy in itself, it is now become venerable by its Antiquity; and is, perhaps, the only Thing left that gives any Notion of the *Ufford*'s Magnificence.

Old Wills mention a Chauntry in the Manor of *Ottleys*, in this Parish.

The Reverend *Richard Lovekin* was Rector of this Parish *Fifty-seven* Years; for the Mandate of his Induction bears Date 2 *June*, 1621; and he was buried 23 *Sept.* 1678, in the *One Hundred and Eleventh* Year of his Age. It is said he performed all the Offices of his Function to the last, and preached the *Sunday* before his Death. This Gentleman was plundered in the grand Rebellion, and lost all his Goods except one Silver Spoon, which he hid in his Sleeve.

This Parish furnished *London* with a Lord-Mayor as early as the Year 1434, who was *William Ottley*, Son of *Roger Ottley*; from whom, we suppose the Manor abovementioned might take its Name.

The Family of *Hammond* had their Seat here, which is now vested in *Francis Brook*, Esq;

WICKHAM-*Market*, seems now to be only called so to distinguish it from *Wickham-Brook* and *Wickham-Skeith*; but it had a Market formerly, tho' it has been long disused. The Quarter-Sessions were formerly held here, where there was a Shire-Hall for that Purpose; but it was removed by Order of the Lord of the Manor, and a Farm-house therewith built at *Letheringham*, called the *Old Hall*. The Church and Spire-steeple are situated upon a Hill; and tho' the Steeple be not above Twenty-three Yards high: It affords the best Prospect of any in the County; and in a clear Day you may easily view from thence very near, if not altogether, Fifty Churches.

The Family of *Ufford* had this Manor till it was given with the Church to the Nuns at *Campess*. The Manors of *Wickham*, *Gelham*, *Harpole*, and *Bing*, late belonging to the Nunnery of *Campess*, were granted 30 *Henry* VIII. to *Anthony Wingfield*; they belong now to the Earl of *Rochford*; but the Advowson of the Vicarage is still in the Crown. As to the Rectories of *Wickham*, *Pettistree*, and *Bing*, they are vested in the Trustees of Mr. *John Pemberton*, formerly of *Ipswich*, who bequeathed them to charitable Uses in the Year 1718, viz. He directed that out of the Profits 25 *l. per Ann.* should be given to poor Widows and Orphans of deceased Clergymen, within *fifteen* Miles of *Ipswich*; and the Residue thereof, after Taxes, Repairs, and all other Out-goings are discharged, he gave to the Charity-Schools of *Grey-Coat Boys* and *Blue-Coat Girls* in *Ipswich*.

The Isle or Chapel on the South-side of the Church was built by *Walter Fulburn*, of *Wickham*, who was therein buried *A. D.* 1489.

PLOMESGATE.

THE Hundred of *Plomefgate* contains Twenty-four Parishes and Hamlets, is bounded on the *East*, by the Ocean; on the *West*, by the Hundred of *Loes*; on the *North*, by the Hundred of *Blything* and *Hoxne*; and on the *South*, by *Willford*.

ALDBOROUGH, has its Name from the River *Ald*, which runs near the South End of it, affording a good Quay at *Slaughden*; the Sea washes the East-side of it, and hath in this Age swallowed up one whole Street. The present Town consists of two Streets only, which are near a Mile in Length; it stands pleasantly, and is well situated for Strength, having several Pieces of Cannon for its Defence. The Church stands on a Hill to the West of the Town, and is a good Structure.

William Martel gave the Manor of *Aldebure* to the Abbot and Convent of St. *John*'s in *Colchester*, A.D. 1155. The Manor of *Aldeburgh*, with the Manors of *Scoto* and *Taftards* in this Neighbourhood, were granted to Cardinal *Wolsey*, as Parcel of the Possessions of the Priory of *Snape*, which was a Cell to the Abbey of *Colchester*, and they were granted to *Thomas* Duke of *Norfolk* 24 *Henry* VIII. The Rectory and Advowson of the Vicarage, which belonged to the said Abbey, were granted to *Edward Downing* and *Peter Ashton* in Exchange, in 23 *Elizabeth*. They are now vested in the Right Hon. the Earl of *Strafford*.

Aldborough is a Town Corporate, governed by two Bailiffs, twelve capital Burgesses, and twenty-four inferior Officers; but it did not send Members to Parliament before 13 *Elizabeth*. Mr. (a) *Willis* supposes it was made

a

(a) See *Willis*'s Not. Parl.

HUNDRED *of* PLOMESGATE. 119

a Borough in 10 *Elizabeth*; when she granted the Duke of *Norfolk* a *Saturday* Market at this his Manor.

BENHALL. King *Henry* II. gave the Manor to *Ranulf Glanvile*, who gave it to his Daughter *Maud*; and her Grandson sold it to *Guido Kerr*, who obtained in 20 *Ed.* I. a Grant of a Fair at *Benhall*, and a Market and Fair at *Kelton*, within his said Manor. *Guido* dying without Heirs, it escheated; and *Robert de Ufford* had a Grant of this Manor 2 *Edward* III. In 13 *Richard* II. *John de Holand* Earl of *Huntingdon*, is said to have obtained a Grant of the Manors of *Benhall* and *Stratford*, which came to the Crown by the Attainder of *Michael de la Pole*. But *Michael de la Pole*, his Son, died seised of both these Manors 3 *Henry* V. and *William de la Pole* died seised of them 28 *Henry* VI. The Rectory and Advowson of the Vicarage belonged to the Priory of *Butley*, and were granted 37 *Henry* VIII. to *Thomas* Duke of *Norfolk*.

The Hall and chief Estate here is said to have belonged to the *Glemhams*, in Queen *Elizabeth*'s Time, who sold it to the *Dukes*. Sir *Edward Duke* built *Benhall* Lodge, in 1638; in 1661 Sir *Edward* was created a Baronet, and his Grandson dying without Issue, the Estate went to his Sister's Son *Edmund Tyrrel*, Esq; of *Gipping*, who sold it to *John Rush*, Esq; who now enjoys it.

BLAXHALL. *Bartholomew Burghersh* died seised of this Manor, in Right of his Wife, 43 *Edward* III. *Edward le Despenser* died seised 49 *Edward* III. In these latter Times it belonged to ——— *Warryn*, Esq; who sold it to Mr. *John Bence*; and he again to *Dudley North*, of *Glemham*, Esq; in whose Son it is now vested. The Advowson of the Rectory is in the Heirs of the Reverend Mr. *Jackson*, the late Incumbent.

I 4 BRUIS-

BRUISYARD, is chiefly memorable for the Collegiate Chantry of a Warden and four Secular Priefts, tranflated hither from *Campfey-Afh*, A.D. 1354. About eleven Years after that, it was changed into a Nunnery, of the Order of St. *Clare*; and was of the yearly Value of 56*l.* 2*s.* 1*d.* It was granted to *Nicholas Hare*, 30 *Henry* VIII. and hath been for fome Time in Sir *John Rous*'s Family, who now poffeffes it.

BUTLEY, was noted for a Priory of Black Canons of St. *Auftin*, founded by the famous *Ranulf Glanvile*, Chief Juftice of *England* about the Year 1171. The Revenues of this Priory became very large, for they were at the Diffolution found to be of the yearly Value of 318*l.* 17*s.* 2*d.* The Priory was granted to *William Forthe*, in whofe Family it long continued: It was Mr. *Clyat*'s afterwards; and is now the Eftate of Mrs. *Wright*. In the Church of this Priory *Michael de la Pole*, the third Lord *Wingfield* and Earl of *Suffolk*, was interred; he was flain at the Battle of *Agincourt*, with *Edward Plantagenet* Duke of *York*. The Ruins of the Priory, which are ftill to be feen, fhew it to have been very large; and the Gate-houfe, which is ftill entire and embellifhed in the Front with many Coats of Arms finely cut in Stone, fhews it to have been a very magnificent Building. This was repaired and beautified in an elegant manner by the late *George Wright*, Efq; and is now become a very handfome Seat. But the Advowfon of the Church is in the Rev. *Eden Howard*, the prefent Incumbent.

CHILLESFORD. *Robert de Ufford* died feifed of this Manor 5 *Richard* II. but, before the Diffolution of Religious Houfes, it belonged to the Priory and Convent of *Butley*, given by *John Staverton*; and was granted as Parcel of their Poffeffions to *John* Earl of *Warwick*, 1 *Edward* VI. It is now vefted in ―――――

The

HUNDRED of PLOMESGATE. 121

The Advowfon of the Church belonged to the *Weylands*, about the Year 1300; and afterwards to the *Beauchamps* Earls of *Warwick*, and the *Nevils* Lords *Bergavennys*.

CRANSFORD. This Church was appropriated to *Sibton* Abbey, and the Impropriation and Advowfon of the Vicarage granted to the Duke of *Norfolk*. The Manor now belongs to Mr. *Moore*.

DUNNINGWORTH. The Manor and Advowfon of the Rectory belonged to the Earls and Dukes of *Norfolk* from A.D. 1300, to the Reign of *Henry* VIII. or after. The Church was ftanding and in Ufe in the Year 1561; but feems to have fallen into Decay foon after; and hath been fo long down, that there are fcarce any Ruins of it left; fo that this Place is now confidered as a Hamlet of *Tunftall*. The Manor belonged to *Charles Wood*, Efq; it is now vefted in *William Chapman*, Efq. Here is a confiderable Fair for Horfes, which begins annually on *Aug.* 11. and holds two Days.

FARNHAM. *Ranulf Glanvile* gave this Church to his Priory of *Butley*; the Impropriation was granted 19 *Eliz.* to *Edward Grimfton*. *Robert de Sackville* is faid to have had this Manor in the Time of *Henry* I. It now belongs to *Dudley North*, Efq; whofe Father bought it as Part of the *Glemham*'s Eftate.

FRISTON, belonged to *Snape* Priory. Sir *Henry Johnfon* having purchafed the faid Priory and its Appendances, built *Frifton* Hall, and made it his Seat. His Daughter and Heirefs marrying the Right Hon. *Thomas* the late Earl of *Strafford*, carried this delightful Seat and a plentiful Eftate into that noble Family. It is now vefted in the Earl of *Strafford*.

GEDGRAVE,

GEDGRAVE, was lately the Lordship of *George Wright*, Esq; in Right of his Wife, who was only Daughter and Heiress of Mr. *Clyatt*, at *Butley*; then of the Lord Viscount *Hereford*; and now, by Purchase, belongs to the Earl of *Hertford*.

GLEMHAM MAGNA, or *North Glemham*, is of Note for the Family of *Edgar*; who, for many Generations, have had their Seat here. The Manor and great Tythes did belong to *Butley* Priory, but were granted to *William Edgar* 37 *Henry* VIII or *A.D.* 1545. This Family was extended into three Branches: 1. This at *Glemham*, of which is *William Edgar*, now living at *Sutton*. 2. That at *Ipswich*, of which are *Robert Edgar*, Esq; and *Milleson Edgar*, Esq. And, 3. Another at *Cranby* Hall, in *Eye*. The Heiress of which last Family married *Arthur Jenney*, of *Bredfield*, Esq. The Estates lately belonging to Mr. *Edgar* in this Parish, are now vested in the Hon. Mr. *Nicholas Herbert*, Uncle to the present Earl of *Pembroke*. But the great Tithes were sold to Mr. *Manning*, of *Peasenhall*.

GLEMHAM PARVA, was famous for a Family who took their Names from the Town, and continued here till the Middle of the last Century. This Family ended with two Persons of great Eminence in their several Professions; they both were great Sufferers in those unhappy Times of Disorder, and both were buried in the Family Vault in this Church. Sir *Thomas Glemham*, with his two gallant Countrymen Colonel *Gosnold* of *Ottley*, and Major *Naunton* of *Letheringham*, defended *Carlisle* for the King, with remarkable Circumstances of Resolution and Patience. He died in *Holland* in the Year 1649, and his Body was brought over hither. His Brother *Henry Glemham*, D.D. survived the Restoration, and by K. *Char.* II. was promoted to the Bishoprick of St. *Asaph*, A.D. 1667.

but

but he died two Years afterwards, and was buried here in 1669. Sir *Thomas Glemham*, Knt. left a Son, who died seised of this Estate, who likewise left it to *his* Son; which last Person was an Officer in Queen *Anne*'s War, and died of a Calenture, in *Spain*. In him the Family failed of Male Issue, and the Estate was purchased by *Dudley North*, Esq; who added greatly to the Beauty of the Hall, where his Son doth now reside.

HASLEWOOD, is a Hamlet of *Aldborough*; the Church is in Ruins; how long it has been so, we know not; but within forty Years they buried their Dead there.

IKEN, formerly the Lordship and Demesne of the *Wingfields*. It is now vested in the Earl of *Hertford*.

ORFORD, is situated on the North-west Side of the River *Ore*, and probably took its Name from it. According to *Leland*'s Rule, it should be no ancient Town; because it is properly a Hamlet only, and a Chapel of Ease to *Sudborn*, as *Harwich* is a Hamlet to *Dovercourt*; yet it had a Market in King *Stephen*'s Reign, when the Toll of it was given to the Priory of *Eye*.

The Castle must have been as old as King *Henry* I. if the Fishermen caught the wild Man in their Nets in that King's Reign, as *Cambden* relates from *Ralph Coggeshall*; but other Writers place that Story almost a hundred Years later, *viz.* in the sixth Year of King *John*, or *A.D.* 1204. *Hugh Bigod* and *John Fitz-Robert* were made Governors of *Norwich* and *Orford* Castles, *A. D.* 1215; and upon their Removal *Hubert de Burgh* was made Governor of both those Castles, that same Year. *Philip Marmion* was made Governor of this Castle 45 *Henry* III. And three Years afterwards when the Barons took the King Prisoner at the Battle of *Lewes*, they made *Hugh le Despenser* Governor of it. Sir *William Dugdale*

Dugdale faith, that the Defcendants of *Peter de la Valoines*, who came in with the Conqueror, made the Caftle of *Orford* the capital Seat of their Barony; which probably muft have been in the Time of *Edward* I. or *Edward* II. For in 4 *Edward* III. *Robert de Ufford*, who married *Cecilia* Daughter and Coheir of *Robert de Valoines*, had a Grant for Life of this Town and Caftle. *William de Ufford* died feifed of it 5 *Richard* II. and *Ifabel* his Wife had it affigned, among other Things, for her Dowry. Upon her Death *Robert* Lord *Willoughby* of *Erefby*, whofe Anceftor married *Cecilia* Daughter of *Robert de Ufford* before-mentioned, had Livery of this Town and Caftle 4 *Henry* V. *William* Lord *Willoughby* died feifed of the Lordfhip of *Orford*, 18 *Henry* VIII. and affigned it to his Wife for Life. It probably came afterwards with the Eftate at *Sudborn* to Sir *Michael Stanhope*, and defcended as that did to the Right Hon. *Pryce Devereux* Lord Vifcount *Hereford*; and was lately fold by his Executors to the Right Hon. the Earl of *Hertford*, who now poffeffes it.

This Place is a Town Corporate, governed by a Mayor, eight Portmen, and twelve chief Burgeffes; and fends two Members to Parliament. *Monday* is the Market-Day; and there are two yearly Fairs, one on *Midfummer-Day*, and the other on *Shrove-Monday*.

Orford fent Members to Parliament in *Edward* the Firft's Time. But we have no Account of any others fent from hence till 3 *Henry* VI. After this Difufe, the Privilege was probably reftored (as Mr. *Willis* thinks) by King *Richard* III. who in his firft Year granted a Charter here, with great Privileges.

It was certainly a much larger Place formerly, than it is at prefent; for, befides the Church, or rather the Parochial Chapel, here was one Chapel dedicated to St. *John Baptift*, and another to St. *Leonard*; thefe were ftanding fince the Year 1500; and there is a Piece of Land

Land on the North-side of the Town, now called St. *John's Chapel Field*. *A. D.* 1359, *Orford* sent three Ships and Sixty-two Men to the Siege of *Calais*. There are several Lanes which retain the Names of *Bridge-street, Church-street, Broad-street,* and the like, tho' there are now scarce any Houses in them. Here was a House of *Austin* Friers, an Hospital of St. *Leonard,* and a Chauntry of the yearly Value of 6*l.* 13*s.* 11½*d.*

PARHAM, was the Lordship of *Robert de Ufford* Earl of *Suffolk,* 9 *Edward* II. He died seised of it 43 *Edw.* III. and left it to his Son *William*, who built the Church; but, dying suddenly in the Parliament-House, it went to his Sister *Cicely,* who married Sir *Robert Willoughby,* and carried it into that Family. Their Descendants became afterwards Lord *Willoughbys* of *Eresby,* and for some Time were in Possession of this Manor; till *Christopher* Lord *Willoughby* of *Eresby,* gave it to his youngest Son *Christopher,* who took up his Residence here. This *Christopher,* in his last Will dated 8 *May,* 18 *Henry* VIII. gave Four Pounds *per Annum* to the Church of *Parham,* in satisfaction of all Tithes and Offerings by him negligently forgotten. Sir *William Willoughby* his Son, was 20 *Feb.* in 1 *Edward* VI. created Lord *Willoughby* of *Parham*; whose Successors now enjoy that Honour. The Hall and Manor of *Parham* have been in several Families since the *Willoughbys*; the Estate is now in Mrs. *Long,* the only surviving Daughter of ⸺ *Corance,* Esq;

In 1734, the Bones of a Man, an Urn, and the Head of a Spear, were taken out of a Gravel-pit in a Field called *Fryers Close,* in this Parish; which were supposed to have belonged to some *Danish* Commander.

RENDHAM. The Manor of *Barnies* in this Parish, belonged formerly to *Sibton* Abbey, and was granted 1 *Edward* VI. to *Anthony Denney.* It is now Mr. *Powel*'s.

SAX-

SAXMUNDHAM. Here is a small Market on *Thursdays*, and a Fair on *Ascension*-Day, granted 4 *Edward* II. or *A. D.* 1310, at the Request of *Thomas de Verley*. The Manor of *Hurts*, to which the Advowson is appendant, was formerly the Earl of *Suffolk*'s; then Sir *Nicholas Hare*'s; then Mr. *Cutler*'s, of the Chantry by *Ipswich*; then Mr. *Basse*'s, who built the Seat about the Year 1650, which is now vested in *Charles Long*, Esq;

A Chantry was founded here by *Robert Swan*, Lord of a Manor in this Town about the Year 1308. The Manor of *Swans*, in *Saxmundham*, belongs to *Dudley North*, Esq.

SNAPE, was formerly noted for a Monastery of Black Monks, founded *A. D.* 1155, by *William Martel* and *Alfred* his Wife, and *Jeffery Martel* their Son. It was at first made a Cell to the Abbey of St. *John*, in *Colchester*; but afterwards became almost independent of it; being, as it is said, in no more Subjection than that of paying half a Marc as an Acknowledgment, and that the Abbot of *Colchester* might visit them twice a Year, and abide there four Days with twelve Horses. King *Henry* VII. gave the Priory of *Snape* to the Canons of *Butley*; but it was dissolved in 1534, by the Bull of Pope *Clement* VII. and given by King *Henry* VIII. to Cardinal *Wolsey*: After the Cardinal's Fall it was granted to *Thomas* Duke of *Norfolk*: At the Dissolution it was of the yearly Value of 99 *l.* 1 *s.* 11½ *d.* It was lately the Estate of Sir *Henry Johnson*, and came with the rest of that to the Earl of *Strafford*. See *Friston*.

The Manor of *Snape* belonged to the Priory, was granted with that to the Duke of *Norfolk*, and came with the rest to Lord *Strafford*.

STERNFIELD. The Manor of *Maunde Villes* in this Parish, with the Advowson of the Rectory, belong to
Dudley

Dudley North, Efq. They were formerly the Eftate of *Verlies*, who probably built the Church; from them the Eftate came to the *Framlinghams*; and, by Marriage, from them to the *Gaudy's*, of whom Mr. *North* purchafed it.

STRATFORD ST. ANDREW. The Manors of *Grifton* and *Stratford* in this Parifh, are vefted alfo in *Dudley North*, Efq;.

SUDBORN. The Manor and Advowfon belonged formerly to the Prior and Convent of *Ely*. The Advowfon is now in the Crown. The Manor was granted to the Bifhop of *Norwich* 4 *Edward* VI. but refumed and probably granted to Sir *Michael Stanhope*, who built the Hall. Sir *Edmund Withipole* married Sir *Michael Stanhope's* Daughter, who had Iffue only one Daughter, married to *Leicefter Devereux* Lord Vifcount *Hereford*; from whom it came to *Pryce Devereux* Lord Vifcount *Hereford* his Son; and his Executors fold it to the Right Hon. the Earl of *Hertford*.

SWEFFLING. The Manor of *Dernford*, alias *Derneford* Hall, in *Sweffling*, belonged to the Priory of *Leighs* in *Effex*; and was granted to R. *Cavendifh*, Efq; 28 *Hen.* VIII. It is now in *William Plumer*, Efq.

TUNSTALL. The Manor of *Banyard* in this Parifh is now vefted in *Dudley North*, Efq.

WANTISDEN. The Manor and Rectory belonged to *Butley* Abbey, and were granted to *Lionel Talmach* 36 *Henry* VIII. They are now vefted in *William Chapman*, Efq; as Part of Mr. *Wood's* Eftate.

BLITHING.

BLITHING.

THE Hundred of *Blithing* is bounded on the East by the Ocean, on the West and South by the Hundreds of *Hoxne* and *Plomesgate*, and on the North by *Wangford* and *Mutford*. In this are contained forty-eight Parishes, and six Hamlets, *viz.*

ALDRINGHAM, at present a mean Village, of which *Hamo de Masey* seems to have been Lord in the Reign of King *Edward* II. for in the twelfth Year of that King he obtained a Grant for a Market and Fair to be held here; and there is still a little Fair on a Green within this Parish on St. *Andrew*'s Day. The Church was given to the Abbey of *Leiston* by *Ranulf Glanvile*, the Founder; and the Impropriation, which was granted 28 *Hen.* VIII. to *Charles* Duke of *Suffolk*, belongs now to the Heirs of the late *Daniel Hervey*, Esq;

BENACRE, anciently the Lordship and Demesne of *Simon de Pierpoint*. About the Year 1400 it came to Sir *William Bowet*, and soon after to *Fines* Lord *Dacres*, in which Family it continued till about the Middle of Queen *Elizabeth*'s Reign, when *William Playters* and *Henry Yarmouth* had it. *Henry North* of *Laxfield*, purchased it in King *Charles* the First's Time; and it now belongs to Sir *Thomas Gooch*, Bart. who purchased it of ——— *Carthew*, Esq.

BLIBURGH, tho' now a mean Village, seems to have been of great Antiquity and Note; for several *Roman* Urns

Urns were here dug up about the Year 1678. *Anna* King of the *East-Angles* and *Firminus* his Son, who were slain in fighting against *Penda* King of the *Mercians*, A. D. 654, or 655, were here buried: So faith *Cambden*, and almost all our Historians; but it may be doubted, whether the Tomb now shewn at *Blithburgh* for King *Anna*'s, be really his; for the present Church is certainly a modern Building. There are several Legacies in Wills between the Years 1450 and 1480, towards building the Chancel at *Blithburgh*; and yet it seems to be exactly the same kind of Building with the Church, so that probably it is little more than Three Hundred Years old. The Body of *Firminus* was afterwards translated to *Bury*. The Sessions for the Division of *Beccles*, were certainly held here formerly; and *John de Clavering* (so called from his Manor in *Essex* of that Name,) who was Lord of this Manor 17 *Edward* II. obtained a Grant for a Weekly Market on *Mondays*, and two Yearly Fairs; one, on the Eve and Feast-day of the *Annunciation, Feb.* 2. the other on the Eve and Day of the *Nativity* of the Virgin *Mary, Sept.* 8. The Name of the Town by its Termination *Burgh*, which signifies a Town or Castle, and the Stateliness of its Church, argue its former Greatness; and as late as the Year 1677, there was a Collection made for a Loss by Fire, to the Amount of 1803 *l*. Here was a Priory of Black Canons, a Cell to the Abbey of St. *Ositb* in *Essex*, founded in the Time of King *Henry* I. and valued at the Dissolution at 48 *l*. 8 *s*. 10 *d*. *per Annum*. This was granted 30 *Henry* VIII. to Sir *Arthur Hopton*, Knt. then Lord of the Manor; considerable Remains of which are standing near the Church. Sir *John Blois*, Bart. is the present Lord. In *Stow*'s Annals is an Account of a terrible Thunder-Storm, which happened here on *Sunday* 4 *August* 1577, in the Time of Divine Service, when the Lightning damaged the Church, struck down and scorched several Persons, and killed one Man and a Boy.

BRAMPTON. The chief Manor and Advowson of the Church have belonged to the Family of *Leman*, ever since the Year 1600. *Robert Leman*, Esq; is the present Lord and Patron, who having his Hall or Manor-house here burnt down in 1733, resides now at *Wickham-Market*, in *Suffolk*. The Manor of *Hales Hall* in this Parish, was lately vested in Sir *Edward Duke*, Bart. and now belongs to *William Chapman*, Esq; of *Loudham*.

BLYTHFORD. *Ralph de Criketot* gave this Church to *Blithburgh* Priory before the Year 1200, and the Impropriation was granted 30 *Henry* VIII. to Sir *Arthur Hopton*; and belongeth now, as the Manor also doth, to *William Chapman*, Esq.

BRAMFIELD, was the Manor of *Nicholas de Seagrave*, 9 *Edward* II. but soon after of *Walter de Norwich*. He dying 2 *Edward* III. left it to Sir *John de Norwich*, whose Executors made it Part of the Endowment of the College of *Mettingham*, built by his Order. At the Dissolution of that College this Manor was granted to *Thomas Denney*; but came shortly after to the *Rous's*, of *Henham*; and is now vested in Sir *John Rous*, Bart. *Brookhall* belonged also to *Mettingham* College; and, in a Register belonging to the late *Peter le Neve*, Esq; there was an Extent of the Manors of *Bromfield* and *Brook-hall*, made 18 *Edward* IV. The Stile of the Manor now is *Bramfield cum Brook-hall*.

This Church was impropriated to *Blithburgh*. In the Chancel of it there is a noble Monument erected to the Memory of *Arthur Coke*, third Son of Sir *Edward Coke* and —— his Wife, not unworthy even of *Westminster-Abbey*; and on the Pavement there are several black Marble Stones, for the two ancient Families of this Parish, *Rabbet* and *Nelson*. The *Rabbet's* Estate is now vested in *Reginald Rabbet*, Esq; not long since High-Sheriff

Sheriff of this County, and hath a good old Seat near the Church. There was also another good old Seat in this Parish, about a Mile from the Church, which formerly belonged to *Thomas Neale*, Esq; and now to Mr. *Neale Ward*, Attorney at Law in *Bury*; but that hath lately been reduced to a Farm-house. The said *Thomas Neale* left Orders at his Decease for erecting and endowing an Alms-house here, for four single Persons, who have each of them a Room and about a Rood of Land, and one of them hath a Rent-charge of Three Pounds *per Ann.* more, for teaching six poor Children to read the Bible. *Mary*, the Relict of the said *Thomas Neale*, and afterwards Wife of *John Fowle*, Esq; left an Estate at *Metfield*, of about 10*l. per Ann.* to keep the said Alms-houses in Repair; and to teach six other poor Children to read, according to the Will of Mrs. *Elizabeth Archer*, Spinster. The Impropriation was granted 30 *Henry* VIII. to Sir *Arthur Hopton*, and belongs now to *William Plumer*, Esq.

BULCHAMP, is a Hamlet of *Blithburgh*, and a Lordship, which had for many Years the same Lords with *Henham*.

BUXLOW, was a Parish by itself, when the Church was standing; but, since the Decay of that, it has been consolidated with *Knoddishall*, viz. by *Bishop Green*, 22 *Feb.* 1721. The Family of *Jenney* have been Patrons of the Church; and therefore, probably, Lords here, ever since the Year 1435.

CHEDDISTON. *Robert Vaux* or *de Vallibus*, who came over with the Conqueror, and founded a Religious House at *Pentery* in *Norfolk*, was probably Lord here, by his giving the Church to that Priory. At the Dissolution, the Rectory and Advowson of the Vicarage were granted to *Thomas Sidney* and *Nicholas Haleswelle*. The *Pettus*'s were formerly Lords here; afterwards the *Fleetwoods*; then *Walter Plumer*, Efq; who beautifully rebuilt the Hall; at his Death he gave it to his Brother *William*.

COOKLEY. The same Patrons presented to this Church who presented to *Huntingfield*. There are two Manors here: That of *Cookley* belongeth to Sir *Joshua Vanneck*, Bart. and that of *Cookley-Grange*, belonging to *William Plumer*, Esq; which last formerly belonged to *Sibton* Abbey, and was granted to *Thomas* Duke of *Norfolk*, 28 *Henry* VIII.

COVEHITHE. See *Northales*.

CRATFIELD. *Ralph Barnard* held *Cratfield* when Domesday-Book was made. It was afterwards separated into three Parts. For *A.D.* 1140, *Maud de St. Liz*, Daughter of *William St. Liz* Earl of *Northampton*, and Wife of *William Abenni*, gave one third Part of her Manor of *Cratisfield* in *Suffolk* to the Priory of St. *Neots* in *Huntingdonshire*; and *William Abenni* her Son, gave the Church of *Cratfield* to the Monks of St. *Neots*, who had the Profits of the Rectory, and were Patrons of the Vicarage till the Dissolution; when the Rectory and Advowson of the Vicarage were granted by K. *Edward* VI. to *Thomas Sidney* and *Nicholas Halefwelle*, who shortly after sold them to Mr. *John Lany*; and being in the Hands of *John Lany*, Esq; of *Ipswich*, in 1635; he piously and generously conveyed the Rectory-House, with two Acres of Glebe and all the Tythes, except the Tithes of Corn, and twenty Marks *per Ann.* out of the Rectory, to the Vicar for the Time being for ever.

2. *Robert de Tateshall* departing this Life 28 *Edward* I., his Relict *Eve* was endowed, amongst other Things, with the Manor of *Cratefield*, in *Suffolk*; and this we suppose to have been the second Part of the Manor. *Henry Piercy* Earl of *Northumberland*, died seised of a Manor in *Cratfield*,

HUNDRED of BLITHING. 133

field, 43 *Edward* III. and out of this the Priory of *Buckenham* in *Norfolk* had a yearly Rent of 3*l*. 1*s*. 7¼*d*. which Rent of 3*l*. 1*s*. 7¼*d*. issuing out of a Manor in *Cratfield*, was granted in 8 *James* I. to *John Eldred*, Esq; and *John Verdon*, Gent. as Part of the Revenues of the Priory of *Buckenham*.

3. A third Part of this Manor seems to have been in *Thomas de Brotherton* Earl of *Norfolk*, who died 12 *Ed.* III. and after his Wife's Decease 36 *Ed.* III. to have descended to his Grand-daughter *Joan*, married to *William de Ufford*. The Earl of *Leicester* lately sold all these Manors to Sir *Joshua Vanneck*.

DARSHAM. *William* the Son of *Roger Bygot*, Founder of the Priory of Cluniac Monks at *Thetford*, gave those Monks about the Year 1110, all the Land of *Asceline de Dersham*, with its Appurtenances, and the Church of the same Village. And, upon the Dissolution of that House, the Manor, Rectory and Advowson of the Vicarage, were granted 32 *Henry* VIII. to *Thomas* Duke of *Norfolk*. Another Manor here was granted 28 *Henry* VIII. to *Charles* Duke of *Suffolk*; and 36 *Henry* VIII. to *Thomas Denton* and *Richard Nottingham*, as Parcel of the Possessions of the Abbey of *Leiston*. There are now four Manors here: *Darsham cum Yoxford*, which is the first before-mentioned. 2. *Abbots*, which might probably be the second. 3. *Austins*. And, 4. *Gerrards*. All which were lately the Estate of the *Beddingfields*, and now of Sir *John Rous*, Bart.

There seem formerly to have been several Hamlets in this Parish; for we have met with *Cheyneys*, in *Darsham*; *Buckles*, in *Darsham*; and *Barstill*, in *Darsham*. There were also several Legacies given in Wills, between the Year 1460 and 1505, towards building the Steeple.

DUNWICH. Tho' the traditionary Accounts of this Place are probably fabulous, it hath certainly been very ancient

ancient and confiderable; from the finding *Roman* Coins here, it may reafonably be thought to have been a *Roman* Station. *Felix* the *Burgundian* Bifhop, whom *Sigebert* King of the *Eaft-Angles* brought hither to reduce his Subjects to Chriftianity, which they had almoft forfaken, fixed his Epifcopal See here, *A. D.* 636. After him fate three Bifhops here, who had Jurifdiction over the whole Kingdom of the *Eaft-Angles*; but in the latter Part of his third Succeffor's Time, and perhaps about fifty Years from the Erection of the See, it was divided; and a Bifhop for the *Norfolk* Part of the Kingdom being placed at *Elmham*, the Bifhop of *Dunwich*, or (as it was then called) *Domoc*, and *Donmuc*, had the *Suffolk* Part only. After this Divifion of the See, there fate, as 'tis faid, eleven Bifhops at *Dunwich*, 'till about the Year 820, or fhortly after, when the troublefome Times put an end to this Bifhopric, before it had ftood 200 Years. When Domefday Book was made, this Place was valued as yielding 50 *l. per* Year to the King, and 60,000 Herrings. In King *Stephen*'s Time they feem to have had fome Toll paid them by Ships at *Oreford*, which is mentioned in his Grant to the Monks of *Eye*, as valued at 30 *s. per Annum*. In King *Henry* the Second's Time it was a famous City, well ftored with Riches of all Sorts. In the firft Year of King *John*, it had a Charter of Liberties, and a Grant of Wreck of the Sea. It is faid, that there was fometime a Mint here; but I meet with no Money coined here, either in *Thorefby*, *Nicholfon*, or the *Nummi Britan-Hiftoria*. It fendeth two Members to Parliament, and is governed by two Bailiffs, *&c.* King *John*, among other Things mentioned in his Charter, granted to the *Burgeffes* the Liberty of marrying their Sons and Daughters as they would; and alfo the Liberty of giving, felling, or otherwife difpofing of their Lands and Houfes within their Town, at Pleafure. This Charter is dated at *Gold Cliff*, 29 *June*, 1 *Johan*. and it coft

them

them 300 Marks, besides ten Falcons and five Gir-Falcons.

Here were certainly six, if not eight Parish Churches, *viz.* 1. St. *John's*, which was a Rectory, and seems to have been swallowed up by the Sea, about *A. D.* 1540. In a Will dated 1499, and proved 1501, there is a Legacy of ten Marks for some Ornaments in this Church, with this Clàuse, " If it fortune the Church to decay by " Adventure of the Sea, the ten Marks to be disposed of " by my Attornies *(i. e.* Executors) where they think " best." About 1510 two Legacies are given towards building a Pier against St. *John's* Church: The last Institution to it was in 1537, and the last Time it is mentioned is in 1538, when *Margaret Haliday* ordered her Body to be buried in the South Isle of it.

2. St. *Martins*, which was likewise a Rectory; but the last Institution we can find to it was in *A. D.* 1335.

3. St. *Nicholas*, a Rectory also; but no Institution to it occurs since *A. D.* 1352.

4. St. *Leonards*, impropriated, and probably early lost; for in a Will dated *A. D.* 1450, the Testator deviseth his House in the Parish *anciently* called St. *Leonard's*.

5. St. *Peter's*, a Rectory, last instituted into, in *A. D.* 1609; but standing since the Restoration.

6. *All Saints*, impropriated; the only Church now standing, and that in a mean Condition.

These and all other Churches here were given by *Robert Mallet* to his Priory at *Eye*, in his Foundation or Endowment Charter. (*Temp. Will. Conq.*) And the said Prior and Convent presented to all the instituted Churches, and had Portions of Tithes out of most of them; and all the Revenues of the impropriated ones, finding a secular Priest to serve the Cures.

The Register of *Eye* mentions also the Churches of St. *Michael* and St. *Bartholomew* in *Dunwich*, which were swallowed up by the Sea before *A. D.* 1331; when the

Prior and Convent of *Eye* petitioned the Bishop of *Norwich* to impropriate the Church of *Laxfield* to them; and, amongst other Reasons for it, alledged that they had lost a considerable Part of their Revenues at *Dunwich* by the breaking in of the Sea. However, in A.D. 1359, *Dunwich* sent to the Siege of *Calais* six Ships and 102 Mariners; when *Ipswich* sent twelve Ships, and 239 Men; and *Orford*, three Ships and 62 Men.

Besides these Churches, *Weaver* mentions three Chapels here dedicated to St. *Anthony*, St. *Francis*, and St. *Catharine*. The last is often mentioned in old Wills: It was in St. *John's* Parish, and had a Guild of St. *Catharine's* belonging to it; and was standing and in use in King *Henry* VIIIth's Reign. But the other two we have yet met with nothing of.

Here was also, 1st, The *Temple* Church, dedicated to St. *Mary* and St. *John Baptist*, which probably belonged first to the *Templars*, and afterwards to the *Hospitalers*, who had a good Estate hereabouts; and might, as other Lords often did, build a Church for the Use of their own Tenants: For we don't find that they had ever any Preceptory, or Commandery here. The *Temple* Manor of Lands hereabouts being granted as Parcel of the Possessions of the Preceptory at *Batisford*, to *Thomas Andrews*, 4th *Elizabeth*.

2dly. A noble ancient Church belonging to St. *James's* Hospital; the Ruins of which yet remain.

3dly. Another Church dedicated to the *Holy Trinity*, for the Use of another Hospital, called *Maison Dieu*, or *God's House*. Some Part of the Revenues of these ancient Hospitals, (which we can say nothing of, but that the former seems to have been chiefly for Men, and the latter wholly for Women,) are yet remaining.

Here were also two Houses of Friers; one of *Franciscan* or *Grey Friers*, founded by *Henry Fitz-John* and *Alice* his Wife, and enlarged by King *Henry* III. and the other of
Dominicans

Dominicans or *Preaching Friers*, founded by Sir *Roger Holiſhe*, Knt. Both theſe Houſes had fair Churches belonging to them.

But whatever the ancient State of this Place was, it is at preſent but a ſmall Village, conſiſting of a few mean Houſes: It hath a mean Market on *Mondays*, and a Fair (which was probably granted to the Hoſpital) on St. *James*'s Day, *July* 25th.

It ſeems to have been at its Height in King *Henry* the Third's Time, when it paid One Hundred Marks to the King's Tax; and to have declined alſo in that Reign, when the Sea made ſo great a Breach here that the King wrote to the Barons of *Suffolk*, to aſſiſt the Inhabitants in ſtopping it. And *Stow* mentions an high Wind and great Tide on New-year's Day, 15 *Edward* I. or *A.D.* 1287; which did great Damage to the Churches here.

EASTON BAVENT. The Lordſhip of *Thomas de Bavent*, 9 *Edward* I. one of whoſe Deſcendants had a Grant 4 *Edward* III. for a Weekly Market here on *Wedneſdays*, and a Yearly Fair on the Eve, Day, and Morrow of the Feaſt of St. *Nicholas*. It came afterwards to the *Argentines*, *Schardelowes*, *Hoptons*, *Robards's*, and *Howlands*. What remains of it is now veſted in Sir *Thomas Gooch*, Bart. for the Sea hath waſhed away almoſt all the Pariſh, leaving only two Houſes and ſome Land. The Church was ſtanding in 1638; and, beſides the Pariſh Church, there was formerly a Chapel of St. *Margaret*'s.

FORDLEY. In the Time of King *Edward* II. this was the Lordſhip of Sir *John de Weyland*, Knt. it afterwards came to *Elizabeth* Lady *Deſpenſer*. In Queen *Elizabeth*'s Time it belonged to Mr. *Edward Hunnings*; and now to Mrs. *Freake*. The Church hath long been in Ruins; it ſtood in the ſame Yard with *Middleton* Church, and ſo near it, that Complaint was made to the Biſhop of
Norwich

Norwich in *Feb.* 1620, that when Service did not begin and end at both Churches exactly at the same Time, the Bells and People of the one Church disturbed those of the other; and an Order was made thereupon, that the same Minister should serve them both, and officiate in *Fordley* Church one Week, and in *Middleton* the other; and this, perhaps, might occasion the letting down of *Fordley* Church, which was but small.

FROSTENDEN, formerly the Lordship of *Robert de Biskele*; *William de la Pole* died seised of it 28 *Hen.* VI. and *Edmund de la Pole* being attainted of high Treason, *A.D.* 1510, the Crown seised it; and the next Year granted it to *Thomas* Lord *Howard* and *Ann* his Wife, and the Heirs of their Bodies; but they dying without Issue, it came again to the Crown, and was granted towards the latter End of Queen *Elizabeth*'s Reign to ———— *Morse*, who sold it to *John Glover*, Esq; and in this Family it still continues.

HALESWORTH, is a well built Town, situated on the Borders of the River *Blythe*, which hath lately been made navigable up to this Town. It has a considerable Weekly Market on *Thursdays*, and a good Fair yearly for lean Cattle on the Feast-Day of St. *Luke*, *Oct.* 18, obtained from *Henry* III. by *Richard de Argentin*, then Lord of the Manor. From the *Argentins* it descended to the *Allingtons*, who sold it. Afterwards the Family of *Betts* had it. *Walter Plumer*, Esq; bought it of *Thomas Betts*; and his Brother *William* is now Lord of this Manor, together with the Manor of *Dame Margery*, in this Town. There is also a Manor belonging to the Rectory of this Parish. Sir *Robert Bedingfield*, who was Lord-Mayor of *London*, A.D. 1707, was fifth Son of *John Bedingfield*, of this Parish.

HENHAM,

HENHAM, is a Hamlet of *Wangford*. *Ralph Baynard* had the Lordships of *Henham* and *Wangford*, when Domesday-Book was made. In the Time of King *Edward* I. it belonged to *Robert* Lord *Kerdeston*, and continued some time in his Family. About the Year 1440, it came to the *De la Poles*; and in the Time of King *Henry* VIII. to the ancient Family of *Rous*, who had long before considerable Possessions at *Dennington* in this County. In the Archdeacon's Office, *A. D.* 1550, is the Will of *William Bennet*, Servant of *Thomas Rous*, Esq; of *Henham*. We meet with *Edmund Rous*, Knt. in 1588; and Sir *John Rous*, Knt. in 1623; but the Title of Baronet was not granted to this Family before 17 *Aug.* 1660.

HENSTEAD. The Manor of *Robert de Pierpoint*, in the Time of *William* the Conqueror. It continued in that Family till about the Year 1340. It came to the *Cloptons* of *Long Melford*, about the Year 1500. The *Sydnors* of *Blundeston*, had it in Queen *Elizabeth*'s Time. About the Restoration it was in Sir *Robert Brook*, of *Yoxford*; since in *Mildmay*; and now it is in Mrs. *Haloday*.

HEVENINGHAM. *Walter Fitz-Robert*, who gave the Advowson of this Church to the Priory of St. *Neots*, and died *A. D.* 1198, was probably then Lord. It was afterwards for many Years in a Family, who took their Name from the Place; and when that failed, about the Year 1700, it became the Estate of *John Bence*, Esq; and belongs now to Sir *Joshua Vanneck*, who hath a handsome Seat here.

HINTON, is a Hamlet of *Blithburgh*.

HOLTON. *Alan* Earl of *Richmond*, was probably Lord here in the Time of *William Rufus*; for he then gave this Church to St. *Mary*'s, in *York*.

HUNTING-

HUNTINGFIED. *William de Huntingfield* (Founder of *Mendham* Priory in King *Stephen*'s Time) and his Heirs had the Manor and Advowfon here till about 50 *Edw.* III. when *William de Huntingfield* dying without Iffue, left *Alice* the Widow of Sir *John Norwich* his next Heir. *William de la Pole* married *Catherine*, Daughter of Sir *John Norwich*, by the faid *Alice*; and after *Catherine*'s Deceafe, 5 *Richard* II. *Michael de la Pole* her Son entered upon her Lands, and had Licence to make Caftles of his Manor-Houfes of *Wingfield*, *Sternfield*, and *Huntingfield*, in *Suffolk*, 8 *Richard* II. *Michael de la Pole* died feifed of this Manor 28 *Henry* VI. or 1449; and it continued in the *Dukes* of *Suffolk* till Queen *Elizabeth*'s Time, when *Henry* Lord *Hunfdon* had it; and foon after it became the Eftate of that great Oracle of the Law Sir *Edward Coke*, whofe Defcendant the Earl of *Leicefter* lately fold it to Sir *Joſhua Vanneck*, Bart.

Before the Reformation there was a Chauntry here, of the yearly Value of 4*l.* 17*s.* 6*d.* the Lands belonging to it were granted by King *James* I. to Sir *Edward Coke*, A. D. 1604.

KNOTTISHALL. The Family of *Jenney* were Lords here before the Year 1480. Mr. *Blomfield* mentions one Sir *Thomas Jenney*, of *Suffolk*, Knt. *A. D.* 1401; and there was a Sir *Chriſtopher Jenney*, Baron of the Exchequer, in the Reign of *Henry* VIII. *Arthur Jenney*, of *Knotteſhall*, was knighted 26 *March*, 1639. The Eftate is now in *Edmund Jenney*, of *Bredfield*, Efq.

LEISTON. Here was formerly an Abbey of *Præmonſtratenſian* Canons, founded by *Ranulph Glanvile*, about the Year 1183. The Abbot obtained a Charter for a Market and Fair here 6 *Edward* II. or *A. D.* 1312; but both have been long difufed. This Abbey being probably decayed and feated in an inconvenient Place, another

HUNDRED *of* BLITHING. 141

ther was erected at some Distance from the former by *Robert de Ufford* Earl of *Suffolk*, about the Year 1363; and the Canons removed into it. The new, as well as the old House, was dedicated to the *Blessed Virgin*, and endowed at the Dissolution with the yearly Revenue of 181 *l.* 17 *s.* 1½ *d.* It was granted 28 *Henry* VIII. to *Charles Brandon* Duke, of *Suffolk*; and was lately the Estate of *Daniel Harvey*, Esq; in Right of his Wife; and is now, with the Manor of *Leiston*, vested in the Hon. *Elizabeth* Relict of *Kellond Courteney*, Esq; who was Daughter of the Viscountess *Hinchinbrooke*, and Grand-daughter of the Right Hon. Lady *Ann Harvey*.

LINSTEAD *Great*, and LINSTEAD *Little.* The Church of St. *Margaret* of *Linstead*, and half the Church of St. *Peter*, were given to the Priory of *Mendham* by *Roger de Huntingfield.* Both of them came in time to be wholly impropriated to that Priory. The Manor of *Little Linstead* belonged to *Sibton* Abbey, and was granted to *Thomas* Duke of *Norfolk* 28 *Henry* VIII.

MELLS, a Hamlet of *Wenhaston*; the Manor belonged formerly to *Mettingham* College, and at the Dissolution was granted to *Thomas Denney.*

MIDDLETON. This Church was given by *Roger de Glanvile* and *Robert Crec*, to the Abbot and Convent of *Leiston*, who got it impropriated to them; the Impropriation was granted 28 *Henry* VIII. to *Charles* Duke of *Suffolk*; and, with the Manor, belongs now to Mr. *Freake.*

NORTHALES, commonly called *Cove-Hithe*, probably from *John* and *Walter Cove*, who were Lords here in the Time of King *Edward* I. and had a Hithe or Quay for loading and unloading small Vessels; for here the River formerly emptied itself into the Sea. *John de Cove* and
Eve

Eve his Wife had free Warren in their Lands at *Cove* and *Northales* in *Suffolk*, in *A.D.* 1308; and the Grant of a Fair here, *A.D.* 1328, which is still kept upon St. *Andrew*'s Day. The Church was impropriated to the *Cluniac* Cell of *Wangford*, and granted therewith to the Duke of *Norfolk*, in whose Family it still continues. This was a considerable Fishing-Town formerly, and had a noble Church belonging to it; but by the Decay of that Business, it is reduced to a very mean Village. The Ruins of the Church are extremely fine, and well worth the Observation of the curious. The South-Isle is preserved, and inclosed into a neat little Church. *John Bale*, whose Book *De Scriptoribus Britannicis* was printed at *Ipswich* by *John Overton*, A.D. 1548, was Rector of this Church, if not a Native of the Town.

PEASENHALL. This Lordship belonged to *Roger Bygod*, 18 *Edward* I. *Nicholas de Segrave* died seised of it 15 *Edward* II. leaving *Maud* his Daughter and Heir, then married to *Edmund de Bohun*. It now belongeth to *Mileson Edgar*, Esq.

RAYDON, is the Mother-Church to *Southwold*; the Manor belongs to Sir *John Rous*.

RUMBURGH. Here was a *Benedictine* Monastery founded about the Time of the Conquest, and dedicated to St. *Michael*; but by *Stephen* Earl of *Brittany*, given as a *Cell* to the Abbey of St. *Mary*'s in *York*. It was granted before the general Suppression of these Houses to Cardinal *Wolsey*. It was afterwards the Estate of the Earls of *Oxford*, and lately purchased by Mr. *Cobbold*, a wealthy Quaker; and now belongs to Mr. *Jessup*, a Quaker, at *Leiston* Abbey.

SIBTON. *William de Casineto* or *Cheny*, founded a *Cistertian* Abbey here, about the Year 1150, and dedicated
it

HUNDRED *of* BLITHING. 143

it to the Bleffed Virgin. The Revenues of it were valued at 250 *l*. 15 *s*. 7½ *d. per Ann.* and granted away by the Abbot and Convent themfelves to *Thomas* Duke of *Norfolk*, *Anthony Roufe*, Efq; and *Nicholas Hare*, Gent. 31 *July*, 1536. It is at prefent a good old Houfe; and, with the Manor, belongs to *Charles Scrivener*, Efq. The Church was built by *Robert* the Son of *Walter de Cadom*, in the Reign of *William Rufus*; but the North Ifle was built by the Executors of *Robert Ducket*, whofe Will is dated 24 *Jan*. 1533. The *Barkers* of this Parifh are mentioned in old Wills, as Perfons of good Subftance, ever fince the Year 1500. Their Eftate is now vefted in *Milefon Edgar*, Efq.

SIZEWELL, is a Hamlet of *Leifton*, where there was a Chapel for Divine Service as late as Queen *Elizabeth*'s Time, and in the preceding Times probably, a confiderable Number of Houfes; but at prefent one Farm-houfe only.

SOTHERTON. Here were two Manors: One of which had the Patronage of the Church, and belonged formerly to *Walter de Bernham*. *John Brightyere* (or *Britiffe*) of *Bernham-Broom*, in *Norfolk*, had it in the Time of *Edward* IV. and dying in 1497, left it to *Agnes* his Daughter; and foon after it came to the *Rous's*. The other Manor belonged to the Prior and Convent of *Ely*, and was granted 37 *Henry* VIII. to *Anthony Roufe*. They are now both in Sir *John Rous*.

SOUTHWOULD, is pleafantly fituated upon a Hill, being almoft furrounded with the Sea, and the River *Blythe*, over which it hath a Bridge for Entrance into the Town.

The Bay, corruptly called *Sowl* Bay, is a commodious Place for Anchorage, and was made memorable by a fharp Engagement between the *Englifh* and *Dutch* Fleets on 28 *May*, 1672; in which the Earl of *Sandwich* loft his Life.

It

It is a Town Corporate, being made so by Act of Parliament in 1489; and is governed by two Bailiffs, and other Sub-officers; but sends no Members to Parliament. It has a tolerable Market Weekly on *Thursdays*, indifferently served with Provisions; and two Fairs Yearly, one on the *Monday* after *Trinity-Sunday*, and the other 24 *August* being St. *Bartholomew*'s Day. It drives a considerable Trade in Salt, and old Beer; having excellent Springs of good Water, which may be one Reason why their Beer is so much esteemed.

SOUTH-COVE. Here are two Manors: *South-Cove* with *Northale*, which was probably the Manor of *John de Cove* and *Eve* his Wife; and *Polfrey*, or *Blueflory-Cove*, both belonging to Mr. *Cowling*.

SPECKSHALL. The Earl of *Richmond* was probably Lord here, by his giving the Advowson of this Church to the Priory of St. *Mary*'s, at *York*.

STOVEN. This Church was impropriated to *Wangford* Cell or Priory, and the Impropriation was granted with that Cell to the Duke of *Norfolk*.

THEBERTON, seems anciently to have been Part of the *Bygods* and *Segraves* Estate; for they presented to the Church till after the Year 1350: But soon after the Abbot and Convent of *Leiston* became Patrons.

THORINGTON, was formerly the Lordship and Demesne of *Walter de Norwich*; afterwards of the *Uffords*; then of the *Cokes*; but for some Time hath been in the Family of *Bence*, and was lately vested in *Alexander Bence*, Esq; who made the Hall his Seat. His only Daughter is now Lady of this Manor, called by the Name of *Thorington Wimples*. The Advowson of the Church was given to the Priory of *Blythburgh*, by *William* the Son of of *Walter de Sadenefield*, before the Year 1200; for this Gift was confirmed by *Richard* I. who died in 1199. At the Diffolution it was granted to Sir *Arthur Hopton*, Knt. but is now in Mrs. *Bence.*

THORP, is a Hamlet of *Aldringham*, which had a Chapel belonging to it ftanding fince the Reftoration; but it is now in Ruins.

UBBESTON. This Church and Manor were given with *Henningham*, to the Priory of St. *Neots*; the Manor, Rectory, and Advowfon of the Vicarage were granted as Parcel of the Poffeffions of that Priory 36 *Henry* VIII. to *John Pope*, Efq. It hath for fome time been the Seat of the Family of *Kemp*; which ancient Family is defcended from *Normannus de Kempe*, whofe great Grandfon was *Allen Kempe*, of *Wefton* in this County, Efq; from whom defcended Sir *Robert Kemp*, of *Giffing* in *Norfolk*, Knt. one of the Gentlemen of the Bedchamber to King *Charles* the Firft; who, for his eminent Loyalty to the faid King, was, by him created a Baronet 14 *March*, 1641. He died 20 *Auguft*, 1647; having fuffered very much both in his real and perfonal Eftate, from the Sequeftrations of thofe unhappy Times. To him fucceeded his Son Sir *Robert Kemp*, who marrying *Mary* the only Daughter and Heirefs of *John Sone*, of *Ubbefton*, Efq; removed from *Giffing* hither, and made *Ubbefton* Hall his Seat. He was fucceeded by his Son Sir *Robert Kemp*, who, on the Death of Sir *William Barker*, was elected Reprefentative of this County, and left a numerous Iffue. The prefent Heir of this Family is the Rev. Sir *Thomas Kemp*, Bart.

The Rectory was pioufly and generoufly given to the Vicar by the laft Will and Teftament of Mrs. *Mary Sone*, Widow, proved in the Archdeacon's Office A.D. 1685.

UGGESHALL. The Manor of *Ugghall* in this Parish, was formerly the Lordship of *Catharine Fitz-Osborn*, of *Somerly*; afterwards in the *Playters*; and at prefent is vefted in Sir *John Rous*; as is alfo the Manor of *Ugghall ex parte Northalys* in this Parish.

WALDERSWICK, formerly a large Place which traded confiderably to Sea, but now is very mean; and only a Chapel and Hamlet to *Blithburgh*.

WALPOOLE. Sir *Joshua Vanneck*, Bart. is now Lord of the Manor of *Walpoole* with *Chickering*. This Church was impropriated to the Nunnery of *Redlingfield*, and granted in 37 *Henry* VIII. to *Robert* and *Richard Taverner*.

WANGFORD. Here was formerly a Priory or Cell of Cluniac Monks, fubordinate to *Thetford*, dedicated to the Virgin *Mary*. It was valued at 30 *l*. 9 *s*. 5 *d*. *per Ann*. and fuppreffed 16 *Feb*. 32 *Henry* VIII. and granted foon after with the Monaftery of *Thetford* to *Thomas* Duke of *Norfolk*, whofe Son fold it to Sir *John Rous*, Knt. *A. D.* 1612. It is now vefted in Sir *John Rous*, who is alfo Lord of the Manor of *Wangford*.

WENHASTON, the Lordship of *William Strode*, Efq; befides the Chapel of *Mells* in this Parish, which was dedicated to St. *Margaret*, there was a Chapel of St. *Bartholomew* near the old Site of *Wenhafton* Hall. The North Ifle of this Church feems to have been built about the Year 1530. For *Robert Pepyn*, Rector of *Knoddifhall*, in his Will dated 19 *Jan*. 1535, orders his Body to be buried in the new Ifle at *Wenhafton*, at the Feet of the Vicar of that Parish lately deceafed. And in the Year following a Legacy was given towards paving the new Ifle at *Wenhafton*. Several of the ancient Family of *Le-man*,

HUNDRED *of* BLITHING. 147

ixan, who have a Seat in this Parish, are buried at the East-end of this Isle. The Manor of *Wenhaston* belonged to the Abbot and Convent of *Sibton*, who sold it to *Thomas* Duke of *Norfolk*. It is now vested in *Robert Sparrow*, Esq; of *Worlingham*. The Hall belongs to the Rev. *John Leman*, who resides there.

WESTHALL. *Hubert de Burgh* Earl of *Kent*, had a Grant of the Manor of *Westhall*, in *Suffolk*, made to him 13 *Henry* III. but ever since the 25 *Henry* VIII. it hath belonged to the Family of *Bohun*, (of whom *Edmund Bohun* was a noted Writer) and is now vested in *William Bohun*, of *Beccles*. The Prior and Convent of *Hulverstain* in *Lincolnshire*, were formerly Patrons of this Church; and the Prior and Convent of *Norwich* bought the Advowson of them. *John Salmon*, Bishop of *Norwich*, impropriated it to the Use of the Chauntry of Four Chaplains, at the West-end of the Cathedral Church at *Norwich*.

WESTLETON. In this Parish there was formerly a Hamlet, which had a Chapel belonging to it, named *Dingbe*. Two Manors are mentioned here; *Westleton-Grange*, which anciently belonged to the Abbey of *Sibton*, and was granted to *Thomas* Duke of *Norfolk*, 28 *Henry* VIII. and the Manor of *Westleton-Clevis*.

WESTWOOD-LODGE. A single House near *Blithburgh*. *Michael de la Pole* died seised of the Manors of *Westwood* and *Blyburgh* 3 *Henry* V. or 1414. It now belongs to Sir *John Blois*, Bart. The Family of *Brookes*, who had it before the *Blois's*, used to reside here.

WISSET. This was the Lordship of the Earls of *Britany* and *Richmond* till 25 *Henry* III. when it was granted to *Peter* Earl of *Savoy*. *John de Vallibus* or *de Vaux* died seised of it 16 *Edward* I. or 1287, leaving Issue two

L 2 Daughters,

Daughters, *viz. Petronil* married to *William de Nerford*, and *Maud* married to *Thomas* Lord *Rofs*. Upon Partition *William* and *Petronil* had this Manor; but *Thomas* Lord *Rofs* is faid to have died feifed of it 8 *Richard* II. or 1384. It now belongs to the Heirs of *Smith Heelwood*, Efq.

WRENTHAM. *Robert de Pierpoint* who came in with the Conqueror, held the Manors of *Wrentham* and *Henfled*, of the famous *William* Earl *Warren*, at the making of Domefday-book. *Michael de Poinings* died feifed of it 43 *Edward* III. or 1368. *Richard de Poinings*, by his Will dated 10 *June* 1387, gave his Manor at *Wrentham*, called *North-hall*, to the Lady *Ifabel* his Wife, for her Life. *Robert de Poinings*, who was flain at the Siege of *Orleans*, died feifed of it 2 *Oct.* 1446. In the Time of King *Edward* VI. it was purchafed by the Family of *Brewfter*, who built the Hall, and have refided here ever fince. *Philip Brewfter*, Efq; is the prefent Lord.

YOXFORD. On the North-fide of this Village is *Cockfield-Hall*, which was formerly the Seat of the Family of *Brook*; and paffed from them to the *Blois's*. Sir *John Blois*, Bart. hath his Refidence here. Befides the Manor of *Darfham* with *Yoxford*, which belonged to the Monks at *Thetford*, here was alfo a Manor that belonged to the Abbot and Convent of *Sibton*; and was by them granted 28 *Henry* VIII. to *Thomas* Duke of *Norfolk*. Here are two other good Houfes, one belonging to ——— *Clutterbuck*, Efq; the other to Mr. *Ingham*.

MUTFORD.

MUTFORD Hundred is bounded by the Sea on the *East*; on the *West* by the *Waveney*; on the North by the Lake *Luthing*; and on the *South* by *Blithing* Hundred.

This Hundred being Part of the Demefne of the Crown, it appears by *Rot. Clauf.* 14 *Henry* VI. that the Inhabitants are to be free from Toll, and from the Expences of the Knights of the Shire. There is no Market-Town in it. The Villages are,

BARNBY, confolidated to *Mutford*.

CARLTON-COLVILE, fo called from the Family of *Colviles*, who were anciently Lords of one Part of it. The Prior of *Bromholm* was Lord of the other Part. Both Parts now belong to Sir *Thomas Allen*.

GISSLEHAM. The prefent Lord of this Manor is *Richmond Garneys*, Efq.

KESSINGLAND. Here was formerly a Market on *Tuefdays*, and a Fair on *Nov.* 20; the Church being dedicated to St. *Edmund*. There are four Manors in this Parifh, which have belonged to the Family of *Proctor* above One Hundred Years. *Daniel Proctor*, Efq; of *Norfolk*, is now Lord of them.

KIRKLEY. *Richmond Garneys*, Efq; is Lord of this Manor. The Church was for many Years dilapidated; but, as it ftood in the fame Church-yard with that of *Pakefield*, the Lofs of it was eafily fupplied by the Minifter of *Kirkley*'s being permitted to ufe the Church of *Pakefield* on one Part of each *Sunday*, and the Minister of *Pakefield* using it on the other. It happened afterwards that both these Parishes went together for many Years, and had the same Incumbent; but at length they were parted again. And then, the Incumbent of *Kirkley* refused to make use of *Pakefield* Church, neither would he allow any thing to the Incumbent of that Parish, for officiating on both Parts of each Lord's-day; alledging, that he could not legally be compelled to it. The Rev. *John Tanner*, Vicar of *Lowestoft*, was at that time Commissary and Official in the Archdeaconry of *Suffolk*; and he failed not to use all the mild and persuasive Arguments he could think of to the Incumbent of *Kirkley*, but to no Purpose; so at last finding him continue obstinate, he left him with this Threat, " Sir, if you will not officiate in *Pakefield* " Church, I will build you a Church at *Kirkley*, and in " that you shall officiate." Mr. *Tanner* was as good as his Word; for chiefly at his own Expence, but with some little Assistance from his Friends and Acquaintance, he did build the present Church at *Kirkley*, and Divine Service is performed in it accordingly.

MUTFORD, which gives Name to the Hundred.

PAKEFIELD, a pretty large Fishing-Town. See *Kirkley*.

RUSHMERE.

LOTHING.

THE Hundred of *Lothing*, or *Luthing-land*, probably took its Name from that spacious Lake called by *Cambden*, the Lake *Luthing*. It is bounded on the *East* by by the Ocean; on the *West*, by the *Waveney*; on the *North*, by *Breydon-Water*; and, on the *South*, by the Lake *Luthing*. It contains the following Parishes.

ASHBY, or *Haskely*. The Estate here belonged formerly to the ancient Family of *Ingeloſſe*; but about the Year 1520 it came to the *Jernegans*, and hath ever since had the same Owners with *Somerliton-Hall*.

BELTON. The Manor of *Gapton* in this and the neighbouring Parishes belongs to Sir *Thomas Allen*.

BLUNDESTON. A Family which took their Name from this Place, were formerly Lords and Patrons here. After them a Family of the Name of *Yarmouth*; then the *Sydnors*, since *Allens*. The Manor now belongs to Sir *Thomas Allen*; but the Hall and chief Estate to Mr. *Robert Lufon*, of *Yarmouth*, who generally resides there every Summer. Besides the Manor of *Blundeston*, here was also formerly another Manor called *Gunviles*, belonging probably to the *Gonviles*, of *Rushworth*; one of whom married a Daughter of Sir *John Jernegan*, of *Somerley*, A. D. 1402.

BRADWELL. *Caxton* Hall here belonged to the Prior of St. *John*'s, of *Jerufalem*; and *Gapton* Hall to the Priory of *Leigh*, in *Eſſex*; and were both granted by King *Henry* VIII. to ―――― *Cavendiſh*, Esq;.

BURGH-*Caſtle*, or *Cnoberſbourge*, was a Place of considerable Account in the Time of the *Romans*, as may be conjectured from the *Roman* Coins often found within the Walls of the Castle. This Castle is in the Form of a Parallelogram; the Length of the Wall on the East-side is 220 Paces, the Breadth of it 120; the Entrance was on the East-side. The Walls are still standing on the East, North, and South; and it is probable it was never

walled

walled on the West, the River being a sufficient Defence. *Robert de Burgh* had anciently the Manor and Castle here; then *Gilbert de Wesham*; but King *Henry* III. gave it to the Priory of *Bromholme*, which enjoyed it to the Dissolution; when Queen *Elizabeth* granted it to *William Roberts*. It now belongs to *Joshua Smith*, Esq. A little North of the Castle appear the Ruins of a Monastery, built by *Furseus*, a *Scotchman*, in the Time of King *Sigebert*, about the Year 636, as is mentioned by *Speed*; which probably dwindled away in a few Years, as we meet with little or nothing of it afterwards.

The Advowson of the Church was given to the Prior and Canons of St. *Olaves*, who got it impropriated to them about the Year 1400; but gave up the Impropriation again in a short time, for a yearly Pension. The Advowson was not granted away at the Dissolution, but is still in the Crown.

CORTON. This Church is in Ruins; but the Chancel is kept up. Sir *Thomas Allen*, Bart. is Lord of the Manor.

FLIXTON. This Church is also in Ruins. The Roof of it was blown off in the great Storm 27 *Nov.* 1703. It is consolidated with *Blundeston*. The Manor belonged formerly to *Robert Mighells*, of *Chelmondiston*; who sold it to *John Wantworth*, Esq; of *Somerlyton*. It is now in Sir *Thomas Allen*.

FRITTON. The Manor of *Fritton* was formerly *Sydnor*'s, then *Allen*'s, and now *Richard Fuller*'s, Esq; but the Manor of *Caldecot* Hall belongs to *Magdalen* College, in *Oxford*.

GORLESTON. Nothing is remarkable here but the Ruins of an old Building, supposed by Mr. *Cambden* to have been some religious House. In fact, they are the Ruins

HUNDRED of LOTHING.

Ruins of the Church of St. *Nicholas* of *South-Town*, an adjoining Hamlet. Next to *Yarmouth* Bridge is another Hamlet called *West-Town*. These two Hamlets are called in old Writings, *Little Yarmouth*. Great *Yarmouth*, on the other Side of the River, being often called in such Writings, the *East-Town* of *Yarmouth*.

GUNTON. The Estate here belonged formerly to the *Lowdhams*, then to the *Ingeloses*, *Blomviles*, *Wroths*, *Holles*, in this Order; and it doth now belong to Vice-Admiral Sir *Charles Saunders*, Knight of the Bath.

HOPTON. The Manor and Impropriation belonged anciently to the Prior and Convent, and now to the Dean and Chapter of *Norwich*.

HERINGFLEET. Here was a religious House of Canons Regulars of St. *Austins*, dedicated to the Honor of St. *Olave*, and founded by *Robert Fitz-Osbert*, of the yearly Value of 49*l*. 11*s*. 7*d*. It was granted to *Henry Jerningham*, 28 *Henry* VIII. It was lately the Estate of Mr. *Taverner*, since of Sir *Edmund Bacon*, of *Gillingham*, Bart. and now of *Henry Hills Muffenden*, Esq;

LOUND. Sir *Thomas Allen*, Bart. is Lord of this Manor.

LOWESTOFT, is a considerable large Town, standing near the Sea: It is pretty well built, and the chief Street is paved throughout. The Church, which is situated near a Mile from the Town, is a good Building; but for the Ease of the Inhabitants there is a Chapel in the Town, wherein Divine Service is often celebrated. The Ness below the North End of the Town, is, since the washing away of *Easton* Ness, the most Eastern Point of Land in *Great-Britain*. The chief Employment here is Fishing. The Market-day is *Wednesday*; and here are two annual Fairs, viz. on *May*-day, and *Michaelmas*-day. Besides
the

the present Chapel, here was formerly at the South-end of the Town another, called *Good-Cross Chapel,* which hath long been destroyed by the Sea.

This Town, having been Part of the ancient Demesnes of the Crown, hath a Charter and a Town Seal; but the greatest Privilege they now enjoy from their Charter, is that of not serving upon Juries, either at the Assizes or Sessions. Sir *Thomas Allen,* Rear-Admiral *Utler,* Sir *John Ashley,* Vice-Admiral *Mighells,* and other noted Men in the Sea-service, were either Natives or Inhabitants of this Town.

OULTON. The Manor and Estate here formerly belonged to the *Bacons,* then to the *Fastolfs,* then the *Hobarts,* since to the *Reeves,* and now belong to *Gerard Van Heythuysen,* Esq; but he is only the mean Lord, Sir *Thomas Allen* hath a Paramountship over him.

SOMERLITON, now for Shortness called *Somerly,* is most remarkable for a beautiful old Seat called the *Hall,* which was anciently the Seat of the *Fitz-Osberts,* or *Fitz-Osbourns;* then the *Jernegans, Wentworths,* and *Garneys;* of whom it was purchased by Sir *Thomas Allen,* who was created a Baronet 7 *Feb.* 1672; which Sir *Thomas,* or his Successor, for want of Issue gave his Seat to his Nephew *Richard Anguish,* Esq; who was created a Baronet 15 *Dec.* 1699, by the Name of *Richard Anguish,* alias *Allen.* This noble Seat is now vested in his Son Sir *Thomas Allen,* Bart. See *Horham,* in *Hoxne* Hundred.

Besides the sixteen Parishes, and the Hamlets before-mentioned, there are several other Hamlets in this Hundred; such as *Brotherton,* a Hamlet of *Hopton; Browston,* a Hamlet of *Belton. Browston-Hall* is the Seat of *Nathaniel Symonds,* Esq; and *Normanston,* corruptly called *Nomanstown,* which lieth between *Mutford*-Bridge and the Town of *Lowestoft.* It is the Estate of *Richard Jenkinson,* Gentleman.

WANG-

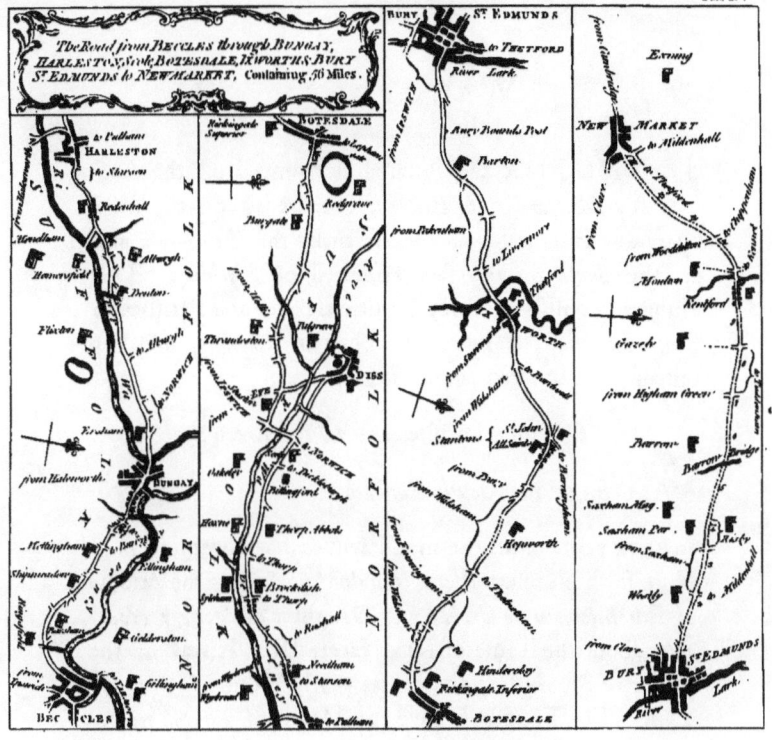

WANGFORD.

WANGFORD Hundred is bounded on the *East* by *Mutford* and *Blything* Hundreds; on the *West* by *Hoxne* Hundred; on the *North* by the *Waveney*; and on the *South* by the said Hundred of *Blything*. This Hundred consists of three Partitions; the *nine* Parishes or *South-Elmhams*, the *seven* Parishes or *Ilketsals*, and the rest of the Hundred about *Beccles*.

The nine Parishes are as followeth:

ALL-SAINTS, *South-Elmham.*

FLIXTON, of all the nine Parishes hath been of most Note for a Nunnery there, founded by *Margery* the Widow of *Bartholomew de Creke*, and Daughter of *Jeffery Hautvile*, about the Time of King *Henry* III. It was of the Order of St. *Austin*, and of the yearly Value of 23*l*. 4*s*. 1½*d*. The Foundress gave the Manor of *Flixton* to this House, which was dissolved by the second Bull of Pope *Clement* VII. in 1528, and intended for Cardinal *Wolsey*. But he declining in the King's Favour, it was granted to *John Tasburgh*, whose Descendants long had their Seat at *Flixton* Hall. That Family being extinct, it descended to the Family of *Wyburn*; but hath since been purchased by *William Adair*, Esq. The Manor of the nine Parishes belonged to the Bishop of *Norwich*, with the Advowson of all the Churches, except *Flixton*, (which he had granted to the Nuns, in Exchange for *Holmingham-Sancroft*, which belonged to the *Batemans*,) and St. *Michael*, which was impropriated to the Priory of *Rumburgh*, till A. D. 1335; when it was granted by Act of Parliament to King *Henry* VIII. who granted the Manor with the Advowsons of St. *James*, St. *Peter's*, St. *Margaret's*, St. *Nicholas, All Saints*, and *Homersfield*, to Sir *Edward Northe*, Knt. in Exchange. The whole is now vested in Mr. *Adair*.

SAN-

SANCROFT, or St. *George Southelmham.*

HOMERSFIELD, or St. *Mary Southelmham.* A Market and a Fair here were granted to the Bishop of *Norwich* 2 *Henry* III. The Manor of *Limborne* in *Homersfield* belonged formerly to the Nuns of *Bungay*, and was granted 29 *Henry* VIII. to *Thomas* Duke of *Norfolk*, and 7 *Ed.* VI. to *John* and *Thomas Wright.* Sir *Basingburn Gaudy* died seised of it *A. D.* 1569. It belongs now to ——— ———; but there are few or no Tenants to it, and it would scarce be known, if it were not for the Water-Mill, which still retains the Name of *Lymborn* Mill.

ST. JAMES, *Southelmham.*

ST. MARGARET, *Southelmham.*

ST. MICHAEL, *Southelmham.* The Earl of *Brittany* and *Richmond* had Lands here when Domesday-Book was made, and by his means probably this Church became early impropriated to *Rumburgh Priory.*

ST. NICHOLAS, *Southelmham,* whose Church is so entirely demolished that hardly any Rubbish of it remains.

ST. PETER, *Southelmham.*

These nine Parishes which are called the Deanery of *Southelmham*, are represented in old Wills as one Township; and as such they have an Estate in *Aldborough* and *Wortwell* in *Norfolk*, common to them all. For we frequently meet with *Homersfield*, in the Town of *Southelmham*; and St. *James*, in the Township of *Southelmham*; and the like.

The seven Parishes are these:

ST. ANDREW ILKETSAL, is one of the Duke of *Norfolk*'s Towns.

BUNGAY

BUNGAY *St. Mary*, and BUNGAY *Trinity*. *Bungay* is a pleasant Town, situated on the River *Waveney*, which is navigable for Barges from *Yarmouth* hither. A great Fire broke out on 1 *March* 1688, in a small un-inhabited House, which raged so furiously, that in four Hours Time it consumed the whole Town, except one small Street: The whole Loss was computed at 29,896*l.* and upwards. By this terrible Accident, it has happened that the Town is well built. St. *Mary*'s Church is a sumptuous Structure, and, with its beautiful Steeple, is a great Ornament to the Town. Between the two Churches the Ruins of a *Benedictine* Nunnery appear; it was founded by *Roger de Glanvile* and the Countess *Gundreda* his Wife, to the Honour of the Blessed Virgin *Mary*, and the *Holy Cross*. It was endowed by a great Number of Benefactors, all whose Gifts were confirmed by 19 King *Henry* II. At the Suppression it was of the yearly Value of 62 *l.* and was granted to *Thomas* Duke of *Norfolk*; in which Family, with a Manor in this Town, it now remains.

The Church of the *Holy Trinity* in *Bungay* was impropriated to the Priory of *Barlynch*, in *Somersetshire*. The Impropriation now belongeth to the Bishop of *Ely*, who leaseth it to the Vicar. Besides these two Churches, there was also a Church of St. *Thomas*, which was impropriated to the Nunnery: It was standing and in use since the Year 1500; but hath been so long down, that no Man now knows where it stood.

Here are also the Ruins of a very strong Castle, supposed to have been built by the *Bygods*, Earls of *Norfolk*. In the Barons Wars it was fortified, and made so strong by *Hugh Bygod*, that he was wont to boast of it as impregnable; saying, in the Wars of King *Stephen*, as is reported,

Were I in my Castle of *Bungay*,
Upon the River *Waveney*,
I would ne care for the King of *Cockney*.

But

But notwithstanding his great Confidence in this Castle, he was forced to compound with King *Henry* II. for a great Sum of Money, with sufficient Hostages, to save it from being demolished. But afterwards the said Earl siding with *Richard* Son of *Henry* II. against his Father, King *Henry* took from him his Castles of *Framlingham* and *Bungay*. In the Reign of King *Henry* III. this Castle was demolished, and *Roger Bygod* Earl of *Norfolk* obtained a Licence 10 *Edward* I. to embattle his House in the Place where this Castle stood; afterwards it reverted to the Crown. In the 4th *Richard* II. *William de Ufford* Earl of *Suffolk*, died possessed of the Castle, Borough, and Manor of *Bungay*: He married *Joan* Daughter of *Edward Montacute*, by *Alice* his Wife Daughter and Coheiress of *Thomas Brotherton*, fifth Son of King *Edward* I. on whom it is probable that King settled them.

Here is a good Market on *Thursdays*, well served with all manner of Provisions: There are also two yearly Fairs on 3d *May* and *Sept.* 14; both Festivals of the *Holy Cross*, to which the Nunnery was dedicated. The Inhabitants of *Bungay* have the Privilege of a large Common belonging to this Town, and almost encompassed with the River *Waveney*, which is of great advantage to them.

ST. JOHN ILKETSAL, ST. LAURENCE ILKETSAL, ST. MARGARET ILKETSAL, METTINGHAM. The Churches of *Mettingham, Ilketsal St. Andrew's, St. Margaret*, and *St. Laurence*, were given by *Roger de Glanvile* and *Gundreda* his Countess to the Nuns of *Bungay*, who got them impropriated to them. And the Impropriations and Advowson of the Vicarages were granted to *Thomas* Duke of *Norfolk* 29 *Henry* VIII.

The Manor of BARDOLF in *Ilketsal St. Laurence* and *Bungay Trinity*, was obtained 2 *Edward* III. with the Manor of *Clopton*, by *Elizabeth de Burgh* the Relict of *Roger de Amorie*, for herself for Life; and the Remainder

to

HUNDRED *of* WANGFORD. 159

to *John* Lord *Bardolf* and *Elizabeth* his Wife, (who was her Daughter) and the Issue by the said *Roger*; in Exchange for the Manors of *Kennington* and *Fankshall*, in *Surry*.

The remaining Parishes in that Hundred about *Beccles*, are,

BARSHAM, anciently the Lordship and Seat of the *Itchinghams*; *John Blennerhasset*, Esq; about the Time of *Edward* VI. acquired it by marrying one of the Coheiresses of Sir *Edward Itchingbam*, and made it the Seat of his Family. It now belongs to the *Sucklings*.

BECCLES, is a large well-built Town, situated on the *East* and *South* Sides of the River *Waveney*, which is navigable beyond the Town: The chief Streets are well paved: The Church and the Steeple, which last stands at some Distance from the *South East* Corner of the Chancel, are noble Structures, and great Ornaments to the Town. On the *South* Part of the Town are the Ruins of another Parish Church, called *Endgate*, which was taken down by Order of Queen *Elizabeth*: " For that " the Parishes of *Beccles* and *Endgate* had been for many " Years so blended together, that the Bounds and Limits " of them could not be known in *A. D.* 1419; when a " legal Agreement was made by the Bishop, Patron, and " Rectors of both Parishes, That the Rector of *Beccles* " should take the whole Tithes of both Parishes, and " pay the Rector of *Endgate* 6*l.* 13*s.* 4*d.* yearly, in the " Parish Church of *Endgate*. So that the Inhabitants of " *Endgate* have Time out of Mind been esteemed Pa" rishioners of *Beccles*."

It seems probable from what is said in *Mon. Angl.* Vol. I. p. 408, that *Beccles* was very early a Place of some Note; for, speaking of the Citizens of *Norwich*, it is said, " Nunquam ante Conquestum, nec post per cen-

4 " tum

" tum & plures annos, habuerunt Coronatores, nec Bal-
" livos de feipfis, fed folummodo unum Ballivum, qui
" nomine Regis curias tenebat et amerciamenta collige-
" bat, *ficut fuit in* Beccles *feu in* Bungay, *five in aliis*
" *villis ubi merchandifiæ venduntur.*" They had not before the Conqueft, nor for a hundred Years or more after it, any Coroners or Bailives from among themfelves ; but they had one Bailiff only, who in *the King's Name* held Courts, and collected Amercements, *as it was in* Beccles *or* Bungay, *or other Towns where Merchandize is fold.*

The Manor of *Beccles* was given to the Abbey of *Bury* by King *Edwin* Brother of King *Edgar*, who enjoyed it till the Diffolution; when it was given by K. *Hen.* VIII. to *William Rede*, Gent. from whom it came to the *Yallops*; and from them to Mr. *Bence*, of *Henftead.*

The Manor of *Roos* or *Rofs* in *Beccles*, was formerly the Eftate of *Peter Garneys*, Efq; then of the *Tollbys* ; after that of the *Sucklings* ; and is now the Seat of Sir *Robert Rich*, Bart.

The Common belonging to this Town contains about 1400 Acres, and was likewife Part of the Poffeffions of *Bury Abbey*, and granted to the aforefaid *William Rede*, for the Ufe of the Inhabitants. For the better Prefervation and Improvement of this Common Queen *Elizabeth* A. D. 1583, incorporated a Body Politick, by the Name of, *The Corporation of* Beccles *Fenn* ; confifting of a Portreve, a Steward, twelve capital and twenty-four inferior Common-Councilmen, to overlook and regulate all Matters relating to it.

Here is a plentiful Market every *Saturday*, and three yearly Fairs; the firft on *Afcenfion-day* ; the fecond on *June* 29, granted by King *John* to be held eight Days; and the third on *September* 21.

Befides the Parifh Church, here was formerly a Chapel of St. *Peter*, near the Old Market ; a Chapel of St. *Mary Magdalene*, belonging to a fmall Hofpital on the Hill near the Free-School; and a Chapel or Hermitage near the Bridge over the *Waveney*, as there was alſo formerly at *Bungay*, and upon almoſt all great Bridges in *England*.

Sir *John Leman*, Knt. Alderman of *London*, in the Reign of King *James* I. built a Free School and endowed it with an hundred Acres of Land, for the Maintenance of a Maſter and Uſher, to teach forty-eight Boys Writing and Arithmetick. And *Henry Falconberge*, L.L.D. Chancellor of the Dioceſe of St. *David*'s, Regiſtrary of the Faculty-Office, and Commiſſary and Official of the Archdeaconry of *Suffolk*, who lived ſeveral Years, and died in this Pariſh *A.D.* 1713. bequeathed an Eſtate at *Corton* in this County of the yearly Rent of 40 *l.* for the Endowment of a Grammar-School here: The Maſter whereof is to be elected by the Biſhop of *Norwich*, the Archdeacon of *Suffolk*, and the Rector of *Beccles* for the Time being.

ELLOUGH, or WILLINGHAM *All-Saints*. The Lordſhip of this Place, and the Advowſon of the Church, hath been in the Family of *Playters* above two hundred Years. Sir *John Playters*, of *Satterly*, is now Lord and Patron.

ENDGATE. See *Beccles*.

HULVERSTREET, is a Hamlet of *Henſtead*.

NORTH-COVE. The Manor of *Wade-Hall* in *North-Cove*, belonged anciently to *Robert Waſhby*, of *Cumberland*. *Hubert Jernegan* obtained it about the Year 1200, by marrying *Waſhby*'s Daughter. Sir *John Jernegan*, upon the Marriage of his Sons, *A.D.* 1456, ſettled at *Cove* by *Beccles*, and gave the Manor of *Waſhe* or *Wade-Hall* to his Son *Oſbert*. Sir *Edward Jernegan* died ſeiſed 1515: It lately belonged to the *Yallops*; and is now in the Heirs of Mr. *Robert Bence*, late of *Henſtead*.

REDISHAM *Magna.* This Church was impropriated to the Priory of *Butley,* and the Impropriation was granted 20 *Elizabeth* to *John Hercy* and *John Hayward.* The Church of *Little Redisham* hath been many Years down. The Rectory hath been confolidated to *Ringsfield.* The Lordship is in *Edmund Tyrrel,* Efq; of *Gipping.*

RINGSFIELD. The Prior and Convent of *Butley* were Patrons both of *Little Redisham* and *Ringsfield* before the Reformation.

SATTERLY, is chiefly remarkable for the Family of *Playters,* which is very ancient, having had their Seat at *Satterly* ever fince the Reign of King *Edward* II. This Family were early in the Lift of Baronets; for Sir *Thomas Playters,* of *Satterly* was created a Baronet 13 *Aug.* 1623; which Honour is now vefted in Sir *John Playters;* but the Manor in *Miles Barnes,* Efq;

SHADDINGFIELD. The Family of *Cuddon* had for many Years their Seat at this Hall; which, with their Eftate in this Parifh, was lately fold by *Eleazor Cuddon* to ―― ――――.

SHIPMEADOW.

WESTON. Here is a Seat which for fome time has been in the Family of *Leman,* and is now vefted in *William Leman,* Efq. There is alfo another Seat which belongs to ―― ――――.

WILLINGHAM *St. Mary.* This Church was ftanding *A. D.* 1529; but is now in Ruins. The Lordship was lately in Sir *Thomas Robinfon;* now in *Robert Sparrow,* Efq.

WORLINGHAM, was formerly two Parifhes, St. *Mary* and St. *Peter.* The Church of *Worlingham* St. *Peter* hath been

been many Years down, and it is now accounted but one Parish. The Advowson was formerly in the Prior and Convent of *Butley*, but was not granted away at the Dissolution of that; so it remains still in the Crown.

The Hall is a neat Mansion, and was for some time the Seat of *John Felton*, Esq; whose only Daughter married to Sir *John Playters*; and he sold this and some other Estates to Sir *Thomas Robinson*, Bart. who made it his Seat. It is now by Purchase the Seat of *Robert Sparrow*, Esq.

HOXNE.

THE Hundred of *Hoxne* is bounded by the Hundreds of *Loes* and *Plomesgate*, on the South; on the *West*, by *Loes* and *Hartifmere*; on the North, by the River *Waveney*, which parts it from *Norfolk*; and on the *East*, by *Wangford* and *Blything*. It contains the Parishes following, viz.

ATHELINGTON. The Prior and Convent of *Butley* were Patrons of this Church before the Reformation; the Crown did not present to it before the Year 1555.

BADDINGHAM. The Hall was for many Years the Seat of the Family of *Rous*, and is now vested in the Heirs of the Rev. Mr. *Fynn*, who married a Lady of that Family. The Family of *Alexander* hath long resided here; also *Colston* Hall here belongs to *Rowland Holt*, Esq; and the Manors of *Colston*-Hall and *Baddingham*-Hall to *Mileson Edgar*, Esq. The Patronage of the Church is now vested in the Rev. Mr. *Chevalier*. The late Rector Dr. *Blomfield*, built a neat Rectory-House not far from the Church.

BEDDINGFIELD, was remarkable for a Family of that Name, who were Lords of this Manor, and had their Seat at *Redlingfield*. The Manor did belong to the Priory of *Snape*, and was granted 17 *Henry* VIII. to Cardinal *Wolsey* towards the Endowment of his College at *Ipswich*. After the Dissolution of that College, it was granted to *Thomas* Duke of *Norfolk*; and in 7 *Edward* VI. to *Thomas* and *George Golding*; and came to the *Beddingfields* soon after.

It

HUNDRED *of* HOXNE. 165

It is now vested in —— *Beddingfield*, of *Ditchingham*, Esq; who is Patron likewise of the Benefice.

BEDFIELD. The Manor and Advowson was given to the Priory of *Eye*, by *Robert Mallet*, and granted 31 *Henry* VIII. to *Anthony Rous*, Esq. They are now vested in Sir *John Rous*, Bart.

BRUNDISH. Here was a famous Chauntry, founded by Sir *John Pyshall*, Rector of *Caston*, one of the Executors of *Robert de Ufford* Earl of *Suffolk*, in 7 *Richard* II. for six Chaplains to pray for the Soul of the said Earl, and all his Benefactors: It was of the yearly Value of 13 l. 7$\frac{1}{2}$ d. and surrendered 25 *June* 1545, by *William* Bishop of *Norwich* and *John Person* Incumbent, with the Consent of *Richard Fulmerston* Patron, and granted on the first of *August* following to the said *Richard Fulmerston*. It is now vested in —— *Gooch*, Gent. who resides in a Mansion near the Church: Here is also the Seat of *Turner Calvert*, Esq; called the *Lodge*. It is remarkable, that all the Land within this Parish is Freehold.

CARLETON. A Chauntry was founded here about the Year 1330, by *John Framlingham*, Rector of *Kelsale*, for three Chaplains to pray for the Soul of *Alice* of *Hainault*, Countess of *Mareschall*. It was granted 36 *Henry* VIII. to *William Honing*.

DENHAM. The Manor is vested in Lord *Maynard*.

DENNINGTON. In this Church is the Burial-place of Lord *Bardolph*, who had his Seat at the Hall, which by the Ruins appears to have been a sumptuous Building. Here were two Chauntries, one called our Lady's Chauntry, as belonging to the Altar of St. *Mary*, this is mentioned in 1306, and was of the yearly Value of 9l. 7$\frac{1}{2}$$d$. the other to the Altar of St. *Margaret*, founded in 1437, by Sir *William Philips*, who by marrying the Daughter of

M 3   Lord

Lord *Bardolph*, was Lord *Bardolph* in her Right, and called *Philips*'s *Chauntry:* This was for two Priests to pray for his and his Wife's Welfare during their Lives, and for their Souls, &c. after their Decease; it was of the yearly Value of 26*l*. 4*s*. 7*d*. They were both granted to *Richard Fulmerston*. The Hall with several Estates and the Lordship of this Parish and the Advowson of the Rectory, have been long in the Family of *Rous*, and are now vested in Sir *John Rous*, Bart. *Leland* says, " All the *Rous's* that be in *Suffolk*, come, as far as I can " learn, out of the House of *Rous* of *Dennington*. Divers " of the *Rous's* of this eldest House lie in *Dennington* " Church, under flat Stones. *Anthony Rous*, now Heir of " *Dennington* Hall, hath much enlarged his Possessions." *Leland*'s *Hen.* VI. p. 10.

FRESINGFIELD. Here are, or were several Manors: 1. Belonged to *Michael de la Pole*, who died seised of it 12 *Richard* II. and *William de la Pole* died seised of the same when he was beheaded, 28 *Henry* VI. 2. A Manor which belonged to the Priory of *Eye*, and was granted 28 *Henry* VIII. to *Edmund Bedingfield*. 3. The Manor or Hamlet of *Chepenhal*, which was given to *Bury* Abbey by one *Swarting stone*. 4. The Manor or Hamlet of *Witingham*, which had anciently a Chapel belonging to it: Part of this Lordship was given to *Bury* Abbey, by *Thirketel*; but Part of the Tythes to *Eye* Priory. It is now chiefly of Note for being the Birth-place and Burial-place of that truly pious and most reverend Dr. *William Sancroft*, Lord Archbishop of *Canterbury*, who had a Seat in this Parish, and lieth buried in the Church-yard under a handsome Monument. ―― *Sancroft*, Esq; a Descendant of the Bishop's, now resides in the Family Seat. The Advowson of the Church is, by the Bishop's Donation, in *Emanuel* College, *Cambridge*; and the Manors of *Chevenhall* alias *Chepenhall*, and *Ufford* Hall in *Fresingfield*, are now in the *Sancroft* Family.

HORHAM.

HORHAM. Here are, or were three Manors: *Horham-Brodocks*, late *Copleditche*, *Horham-Comitis*, and *Horham-Shermans*, late *Jernegan*'s. Sir *Hubert Jernegan*, who died A. D. 1239, had his capital Seat at his Manor of *Horham*. Sir *Hugh Jernegan* his Son, made *Stonham Jernegan* the chief Seat of the Family. Sir *Peter Jernegan*, Grandson of Sir *Hugh*, whose Mother was Heiress of the *Fitz-Osberts* of *Somerley*, made *Somerley* the chief Seat of the Family. All these Manors are now said to be in the Earl of *Leicester*.

HOXNE gives Name to the Hundred, but is more remarkable for being the Place where the *Danes* martyr'd *Edmund* King of the *East-Angles*, because he would not renounce his Faith in Christ, by binding him to a Tree, and shooting him to Death with Arrows: His Death happened A. D. 870. His Body was removed to *Bury*, and there buried. A Chapel was built on the Spot where he was slain, which was dedicated to him; and afterwards improved to a House of *Benedictine* Monks, as a Cell to *Norwich*; it was of the clear Value of 18 *l*. 1 *s*. per *Ann*. It is now converted into a Farm-house; and that, with the Estate belonging thereto, lately vested in *John Thruston*, Esq; is now the Estate of Lord *Maynard*. The Hall, the Manor, the Rectory, and Advowson of the Vicarage, belonged to the Bishops of *Norwich*; who used frequently to reside here, till the Year 1535; when it was given up by Act of Parliament to King *Henry* VIII. who shortly after granted them to Sir *Robert Southwell*. It is now the Mansion of the Right Hon. the Lord *Maynard*.

Here is a considerable Fair for Cattle, beginning yearly on *November* 20, being St. *Edmund*'s Day.

KELSALE near *Saxmundham*, was anciently the Demesne of *John* Duke of *Norfolk*, which he had with the Countess *Mareschal*, as her Portion; till being attainted for siding with the House of *York* against *Henry* Duke of *Richmond*, this Manor was given to *John de Vere*, Earl of *Oxford*; but it is probable it did not remain long in that Family, for it was in the Duke of *Norfolk*'s Family again *A.D.* 1545; and his Trustees presented to the Church all Queen *Elizabeth*'s Reign. In King *James* the First's Time Sir *Thomas Holland* had it; and in King *Charles* the Second's Reign, *John Bence*, Esq. It is now vested in *George Golding*, Esq; in Right of his Lady the Heiress of that Family.

KELSALE-*Lodge*, did also formerly belong to the Dukes of *Norfolk*, and passed from them to the Family of *Weakenham*, and from them to the *Hobarts*. It is now Sir *John Blois*'s.

LAXFIELD. *Robert Mallett* gave what he had in this Place to the Priory of *Eye*; and a Manor, the Rectory, and Advowson of the Vicarage were granted as Parcel of the Possessions of that Priory, 28 *Henry* VIII. to *Edmund Bedingfield*. Another Manor in *Laxfield* was granted as Parcel of the Possessions of *Leiston* Abbey to *Charles* Duke of *Suffolk*, 28 *Henry* VIII. *John Wingfield* obtained a Grant for a Market at *Laxfield* in King *Edward* IVth's Reign; and there are two Fairs here yearly, *May* 1st, and *October* 13th; from whence we may suppose that this Place was of more Note formerly, than it is now. The Church and Steeple are very beautiful Edifices. There were many Legacies in old Wills about the Year 1445, given to the Building the Steeple here. The Family of *Jacobs* have long had their Seat in this Town, which is now vested in the Heirs of that Family.

MENDHAM, is situated on both Sides of the River *Waveney*, taking into its Bounds Part of the Town of *Harleston*: There was formerly a Chapel in this Churchyard, at a little Distance from the Church: And in the *Suffolk* Part of this Parish, *William* the Son of *Roger de Hunt-*

HUNDRED of HOXNE.

Huntingfield founded in King *Stephen*'s Reign a *Cluniac* Priory, dedicated to the Blessed Virgin, and subordinate to *Castleacre* in *Norfolk*; which, at the Dissolution, was granted to *Richard Freston* and *Ann* his Wife. Sir *John Howard* had a Grant of the Manor of *Mendham* in *Suffolk* 15 *Edward* IV. which was lately the Estate of *John* Earl of *Oxford*, attainted. And the Manor of *Winchenden*, in this Parish, was granted to *Richard* and *William Freston*, 1 *Edward* VI. as Parcel of the Possessions of the Prior and Convent of the *Holy Trinity* in *Ipswich*, who had a Share of the Church here by the Gift of *Robert* the Son of *Angot*, and is now vested in *Cook Freston*, Esq; who resides in a good Seat here.

METFIELD, is sometimes called a Chapel to *Mendham:* The Lordship is in *William Plumer*, Esq;

MONK-SOHAM, so called because the Monks of *Bury* were Patrons of the Rectory, and had the Manor here by the Gift of *Alfred*, Bishop of the *East-Angles*. It was granted 37 *Henry* VIII. to *Anthony Rous*, and sold by *Thomas Rous* in 3 *Elizabeth*, to *Lionel Talmach*. The Manor of *Blomviles*, or *Woodcroft-Hall*, in this and the neighbouring Parishes, belonged to *John Caldwell*, in *A. D.* 1460; and is now vested in *Anthony Deane*, Esq;

SAXSTEAD, is the Lordship of the Master and Fellows of *Pembroke-Hall*, in *Cambridge*.

SYLEHAM. In this Parish there is a Hamlet called *Esham*, in which there was formerly a Chapel. The Manor of *Syleham Comitis* is now vested in *William Chapman*, Esq; this is probably the Manor which belonged to *Michael* and *William de la Pole*, as mentioned in *Dugdale*'s Baron. *Roger Bygod* had Lands here, by Exchange with Bishop *Herbert*, which he gave to his *Cluniac* Monks at *Thetford*, upon whose Dissolution a Manor in *Syleham* (perhaps that which

which is now called *Monks-Hall*) was granted to *Thomas* Duke of *Norfolk*, 32 *Henry* VIII. *Henry Jernegan*, Efq; who died *A. D.* 1619, had a Manor in *Syleham*; but which of thefe it was, does not appear. In this Parifh is the Seat of *Lamb Barry*, Efq;

SOUTHOLT, is but a Kind of Hamlet and Chapel of Eafe to *Worlingworth*, and feems to have belonged to *Bury* Abbey, as that did.

STRADBROOK, is a confiderable and large Village. There is a Patent granted by King *Henry* III. for a Market here on *Fridays*, but it hath long been difufed; but the Fair on *Sept.* 21, is kept up. Here are two Manors, 1ft. *Schelton*'s, in which *John de Schelton* had a Chapel, which was inftituted to for about 150 Years, *viz.* from the Year 1306, to the Year 1455. 2. A Manor which *Michael de la Pole* died feifed of 12 *Richard* II. *William de la Pole* died feifed of it 28 *Henry* VI. and *Thomas* Lord *Howard* and *Ann* his Wife, probably had this granted to them *A. D.* 1511. *Robert Grofthead*, Bifhop of *Lincoln*, was a Native of this Parifh; he died in 1253: He was a Man of good Learning, the Age confidered, (faith *Lambard*) and was fuch an Adverfary to the unholy Proceedings of Pope *Innocent* IV. that, after his Death, the holy Father confulted to have him taken up, and burnt.

TANNINGTON. Here the Family of the *Dades* have long had their Seat in a good Manfion, now vefted in the Relict of Dr. *Dade*.

WETHERSDALE. The Patronage of this Church is in *Emanuel* College, *Cambridge*; and it is held with *Frefingfield*.

WEYBREAD. *Oliver de Ingham* died 18 *Edward* III. feifed of the Manor of *Weybread*, in *Suffolk*. The Patron of of this Church is *Philips Coleman*, Efq; of *Ipfwich*, who is likewife Lord of the Manor.

WILBY. *John Nevil* Marquis *Montague*, had a Grant of the Manor of *Wilby*, 8 *Edward* IV. It was Part of the *Wingfield*'s Eftate, and doth now belong to the Earl of *Rochford*. Here is alfo a Manor called *Ruffels*, in *Wilby*, belonging to *William Stane*, Efq;

WINGFIELD, was fometime the Eftate of *Richard de Brews*, who had a Grant for a Fair here 3 *Edward* III. or 1328; but more anciently it belonged to a Family who took their Name from it, and were in great Reputation here for many Ages: In After-times they had their Habitation at *Letheringham* and *Eafton*, in the Hundred of *Loes*. It is faid, that in the Reign of *Henry* VIII. there were eight or nine Knights at the fame time, all Brothers, and two Knights of the Garter of this Family. That noble old Building called *Wingfield-Caftle*, was the Seat of this Family before the *Norman* Conqueft, as appears by an ancient Pedigree now in that Family. It was for a long time and till lately vefted in the Family of the *Catalynes*. The Lady of the late Sir *Charles Turner*, Bart. was the Relict of Sir *Nevil Catalyne*, after whofe Death it defcended to the Heirs of *Thomas Leman*, of *Wenhafton*, Efq; in whom it now is.

At the South weft Corner of the Church-yard the Executors of Sir *John Wingfield* erected a College about the Year 1362, for a Provoft or Mafter, and feveral Priefts: It was dedicated to St. *Mary*, St. *John Baptift*, and St. *Andrew*, and was valued at the Suppreffion at 50 *l*. 3 *s*. 5½ *d*. and was granted by K. *Edw*. VI. to the Bifhop of *Norwich*, probably in exchange for fome Manor taken from him.

WORLINGWORTH. Bifhop *Alfric* gave this Lordfhip and Church to *Bury* Abbey; and the Manor and Advowfon of the Rectory were granted in 31 *Henry* VIII. to

Anthony

Anthony Rous. John Major, Efq; is now Lord of the Manor.

HARTISMERE.

HARTISMERE Hundred is bounded on the *Eaft,* by the Hundred of *Hoxne;* on the *Weft,* by *Blackbourn;* on the *North,* by the River *Waveney,* which parts it from *Norfolk;* and, on the *South,* by the Hundreds of *Bofmere, Claydon* and *Stow.* It contains the following Parifhes.

ASPALL, is fituated at the Head of the River *Deben:* The Hall was formerly the Seat of the noble Family of *Brooks,* Lords *Cobham: Edmund Brook* Lord *Cobham,* died 29 *May,* 4 *Edward* IV. feifed of the Manors of *Herdeburgh* and *Afpall,* in *Com. Suff.* but this laft is now vefted in the Rev. Mr. *Chevalier,* who hath his Seat here. The Church feems to have belonged firft to the Prior and Convent of *Caftleacre,* and to have come afterwards to the Prior and Convent of *Butley;* for the Impropriation was granted as Parcel of the Poffeffions of *Butley,* to *Francis Framlingham,* 34 *Henry* VIII. but Sir *Charles Gawdy* generoufly fettled it upon the Minifter for the Time being for ever.

BACTON, was the Lordfhip and Demefne of the Bifhop of *Norwich* till about the Year 1535, when it was given up to King *Henry* VIII. who, probably, granted it to the Duke of *Norfolk;* for *A. D.* 1558, the Duke of *Norfolk* conveyed the Manors of *Bacton* and *Cotton* to Sir *John Tyrell,* of *Gipping,* in exchange for the Manor of *Banham* in *Norfolk.* Here is now a neat Manfion built by *George Pretyman,* Efq; and is now the Seat of ———— ————.

In

In the Year 1739 *Henry Howard* died in this Parish, aged Ninety-five Years, whose Wife bare him a Daughter in the Fifty-eighth Year of her Age.

BOTESDALE, or BOTULPHSDALE, is a long Thorough-fare Town; but the greater Part of the Houses, altho' so called, stand in *Rickengale inferior*; the Mother Church to *Botesdale*, is *Redgrave*. There is a Market Weekly on *Thursday*, which was granted to the Abbey of *Bury*, as Lord of *Redgrave* with *Botesdale*, and *Gislingham*. (See *Redgrave*.) There is also a Fair yearly on *Holy Thursday*; but by the Charter of *Henry* III. by whom it was granted, it is to be held on the Eve and Day of St. *Botulph*, viz. *May* 17 and 18.

Here is a free Grammar School, founded by Sir *Nicholas Bacon* about the Year 1576, and established by Queen *Elizabeth*'s Letters-Patent. The Master and Usher are to be elected out of *Bennet* College *Cambridge*, where Sir *Nicholas* was educated; and there is 20*l*. *per Annum* given by Sir *Nicholas* to the said College for six Scholars out of the said School. It is said Archbishop *Tennison*, by his last Will, gave six Pounds yearly to these six Scholars. At the East-end of the School-House was formerly a Chauntry, built by *John Sheriff*, for the Benefit of his and his Wife's Soul; in which the School is now kept.

BREISWORTH. Sir *Robert de Sacvill* had the Lordships of *Breisworth*, *Cotton* and *Brachford*, in *Suffolk*, in the Time of *Henry* I. probably *Breisworth*, *Cotton*, and *Brockford*. Earl *Cornwallis* has this Lordship and Advowson now.

BROOME. Here is a fine old Mansion, which has long since been the Seat of the noble Family of *Cornwallis*. This Family has furnished the State with many worthy and respectable Men. Sir *John Cornwallis*, of *Broome-Hall*,

Hall, was knighted for his Courage and Conduct at the Siege of *Marlaix* in *Britany*; and was made Steward of the Houshold to Prince *Edward*, who was afterwards King *Edward* VI. His Son Sir *Thomas* being High-Sheriff of *Norfolk* and *Suffolk* in the last Year of *Edward* VI. raised considerable Forces against the Opposers of Queen *Mary*'s Title, and by their Assistance, set her on the Throne of her Ancestors: He was promoted by Queen *Mary* to be Privy Counsellor, Treasurer of *Callice*, and Comptroller of her Houshold. A second Sir *Thomas Cornwallis* was Ambassador to the King of *Spain* in the Reign of *James* I. and Mr. *Cottington*, afterwards Lord *Cottington*, was his Secretary: From him descended *Frederick Cornwallis* of *Broome*, who was created a Baronet 4 *May*, 1627 : He suffered much in the great Rebellion by the Sequestration of his Estate, and the Imprisonment of his Person: He attended the King in all his Wars ; and in particular at the Battle of *Copredy-Bridge*, against Sir *William Waller*, he rescued a General Officer, who was fallen into the Hands of the Rebels. King *Charles* II. in reward of his Merit, not only made him Treasurer of his Houshold, Comptroller and Privy Counsellor, but created him a Baron of this Realm in 1661, by the Stile of Lord *Cornwallis*, of *Eye*. To him succeeded *Charles* Lord *Cornwallis*, who was one of the Lords of the Admiralty, and Lord Lieutenant of the County of *Suffolk* in the Reign of King *William* III. His Son *Charles* Lord *Cornwallis* was Postmaster-General of *England*, and Paymaster of the Army in the Reign of King *George* I. He left nine Sons and one Daughter: His eldest Son *Charles* was by his late Majesty King *George* II. advanced to the Dignity of an Earl, by the Style of Lord Viscount *Broome* and Earl *Cornwallis*, and was in the Reign of King *George* III. Constable of the Tower of *London*, and one of his Majesty's most Honourable Privy Council ; and the fine old Seat, together with the Lordship of *Broome*, is now vested in his Son the present Earl *Cornwallis*. There

HUNDRED of HARTISMERE. 175

There were formerly two Medieties in the Church of *Broome*; the Prior of *Thetford* was Patron of one, and Mr. *Calthorp* Patron of the other. They were confolidated *A. D.* 1448, and Earl *Cornwallis* prefents.

BROCKFORD. See before *Breifworth*. Some Part of this formerly belonged to *Bury* Abbey. It is a Hamlet of *Wetheringfett*.

BURGATE, formerly the Lordfhip of Sir *William de Burgate*, who refided in this Parifh, and lies buried under a very good Tomb in the Chancel. This Lordfhip, and alfo the Advowfon of the Church, are now vefted in *Rowland Holt*, Efq.

COTTON. *William de la Pole* died feifed of this Manor, 28 *Henry* VI. It came afterwards to the Duke of *Norfolk*, who, *A. D.* 1558, affigned it to Sir *John Tyrell*.

The Country hereabouts feems to be remarkably healthy, if we may judge by the Longevity of the Inhabitants; for in the Year 1739, the Widow of one Dr. *Ellis*, a Practitioner in Phyfick, died in the Ninety-fifth Year of her Age; and, fince that, one *Woods* died in this Parifh, aged One Hundred and Two Years.

EYE, is fituated in a Bottom, and is a Town Corporate, governed by two Bailiffs, ten principal Burgeffes, and twenty-four Common Council-men: It enjoys divers Privileges now, but they were more extenfive formerly; they are faid to have reached even to the Gates of *York*. It fends two Members to Parliament, is faid to have been a Borough before the Reign of King *John*, and to be called in old Writings the Town and Borough of *Aye*; but it did not fend Members to Parliament before the 13th Year of Queen *Elizabeth*. This Town is improved in its Buildings of late Years, but from its Situation it is dirty.

dirty. There is a fmall Market Weekly on *Saturdays*, and one Fair Yearly on *Whitfon-Monday*.

Robert Mallet, a *Norman* Baron, whofe Father came in with the Conqueror, obtained of him the Lordfhip of *Eye*, with all the Appendages of it: He being poffeffed of this Lordfhip built the Caftle here, near the Weft-end of the Church; fome of the ruinous Walls of which are ftill to be feen. But this *Robert* was deprived of the Lordfhip and Honor of *Eye* by *Henry* I. and it was given by him to *Stephen* Earl of *Bologne*, who was afterwards King of *England*. He left it to his natural Son; but, he dying without Heirs, it reverted to the Crown. *Richard* I. gave it to *Henry* the fifth Earl of *Brabant* and *Lorain*; yet it was in the King's Hands 9 *Edward* II. and fo continued, until *Edward* III. granted it to *John* of *Eltham*, Earl of *Cornwall*; but he dying without Iffue, the fame King granted it to *Robert de Ufford*, whom he had lately made Earl of *Suffolk*. The Honor and Manor of *Eye Sokemere* belongs now, but not in that vaft Extent which *Robert Mallet* had it in, to the Right Hon. Earl *Cornwallis*. There is alfo another confiderable Manor in this Town, called *Netherhall* in *Eye*, belonging to Sir *John Rous*, Bart. and another Manor called *Eye Priory*, belonging to ———.

On the Eaft-fide of the Town appear the Ruins of a *Benedictine* Monaftery, founded by the faid *Robert Mallet*, who gave it to the Church of St. *Peter* in *Eye*, with divers other Churches, Lands, &c. No fooner were the Foundations of this Houfe laid, than it found confiderable Benefactors; for *Ranulph de Glanville*, one of the Barons (fo Lords of Manors were then called) of *Robert Mallet*, Chief Lord of the Honor of *Eye*, gave it his Houfe in *Jakefly*. *Hubert de Monchenfy* gave about the fame time, his own Houfe in the fame Place. *William* Earl of *Bologne* confirmed to thefe Monks the Lordfhip of *Acol*, (we fuppofe *Occold*) and *Stoke*. In the Reign of King *Stephen* all thefe Benefactions were confirmed to this Houfe, with a grievous

Curfe

HUNDRED *of* HARTISMERE. 177

Curse upon the Violators of them. This Monastery was at first an alien Monastery, subordinate to the Abbey of *Bernay* in *Normandy*, whose Abbots were the Patrons of this at *Eye*; and in token of their Dominion, during the Vacancy of a Prior, they used to place a Porter at the Gate, to be maintained out of the House; and who, at the Instalment of the next Prior, was to receive Five Shillings to buy him an Ox. But it was made Denison by King *Richard* II. and granted at the Dissolution, when it was valued at 161 *l*. 2 *s*. $3\frac{1}{4}d$. clear of Reprises, to *Charles* Duke of *Suffolk*. This is also now the Estate of the Right Hon. Earl *Cornwallis*.

FINNINGHAM-*Hall*, is the Seat and Lordship of *Edward Frere*, Esq. Here is a considerable Fair for Cattle, beginning every Year on *August* 24.

GISLINGHAM. The Manor-Seat called *Swatsal-Hall*, was lately re-built by *Charles Beddingfield*, Esq; but Part of the Lands in this Parish hold of the Manor of *Rushes* and *Jenneys*, which belong to *Rowland Holt*, Esq. There is a School here.

MELLIS, is the Lordship of *Rowland Holt*, Esq.

MENDLESHAM, is a dirty Town; for which *Hugh Fitz-Otho* procured the Privilege of a Market and Fair from King *Edward* I. The Market is on *Tuesday* Weekly, and the Yearly Fair on *September* 21. The Lordship of this Town has for some time been vested in the Family of *Duke*, and now belongs to *Edmund Tyrell*, Esq. King *William Rufus* gave the Church of *Mendlesham* with *Andreston*, to the Abbot and Convent of *Battel* in *Sussex*, who had the Impropriation and Advowson of the Vicarage until the Dissolution.

N   OAKLEY.

OAKLEY. Here were formerly two Churches and Parishes; *Great Oakley*, dedicated to St. *Nicholas*; and *Little Oakley*, dedicated to St. *Andrew*: They were confolidated 27 *Oct.* 1449. The Lordfhip is in Earl *Cornwallis*.

OCCOLD. The Manor of *Occolde* belongs to *Milefon Edgar*, Efq; alfo here are two other Manors belonging to the *Malyn* Family.

PALGRAVE. The Lordfhip of the Abbot of *Bury*, given thereto by Earl *Wolfflan*, and others. In the Weft Part of this Parifh was a Chapel of St. *John Baptift*, fubordinate to the Abbey of *Bury*, where five fecular Priefts had their Refidence, and faid Mafs daily. The Manors of *Palgrave* and *Fenhoufe* in this Parifh, are now vefted in Earl *Cornwallis*.

REDLINGFIELD, is chiefly memorable for a Monaftery of *Benedictine* Nuns, founded by *Manaffes de Gratia* Earl of *Guifnes*, and *Emma* his Wife, *A.D.* 1120, and endowed by them with the Manor of this Parifh. This Houfe was valued upon the Diffolution at 67 *l.* 1½ *d.* It was granted 28 *Henry* VIII. to *Edmund Beddingfield*, which Family enjoyed it till it was fold to *John Willis*, Efq; who now hath it.

REDGRAVE, was anciently the Lordfhip of the Abbot of *Bury*, to whom it was given by *Ulfketel* Earl of *Eaft-England*. It was granted by *Henry* VIII. in the laft Year of his Reign to *Thomas Darcy*, from whom it came fhortly into the Family of the *Bacons*. Sir *Nicholas Bacon*, Lord-Keeper, made it his Seat; and his Defcendant Sir *Nicholas Bacon*, of *Redgrave*, was created by K. *James* I. the firft Baronet in *England*, 22 *June*, 1611. The late Sir *Edmund Bacon* removed to *Garboldifham* in *Norfolk*, and fold this Eftate to Sir *John Holt*, Lord Chief Juftice of the King's-Bench; in whofe Family it now is, being the

the Seat of *Rowland Holt*, Efq; one of the Reprefentatives in Parliament for this County.

Thomas Wolfey Chaplain, afterwards the famous Cardinal and Archbifhop of *York*, was inftituted to the Rectory of *Redgrave*, 8 *June* 1506, upon the Prefentation of the Abbot and Convent of *Bury*. This Church, for beautiful Monuments, may vie with that of any other Village in *England*. There are feveral to the Memory of the ancient and honourable Family of the *Bacons*; particularly in the Right-Ifle is the Effigies of Sir *Nicholas Bacon* and his Lady, raifed on a Tomb, which for Beauty of Marble is very fine. In the Chancel is the Effigies of Lord Chief Juftice *Holt*, fitting in his Chair and dreffed in his Robes, which, as it is faid, coft 1500 *l*.

Near this Parifh is *Lopham* Gate, where is a great natural Curiofity; for two Springs rife, one on each Side of the Gate; and one of thefe running Eaftward forms the River *Waveney*, which emptieth itfelf at *Yarmouth*; the other running Weftward forms the little *Oufe*, which emptieth itfelf into the Sea at *Lynn*. But the chief Springhead of the *Oufe* rifes at *Whattisfield*, and joins this Spring about a Mile Weft from *Lopham* Gate.

RICKINGALE-*fuperior*. The Manor of *Facon's Hall* in this Parifh, is now vefted in *Rowland Holt*, Efq;

RISHANGLES. The Manor and Advowfon of the Rectory belonged to the Nunnery of *Redlingfield*, and were granted as Parcel of the Poffeffions of that Houfe to *William Honing* and *Nicholas Cutler*, 4 and 5 *Philip* and *Mary*. They now belong to the Right Honourable Lord *Orwell*.

STOKE-*Afh*. This Manor was given to the Priory of *Eye* by the Founder, and granted 28 *Henry* VIII. to *Edmund Bedingfield*. *Thomas Tyrel Bokenham*, Efq; hath the Manor now. Another Manor here, called *Stoke-Hall*, with *Thorpe*, late in *Charles Killegrew*, Esq; is now vested in *John Major*, Esq.

STUSTON. The Hall is a good old Seat, and did belong to the knightly Family of the *Castletons*; after that to the *Mariots*; then it was purchased by *Samuel Traverse*, Esq; and the Trustees of the said *Samuel* are now Lords of the Manor of *Hugh Margarets*, and Earl *Cornwallis* is Lord of *Boylands Beauchamps*, and *Faucons*. The Manor of *Faucons* in *Stuston*, was granted as Part of the Possessions of the Nuns of *Flixton* to *John Eyre*, 36 *Hen.* VIII. and most of this Village was Church-Land before the Reformation. The middle Part of the Hall was built by Bishop *Nix*, the two Wings are of later Date. There was an Oratory on the North-side of the Chancel, dedicated to St. *Katharine*; and the Field adjoining Northward to the Church-yard called *Golds*, was tied for the Payment of Three Shillings yearly, to supply the Lamp of the Virgin *Mary* with Oil.

THORNDON. *Edmund* Earl of *Cornwal* died seised 29 *Edward* I. and *Robert de Ufford* died seised of the Manor of *Thorndene* 43 *Edward* III. *William de la Pole* had it when he was put to Death, 28 *Henry* VI. It is now vested in *Rowland Holt*, Esq; and hath Jurisdiction of Courts-Leet within the Parishes of *Occolt*, *Rishangles*, and *Aspel*.

THORNHAM-*Magna*, late the Lordship of *Charles Killegrew*, Esq; descended from the famous *Killegrew* in the Time of King *Charles* the Second. This Estate, and a good Seat, there are now vested in *John Major*, Esq; Member for *Scarborough*.

THORNHAM-*Parva*.

THRANDISTON. This Place in former Accounts has been mistaken for *Thurston* in *Thedwastre* Hundred, called ancietnly anciently *Thurstaneston* (fee the Account there). For *Thrandiston* Fair is on the Feast of St. *Margaret*, and not of St. *Mary Magdalene*, which was the Day of the Fair granted to *Thurstaneston*. *William Smith*, of *Thetford*, died possessed of the Manor of *Welholmes* in *Thrandiston*, A.D. 1622; and the Hall in this Parish doth now belong to *Sheppard Frere*, Esq; the Grandson of *Thomas Smith*.

THWAITE. This Village was honoured with the Residence of the Family of *Reeve*. Sir *George Wright*, alias *Reeve*, was created a Baronet 22 *Jan*. 1661. This Family is extinct; but the Manor and Estate were lately vested in *John Sheppard*, Esq; who married the Countess Dowager of *Leicester*, a Daughter of Sir *Robert Reeve*, Bart. The Lady of Sir *Samuel Prime* has this Estate for her Life, and the Reversion is in *John Shepherd*, of *Campsey-Ash*, Esq. Here are two Fairs, one on 20 *June*, the other *November* 15.

WESTHORP. *Robert de Blund* had this when Domesday Survey was taken. *William de Ellingham*, or *Elmham*, had the Grant of a Market and Fair here 46 *Edward* III. or 1371. Sir *William de Elmham*, Knt. died possessed of this Manor, *A.D.* 1403, and left it to his Wife *Elizabeth*, who died here in 1419, and was buried by her Husband in *Bury* Abbey. *William de la Pole* died seised of the Manor of *Westhorp*-Hall, when he was beheaded 28 *Hen*.VI. or 1448. By the Ruins of this Hall it seems to have been a noble Structure, and it was afterwards granted to *Charles Brandon*, Duke of *Suffolk*. This Estate has been for a long time in the Family of the *Sheltons*, from whom it passed to *Thomas Taylor*, Esq; and is now vested in *John Reilly*, Esq.

WETHERINGSETT. The Lordship of this Town did anciently belong to the Bishop or Church of *Ely*, given to

St. *Etheldred* in *Edward* the Confeffor's Time by *Thurſtan*; but now it belongs to the Right Hon. Lord *Maynard*. *Richard Hackluyt*, Prebendary of *Weſtminſter*, who wrote *Engliſh* Voyages, &c. in 1598, was Rector of this Church.

WICKHAM-SKEITH. *Robert de Sackville*, Lord of this Place, gave the Manor to St. *John*'s Abbey in *Colcheſter*, in the Time of *Henry* I. and the faid Manor with the Rectory and Advowfon of the Vicarage were granted as Parcel of the Poffeffion of that Abbey to *Richard Freſton*, 34 *Henry* VIII. The Manor of *Wickham*-Hall, with the Rectory and Advowfon of the Vicarage, are now vefted in Sir *Armine Woodhouſe*, Bart. in Right of his Lady, who was a Daughter of the late Sir *Edmund Bacon*, of *Garboldiſham*: And the Farm called the *Abbey*, was in the *Harveys*, by whom it was fold to *Richard Canning*, of *Ipſwich*, Efq; in 1716; and now continues in his Heirs.

WORTHAM. *A.D.* 1272, *Giles de Wacheſham* had this Manor, and *Hugo de Creping* held Part of *Blomviles* in *Deopham Norfolk*, of the faid *Giles*, as of the Manor of *Wortham* in *Suffolk*. A.D. 1358, Sir *Robert de Wacheſham* had the Manor and the Advowfon of one Mediety of the Church.

One Manor here called *Wortham*, late the *Abots*, is now vefted in *Rowland Holt*, Efq; and another Manor called *Wortham*-Hall, in *Edmund Jenney*, Efq. The Advowfon of the Church of *Wortham* is in Moieties; one of which was lately in *Barnaby Gibſon*, Efq; who fold it to Mr. *Holt*, who before was poffeffed of the other Moiety.

WYVERSTON. *Gilbert de Bland* had this Lordfhip in the Time of *William* the Conqueror. *William de la Pole* died feifed of it 28 *Henry* VI. The Tenants of this
Manor

Manor enjoy several Privileges, said to be granted by the Dukes of *Suffolk*. It is now vested in the Right Rev. *John (Ewer)* Bishop of *Landaff*, by Marriage of *Elizabeth*, one of the Coheiresses of *Thomas Barnardiston*, Esq.

YAXLEY.

THREDLING.

THREDLING Hundred lieth *South-East* of *Hartismere*; and contains only five Parishes, and one Hamlet, *viz.*

ASHFIELD. The Church is now in Ruins: The Manor and Impropriation did belong to the Priory of *Butley*, and were granted 34 *Henry* VIII. to *Francis Framlingham:* They now belong to *James Bridges*, Esq.

DEBENHAM, is so called from the River *Deben*, which rises near it. The Country round this Town is very deep and dirty, but the Town itself is clean, standing on a rising Hill. The Church is a good Building. Sir *Robert Hitcham*, by his Will, ordered that Twenty poor Children of the Parish of *Debenham*, should be taught at his School at *Framlingham*; which being impossible, an Ordinance was obtained from *Oliver Cromwell*, for a School and Maintenance of a Schoolmaster at *Debenham*, out of the Estate of the said Sir *Robert Hitcham*. In consequence whereof 20 *l. per Ann.* was appointed for a Master at *Debenham*. Here is a mean Market on *Fridays*, and a Fair *June* 24.

The Manor, Impropriation and Advowson of the Vicarage did belong to the Priory of *Butley*, and were granted by *Henry* VIII. *A.D.* 1542, to *Francis Framlingham*; from whom they came about the Year 1600 to the *Gaudys*, who had their Seat at *Crows*-Hall, in this Parish. Sir *Charles Gaudy*, of *Crows*-Hall was created a Baronet 29 *April* 1661. From the *Gaudys* they came by Purchase to *John Pitt*, Efq; and from the *Pitts* by Purchafe likewife to *James Bridges*, of *Bealings*, Efq; who now poffeffes them.

Mr. *Bridges* hath alfo the contiguous Manors of *Scotnetts* and *Bloodhall*.

The Prior and Convent of *Ely* had Poffeffions here in the Time of *Edward* the Confeffor.

Befides the Manors before-mentioned, here are alfo two others, *Ulverfton*-Hall and *Sackvyl*'s, which the Corporation of *Ipfwich* hold by the Will of *Henry Tooley* (who died in 1551) for charitable Ufes.

FRAMSDEN. *Roger de Montealto* or *Monthalt*, paid a Fine to *Ipfwich* in King *John*'s Time, for Freedom from Toll for his Villains in *Framfden*; and *Roger Montcalto* died 25 *Edward* I. feifed of the Manor of *Framfden* in *Suffolk*, leaving his Brother *Robert* his Heir; who, for want of Iffue, fettled this Manor 1 *Edw.* III. upon *Ifabel*, Mother to the King, for Life; and, after her Deceafe, to *John Eltham*, Brother to the King, and his Heirs for ever. The Church was impropriated about 20 *Edward* III. to the Minoreffes without *Aldgate, London*. They both belong to the Right Hon. the Earl of *Dyfart*. Here is a Yearly Fair upon *Afcenfion*-Day.

PETTAUGH. This Manor belonged formerly to *Leifton*-Abbey, and was granted 28 *Henry* VIII. to *Charles Brandon* Duke of *Suffolk*. It is now, with the Advowfon of the Church, vefted in ——— *Bennet*, of *Bath*, Efq;

THORP, is a Hamlet of *Afhfield*, and belongeth to *James Bridges*, Efq;

WINSTON. One Manor and the Impropriation of this Church, with the Advowfon of the Vicarage belongeth to the Dean and Chapter of *Ely*. But there is another Manor which belonged formerly to the Nuns of *Brufyard*, and was granted 30 *Henry* VIII. to *Nicholas Hare*.

STOW.

Stow.

THE Hundred of *Stow* is bounded on the *North* by *Hartifmere*; on the *Weſt* by *Blackbourn* and *Thredwaſtre*; on the *South* and *Eaſt* by *Cosford*, *Boſmere*, and *Claydon* Hundreds.

BUXHALL, was the Eſtate of *Bartho. de Burgherſh*, 23 *Edward* III. It is moſt remarkable as the Birth-place of Sir *William Coppinger*, Lord-Mayor of *London*, A. D. 1512. At his Death he gave half his Eſtate to charitable Uſes, and half to his Relations, who lived here in plentiful Circumſtances.

COMBS, in 43 King *Edward* III. was the Lordſhip of *Robert de Ufford*; then it came into the Family of *Willoughbys* Lords of *Ereſby*; and from them to *Charles Brandon* Duke of *Suffolk*, who married the Heireſs of the other Family: It came afterwards into the Poſſeſſion of the *Dandys*. It was for ſome Time the Seat of the *Bridgmans*. *William Bridgman* (Son of the Right Rev. the Lord Biſhop of *Cheſter*, who was Brother of Sir *Orlando*, Keeper of the Great Seal in the Reign of King *Charles* II.) was Clerk of the Council in the Reigns of King *Charles* II. King *James* II. King *William* and Queen *Mary*. His Son *Orlando Bridgman*, Eſq; rebuilt the Hall; which, after his Death, was ſold to Mr. *Crowley*; and by his Heirs not long ſince pulled down.

Another Manor here was granted to *Dartford* Nunnery; and afterwards in 35 King *Henry* VIII. to Sir *Richard Greſham*, Knt.

CHILTON,

CHILTON, is now a Hamlet of *Stow*.

CREETING *St. Peter*, or *West-Creeting*, is a Rectory in this Hundred: The three other *Creetings* are in the Hundred of *Bosmere*. The Manor and Advowson of this Church were very lately vested in the Heirs of Mr. *Glover*, of *Frostenden*; and the Manor is now vested in Mr. *Brograve*. See Hundred of *Bosmere* and *Claydon*.

DAGWORTH, is a Hamlet of *Newton*. *William* Lord *Furnival* married *Thomasine*, Daughter of Sir *John de Dagworth*, and thereby obtained this Manor; he died seised of it 6 *Richard* II. *Thomas Nevil*, Brother to *Ralph* Earl of *Westmorland*, having married *Joan* the Heir of the said Lord *Furnival*, had Livery of this Manor 7 *Ric.* II. and *William de la Pole* died seised of it 28 *Henry* VI.

EXNING, or IXNING, a Village situated in the very utmost Bounds of this County towards *Cambridgeshire*, is with *Newmarket* reckoned in this Hundred of *Stow*. It was formerly of greater Note than it is at present. It is said, here *Ethelreda* Daughter of King *Anna*, was born. Here *Ralph* Earl of the *East-Angles* conspired against *William* the Conqueror; and from hence *Harvey*, first Bishop of *Ely* made a Way to *Ely*; and in digging thro' Devil's Dyke near *Ixning* some Pieces of ancient Coins were found; but now it is a Town of no Note. King *William Rufus* gave the Church of *Exelinges*, in the Diocese of *Norwich*, to the Abbey of *Battel* in *Sussex*; and the Rectory and Advowson of the Vicarage of *Exning* in *Suffolk* were granted to the Dean and Chapter of *Canterbury* 33 *Henry* VIII. as Part of the Possessions of *Battel* Abbey. *Elizabeth*, the Wife of *John* Lord *Comyn*, and afterwards the Wife of *Richard Talbot*, being one of the Heirs of *Audemere de Valence*, 18 *Edward* II. as her Purparty, *inter alia*, had the Manor of *Ixning* in *Suffolk*.

Great FINBOROUGH. The Defcendants of *Ranulf Glanvile* gave Poffeffions here to the Prior and Convent of *Butley*, who had the Rectory and Advowfon of the Vicarage till the Diffolution; but *A. D.* 1559, they were granted to the Bifhop of *Ely*, in Exchange. The Manor was 3 *Edward* II. in *Ralph* Lord *Pipard*. *William Wollafton*, Efq; hath a fine Seat in this Parifh, which hath been greatly improved by him.

Little FINBOROUGH. This Church was impropriated to *Bricet* Priory, and given with that to King's College, *Cambridge*.

GIPPING, is a Hamlet of *Newton*; it hath its Name from its Situation near the Rife of one of thofe Springs, which form the River *Gippen*. It is chiefly noted for being the Refidence of the Family of *Tyrell*. They are defcended from Sir *Walter Tyrell*, Knt. who held the Lordfhip of *Langham* in *Effex*, at the Time of the general Survey. *William Tyrell*, of *Gipping*, was the fecond Son of Sir *Walter Tyrell*, who was the eighth Knight in a lineal Defcent from Sir *Walter* firft named. He was the Father of *James Tyrell*, Captain of *Guifnes* in *France*, in the Reign of King *Henry* VII. and from him is defcended the prefent Proprietor of *Gipping*, now a Minor.

HALSTON, or HARLESTON. The Manor and Advowfon of the Rectory were granted, as Parcel of the Poffeffions of *Butley* Priory, to *Charles* Vifcount *Lifle*, 31 *Henry* VIII.

HAUGHLEY, is varioufly written in old Records: Near the Church are the Remains of a very ftrong Caftle, which was, moft probably, a *Saxon* Work. It is of a Figure inclining to a Square, fortified with a deep Ditch or Moat, and (except on the North-fide) a Rampire proportionable,

tionable, and still entire. Towards the North upon a high artificial Hill, surrounded also with a deep Moat, and of steep Ascent, stood the Keep, or strong Tower; the Foundation of which, now remaining, is of great Thickness, and in a manner circular. On the West-part is a pretty large Spot of Ground, in Form resembling an oblong Square, which seems to have been an Out-work of the Castle; the East-side thereof abuts upon the Moats beforementioned, and is somewhat irregular. The North and West Sides are rectangular, and encompassed with a lesser Moat; as was, perhaps, the South-end, or Side; tho' there is now no appearance of it. The Ground which these several Works take up, and the Areas they inclose, amount in the whole to upwards of seven Acres. This, without doubt, was called *Hageneth*-Castle, which was in the Custody of *Ralph de Broc*, and was demolished by *Robert* Earl of *Leicester*, 13 *Oct.* 1173. (See *Fornham*, in *Thedwastre*.) This Castle afterwards belonged to the *de Uffords*, Earls of *Suffolk*; the last of whom is said to have died seised of it 43 *Edward* III. The present Proprietor is *Richard Ray*, Esq.

The Manor and Park were the Estate of *Charles Brandon* Duke of *Suffolk*, and came to the Crown by Purchase or Exchange with him. Afterwards they were granted to Sir *John Sulyard*, of *Wetherden*. (See p. 193.) The Manor is very large and extensive: The Lord of it had formerly a Jurisdiction of *Oyer* and *Terminer*, trying all Causes in his own Court. At a Court holden 15 *Edw.* IV. the Lands, Tenements, &c. of *John Buxton* of *Stow*, were seised; for that he had vexed one *William Turner* by the Writ of our Lord the King, contrary to the ancient Custom of the Manor, that no Tenant should prosecute any other Tenant, in any Court saving this. And there are other like Instances, so late as the eleventh Year of Queen *Elizabeth*.

At another Court in the same Year it was ordered, that the Abbot of *Hales* in *Gloucestershire*, to whom the Parishes

rishes of *Haughley* and *Shelland* were impropriated, should erect a new Pair of Gallows in *Luberlow*-Field in *Haughley*, under the Penalty of Forty Shillings. And, in the 8th Year of King *Edward* IV. *William Baxteyn* held certain Lands by the Service of finding a Ladder for the Lords Gallows.

This was an ancient Market-Town, out of the Ruins of which *Stow* seems to have risen. For in 3 *Edward* IV. *William Hoxon* of *Stow*, was fined, for lying in wait near the Town of *Haughley*, and buying Chickens, Eggs, &c. And in 31 *Henry* VIII. the Butchers of *Stow* were amerced 3*s*. 4*d*. because they sold the Meat out of the Market on a Market-day, contrary to the Custom of this Manor. In the Year following the Amercement was advanced to 6*s*. 8*d*. but the Market hath been long disused. Here is a Fair Yearly on *August* 15, being the Assumption of the Virgin *Mary*; to whom the Church is dedicated.

NEW-MARKET, at the Extremity of the County, is a well-built Thorough-fare Town, consisting chiefly of one long Street, so situated that the *North*-side of the Street is in *Suffolk*, and the *South*-side in *Cambridgeshire*. There are two Churches, St. *Mary*'s in *Suffolk*, and *All-Saints* in *Cambridgeshire*. His Majesty hath a House here for his Residence during the Races; and there are many good modern Houses built by Noblemen and Gentlemen, who delight in Horse-coursing, and sometimes condescend to countenance that Sport with their Presence.

There are two annual Fairs, one on the *Tuesday* in *Whitsun*-Week; the other *October* 28. Here is also a good Market on *Tuesdays*; and a Free-School, which was endowed by King *Charles* II. The Town is supported not by Merchandise or Manufactures of any Kind, but by its Situation upon a considerable Road, and by the Company which frequent the Horse-Races on the neighbouring Heath.

About

About two Miles *West* of the Town is the *Devil's-Dyke*, by the Vulgar so called, who readily ascribe to him what they cannot account for. It is also called *Reche-Dyke*, from a little Market-Town at the Beginning of it. From *Reche* it crosses the Heath near to *Stickworth*. It was formerly the Boundary between the *East-Angles* and the *Mercians*; and is now the Boundary between the Bishopricks of *Norwich* and *Ely*. It is uncertain who was the Founder of so great a Work; some ascribe it to King *Canute*, but that cannot be true; for *Abbo*, who mentioned it, died before *Canute* began his Reign: Besides, the Purpose for which he is said to have done it, was far from being equivalent to the Expence of such a Work, *viz.* as a Mark beyond which the King's Purveyors were not to come towards *Bury*. It is most probable, it was cast up in the Reign of King *Edmund*; for *Matthew Florilegus* declares, that the Battle against *Ethelwolf* was fought between St. *Edmund*'s two Ditches. The other Ditch is about five Miles farther towards *Cambridge*, now called *Seven-mile* Dyke; formerly *Fleam* Dyke.

NEWTON. *Margaret Pole*, Mother of Cardinal *Pole*, and Countess of *Salisbury*, who was beheaded in the Seventieth Year of her Age, died seised of *Newton*-Hall in *Suffolk*, then valued at 17 *l. per Ann.* See *Stow*.

ONEHOUSE, probably belonged formerly to the *Weylands*; it was certainly the Estate of *Bartholomew Burgbersh*, for he died seised of it 43 *Edw.* III. See *Witnesham*.

SHELLAND, was the Lordship of the *Bourchiers*, Earls of *Essex*; from whom it descended to the Family of *Devereux*, and was sold in 1591 by that great, but unhappy Favourite of Queen *Elizabeth*, *Robert Devereux*, Earl of *Essex*. The Manor of *Rockylls* in *Shelland*, formerly belonged to the *Drurys*; a Family of great Note in this County. These Manors, with their Demesnes, are now the Estate of *Richard Ray*, Esq.

STOWMARKET, is so called to distinguish it from *Stowlantoft*, *Stow-Upland*, *West-Stow*, &c. and stands very near the Centre of the County; but *Needham* is something nearer it. It is also situated near the Junction of the three Rivulets, which form the River *Gippen*. Those which rise near *Gipping* and *Wetherden* wash the *East*-side of the Town, and the other which rises at *Rattlesden* meets them on the *South*-End of the Town at *Combs-Ford*. The chief Ornament of this Town is the Church and Spire-steeple. The Parishes of *Stow-market* and *Stow-upland*, are now consolidated; but they have still distinct Officers for each Parish. K. *Henry* II. gave the Churches of *Blyburgh* and *Stow-market*, with all the Chapels thereunto belonging, to the Abbey of *Chick*, or *St. Osyth*, in *Essex*; and the Manor of *Stow market*, the Rectory and Advowson of the Vicarages, the Rectory of *Newton*, and the Advowson of the Vicarage, and the Rectories or Impropriations of *Gipping* and *Dagworth* (Chapels of *Newton*) were granted 38 *Henry* VIII. as Parcel of the Possessions of *St. Osyth*, to *Thomas Darcie*. The Manor of *Thorney* near *Stow-market*, belonged to the Nuns of *Campesse*, and was granted 37 *Henry* VIII. to *Thomas* Duke of *Norfolk*; and is now vested in the Earl of *Jersey*.

Richard de *Amourdevil* obtained a Grant of a Market and Fair here, 12 *Edward* III. The Market is on *Thursday*; and they have now two Fairs, one on *June* 29, St. *Peter*'s Day, to whom the Church was dedicated; the other is a Lamb Fair, on *Lammas* Day *August* 1. The Manor of *Stow-market*, otherwise *Abbots*-Hall, and the Fairs and Markets, are now vested in *William Lynch* of *Ipswich*, Esq.

WETHERDEN. *Roger de Scales* obtained a Grant of Free Warren here, 18 *Edward* I. This Grant was confirmed to *John Sulyard*, who was seised of the said Warren 8 *Edward* IV. and confirmed again to *John Sulyard*
and

and *Ann* his Wife 1 *Richard* III. This was Judge *Sulyard* afterwards mentioned; and his Lady was the Daughter of *John Andrews*, of *Bailham** in *Suffolk*, by *Elizabeth Scratton*; which *Elizabeth* was lineally descended from *Humfrey Bohun*, Earl of *Hereford* and *Essex*, by his Countess *Elizabeth* Daughter of King *Edward* I. We have lately received the following Account of this respectable Family, which we shall insert pretty nearly in the Words it was sent.

In this Village is a very neat Church, the Porch of which, and a very large Isle continuing from thence to the Chancel, was built by Sir *John Sulyard*, of *Wetherden-Hall*; which Sir *John*, in the Pedigree of the *Sulyards*, is called only a Judge; but in the Baronetage of *England*, under the Title of *Rous*, is said to have been *Lord Chief Justice* of *England*. Round the Porch and along to the Chancel on the Stones next above the Ground, are finely carved the Arms and Quarterings of this ancient Family, to the Time the Isle was built. In this Parish is the Place called *Wetherden*-Hall, which was the Seat and Residence of the said Sir *John*; and, by the Ruins of it, appears to have been a very large and noble Building. It remained the Seat of this Family until the Reign of Queen *Mary*, and was at that time inhabited by Sir *John Sulyard*, the Descendant of the first-mentioned Sir *John*. This last Gentleman was a Soldier, and by the Memoirs now extant in the Family, he appears to have been the first who took Arms, and levied Men, in the Defence of his Sovereign, when she fled from the Usurpation of Lady *Jane Grey*. The underwritten is the Mandate (in the very Words

---

* The other Daughter of *John Andrews*, and Co-heiress with Sir *John Sulyard*'s Lady, married *Thomas Windsor*, whose Son Sir *Andrews Windsor* was afterwards created Lord *Windsor*. The Family of *Andrews* removed their Seat to *Bailham*, from *Ipswich*. See p. 42.

Words and Spelling of that Time) he carried from the Queen, when he guarded and protected her Person in the Castle of *Framlingham*.

" *Mary*, the Queen,
" *Henry Bedingfielde*,
" Theys ar to require and comaunde you to give most
" faythfull and assured Orders to this Berer our trustie
" and well-beloved Svient Sur *John Sulyard*; and in any
" wyse as ye love us and tendre our Favor not to fayle
" to accomplish and putte in execution that which he
" shall declare unto you from us to be our Pleasure, so
" fare ye hartylye well. From *Fframsn*. the 23 off *Jan*."

So soon as the Queen was restored to her Throne, she made a Grant to Sir *John* of the Park and Manor of *Haughley*, for the eminent Services he had done her; and he built the fine old Seat that is now standing in the Park. This Gentleman lived until the 12th Year of Queen *Elizabeth*; and to him succeeded his Son *Edward*, who suffered much in this Reign for Recusancy, both in his Person and Fortune: Having been a Prisoner a great Part of his Life, as appears by Transcripts from the Roll of Recusants. He was one of the first, if not the *very first*, who was convicted. And this is to be observed to his Honour, that though he adhered, under every Disadvantage, to the Religion of his Ancestors, he held their Loyalty as firmly evidenced, by his Denial of the Power of the See of *Rome* to depose the Queen, in the following Declaration: " I *Edward Sulyarde*, of *Suff*. Esquier, doe
" acknowledge our most gratious Sov'eigne Ladie Queene
" *Elizabeth*, to be our undoubted lawfull and onlie Queene
" of *Englande* and *Irlande*, and no other forreyne Prince,
" notwithstandinge any Excommunication, under whose
" Power are all Persons both Ecclesiasticall and Tem-
" porall, within any her Majesties Dominions. And also
" by this doe manifest myselfe bounden and readie, as
" becometh

" becometh a true and duetifull Subject, with Body,
" Lands and Goodds, to defend her Highnefs againft the
" Force of any Prince, Pope, Potentate, Prelate, or what-
" otherfoever her Majefties Enemies, which God graunte
" fhe may overcome, and longe contynue her profperous
" Raigne over us. Written in the xxiiijth of *October*,
" 1588.

" By me *Edwarde Sulyarde*."

Declarations of the fame Tenor were figned by divers other Knights and Gentlemen, of the fame Communion; among whom we muft not omit the Mention of *Edward Rookwood*, Efq; of this County, whofe Family is related to that of *Sulyard*; and the Heir of it now enjoys a fair Fortune at *Coldham*-Hall in *Stanningfield*, near *Bury*.

The following Petition of this Gentleman and Warrant, by that great Minifter *Walfingham*, will evince his Sufferings at that Time.

" To the Right Honourable the Lords of her Majefties
" Mofte Honourable Privie Councell.

" In moft humble wife befeecheth your Lordfhips your
" humble Supplicant *Edward Suliard*, of *Wetherden* in
" the Countie of *Suffolk*, Efquier. That whereas your
" Supplicant, upon the Statute of Recufancie hath paid
" Seaventein hundred and threfcore Pounds, and yet is
" to paie into the Exchequour to her Majefties Ufe in
" *Mighelmas* Tearme, now next commyng the Some of
" C.C.C.C. Marks and vij *l*. and for the Accomplifh-
" ment thereof ftandeth yet utterlie unprovided and dif-
" abled, by reafon of diverfe Chardges which heretofor
" and yet dailie fall upon him, as of late your Supplicant
" having Libertie by your Lordfhips Graunt to repaire
" to his Houfe in the Contrie, to make Provifion of
" ftame Money which he then ftoode chardged to paie
" to her Majefties Ufe for his faid Recufancie, in which

" Tyme

"Tyme of his being in the Contrie he received a Privie
"Seale from her Majeftie for the Loane of L¹. which
"Some according to his Duetue he paid out of the faid
"Money which he had provided for her Majefties Ufe,
"and being enforced to make up that Some againe for
"the Difcharge of the faid Paiment in the Exchequour,
"did fend up to *London* vj fatt Oxen to be fold for pre-
"fent Money, which Oxen comming to *London* v of
"them were taken for her Majefties Provifion, for which
"your Supplicant hath received no Paiment, though they
"weare muche underpraifed, in refpect of that which
"was offered for them in prefent Money; fo that your
"Supplicant for the Difcharge of his faid former Pay-
"ment was conftrained to take up other Sommes of
"Money for the fatisfying again wherof your Suppli-
"cant ftandeth ftill endangered alfo: And moreover,
"may it pleafe your Honours to take fome compaffion
"of your Supplicant's faid Troubles, having ever lyved
"a true Man to her Majeftie; not long before the Time
"of your Supplicant his faid former Commitment, a Sen-
"tence paffed againft him and one other deceafed in the
"Court of Awdience for C.C.C.X.X. *l.* from which
"your Supplicant (by reafon of his Imprifonment) cold
"not apeale, and at this prefent ftandeth in great
"danger to be urged with the Paiment thereof, unlefs
"by your Lordfhips he being allowed Libertie may feeke
"his beft Remedie in that Behalf. It maie therefore
"pleafe your good Lordfhips in regarde of the diftreffed
"Eftate of your faid humble Supplicant to graunt to
"him the Contynuance of his Libertie at his owne Howfe
"within the faid Countie of *Suffolk*, as well for the
"better and more fpeedie preparing of the faid Sommes
"of Money payable to her Majeftie in *Michaelmas* Tearme
"next, as for the obteyning of fome Remedie or Relief
"touching the faid Somme of C.C.C.X.X. *l.* for which
"Sentence is given againft him and the other Partie as
"afore-

"aforesaid, without which your Honors Graunt of Li-
"bertie he shall be forced to bring up his Wyfe, Chil-
"dren, and Famelie to *London*, which he cannot bring
"to pass in anie reasonable Sorte, but to his great Charge,
"extreame Losse, and Hindrance, which in no wise he
"can long endure, but in short Tyme will be his uttre
"Ouerthrow and Undoing; and your Supplicant (as in
"Dutie he is bound) shall daily pray to Almightie God
"for your Lordships in honor and happie Estate long
"to contynew.

"Whereas *Edwarde Syliarde*, of *Wetherden*, in the
"Countie of *Suffolke*, Gent. having ben a long Tyme
"restrayned of his Libertie for Mater of Religion, was
"lately for certain Considerations permitted to remayne
"at his Howse in *Suffolk*; and yet notwithstanding, as
"it is informed, hath synce that Tyme ben troubled and
"molested onely for Recusancy. Thease are in her
"Majesties Name to will and require you, and every of
"you to whom it may appertayne, to forbear to sue or
"trouble him any further in respect of his said Recusancy
"untill you shall understand her Majesties further Plea-
"sure herein, and theas shall be his sufficient Warrant
"in that Behalf. Dated at my Howse at *Barnelmes* the
"19th of *June*, 1586.

"*Fra. Walsyngham.*

"L. S.

"To all Justices of Assize, Justices of Peace, Sheriffs,
"Bayliffs, Pursuivants, and Messeangers of the
"Chamber, and all other her Majesties Officers and
"loving Subjects to whom it may apperteyne, and
"to every of them."

To this *Edward Sulyard* succeeded another Sir *John Sulyard*, to whom all these Forfeitures and Penalties were remitted by King *James* the First; who conferred the Honour of Knighthood, both on the said Sir *John*, and his Son *Edward* in his Father's Life-time; and they lived on their Family Estate in Peace and Quietude till the great Rebellion, when the Loyalty of Sir *Edward* procured the Confinement of his Person, and the Sequestration of two Parts in three of his Estate, during the detestable Usurpation of *Cromwell*. At the Restoration Sir *Edward* was restored to his Estates and Liberty: This Gentleman married the Daughter of *William* Lord *Sturton*; but, dying without Issue, his Estate devolved on his next Brother *Ralph*, who married *Elizabeth* the Daughter of *James Willford*, of *Wansworth*, Esq; and by her had a numerous Issue. To him succeeded *Edward* his eldest Son, who married *Penelope*, the eldest Daughter of Sir *Edward Gage*, of *Hengrave*, and by her had many Children. At the Revolution it does not appear this Gentleman at all meddled, or at all suffered; but continuing obstinately a Papist, he was left out of the Commission of the Peace. His next Brother Lieutenant-Colonel *Thomas Sulyard* followed his unhappy Master abroad, and entered afterwards into the *Dutch* Service, married a Lady of *Boisleduc* in *Brabant*, and there died; his Issue are still living in *Flanders*; and on Failure of the elder Branch are next Heirs of this ancient Family Estate, which is now in the Possession of *Edward Sulyard*, the Grandson of the last mentioned *Edward*. The Sufferings of this Family are here mentioned to induce Gentlemen who are so unhappy as to adhere to the Church of *Rome*, to make a Comparison between the Severity of former Reigns, and the great Clemency and Mercy of the late and present Reigns; which have kept, and still keep the penal Laws, like a sharp Sword in the Scabbard, to be drawn only on Defence and Provocation.

BOSMERE

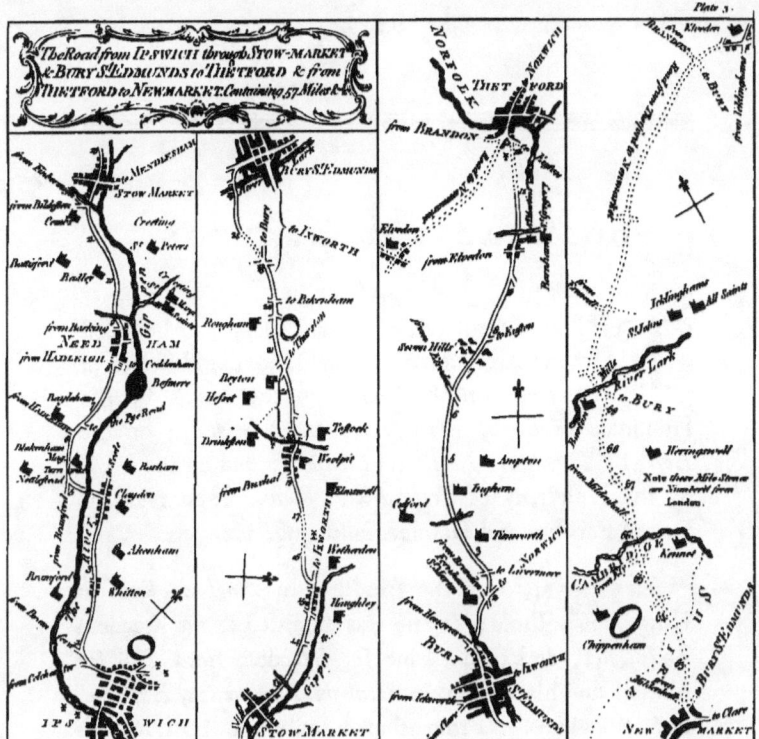

BOSMERE and CLAYDON.

THE Hundreds of *Bosmere* and *Claydon* are bounded by the Liberties of *Ipswich* and the Hundred of *Samford*, on the *South*; on the *North*, by the Hundreds of *Stow*, *Hartesmere*, and *Thredling*; on the *East*, by *Thredling*, *Loes*, and *Carlford*; and on the *West*, by the Hundreds of *Cosford* and *Stow*. It contains the several Parishes and Hamlets following, viz.

AKENHAM, was the Lordship of *Hugh le Rous* in King *John*'s Time; for he was admitted to his Freedom of *Ipswich*, and paid a Fine for Freedom from Toll for himself and his Villains in *Akenham*, *Hemingston*, *Hasketon*, and elsewhere. From that Family the Hall had its Name, now corruptly called *Rice*-Hall. In the Reign of *Edward* IV. it was *Philip Barnard*'s; then *Whitepole*'s, who sold it to Mr. *Hawes*, Town-Clerk of *Ipswich*. It is now vested in *William Plumer*, Esq. This Church was lately consolidated with *Claydon* by Sir *Thomas Gooch*, Bart. Bishop of *Norwich*. The Advowson of both being now vested in the Rev. *George Drury*, late Rector thereof.

ASHBOCKING. This Church was impropriated 24. *July* 1326, to the Prior and Convent of *Christ-Church*, *Canterbury*, who were Patrons of the Vicarage till the Reformation. The Crown is now Patron; and the Vicar enjoys both great and small Tithes.

Here is a Manor called *Ketts de Campo*, now vested in the Earl of *Dysart*; and another Manor called *Ash*-Hall, belonging to Capt. *Cockerell*.

BADLEY, formerly the Seat of the *Mortimers.* The *Pooleys* had it from about the Year 1460. *Richard Gipps,* Efq; married an Heirefs of the *Pooleys,* and fold it to Mrs. *Crowley*; and it is now vefted in the Earl of *Afhburnham,* and *Charles Boone,* Efq; Member for *Caftle-Rifing*; who married the two Heireffes of the *Crawley* Family. The Impropriation was given to the Templars by *Robert Fitz-Jefferey* and *Beatrice* his Wife, and confirmed to them by *Richard Clare* Earl of *Hertford.* There was a Chauntry here valued at 10 *l. per Ann.*

BARHAM. The Manor with the Advowfon of the Rectory belonged to the Prior and Convent of *Ely,* which with a Wood called *Bergham* Coppice, were granted 37 *Henry* VIII. to *John Southwell,* Efq; there is a noble Monument for one of the Family in the Chancel: It was afterwards in the Family of *Wood*; then in the *Webbs,* who fold it to Mr. *Burch,* whofe Son now enjoys it. But the Advowfon of the Rectory is in *Nicholas Bacon,* of *Shrubland*-Hall, Efq.

BARKING. The Manor of *Barking* with the Advowfon of the Rectory belonged to the Church of *Ely,* from the Time of King *Edward* the Confeffor to the fourth Year of Queen *Elizabeth,* when they were alienated from it. Queen *Elizabeth* feems to have kept them in her own Hands; for Sir *Francis Needham* bought them of King *James* I. His eldeft Son fold them to *Francis Theobald,* Efq; whofe Son is mentioned with Honor for his Skill in Oriental Languages by Dr. *Caftle,* in his *Lexicon.* They now belong to Mrs. *Crowley's* Heirs. *(See Badley.)*

BATTISFORD. Here was an Hofpital of St. *John* of *Jerufalem,* of the yearly Value of 53*l.* 10*s.* which at the Diffolution was granted to Sir *Richard Grefham.* One of the Manors in this Parifh belonged formerly to
the

the Bishop of *Norwich*; but it was surrendered by Act of Parliament to King *Henry* VIII. who granted it in 1545 to Sir *Richard Gresham*, and *Richard Billingford*. *Philip Bacon*, Esq; had his Seat at the Hall, in Right of his Mother, which hath lately been taken down.

BAYLHAM, about the Year 1300 was the Lordship of *John de Burnaville* and of his Descendants, till near the Year 1400. About 1450 it came to *John Andrews*, whose Daughter *Elizabeth* marrying to *Thomas Windsor*, Esq; it became the Possession of their Son Sir *Andrews Windsor*, of *Stanwell*, afterwards Lord *Windsor*. The Manor and Advowson is now vested in *Nathanael Acton*, Esq.

BLAKENHAM *Magna*. The Manor and Advowson here was given to the Abbey of *Bece* in *Normandy*, by *Walter Gifford*, Earl of *Buckingham*; and was given by King *Henry* VI. to the Provost and Fellows of *Eaton*.

BLAKENHAM *Parva*. The Lords of *Nettlestead* were Patrons of this Rectory, when the *Tibetots*, *Despensers*, and *Wentworths* had that Lordship. The Manor and Advowson were lately in the *Milners*, but now are vested in the Right Hon. Lord *Orwell*.

BRAMFORD, in 22 *Edward* I. was the Lordship and Demesne of *Robert de Tibetot*; but for many Years the Family of *Acton* has had their Seat here. The Church, with the *Berewick* of *Burstal* and *Albrighteston* belonging to it, was given to *Battle* Abbey by King *William Rufus*; and that Abbey had the Rectory and were Patrons of the Vicarage till 33 *Henry* VIII. when it was granted to *Christ-Church Canterbury*, in Exchange. The Manor here hath an uncommon Tenure belonging to it; for the Tenants hold of the Lord by a Lease of 21 Years, renewed from Time to Time upon a Fine; and, upon

the

the Death of a Tenant, or an Alienation, the new Tenant is admitted to the Remainder of that Term unexpired; so that the Lord hath more Profit from the Lands, than the Tenants have. There was another Manor in *Bramford* belonging to the Bishop of *Ely*, as late as the Year 1547, which seems to have been in the Hands of *Francis Colborne*, in 1593.

BRICET, was remarkable for a Priory founded by *Radulfus Fitzbrian* and *Emma* his Wife, and made a Cell to *Nobiliac* in *France*, which occasioned its being suppressed as an alien Priory; and the Revenues of it were thereupon granted to the Provost and Fellows of *King*'s College in *Cambridge*, who are Lords of the Manor, and Lessors of the Tithes.

BRICET *Parva*. The Prior and Convent of *Cluniac* Monks at *Thetford* had the Advowson of the Church and twelve Acres of Demesne Land, of the Gift of *Robert de Reims*. The Church, having been long down, hath been annexed to *Offton* ever since the Year 1503. *Talmach*-Hall, in this Place, is said to have been sometime the Seat of the *Kemps*, but lately in the Family of the *D'Autreys*; and of *John Luther*, Esq; Member for *Essex*, who is Lord of the Manor of *Little Bricet*, alias *Talmash*-Hall.

CLAYDON, is a thorough-fare Village, where the Road divides; that right forward from *Ipswich*, leads to *Norwich*; and that on the left, to *Bury St. Edmunds*. *Thomas Southwell*, Esq; had the Manor of *Claydon*, 9 *Elizabeth*. The Manor of *Claydon*-Hall is now vested in *Nathanael Acton*, Esq. The Patronage of the Church seems to have belonged to the Manor of *Akenham*; but the Churches are now consolidated, and the Patronage of both is now vested in the Rev. *George Drury*, late Rector thereof.

Con-

CODDENHAM. This Church was given to *Royston* Priory by *Eustachius de Merc*, the Founder of that Priory, about the Year 1220. The Impropriation was granted 36 *Henry* VIII. to *Jo. Atkyns*; and coming into the Hands of the Rev. Mr. *Balthazar Guardemau* Vicar here, was piously by him settled on Trustees for the Use of the Vicar for the Time being for ever. The chief Manor here of *Dennies*, is now vested in *Nicholas Bacon* and *Mileson Edgar*, Esqrs. Another Manor called the *Vicarage*, is vested in the Vicar for the Time being; and the Manor of *Shrubland*-Hall in this Parish, has for some time been in the *Bacons*, now remaining to *Nicholas Bacon*, Esq; whose Grandfather Sir *Nicholas Bacon* was created Knight of the Bath at the Coronation of *Charles* II.

CREETING *All Saints*, and CREETING *St. Olaves*. There are four contiguous Parishes in *Suffolk*, to whom the Names of *Creeting* is common: That of *Creeting St. Peter*, already mentioned in *Stow* Hundred, and those three which will be mentioned here. For, tho' *Creeting All-Saints* is in the Deanery of *Stow* and Archdeaconry of *Sudbury*, it is in the Hundred of *Bosmere*, as well as *Creeting St. Olave*, and *Creeting St. Mary*. The Church of *Creeting All-Saints* is a very ancient Building; but that of *St. Olave* hath been long down; for which Reason those two Rectories were consolidated about the Year 1711. *St. Olave's* was standing in 1532, when *John Pinkeney* ordered his Body to be buried in the Chancel. The Manor of *Gratinges* in *Creeting St. Olave's*, was given by *Robert* Earl of *Moreton* in *Normandy*, and of *Cornwal* in *England*, in the Time of *William* the Conqueror, to the Abbey of *Grestein* in *Normandy*, which in After-times made it a Cell to that Monastery, and annexed the Manor to it, as it was held 9 *Edward* I. It was taken care of by some Monks belonging thereunto, or by their Agent the Prior of *Wilmington* in *Sussex*, their chief Cell in
England.

England. King *Edward* III. granted this to *Tydeman de Lymburgh,* a Merchant; and afterwards, about the Year 1347, the Abbot and Convent sold it, by the King's Licence to Sir *Edmund de la Pole,* by the Names of the Manors of *Mikelfeld* and *Creeting.* The last Priors of *St. Olave*'s were *William Beverley* in 1468, *Thomas Baget* in 1492, and *William Dale* in 1519. The Manor and Advowson of *Creeting All-Saints,* as well as *St. Olaves,* were vested and continued for a considerable Time in the ancient and reputable Family of *Bridgman*; whose Heirs in 1753 sold and conveyed the same, together with their other Estates in these two Parishes, and the other *Creetings,* to *Philip Champion Crespigny,* Esq; of *Doctors Commons,* the present Owner and Possessor thereof.

CREETING *St. Mary,* is also a Rectory; the Parish Church of which is close to *Creeting All-Saints*; and as they stand very near each other upon an Eminence, they are easily seen at some Miles Distance, and are commonly called *Creeting*-two-Churches. *Creeting St. Mary* was in ancient Times most usually styled the Priory of *Creeting,* and was a Cell to the Abbey of *Bernay* in *Normandy*; and, after the Suppression of those foreign Houses, was made Part of the Endowment of *Eton* College; and it now belongs to the Provost and Fellows of that College.

CROWFIELD, is a Hamlet of *Coddenham,* and hath nothing worthy of Remark but the Hall, which formerly belonged to the Family of *Woodhouse,* who sold it to *John Harbottle*; one of whose Daughters and Coheiresses married to *Henry Wingfield.* It was lately the Seat of *Henry Harwood,* Esq; then of *Theodore Eccleston*; and now of *William Middleton,* Esq; who is also Lord of the Manor.

DARMSDEN, is a Hamlet of *Barking.* The Manor of *Tafton-Hall* in *Darmsden* belonged to Lord *Windsor,* A.D. 1596. It is now in the Heirs of Mr. *Crowley.*

FLOWTON.

FLOWTON.

GOSBECK. Here seems to have been three Manors in Queen *Elizabeth*'s Time, *viz.* one belonging to Mr. *Jermyn*, to which the Advowson was appendant; and this, we think, belongeth now to Lord *Orwell*; another belonging to Mr. *Stibes*; and another called *Ketsalfield*, belonging to the *Talmachs*.

HEMINGSTON. Mr. *Cambden*'s Account of this Place is this: "That in it *Baldwin le Pettcur* (observe the "Name) held Lands by Serjeantry, for which he was "obliged, every *Christmas*-day, to perform before our "Lord the King of *England*, one *Saltus*, one *Sufflatus*, "and one *Bumbulus*; or, as it is read in another Place, "he held it by a *Saltus*, a *Sufflas*, and *Pettus*; that is, "(if I apprehend it right) he was to dance, make a noise "with his Cheeks, and let a F—t. Such was the plain "jolly Mirth of those Days. It is also observed that the "Manor of *Langhall* belonged to this Fee." *Cambd.* Vol. I. p. 443. Here is the Seat of *Richard Colville*, Esq.

HELMINGHAM. The Prioress and Nuns of *Flixton* near *Bungay* were Patrons of this Rectory, till about the Year 1320; when they gave this Patronage to the Bishop of *Norwich*, for that of *Flixton*. From that Time the Bishop was Patron till the Reformation, when the Crown claimed it, and hath presented ever since. This Parish hath been remarkable for a Family who took their Name from the Place, and had their Seat at *Crekes*-Hall, now called *Helmingham*-Hall; but it hath for many Years been more memorable for being the Seat of that very ancient and noble Family of *Tallmache*. *Tocdmag*, as the Name was then spelt, was said in Domesday Book, to possess Lands, &c. *Hugh Talmache* subscribed the Charter sans Date (about the Reign of King *Stephen*) made to the Abbefs of *Godflow*, in *Oxfordshire*. The Family was feated at *Bentley* in *Samford* Hundred, until *Lionel Talmache* of *Bentley*, married the Heir of —— *Helmingham*, of *Helmingham*, Efq; whereby he acquired the Inheritance and made this Place his Refidence. *Lionel* his Grandfon, was High-Sheriff of *Norfolk* and *Suffolk* 4 *Henry* VIII. or 1513: Again, Sir *Lionel* the Grandfon of this Gentleman was High-Sheriff of *Suffolk* 34 *Elizabeth*, and knighted by her. He was fucceeded by his Son and Heir *Lionel*, who was created a Baronet at the firft Inftitution of that Dignity, 22 *May* 1611; and was the twelfth Perfon who received that Honour. Sir *Lionel Talmache*, Grandfon of the firft Baronet, married *Elizabeth* Daughter and Heir of *William Murray*, Earl of *Dyfart* in *Scotland*; and his Son and Heir Sir *Lionel Talmache* fucceeded him in Honour and Eftate; and after the Death of his Mother (who had married for a fecond Hufband *John Maitland*, Duke of *Lauderdale*) by the Laws of *Scotland*, he became Lord *Huntingtower* and Earl of *Dyfart*. He was elected Knight of the Shire for *Suffolk* in three Parliaments called by King *William* III. and was again elected Knight of the Shire till the Act of Union 6 Queen *Anne* declared him a Peer of *Great-Britain*. He was in Queen *Anne*'s Reign Lord Lieutenant, *Cuftos Rotulorum*, and Vice-Admiral of *Suffolk*, and High-Steward of the Borough of *Ipfwich*. He had Iffue *Lionel* Lord *Huntingtower*, who died in his Father's Life-time, leaving Iffue *Lionel* his Son, who fucceeded his Grandfather in Honor and Eftate; and is the prefent Earl of *Dyfart*, Knight of the Thiftle, and High-Steward of the Borough of *Ipfwich*. The Lordfhip of this Parifh is vefted in his Lordfhip, called *Creikfhall*.

HENLEY. The *Veres* have for many Years (at leaft 200 Years) had a Seat here, which is now vefted in *Thomas Vere*, of *Norwich*, Efq; and lately one of the Reprefentatives in Parliament for that City.

MICK-

MICKFIELD. Two Manors are mentioned here, *viz.* the Manor of *Wolney*-Hall, and the Manor of *Flede*-Hall*. The firſt of which ſeems to have belonged to the alien Priory of *Greſtein* in *Normandy*, and to have been by that Convent ſold to *Tydemannus de Lymbergh*, about the Year 1347. One of theſe Manors belongeth now to *William Middleton*, of *Crowfield*, Eſq; the other to Lord *Orwell*.

NEEDHAM, is a Hamlet of *Barking*. It hath formerly had a conſiderable Trade in the Woollen Manufactory, but the Trade is now in a manner loſt: However it is pretty well built, and has a mean Market Weekly on *Wedneſdays*, but a conſiderable Fair Yearly on 28, 29, and 30th Days of *October*; which, as we ſuppoſe, is the ſame that was granted to the Biſhop of *Ely*, to be held in his Manor of *Barking*, 10 *Henry* III.

NETTLESTEAD. The Earls of *Richmond* and *Brittany* had the Lordſhip here from the Conqueſt to 17 *Henry* II. when *Conan* the laſt Earl died. Sir *Peter Mauclere* (who married *Alice* the Daughter of *Conſtance*, the only Daughter and Heireſs of *Conan*) had Livery of this Manor 15 *Henry* III. *Peter de Savoy* had a Grant of it 25 *Henry* III. *Robert Tibetot* died at *Nettleſtead*, poſſeſſed of this Manor, 25 *Edward* I. *Pain de Tibetot* died ſeiſed 7 *Edward* II. *John de Tibetot* died ſeiſed 41 *Edward* III. and *Robert de Tibetot* died ſeiſed 46 *Edward* III. leaving no Male Iſſue. After this it belonged a little while to the Family of *Deſpenſers*. About the Year 1450 it became the Eſtate of *Roger Wentworth*, whoſe Deſcendants were created Lords by *Henry* VIII. and it continued in this Family to the Time of King *Charles* I. when *Thomas Wentworth* Earl of *Cleveland* ſold it to *William Lodge*, Citizen of *London*. It ſince belonged to Mr. *John Fuller*, of *Ipſwich*; and is now veſted in the Heir of *William Bradley*,

* See *Creeting St. Olaves*, &c.

Bradley, Efq; who married the only Daughter and Heirefs of Mr. *Fuller*.

OFFTON, is remarkable for a Caftle built on a chalky Hill by *Offa*, King of the *Mercians*, after he had flain *Etheldred* King of the *Eaft-Angles*; and from him it is faid the Town took its Name. The Caftle is now fo entirely demolifhed, that not the leaft Rubbifh of it remains. The Prior and Convent of Monks at *Thetford*, had the Advowfon of the Church, and thirty Acres of Land here; and the Manor, Rectory, and Advowfon of the Vicarage were granted, as Parcel of the faid Monks Poffeffions, to *Thomas* Duke of *Norfolk* 32 *Henry* VIII. in Exchange. The Manor is now vefted in *Gideon Glanville*, Efq.

RINGSHALL. Befides the Parifh Church here was formerly a Free-Chapel belonging to the Prior and Convent of *Norwich*, endowed with thirty Acres of Land: Some Ruins of it are faid to be now remaining. The late Sir *William Barker*, Bart. of *Ireland*, had the Hall and Manor here; but, upon his Death they were fold, and are now vefted in *William Watfon*, Efq.

SOMERSHAM. The Family of *Bohun* Earls of *Northampton*, were many Years Patrons of this Rectory, and Lords of the Manor; which, with that of *Offton*, were granted to *Henry Stafford* Duke of *Buckingham*, by King *Richard* III. in 1423. *Katherine* Queen of *England* prefented to it, in Right of the Manor of *Somerfham*, which fhe had by the Grant of King *Henry* VI. The old Wills make mention of a Chapel in *Somerfham-ftreet*. The Manor and Advowfon are now vefted in *Richard Gideon Glanville*, Efq.

STONHAM-*Afpal*, is fo called from a Family of the Name of *Afpale*, or *Hafpele*, who were for many Years Lords and Patrons here. It was alfo called *Stonham Antegan*.

tegan. The Manor and Advowson of *Stonham-Aspal* is lately vested by Purchase in *William Middleton*, Esq; of *Crowfield*-Hall. In this Parish and very near the Church, a Branch of the ancient Family of *Wingfield* (see p. 171.) had a Seat called *Broughton*-Hall, and were Lords of a Manor here called *Broughton*-Hall Manor. The last Possessor whereof the Rev. *John Wingfield*, M.A. died without Issue Male; as did his Brother *Thomas* not long since, who was the last Heir-Male of this Family. *Philip Champion Crespigny*, Esq; purchased the Estate and Manor of *Broughton*-Hall, and is the present Possessor and Proprietary thereof.

STONHAM-*Earl*, is so called, because it was anciently the Lordship of *Thomas Brotherton*, Earl of *Norfolk*; and afterwards of *William Ufford*, Earl of *Suffolk*, who married the Grand-daughter of *Thomas Brotherton*. It was afterwards Sir *Thomas Gresham's*. It is now vested in *Thomas Driver*. The Duke of *Norfolk* had a Grant of a Market and Fair here, 1 *Edward* III. And all the three Parishes of *Stonham* are still a Part of the Duke of *Norfolk's* Liberty; but the Advowson of this Church is in the College of *Pembroke-Hall*, in *Cambridge*.

STONHAM-*Parva*, or *Stonham-Jernegans*, because the *Jernegans* were Lords here till the Time of *Edward* VI. (see *Horham*, in *Hoxne*;) then the *Goodwyns*, who sold the Manor to Lady *Rivers*. It is now vested in the Right Hon. Lord *Orwell*.

SWILLAND. *Bartholomew Burghersh*, and after him *Edward le Despenser* died seised of this Manor in the Time of *Edward* III. The Church was early impropriated to the Nuns of *Wykes*, in *Essex*; and the Impropriation was granted to Cardinal *Wolsey*, towards the Endowment of his College at *Ipswich*, A.D. 1528; but the Vicar hath now the great as well as small Tithes.

P   WILLISHAM.

WILLISHAM. The Church here was given by *Albert Grelli* to the Prior and Convent of the *Holy Trinity* in *Ipswich*, before the Year 1203; and, at the Diffolution, the Tenement, *Canons*, and the Impropriation, were granted as Parcel of the Poffeffions of that Priory to *Andrews* Lord *Windfor*, 31 *Henry* VIII. It was afterwards Bifhop *Brownrigg*'s; and is now vefted in the Rev. Mr. *John Leake*, and the Rev. Mr. *Upcher*; as is the Lordfhip of *Willifham*.

WESTERFIELD. See *Ipfwich*, p. 51.

WHITTON. In this Parifh is a good old Seat, commonly called the *Sparrows-Neft*, but formerly *Whitton-Hall*; lately the Refidence of *Edmund Hammond*, Efq; and now of *William Hamilton*, Efq. See p. 51.

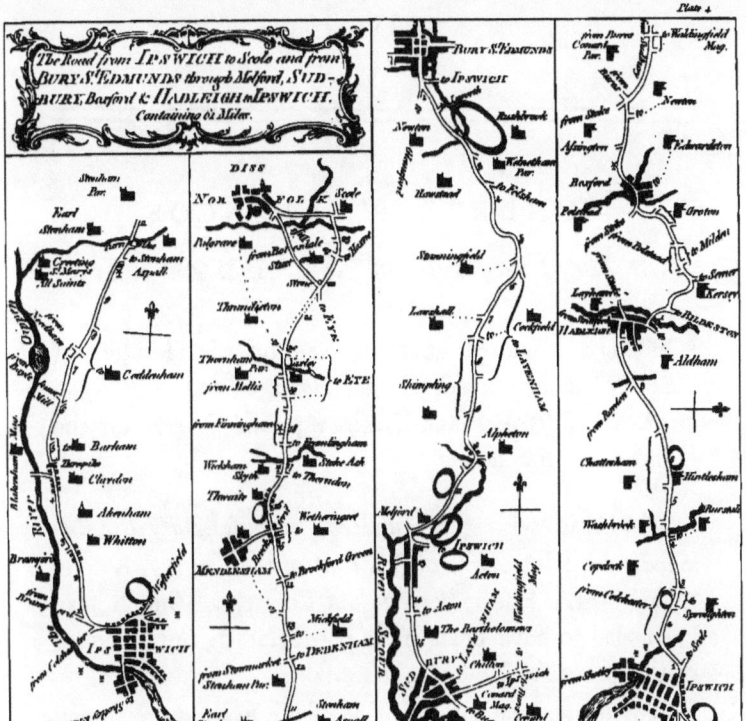

HUNDRED of THINGOE,
in the Franchise of ST. EDMUND.

THIS Hundred abutteth *East* on the Hundred of *Thedwastre*; *South*, on *Babergh* and *Risbridge*; *West*, on *Risbridge* and *Lackford*; and *North*, on the Hundred of *Blackbourn*.

We begin with this Hundred, because *Bury St. Edmunds*, the Metropolis of this Part of the County, is contained in it. Had it been in our Power, we should have been glad to have been more particular in our Account of this beautiful Town.

It is situated on the *West*-side of the River *Lark*, which is now made navigable from *Lynn* to *Fornham*, about a Mile North of this Town. It has a most beautiful inclosed Country on the *South* and *South-West*, and on the *North* and *North-West* the most delicious Champaign Fields, extending themselves to *Lynn*, and that Part of the County of *Norfolk*. The Country on the *East* is partly open, and partly inclosed. *Stow* tells us, " That
" in the Year 1608 *April* 11, being *Monday*, the Quarter-
" Sessions was held at *St. Edmundsbury*, and by Negli-
" gence an Out-Malthouse was set on Fire; from whence
" in most strange and sudden Manner, through fierce
" Winds, the Fire came to the farthest Side of the Town,
" and as it went, left some Streets and Houses safe and
" untouched. The Flame flew clean over many Houses
" near it, and did great Spoil to many fair Buildings far-
" thest off; and ceased not till it had consumed One hun-
" dred and sixty Dwelling-Houses, besides others; and
" in Damage of Wares and Houshold-stuff to the full

P 2 " Value

"Value of Sixty Thousand Pounds." This Accident, however terrible and diftrefsful in itfelf, might poffibly occafion in a good meafure one agreeable Circumftance, which is, the great Regularity of the Streets. For thefe are now feen cutting each other at Right-Angles, which contributes much to the Beauty of them, and as the Town ftands upon an eafy Afcent, it deferves the Encomium which an ancient Writer has given of it, *viz.* "That the Sun fhines not upon a Town more agreeable "in its Situation." *Leland.*

The Abbey which was once fo illuftrious was firft built by *Sigebert* King of the *Eaft-Angles,* foon after Chriftianity was planted here by *Felix* the *Burgundian,* and being finifhed King *Sigebert* about the Year 638 retired into it, and fecluded himfelf from all temporal Affairs.

As to St. *Edmund,* from whom the Town hath taken its Name, we may well fuppofe him to have defcended from the Royal Blood of the *Saxons.* He began to reign as King of the *Eaft-Angles* A.D. 855, in the fourteenth Year of his Age. Some have imagined that he was crowned here; but our Zeal for the Honour of this Town ought not to lead us into fo vulgar an Error, for that Ceremony was performed at *Buers,* as will be mentioned in our Account of that Town. He reigned fifteen Years, being killed *A.D.* 870, in the twenty-ninth Year of his Age; and his Corpfe having lain interred in the Town where he was killed (generally fuppofed to be *Hoxne*) thirty-three Years, was removed to *Bury.* On this Account, and through the Superftition of that Age, the Revenue of the Abbey increafed fo faft, that the Monks, greedy to fwallow all the Prey, accufed the Seculars among other Things of Negligence and Irreverence to the Corpfe of St. *Edmund*; fo petulant was the Accufation, and fo ftrong their Intereft, that they procured Power and Authority to eject all the Seculars, and to fill their Places with thofe of their own; the *Benedictine* Order.

der. This they accomplished about the Year 1020, and in the fourth Year of King *Canute*, who then laid the Foundation of a more magnificent Church, to the Honour of this Martyr; the former in which he had been deposited being but a Wooden Building, or, at best, covered with Wood. The Expence of this Fabrick was raised by an annual Tax of Four-pence on every ploughed Land in *Suffolk* and *Norfolk*. It was finished in the Space of about twelve Years, and consecrated by *Othelnoth*, or *Agelnorth*, Archbishop of *Canterbury*, and dedicated to *Chrijl*, St. *Mary*, and St. *Edmund*.

Uvius, Prior of *Hulm*, was consecrated the first Abbot, *A.D.* 1020; and in the next Year this Abbey was exempted from all Episcopal Jurisdiction by the Council of *Winchester*. He first encompassed the Abbey, and a Part, if not the whole of the Town, with a Wall and a Ditch, the Ruins of which are still to be seen in many Places. Thus was the Grandeur of this Abbey begun: Its Abbots were made Parliamentary Barons, and its Wealth yearly increased, until its final Dissolution by *Henry* VIII. when its yearly Revenues amounted to 2336 *l.* 16*s.* in the whole, and to 1659 *l.* 13*s.* 11½*d.* clear of Reprises. And the Plate, Bells, Lead, Timber, *&c.* yielded 5000 Marks to the King. When the Abbey was in its Prosperity, there was an Hospital or Religious House at every Gate of the Town. There was an Hospital of St. *Peter*, without the *Risby*-Gate, for the Maintenance of leprous and infirm Priests; an Hospital of St. *Nicholas*, without the *East*-gate; of St. *John* within, and St. *Petronilla* without, the *South*-gate: The Ruins of them are at this Day to be seen. But the most famous of the Hospitals was that of St. *Saviour*'s, without the *North*-Gate; an entire Window of which is still remaining. It was in this Building that the Parliament met in *Henry* the Sixth's Time; and it was here that *Humphrey* Duke of *Gloucester* was murdered, at the Instigation of the

Monks. There was alfo a College of Priefts, with a Guild to the holy or fweet Name of *Jefus*, the Situation of which is not known; and a Houfe of *Grey* Friers at *Barwell*, or the Toll-Gate, without the *North*-Gate; whither they retired to, after they were driven out of the Town by the Abbot.

Lands and Tenements called *Hencotes*, near *Bury*, with Pafture for 360 Sheep late belonging to the Abbey, were granted 1 *Mary* to Sir *William Drury* Knt. And a Meadow in *Bury*, *Nowton* and *Whelnetham-parva*, called *Siclefmere*, late belonging to the Abbey, was granted 1 *Mary*, to *Ambrofe Jermyn*. The Site of the Abbey, with two Meadows and a Manor or Farm in *Bury* called *Haldons*, were granted to *John Eyre*, 2 *Elizabeth*. A Parcel of Tithes, the Markets and Fairs and Toll of the fame, and the Toll-Houfe, the Butchers Stalls, Goal, and Goal-Houfe, and Market-Crofs, were granted to the Aldermen and Burgeffes 6 *Jac.* I. as Parcel of the Poffeffions of the Abbot and Convent.

The Abbot, as was faid before, was a Parliamentary Baron; but it is obfervable this Borough made no Return, tho' it had a Precept iffued to it 30 *Edward* I. (except to a Council, 11 *Edward* III.) before the Time of King *James* I. who made it a Parliamentary Borough about the twelfth Year of his Reign.

A Parliament was held here by King *Edward* I, A. D. 1298; and another by King *Henry* VI. A. D. 1447; when *Humphrey* Duke of *Glocefter* was murdered here, as Mr. *Lambard* reports, by the Hand of *Pole*, then Duke of *Suffolk*.

The Civil Government of the Town is now lodged in the Hands of an *Alderman*, a *Recorder*, twelve *Capital Burgeffes*, and twenty-four *Common Burgeffes*: Thefe have the fole Right of chufing their own Burgeffes in Parliament.

King

King *Edward* I. and King *Edward* II. had Mints in *Bury*; and some of their Pennys, coined here, are yet remaining. *Stow* says, here was also a Mint in King *John*'s Time.

Instead of the many Chapels and Oratories which were formerly in this Town, there are now only two magnificent and stately Churches, standing in the same Churchyard: The one dedicated to St. *Mary*, is 139 Feet long by 67 Feet and a half broad, and the Chancel of it is 74 by 68: The Roof of the Nave of St. *Mary*'s Church is truly magnificent: There is a fine Ascent of six Steps to the Altar, on the *North*-side of which is the Tomb of *Mary* Queen of *France*, Daughter of *Henry* VII. and afterwards married to *Charles Brandon*, Duke of *Suffolk*. This Queen of *France* was buried in the great Church of the Monastery, and was removed after the Dissolution of it into St. *Mary*'s Church; her Body is covered with Lead, resembling an human Shape, and on her Breast is inscribed, "*Mary* Queen of *France*, 1533." Her Tomb was not only simple and unadorned, but for a long Series of Years entirely neglected. It was even without any Inscription till the Year 1758, when a Gentleman of the Town, out of a pious Regard for Antiquity, and especially for so valuable a Possession, had the Tomb repaired at his own Expence, and a Marble Tablet inserted into it.

The other Church, dedicated to St. *James*, was finished in the Reign of *Edward* VI. who was himself a Contributor to it, as appears from an Inscription in the Church: It is 137 Feet long by 69 Feet, the Chancel is 56 by 27 Feet; at the *West* End of the *South* Isle are two large Monuments erected to the Memory of *James Reynolds*, Esq; Lord Chief Baron of the Exchequer, and his Lady, who were buried here. In this Church is an Organ lately erected, and a Library convenient enough, but which has no Curiosities, except a M.S. of *Beck*'s Ecclesiastical History, and *Demetrius Chalcondylas*'s Edition of *Homer*.

The Steeple of the Church of St. *James*, and the Abbey-gate, are Buildings which muſt excite the Attention of the Curious: The former was anciently the grand Portal, that led to the great Church of the Monaſtery; the Arches of the Tower are all round of a *Saxon* Form, and ſeem to be much older than *Henry* Third's Time. The Abbey-gate, which conducted you to the private Court of the Abbot, is a Maſter-piece of *Gothic* Architecture; it was built in the Reign of *Richard* the Second, the Townſmen having demoliſhed the former Gate in his Grandfather's Time, upon a Quarrel with the Monks: The Inſide of it is adorned with the Arms of *Holland* Duke of *Exeter*, and of *Edward* the Confeſſor, who was the Favourite Saint of *Richard* II.

The reſt of the public Buildings are the Guild-Hall, the Grammar-School endowed by King *Edward* VI. the Market-Croſs, the Wool-Hall, and the Shire-Houſe; nor muſt we omit the Butchery, which has been lately built at the Expence of the preſent Earl of *Briſtol*, his Majeſty's Embaſſador at the Court of *Spain*.

There are two Market-Days, *Wedneſdays* and *Saturdays*; the chief Market is on *Wedneſday*, which is very well ſerved with all manner of Proviſions. There are alſo three annual Fairs; the firſt on *Eaſter Tueſday*, the ſecond for three Days before the Feaſt of St. *Matthew*, *Sept*. 21, and three Days after; but this is uſually protracted to an uncertain Length, for the Diverſion of the Nobility and Gentry that reſort to it: The third is on St. *Edmund*'s Day, *Nov*. 20.

The other Towns in this Hundred are theſe, *viz*.

BARROW, was anciently the Lordſhip and Seat of the Counteſs of *Gloceſter*; afterwards it belonged to *Bartholomew* Lord *Badleſmere*, who adhering to the Earl of *Lancaſter* againſt King *Edward* II. was taken Priſoner at *Burrow-Brigg* in *Yorkſhire*, and hanged at *Bleen* near *Canterbury*,

HUNDRED *of* THINGOE.

Canterbury, 16 *Edward* II. or *A.D.* 1322. By an Inquisition taken 2 *Edward* III. he died seised jointly with *Margaret* his Wife of the Manor of *Barewe* in *Com. Suff.* and the Advowson of the Church : *Giles*, his Son and Heir, died seised 9 *Edward* III. leaving his four Sisters Heirs : His Widow enjoyed *Barewe* for Life; but, after her Decease, 15 *Edward* III. it was upon Partition assigned to his Sister *Margaret*, then the Wife of *John de Tybetot*. *Robert*, the Son of *John de Tybetot*,, died seised of *Barewe*, 46 *Edward* III. leaving his three Daughters Heirs. The Ruins of their Seat a little *South* of the Church, bespeak it to have been a very noble Structure. The Manor is now vested in the Earl of *Bristol*; the Advowson of the Rectory in St. *John*'s College, *Cambridge*.

BROCKLEY, is the Lordship of *George Thomas*, Esq.

CHEVINGTON. King *William* the Conqueror gave this Lordship to the Abbot and Convent of *Bury*, at the Desire of Abbot *Baldwyn*. The Manor, Park, and Advowson of the Church were granted 31 *Henry* VIII. to Sir *Thomas Kitson*. The Earl of *Bristol* is now Lord of the Manor.

FLEMPTON. This Manor belonged likewise to *Bury* Abbey, and was granted 31 *Henry* VIII. to Sir *Thomas Kitson*. Sir *William Gage*, Bart. now hath it.

FORNHAM *All-Saints*, is the Lordship of Sir *William Gage*; in this Parish is a Seat which belongs to *Thomas Mosely*, Esq. The Advowson of the Rectory is in *Clare*-Hall, *Cambridge*.

HARDWICK-*House*, is extra-parochial, and came by Marriage from the *Drurys* to the *Cullums*. Near it is an Hospital for six Widows, founded by the *Drurys*.

HARGRAVE.

HARGRAVE. This Manor and Advowson belonged to *Bury* Abbey, and was granted 31 *Hen.* VIII. to Sir *Thomas Kitson*; from the *Kitsons* they came to the *Gages* by Marriage, and by Sale from Sir *Edward Gage* to the Earl of *Bristol.*

HAWSTEAD. *Thomas Fitz-Eustace* had this Manor and Estate 9 *Edward* II. but in the Reign of *Edward* IV. it belonged to the very ancient Family of *Drurys*, who had their Seat at the Manor-House called *Hawstead-Place.* This Family produced many famous Men, the greatest of whom was Sir *William Drury*, who atchieved great Things in *Ireland*, mentioned by Mr. *Cambden* in his Life of Queen *Elizabeth.* The *Cullums* are now in Possession of this Manor and Seat, by marrying an Heiress of that Family. The Founder of their Family was Sir *Thomas*, Citizen and Sheriff of *London* 22 *Charles* I. His Son *Thomas Cullum* of this Place, was created a Baronet 18 *June*, 1660. In the Parish Church are some very old Monuments of the *Drurys.*

HENGRAVE, anciently the Lordship of *Edmund de Hengrave*, in the Reign of *Edward* I. *Thomas Hethe* was Lord of *Hengrave*, A. D. 1375. *Henry* Lord *Grey* of *Codnoure*, had a Grant of the Manor 1 *Richard* III. but afterwards it came to the *Kitsons*, who built *Hengrave*-Hall in *Henry* the Eighth's Time, and made it their Seat. It has for some Descents been in the Family of the *Gages*, from *Mary* Daughter and Coheir of Sir *Thomas Kitson* it descended to Sir *Edward Gage*, as Inheritor of his Mother's Estate. *George Gage*, of *Hengrave*-Hall, Esq; was created a Baronet 15 *July*, 1662. The Honour and Estate is now vested in Sir *William Gage*, Bart. The House is extremely large, and deservedly esteemed one of the finest old Fabricks in *England.* There are a few Monuments in the Church, among which those of the *Bouchiers* Earls of *Bath*, are the most famous.

HOR-

HORNINGSHERTH, commonly called *Horringer*. Here were formerly two Parish Churches, distinguished by the Names of *Horningsherth Magna*, and *Parva*: The latter Church is quite demolished. The Parishes were consolidated A. D. 1548. They seem formerly to have belonged to *Bury* Abbey, and are now the Lordship of Sir *Charles Davers*, who is Patron of the Church. Here are two Fairs for Lambs, on St. *John Baptist*'s Day, and St. *Bartholomew*'s Day, upon the Sheep Green; at the upper End of which *Valentine Mumbee*, Esq; hath built a neat Seat.

HORSECROFT, is a Hamlet to *Horringer*, in which the very ancient Family of the *Lucas's* resided. The Estate was purchased by Mr. *Turner*, of *Bury*.

ICKWORTH, formerly belonged to the Abbey of *Bury*, by the Gift of *Theodred*, Bishop of *London*. The whole Parish is now converted into a Park, in which is the Seat of the Family of *Herveys*, who acquired this Estate by their Marriage with the *Drurys*. *John* Lord *Hervey* was created a Baron of this Realm by the Title of Lord *Hervey* of *Ickworth*, by Queen *Anne*; and his Lordship was advanced to the more honourable Title of Earl of *Bristol*, by his Majesty King *George* I. The present Earl is the Grandson of *John* the first Earl. In this Place the late learned Dr. *Battley*, Archdeacon of *Canterbury*, asserts, that in his Memory a large Pot of *Roman* Money was found. The Park is full nine Miles in Circumference, and may justly vie with any one in this Island.

LACKFORD. *Hugh de St. Philebert* died seised of the Manors of *Lackford* and *Blemton* in *Suffolk*, 7 *Edward* III. The Advowson of the Rectory, late belonging to *Bury* Abbey, was granted 2 *Mary* to *Edward* Lord *North*, and *John Williams*. It is at present the Lordship of *Samuel Kent*, Esq.

NOWTON,

NOWTON, is the Lordship of Sir *Charles Davers*, who is Patron likewise of the Church, and of all the Villages near *Bury*; it enjoys the most beautiful Situation.

REED, consisteth of two Manors; *Pickards*, which is the Earl of *Bristol's*; and *Reed*-Hall, which belongs to *Philips Coleman*, of *Ipswich*, Esq. In this Parish is a Mansion called *Downings*, the Inheritance of the ancient Family of *Sparrowe*. The Church is in the Gift of the Crown.

RISBY. King *Edward* the Confessor gave this Manor to *Bury* Abbey; it was granted in 31 *Henry* VIII. to Sir *Thomas Kitson*; and is now vested in Sir *William Gage*, Bart.

SAXHAM-*Magna*. The Manor and Advowson belonged to *Bury* Abbey, and were granted 33 *Henry* VIII. to Sir *Richard Long* and his Wife. It was for many Years the Seat of the Family of *Eldred*. *Revet Eldred*, of this Place, Esq; was created a Baronet 29 *Jan*. 1641; but the Honour is now extinct. The Hall and Estate is now in the Possession of *Hutchinson Mure*, Esq; who purchased it of the late Mr. *Eldred*.

SAXHAM-*Parva*. *Thomas Hethe* was Lord of *Saxham-Parva*, about the Year 1375; but this Place is most noted for having been the Seat of the Family of the *Lucas's*, and afterwards of the *Crofts*; of which *William Crofts*, Esq; was by K. *Charles* II. at *Brussels* in *Brabant*, created Lord *Crofts*, of *Saxham*; he leaving no Male Issue, the Honour became extinct at his Death: But the Hall and Estate here belong now to *William Crofts*, Esq; who is a Gentleman of that Family, and resides chiefly at *Harling* in *Norfolk*.

SOUTH-*Park*,

SOUTH-*Park*, *Southwood*, or *Southwell*-Park, is an extraparochial Place; the greatest Part of which belongs to *Gilbert Affleck*, Esq.

WESTLY, was anciently the Lordship of the Abbot of *Bury*, by the Gift of Bishop *Alfric*, surnamed the *Good*, and granted 31 *Henry* VIII. to Sir *Thomas Kitson*. It is now vested in Sir *William Gage*. The Advowson of the Rectory is in *Clare-Hall*, in *Cambridge*.

WHEPSTEAD. The Manor and Advowson here were given to *Bury* Abbey, by *Theodred* Bishop of *London*, and granted to Sir *William Drury* 31 *Henry* VIII. The first is now vested in Mr. *Grigby*, of *Bury*; and the latter in Mr. *Horrex*, of *London*.

Hundred of Thedwastre.

THE Hundred of *Thedwaſtre* is bounded on the South by the Hundreds of *Babergh* and *Cosford*; on the *Eaſt* by the Hundred of *Stow*; on the *North* by the Hundred of *Blackbourn*; and on the *Weſt* by the Hundred of *Thingoe*.

Ampton, was anciently the Lordſhip of the Abbot of *Bury*. The *Calthorpes* have long reſided at *Ampton*-Hall, which is now veſted in *James Calthorpe*, Eſq.

Barton, called *Great Barton*, to diſtinguiſh it from *Little Barton* or *Barton-Mills*, in *Lackford* Hundred, was formerly the Lordſhip of the Abbot of *Bury*. Biſhop *Theodred* gave one Part of *Barton*; *Edwin*, a wealthy Man, gave another Part; and *Erec* the Provoſt, the other Part: We don't find to whom the Manor, Rectory and Advowſon of the Vicarage of this Place were granted; but a Parcel of Land in *Great Barton*, called *Ox-Paſture*, containing One Hundred Acres, late belonging to *Bury* Abbey, was granted 31 *Henry* VIII. to Sir *Thomas Kitſon*. But ſince this has been the Eſtate of the ancient Family of the *Cottons*, who dwelt at *Neéton*-Hall in this Pariſh, which was purchaſed by *Thomas Folkes*, Eſq; of —— *Audley*, Eſq; by whom the preſent Manſion was built. The Manor and a conſiderable Eſtate with it, was conveyed to Sir *Thomas Hanmer*, Bart. who married the Daughter and Heireſs of Mr. *Folkes*. It is now the Seat of the Rev. Sir *William Bunbury*, Bart. the Nephew and Heir of Sir *Thomas Hanmer*, and of late Years hath been

been very confiderably improved by him; whofe Son is now Reprefentative of the County.

BEIGHTON, though a fmall Village, has a Donation for a Lecture on the firft *Thurfday* in every Month. The Lordfhip of it belongs to the Crown, and the Rectory is in the Gift of the Lord Chancellor.

BRADFIELD-*Combuft*. This Manor belonged to *Giles* Lord *Badlefmere*, whofe Daughter *Margery* married *William* Lord *Roos*, of *Hamelake*; and after her Mother's Deceafe had *Brende Bradfield* affigned to her, 15 *Edw*. III. *Thomas* Lord *Rofs* died 8 *Richard* II. feifed of the Manors of *Wyfette* and *Brende Bradfield*. Mr. *Blomfield* fpeaks of the *Jervaces* of *Sutton*-Hall, in *Burnt-Bradfield*, and of Mr. *Edmund Wright*'s marrying the Heirefs of the Family. The Heir of the late Dr. *Young* has the Advowfon of the Church and Lordfhip.

BRADFIELD *St. Clare*. The Lordfhip belongs to *Edward Wenyeve*, Efq; defcended from an old Family in this County. (See *Brettenham*, in *Cosford*.)

BRADFIELD *St. George*, or *Monks-Bradfield*, fo called for Diftinction; becaufe the Manor and Advowfon of the Church belonged to the Abbey of *Bury*, by the Gift of Bifhop *Alfric*, and Earl *Ulfketel*. They were granted 31 *Henry* VIII. to Sir *Thomas Jermyn*, Knt. and are now vefted in Sir *Charles Davers*, Bart.

DRINKESTON. *Henry* Lord *Bouchier* died feifed of the Manor of *Dringefton* in *Suffolk*, 23 *Edward* IV. The Manor and Advowfon are now vefted in *Thomas Mofeley*, Efq. Here is the new erected Seat of *Jofhua Grigby*, Efq.

FELSHAM. This belonged to the Abbot of *Bury*, by the Gift of Earl *Ulfketel*: There is a neat Manfion here, being lately the Seat of the late Mr. *Reynolds,* and now of Dr. *Scott;* and there is a confiderable Fair for Lambs on the fifth of *Auguft.*

FORNHAM *St. Genoveve.* The Manor formerly belonged to the Abbot of *Bury,* and was granted 31 *Henry* VIII. to Sir *Thomas Kitfon.* It is now vefted in Sir *William Gage,* Bart. *Samuel Kent,* Efq; has a Seat in this Parifh. At this Place 20 *Henry* II. or *A. D.* 1173, *Richard de Lucy* Chief Juftice of *England,* and *Humphrey de Bohun* the King's Conftable, beat *Robert* Earl of *Leicefter* in a pitched Battle, and killed ten thoufand *Flemings,* whom he had got over to his Affiftance. *M. Blomfield* faith, " Their Sepulchres are now to be feen near " a Place called *Rymer*-Houfe, on the Right-hand of the " Road leading from *Thetford* to *Bury,* and are now " called the *Seven Hills,* though there are many more; " but feven of them being much larger than the reft, are " particularly taken notice of by thofe that pafs this Way, " under which, moft probably, the Commanders were " buried."

FORNHAM *St. Martin.* This Manor alfo belonged to the Abbot of *Bury,* and was granted with the other *Fornham* 31 *Henry* VIII. to Sir *Thomas Kitfon.* It is now vefted, as well as the Advowfon of the Church, in *Samuel Kent,* Efq. In this Parifh is the Seat of Mrs. *Ord,* Daughter of the late Mr. *Hutchinfon.*

GEDDING. In this Parifh is the Seat of the Heirs of ———— *Bokenham,* Efq. The Advowfon of the Church was, by the Will of *Jeremiah Catling,* given to the Corporation of *Ipfwich;* and upon a Vacancy the Bailives, the eldeft Portman not being one of the Bailives, the Recorder and the Town-Clerk for the Time being, are to nominate a Clerk. The Manor belongs to the Daughters of the late Mr. *Bokenham.*

HESSET,

HESSET, or HEDGSETT, was the Lordship of the Abbot of *Bury*, by the Gift of Earl *Ulfketel*, and granted 32 *Henry* VIII. to *Thomas Bacon*. *Michael le Heup*, Esq; has a Seat here, and is in Possession both of the Advowson and Manor.

LIVERMORE-*Magna*. *John Bokenham* was Lord of this Manor and Patron of the Church, *A. D.* 1467; his Son *John* died seised 1484; *Thomas Bokenham* died seised 1535; *John Bokenham*, the last Heir Male of this Family, died seised 1551, leaving *Dorothy* his Sister and Heiress, who married *Thomas Caryl* Earl of *Sussex*, who probably sold her Estate here. The Abbot and Convent of *Warden* in *Bedfordshire*, had a Grange at *Livermore* before 10 *Ric.* I. and a Manor or Grange at *Livermore* in *Suffolk*, in the Occupation of *Edward Buckwood* and *Clement Heigham*, was granted 38 *Henry* VIII. to *Richard* and *Roger Taverner*, as late belonging to that Abbey. This Benefice, and that of *Livermore-parva*, are consolidated, and are in the Gift of *Baptist Lee*, Esq; who is likewise Lord of the Manor.

PAKENHAM. The Family of the *Springs* have long had their Seat here, who came originally from *Houghton*, a Village in the Bishoprick of *Durham*; which has been always called *Houghton-le-Spring*, to distinguish it from other Towns of that Name. The first of the Family who made any Figure in this County, was *Thomas Spring*, of *Lavenham*, the rich Clothier, who died *A. D.* 1510; and lies buried in the Church at *Lavenham*, under a Monument of his own Erection. From him descended *William Spring*, of *Pakenham*, who was created a Baronet 11 *August*, 1641. The late Sir *William Spring* dying without Issue, the Honour came to his Uncle, and his Estate to his two Sisters; who were married to the late *Thomas Discipline*, Esq; and the Rev. Dr. *Symonds*. The Vicarage

Vicarage and Manor are vested in the two Daughters of Mrs. *Discipline.*

The ancient Family of the *L'Estranges* had also a Seat here, which was purchased by *John Curwin,* Esq; and now belongs to ——— *Hollingsworth,* Esq. The *Monasticon* saith, King *Edward* gave *Pakenham* to the Abbot and Convent of *Bury;* but perhaps they had little here but the Impropriation and Advowson of the Vicarage.

The Family of the *Ashfields* had formerly their Seat at *Nether-Hall,* in this Parish. *John Ashfield* was the first High-Sheriff of *Suffolk,* (separated from *Norfolk*) 17 *Elizabeth;* from whom descended Sir *John Ashfield,* of *Nether-Hall,* Knt. who was created a Baronet in 1626. That Family is now extinct, and the Vicarage and Manor are vested in *Edmund Tyrrell,* Esq.

RATTLESDEN, belonged to *Ely* in King *Edward* the Confessor's Time: The Manor was alienated from the Bishoprick of *Ely,* 4 *Elizabeth,* and granted 2 *Jac.* I. to *Philip Tyse* and *William Blake;* being then valued at 43*l.* 9*s.* 7½*d per Annum.* It is now vested, as well as the Advowson, in *Thomas Moseley,* Esq.

ROUGHAM, was given to the Abbey of *Bury* by Earl *Ulfketel,* and granted 34 *Henry* VIII. to Sir *Arthur Drury;* in whose Family it continued till 1640: Soon after which it was in the Possession of Sir *Jeffery Benwell,* Knt. whose only Daughter married *Robert Walpole,* of *Houghton* in *Norfolk,* Esq; of whom it was purchased by Sir *Robert Davers,* Bart. who sold it to *Clemence Corrance,* Esq; whose Family hath now Part of the Estate, formerly possessed by the *Drurys,* together with the Lordship and Seat of *Rougham* Place.

Rougham-Hall, formerly part of the Estate belonging to the *Drurys,* was lately the Seat of *John Cooke,* Esq. It is now, with Part of the Manor, vested in Mrs. *Neden,* Daughter of the late *John Cooke,* Esq; and Wife of *Ge-*

rard Neden, D.D. Sir *Robert Davers*, Bart. is Patron of the Church.

Another Manfion in this Parifh was formerly the Seat of the *Maltywards*, and now of *Pell Heigham*, Efq.

In this Parifh is alfo the Manor of *Eldo*, alias *Old-Hall*, or *Oldhaugh*, as it is ftiled in the moft ancient Books. It was a Grange of the Abbot of *Bury*, and was granted by King *Henry* VIII. with other large Demefnes to the *Jermyns*; and is now vefted in Mrs. *Symonds*, who inherited it from her Mother one of the Heirs-General of Lord *Jermyn*.

RUSHBROOK. The Manor here belonged to the Abbey of *Bury*, and was once in the Poffeffion of the *Rufhbrooks*, a very old Family, who took their Name from that Town. It has been remarkable, fince the Diffolution, for the Family of the *Jermyns*, who have had their Seat at *Rufhbrook* Hall. Sir *Thomas Jermyn* was Privy Counfellor and Comptroller of the Houfhold to King *Charles* I. His fecond Son *Henry Jermyn*, was Mafter of the Horfe, and Chamberlain to his Queen: He was created Lord *Jermyn* of *St. Edmondfbury*, 8 *Sept.* 1644; and at *Bredah* in *Brabant* 27 *April* 1660, was by King *Charles* II. created Earl of *St. Albans*; and in the Year 1672, was created Knight of the Garter. He died unmarried, and the Title of Earl of *St. Albans* being limited to him, became extinct. *Thomas* his elder Brother, being then dead, the Title of Lord *Jermyn* Baron of *St. Edmondfbury*, defcended to *Thomas Jermyn*, Efq; the elder Brother's Son; and *Henry* the fecond Son, was by King *James* II. created Baron of *Dover*, and died without Iffue in 1708. This Family concluded in Heirs-General, the eldeft of which was married to *Robert Davers*, Efq; only Son of Sir *Robert Davers*, Bart. of *Rougham*, fo created 12 *May*, 1682; by which means this Eftate and Seat was brought into the Family of *Davers*, and are now vefted in Sir *Robert Davers*, Bart.

Son of the late Sir *Jermyn Davers*, who reprefented the County for many Years. In the Church are feveral Monuments of the *Jermyns*.

TOSTOCK. The Manor here belonged to *Brithulf*, the Son of *Leomar*; and *Baldwin* Abbot of *Bury St. Edmunds*, begged this and fome other Eftates of *William* the Conqueror: Afterwards it came into the Family of the Lords *North* and *Grey*, who had their Seat at *Toftock*-Place, which now is vefted in *Thomas Mofeley*, Efq. But probably here was alfo another Manor; for the Manor of *Toftock*-Hall is faid to have been *William Berdewell's*, *A. D.* 1445.

THURSTON. *Thomas de Multon*, of *Egromont*, 18. *Ed.* I. obtained a Market on *Tuefdays*, and a Fair on the Eve, Day, and Morrow of St. *Mary Magdalen*, at his Manor of *Thurftanefton*, in *Suffolk*; which we take to be this Place. *John de Multon* his Son, died feifed of it 8 *Ed.* III. The Church was impropriated to *Bury* Abbey, and the Rectory and Advowfon of the Vicarage granted 5 *Jac.* I. to *William Blake* and *George Tyte*.

TINWORTH, was lately confolidated with *Ingham*; Earl *Cornwallis* is Patron of the Church, and Lord of the Manor.

WHELNETHAM-*Magna*. In a Chapel here dedicated to *Thomas Becket*, was a fmall Houfe of *Crouched* or *Croffed* Friers, which was granted by King *Henry* VIII. to *Anthony Rous*. Sir *William Bunbury* is now Patron of the Church, and the Manor belongs to Mrs. *Symonds*, Granddaughter of Lord *Jermyn*.

There were found formerly in digging, Abundance of Potfherds and Platters of *Roman* Earth, fome of which had Infcriptions; as alfo Coals, Bones of Sheep and Oxen, many Horns, a facrificing Knife, Urns and Afhes: This

HUNDRED *of* THEDWASTRE.

is *Cambden*'s Account. And, of late Years, some Discoveries have been made of several *Roman* Coins.

WHELNETHAM-*Parva*. *Bartholomew Burghersh*, 23 *Edward* III. had, in Right of his Wife, who was Daughter and Heiress of *Richard de Weyland*, free Warren in the Manor of *Whelnetham*, in *Suffolk* ; and died seised thereof 43 *Edward* III. *Edward le Dispenser*, who married *Burghersh*'s Daughter, died 49 *Edward* III. seised of the Manor of *Whelnetham-Parva*, in *Suffolk* ; and *Edward de Langley* Earl of *Rutland*, died 3 *Henry* V. at the Battle of *Agincourt*, seised of the Manor of *Whelnetham*, in *Suffolk*. The Lordship and Patronage of the Church are now in Sir *Robert Davers*, Bart.

WOOLPIT, or WALPITT. This is said in the *Monasticon*, p. 292. to have been given to *Bury* Abbey by King *Edward* the Confessor ; and p. 294. it is said to have been given by Earl *Ulfketel*. However this be, the Manor, Advowson of the Rectory, a Warren, and a great many Lands, Pastures and Woods, in *Elmswell* and *Walpitt*, were granted 8 *Jac*. I. to Sir *Robert Gardiner*, Knt. as Parcel of the Possessions of *Bury* Abbey. Here is a considerable Fair for Horses and other Cattle, which begins annually on the sixth of *September*, and holds a Week. The Lordship of the Manor belongs to Mr. *Grigby*. It is in this Parish where one sees the Bounds between the Geldable and the Liberty of *St. Edmund*.

HUNDRED of BLACKBOURN.

BLACKBOURN Hundred lieth *East* of *Lackford*, and *West* of *Hartismere*; it is parted on the *North* from *Norfolk* by the *Little Ouse*, and bounded on the *South* by the Hundreds of *Stow*, *Thedwastre*, and *Thingoe*. This Hundred was granted as Parcel of the Possessions of *Bury* Abbey, 3 *Eliz.* to Sir *Nicholas Bacon*, Knt. and is now vested in *Rowland Holt*, Esq; whose great Uncle Lord Chief Justice *Holt* purchased it of the *Bacon* Family. It contains the following Parishes, viz.

ASHFIELD. The *Smiths* have long resided in this Parish, in a Seat called the *Lee*.

BADWELL-*Ash*, or *Little Ashfield*. The Lordship of *William Creketote*, the 9th *Edw.* I. The Manors and Rectories of both these Parishes belonged to *Ixworth* Priory, and were granted at the Dissolution to *Richard Codington*, and *Elizabeth* his Wife. Here is also the Manor of *Shackerland* in this Parish, now belonging to ―― *Clough*, Esq.

BARDWELL, was in the 9th *Edw.* III. the Lordship of *John Pakenham*, and *Isabella de Wykes*; afterwards it came into the Family of *Read*, one of whom married the Daughter and Heiress of *William Crofts*, afterwards created Lord *Crofts*, of *Saxham*; from which Marriage they took the Name of *Crofts*, and it is now the Lordship of *Thomas Crofts-Read*, Esq.

It

It is said there was a Family who took their Name from this Town, where they lived in the Conqueror's Time; and it appears from the Account given of them in Mr. *Blomfield*'s Hist of *Norfolk*, p. 202. that Sir *William Berdewelle*, the great Warrior, whose Effigies still remains in painted Glass in a *North* Window of the Church, died seised of this Manor in King *Henry* VIth's Reign, or *A. D.* 1434.

BARNHAM, consists of two Parishes, St. *Martin* and St. *Gregory*; having formerly had two Parish Churches, but the Church of St. *Martin* is now in Ruins: It was formerly the Lordship of *John de Shyrtle*, and now belongeth to his Grace the Duke of *Grafton*. Here are a Rank of ten or eleven Tumuli between *Rushford*, *Euston*, *Barnham*, and *Thetford*; where, as Mr. *Blomfield* thinks, that great Battle between King *Edmund* and the *Danes* seems to have been fought, *A. D.* 871.

BARNINGHAM, formerly the Lordship of *John de Montfort*, 9 *Edward* I. The Family of the *Sheltons* long resided here; of whom the Duke of *Grafton* purchased the Messuage and Estate in or near this Parish, called *Barningham-Park*.

CONY-*Weston*, formerly the Lordship of the Abbot of *Bury*; and now of *John Reilly*, Esq.

CULFORD, was formerly given to the Abbot of *Bury*, by *Turketel Tyreing*, alias *Dreing*, and granted 32 *Henry* VIII. to *Christopher Cote*. This Village is adorned with a neat Seat, built by Sir *Nicholas Bacon*. It now belongs to the Right Hon. Earl *Cornwallis*, who chiefly resides here, and is Lord of the Manor.

ELMSWELL. This Lordship was given to *Bury* Abbey by King *Edwin*, and granted 8 *Jac.* 1. to *Robert Gardiner*; and is now vested in *William Chapman*, Esq.

EUSTON, was formerly the Lordship of a Family of that Name; afterwards it descended to the Family of *Pattishail*; from them to Sir *Henry Bennet*, who by King *Charles* II. was made Secretary of State, and created Lord *Arlington*, Viscount *Thetford*, and Earl of *Arlington*. He built *Euston* Hall, and leaving only one Daughter *Isabella*, married to *Henry Fitz-Roy*, one of King *Charles* the Second's natural Sons by the Duchess of *Cleveland*, he was by his Father created Earl of *Euston* and Duke of *Grafton*; and this is now the Seat of his great Grandson his Grace the present Duke of *Grafton*.

FAKENHAM *Great*, formerly the Lordship of *Gundred de Warren*, descended from the Earls of *Surry*; afterwards by Marriage it came to the *Nevils*; from them to the Crown. It was granted by *Henry* VI. to *Reginald de Weste*, who died seised of *Fakenham-Aspes* in *Suffolk*, 29 *Henry* VI. His Son, a great Favourite of *Henry* VIII. enjoyed it. Afterwards it was in Possession of the *Talmachs*; from whom it passed through the *Taylors* to the Duke of *Grafton*, who is now Lord of the Manor.

FAKENHAM *Little*, now in part, if not all imparked with *Euston*; there are no Remains of a Church, but there is a Sine-cure in his Grace's Gift.

HEPWORTH. *Gilbert de Blund* had this Lordship when Domesday-Book was made; afterwards it was given to the Abbot of *Bury*; and is now vested in ———— *Ord*, Esq; and Mr. *Nunn*.

HINDERCLAY, was the Lordship and Demesne of the Abbey of *Bury St. Edmunds*, given thereto together with *Redgrave*, *Rickengale*, *Wulpit*, *Rougham*, Part of *Bradfield*, *Heisham* and *Hedgesset*, by *Ulfketel* Earl of the *East-Angles*; afterwards it came into the Family of the *Bacons*, and was sold by Sir *Edmund Bacon*, of *Garboldisham* in *Norfolk*, to

Sir

Sir *John Holt*, Lord Chief Juftice; and is now vefted in *Rowland Holt*, Efq; his great Nephew.

HOPTON. *Henry* Lord *Bouchier* died feifed of the Manor of *Hopton*, 23 *Edward* IV. it afterwards belonged to the Abbot of *Bury*, and is now vefted in ———— *Cavendifh*, Efq.

HONINGTON. The Lordfhip of this Parifh did likewife belong to the Abbey of *Bury*, but now to his Grace the Duke of *Grafton*.

HUNSTON, anciently the Lordfhip and Demefne of *William de Langham*; the Manor and Rectory was granted to *Richard Codington* and *Elizabeth* his Wife, 30 *Henry* VIII. as Parcel of the Poffeffions of *Ixworth* Priory. *Arthur Heigham*, Efq; now refides in a good old Seat in this Parifh.

INGHAM, was formerly the Lordfhip of *John de Ingham*: The Manor and Advowfon of *Ingham* were granted to Sir *Nicholas Bacon*, 31 *Henry* VIII. as Part of the Poffeffions of *Bury* Abbey. The Lordfhip of *Ingham* with *Tunworth*, is now vefted in Earl *Cornwallis*.

IXWORTH, is a Thorough-fair Town, fituated on the Road from *Bury* to *Yarmouth*: It has a mean Market every Week on *Friday*. Here are two Fairs, one on *May*-day, the other on 18 *Octob*. It is a dirty ill built Town, yet it is memorable for a Religious Houfe founded by *Gilbert de Blund*, or *Blount*, about the Year 1100, in a pleafant Valley by the River Side. Its Order was of Canons Regular of St. *Auftin*, and dedicated to the Virgin *Mary*. It had many Benefactions, being valued at its Suppreffion at 280 *l*. 9 *s*. 5 *d*. as *Speed* fays; but at 168 *l*. 19 *s*. 7 *d*. according to *Dugdale*. At the Diffolution, as appears by a monumental Infcription on the *North* Side

of

of the Altar, it was granted by *Henry* VIII. to *Richard Codington* and *Elizabeth* his Wife, in Exchange for the Manor of *Nonesuch*, in *Surry*. Afterwards it was in the Family of *Fiennes*. It has for some time been in the *Norton* Family, who have built a neat Mansion where the Priory stood, which is now the Seat of *Richard Norton*, Esq.

IXWORTH-*Thorp*. The chief Estate and Rectory belonged to *Ixworth* Priory, and were granted to the aforesaid *Richard* and *Elizabeth Codington*. *Thomas Crofts Read*, Esq; is now Lord of this Manor.

KNATTISHALL, or GNATTSHALL. *John de Herlyng*, of *East-Herlyng* in *Norfolk*, was Lord here A. D. 1360; and it continued long in that Name and Family. Sir *Thomas Lovel* died seised of this Manor A. D. 1522, and left it to his Cousin *Francis Lovel*; and it is now vested in ⸺ *Cavendish*, Esq.

LANGHAM, formerly the Lordship of *William de Crikctote*; it is now vested in *Patrick Blake*, Esq; who hath now a Seat here.

LIVERMORE-*Little*, anciently gave Name to *Bartholomew Livermore*, who was Lord of the Manor: Afterwards it was Mr. *Coke*'s, who built the Hall, and left it to the Duke of *Grafton*, who some time resided here. *Baptist Lee*, Esq; has greatly augmented this neat Mansion, inclosed it with a large Park, and has made it his Seat.

NORTON, was the Lordship of *John de Pakenham*, 9 *Edward* III. Here was lately the Seat of the *Millesons*; then of *Milleson Edgar*, Esq; a Descendant from the Heiress of that Family, who sold it to Alderman *Macro*, of *Bury*; whose Son the Rev. *Cox Macro*, D. D. now enjoys it. It goes by the Name of *Little Law*, or *Little Loe*-Hall.

RICHENGALE-*Inferior*, anciently the Lordſhip and Demeſne of *Ulfketel*, Earl of the *Eaſt-Angles:* He being killed in the Battle of *Aſſingdon*, in *Eſſex*, left this Manor to the Monks of *Bury:* Afterwards it was granted to Sir *Nicholas Bacon*, and ſold with divers others to Lord Chief Juſtice *Holt*, by Sir *Edmund Bacon*; and now belongs to *Rowland Holt*, Eſq.

SAPISTON. *Gilbert de Blund* had this Lordſhip when the Survey in Domeſday-Book was taken, and made it Part of the Endowment of his Priory at *Ixworth*. The Manor, Rectory, and a Grange here, were granted to *Richard* and *Elizabeth Codington* before-mentioned, 30 *Henry* VIII. The Manor is now veſted in the Duke of Grafton.

STANTON, conſiſts of two Pariſhes, St. *John* and *All-Saints*, and lieth upon the Road from *Ixworth* to *Boteſdale*. Here is a Fair Yearly on the laſt Day of *May*, and the firſt Day of *June*. King *Edward* the Confeſſor gave the Manor and Advowſon of *All-Saints* to the Abbey of *Bury*; and they were granted 31 *Henry* VIII. to Sir *Thomas Jermyn*, Knt. The Advowſon of St. *John*'s belonged to *Robert Aſhfield*. The two Rectories were conſolidated *A. D.* 1457. The Manor is now veſted in *Edward Capell*, Eſq.

STOWLANGTOFT, ſo called as ſome think, from the Family of *Langtofts* who lived here, to diſtinguiſh it from other Towns named *Stow*, in this County. The Hall or Manor-Houſe, was the Seat of *Jefferey Peche*, 9 *Ed.* III. but afterwards of the *D'Ewes*. The learned Sir *Simon D'Ewes*, Knt. was created a Baronet 15 *July*, 1641. That Family is now extinct. The Lordſhip and Demeſne in this Pariſh was for ſome time the Eſtate of *Thomas Norton*, Eſq; but is now veſted, by Purchaſe, in
Sir

Sir *Thomas Rawlinson*, Knt. Lord-Mayor of *London* in the Year 1754. The Church is said to have been built about 45 *Edw*. III. or *A.D.* 1370, by *Robert Dacy*, of *Ashfield*, who died in 1401; and before his Death was called *Robert Ashfield*. In the Chancel is a noble Monument for that great Scholar Sir *Simon D'Ewes*.

THELNETHAM, corruptly called *Feltham*, anciently the Lordship and Demesne of *John de Thelnetham*. It is now vested in Dr. *Thruston*.

TROSTON, formerly belonged to the Abbot of *Bury*; then it was in the Family of *Maddox*: It is now vested in Mrs. *Brundish*.

WALSHAM *in the Willows*. *Gilbert de Blund* had a Lordship here in King *William* the Conqueror's Time, which he probably made Part of the Endowment of his Priory of *Ixworth*. For at the Dissolution, a Manor in *Walsham*, and the Rectory and Lands called *East-House Lands*, were granted as Parcel of the Possessions of that Priory to *Richard* and *Elizabeth Codington*, so often mentioned, 31 *July*, 30 *Henry* VIII. And this is probably the Manor and Estate now belonging to *Rowland Holt*, Esq. Another Manor in *Walsham* belonged to *William de la Pole* Duke of *Suffolk*, in *Henry* VIth's Reign; and upon the Attainder of some of his Descendants, was granted 6 *Henry* VIII. to *George* Earl of *Shrewsbury*; and this seems to be the Estate which hath for some time belonged to the Family of *Hunt*, and is now vested in a Maiden Lady of that Name.

WATESFIELD, vulgarly called WATCHFIELD, was the Lordship of the Abbot of *Bury*. It is now vested in *Nocold Tompson*, Esq; and Mr. *Samuel Moody*.

WESTOW-

Hundred of Blackbourn. 237

Weston-*Market*, anciently the Lordship of *Hugh Hovel*; afterwards it descended to the Family of *Bokenham*, from them to the *Tyrrels*, and is now vested in Dr. *Thruston*, who has his Seat here.

Westow. It appears by a mural Monument in the Chancel, that the *Crofts* were in Possession of this Manor as early as the Time of *Edward* III. and there is a Roll yet extant of a Court held in his Reign by one of that Family. Afterwards it was the Abbots of *Bury*; then the *Kitson's*; after them the *Bacon's*; and then came into the Family of *Progers*; and is now vested in Sir *Sydenham Fowke*, who married the Heiress of *Progers*, and makes the Hall his Seat.

Wordwell, anciently the Lordship of *Thomas de Wordwell*. It is now vested in Earl *Cornwallis*.

HUNDRED of LACKFORD.

*L*ACKFORD Hundred is parted from the County of *Cambridge* by the River *Cam*, and from the County of *Norfolk* by the *Little Ouse*; and is bounded on the *East* and *South-East* by the Hundreds of *Blackbourn* and *Thingoe*. It contains the following Parishes, *viz*.

BARTON-*Mills*, or *Little*-BARTON, to distinguish it from another Parish of this Name, in the Hundred of *Thedwastre*. The Manor here was given to the Abbey of *Bury*, by one *Robert Hoo*; and at the Dissolution was granted to *Simon Stewart*, 7 *Edward* VI. But the Advowson of the Church was given to the College of *Stoke*, by *Clare*; and at the Dissolution fell to the Crown.

BRANDON, is situated on the *Little Ouse*, which is nagable from *Lynn* to this Town. The Town is pretty well built, and the Road lies through it from St. *Edmundsbury* to *Lynn*. The Manor and Advowson of the Church, which is a very good Structure, belonged to the Bishoprick of *Ely* until the 4th Year of Queen *Elizabeth*, when it was alienated from it. It was granted to *Charles* Duke of *York* 3 *Jac.* I. West from the Church is the Seat of *Joseph Birch*, Esq. This Town has a small Market on *Fridays*, and three Fairs, *viz.* on 14 *February*, 11th of *June*, and the 11th of *November*. The Lordship now belongs to *Rowland Holt*, Esq. The Town was first honoured by giving the Title of a Baron to *Charles Gerrard*, who was by King *Charles* I. created Lord *Gerrard*, of
Brandon.

Brandon. He was afterwards by King *Charles* II. created Earl of *Macklesfield*; but that Family being extinct Queen *Anne* in 1711 created Duke *Hamilton* a Peer of *England*, by the Stile and Title of Baron *Dutton* and Duke of *Brandon*; whose great Grandson now enjoys this Title. The Town furnished *London* with a Lord-Mayor in 1445, who was *John Eyre*, Son of *John Eyre*, Draper. He built *Leadenhall* for the Use of the City, and left besides that five thousand Marks, (a prodigious Sum in those Days) to charitable Uses. He died 18 *Sept.* 1459.

CAVENHAM, for Shortness called CANHAM, was anciently the Lordship and Demesne of *Gilbert* Earl of *Clare*. The Manor of *Shardelowes* in *Cavenham*, belonged to *Humphrey* Duke of *Buckingham* 28 *Henry* VI. The Church was given to *Stoke*, by *Clare*; and the Impropriation was granted to *George Bingley* and *William Blake*, 4 *Jac.* I. The Lordship now belongs to Lord Viscount *Townshend*. —— *Johnson*, Esq; hath a Seat in this Parish, where he commonly resides.

DOWNHAM. A Manor here was granted to Sir *Thomas Kitson* 31 *Henry* VIII. as Parcel of the Possessions of *Bury* Abbey, which had the Manor of *Dunham* given to it by *William* the Conqueror, at the Desire of Abbot *Baldwin*. Another Manor in *Downham*, and the Impropriation of this Parish were granted to *Richard Codington* and *Elizabeth* his Wife, 30 *Henry* VIII. as Parcel of the Possessions of *Ixworth* Priory. It is now very fitly called *Sandy-Downham*, by reason of a Sand-Flood, as it may be called, which happened in the Year 1668; the Circumstances of which are related at large in the following Letter, written by *Thomas Wright*, Esq; then living upon the Spot, and a great Sufferer by it.

In which he says, "He found some Difficulty in tra-
"cing these wonderful Sands to their Original, but he
"found it to be in *Lakenheath*, a Town about five Miles
"South-

"South-weſt of *Downham*, where ſome great Sand-Hills
"having the Superficies broken by the tempeſtuous South-
"weſt Wind, were blown upon ſome neighbouring
"Ground; this being of the ſame Nature, and having
"only a thin Coat of unthrifty Graſs over it, which was
"ſoon rotted by the other Sand lying on it, joined the
"*Lakenheath* Sand, increaſed its Maſs, and accompanied
"its ſtrange Progreſs. Mr. *Wright* ſuppoſes, that at the
"firſt Eruption the Sand did not cover more than eight
"or ten Acres of Ground; but before it had travelled
"four Miles from its firſt Abode, it increaſed ſo much
"that it covered more than a thouſand. All the Oppo-
"ſition it met with from *Lakenheath* to *Downham* was
"from one Farm-houſe which the Owner endeavoured
"to ſecure by building Bulwarks againſt it; but perceiv-
"ing this would not anſwer his Purpoſe, he changed his
"Plan, and inſtead of trying to prevent its Approach,
"he ſlighted all his Works, and every Fence which might
"obſtruct its Courſe; and thus by giving it free Paſ-
"ſage, in four or five Years Time he was fairly rid of it.
"It was about thirty or forty Years before the writing
"of this Account, that the Sand firſt reached *Downham*,
"where it continued for ten or twelve Years in the Out-
"ſkirts of the Town, without doing any conſiderable
"Damage. The Reaſon of which (as Mr. *W.* ima-
"gined) was becauſe its Current was then down-hill,
"which ſheltered it from thoſe Winds which gave it
"Motion; but the Valley being once paſſed, it went
"above a Mile up-hill in two Months Time, and over-
"ran above 200 Acres of very good Corn-Land the ſame
"Year. It is now got into the Body of this little Town,
"where it hath buried and deſtroyed divers Houſes, and
"hath forced them to preſerve the Remainder at a greater
"Expence than they were worth. He at laſt gave the
"Flood of Sand ſome Check, tho' for four or five Years
"his Succeſs was doubtful. It had poſſeſſed all his A-
"venues,

"venues, so that there was no Passage to him, but over
"two Walls that were eight or nine Feet high, and en-
"compassed a small Grove before his House, then al-
"most buried in Sand. Nay, at one time it had possessed
"his Yard, and was blown up almost to the Eves of his
"Out-houses. At the other End it had broken down
"his Garden-wall, and stopped all Passage that Way.
"For four or five Years Mr. *Wright* stopped it as well as
"he could with Furze Hedges set upon one another as
"fast as the Sand levelled them, which he found to be
"the best Expedient. By this means he raised Sand-banks
"near twenty Yards high, and brought the Sand into
"the Compass of eight or ten Acres; then by laying
"some Hundreds of Loads of Muck and Earth upon it
"in one Year, he reduced it again to *Terra firma*, and
"then he cleared all his Walls, and by the Assistance of
"Neighbours who helped him away with 1500 Loads
"in one Month, he cut a Passage to his House thro' the
"main Body of Sand. But the other End of the Town
"met with a worse Fate, where many Houses were over-
"thrown or buried, and their Pastures and Meadows
"which for so small a Town were considerable, were
"over-run and destroyed. That Branch of the *Little*
"*Ouse*, on which this Town borders, (better known by
"the Name of *Brandon* or *Thetford* River) for three
"Miles together was so filled with the Sand, that a
"Vessel with two Loads Weight passed with as much
"Difficulty as before a Vessel would with ten; and had
"not this River interposed and stopped the Progress of
"the Sand into *Norfolk*, great Part of that County had
"been ruined. For (as Mr. *W.* observes) according to
"the Proportion of the Increase of the Sand in those five
"Miles, which was from 10 Acres to 1500 or 2000, in
"a Progress over ten Miles more of the like Soil, it would
"have been swelled to a huge and amazing Quantity."
Mr. *W.* imputes the Cause of this Flood to the Violence

of the South-west Wind passing over the Level of the
Fens without any Check, and to the Sandiness of the
Soil. The Levity of this, he believed, gave occasion to
that Story of the Actions that used to be brought in *Norfolk*, for Ground blown out of the Owners Possession;
but, he says, the County of *Suffolk* was more friendly in
that Particular, for he had possessed a great Quantity of
that wandering Land without Interruption. *Phil. Transf.*
N°. 17.

The Lordship of this Parish now belongs to the Heirs
of *Thomas Wright*, Esq.

ELVEDON. *Alvedon* Manor and the Advowson of the
Rectory, and *Stanes* alias *Monks-Hall* Manor, with the
Tenement called *Walters*, and some other Things in
Alvedon, were granted as Parcel of the Possessions of *Bury*
to *Thomas* Duke of *Norfolk*, 32 *Henry* VIII. and afterwards to *Richard Fulmerston* in Exchange, 3 *Edward* VI.
Another Manor in *Elvedon* was granted, as late belonging
to *Rushworth* College, to *Henry* Earl of *Surry*, 33 *Henry*
VIII. who, about four Years after, alienated it to *Thomas*
Duke of *Norfolk*. It was lately the Lordship of *Thomas*
Crispe, Esq; and is now vested in Sir *John Tyrrel*, Bart.
who married the Heiress of that Family.

ERESWELL. This Manor was held of the King *in*
Capite, as of his Honour of *Boloigne*, by *Ralph* of *Rouceftre*, and his Descendants; and in the first Year of
Edward II. was so held by *Robert de Tudenham*, and *Eve*
his Wife. Besides the Parish Church, dedicated as we
think to St. *Peter*, there was at the *North* End of the
Parish a Chapel dedicated to St. *Laurence*; and in one of
these there was a Chauntry of the yearly Value of 9 *l.*
4 *s.* 6 *d.* The Manor is now in the Dean and Chapter
of *Ely*.

EXNING,

HUNDRED of LACKFORD. 243

EXNING, or IXNING. See p. 187.

FRECKINGHAM, is a Peculiar of *Rochester* Diocese; and has been so from the Time of *William* the Conqueror, as appears from Domesday-Book. It is also the Lordship and Demesne of Sir *Robert Clarke*, Bart.

HERINGSWELL. The Manor and Advowson belonged to the Abbot and Convent of *Bury*, being given thereto by *Ulfric*, a very wealthy Man. The Manor is now vested in *John Holden*, Esq.

HIGHAM-*Green*, is a Hamlet of *Gazeley*.

ICKLINGHAM, consists of two distinct Parishes, St. *James* and *All-Saints*, having two Parish Churches. The Manor and Advowson of *Icklingham St. James* belonged to the Abbey of *Bury*, and were granted to *Anthony Rous* 31 *Henry* VIII. It is now vested in *Daniel Gwilt*, Esq. The Manor of *All-Saints* belongs to the Earl of *Essex*. Near this Village there have been within the Memory of some, now, or very lately living, several *Roman* Coins dug up; which shews the Antiquity of the Place, and that it probably enough has been a *Roman* Station.

LAKENHEATH. The Prior and Convent of *Ely* had a Grant for a Market and Fair here *A. D.* 1309. They had a Grant for a Market here long before; and the Abbot of *Bury* got an Inquisition in the fourth Year of King *John*, to try by a Jury whether the lately erected Market at *Lakinge*, was not to the Detriment of the Town and Market of *Bury*? The Manor and Advowson now belong to the Dean and Chapter of *Ely*. It is a large Village, situated on the Side of the Fens, in an unwholesome Air; at present not remarkable, except it be for the Residence of Sir *Simeon Stewart*, who has a Seat here.

MILDENHALL, situated on the River *Lark*, is a very large Town in Bounds, and a Half-Hundred of itself. The Borough, commonly called High-Town *Mildenhall*, is a pleasant well-built Town; its noble Church and tall Steeple, are good Ornaments to it. There is a plentiful Market Weekly on *Fridays*, well served with Fish, wild Fowl, and all other Provisions. The Fair begins Yearly on *Sept.* 29, and a considerable one it is, lasting four Days. Towards the Fens are several large Streets as big as ordinary Towns, called by the Inhabitants, *Rows*; as *West-Row*, *Beck-Row*, and *Holywell-Row*.

One Manor of this Town was given to the Abbey of *Bury* by King *Edward* the Confessor, that the Religious might eat Wheat, and not as they did before Barley-bread. At the Dissolution it was granted 4 and 5 *Philip* and *Mary*, to *Thomas Reeve* and *Christopher Ballet*: It is now the Estate of Sir *William Bunbury*, Bart. Nephew of Sir *Thomas Hanmer*, Speaker of the House of Commons in the Reign of Queen *Anne*, who constantly resided here in a noble Mansion North of the Church. This Town has furnished *London* with two Lord-Mayors, *Henry Barton*, who was Lord-Mayor in 1428, and *William Gregory*, who was Mayor in 1451. In the Year 1567, *May* 17, great Part of this Town was consumed by Fire. Here is also the Seat of ——— *Rushbrooke*, Esq.

THETFORD. The whole or greatest Part of this anciently famous Place seems originally to have been on the *Suffolk*-side of the River; and there is still one Parish, *viz.* St. *Mary*'s, consisting of about thirty Houses in *Suffolk*, and Part of this Hundred of *Lackford*; tho' as to Ecclesiastical Matters, under the Jurisdiction of the Archdeacon of *Norwich*. In the Reign of King *Edward* III. there were thirteen Parishes on the *Suffolk*-side, and but seven on the *Norfolk*-side.

The

HUNDRED *of* LACKFORD.

The Priory of *Cluniac* Monks was firſt founded on this Side, tho' ſoon removed into the other. The Houſe of *Benedictine* Nuns, and thoſe of the Canons of the *Holy Sepulchre*, and *Dominican* Friers, continued on the *Suffolk*-ſide till the Diſſolution.

TUDDENHAM.

WANGFORD, was the Seat of the Lord Chief Juſtice *Wright*, well known in the Reign of King *James* II. The Lordſhip of this Pariſh is now veſted in *Rowland Holt*, Eſq.

WORLINGTON. This is thought to be the ſame Place which is called *Wredelington*, which *William de Valence* Earl of *Pembroke* had the Advowſon of, 20 *Edward* I. *Iſabel*, Daughter of the ſaid Earl, became the Wife of *John Haſtings*, Lord of *Bergavenny*; and *John Haſtings*, Earl of *Pembroke*, great Grandſon of the ſaid *John* and *Iſabel*, died ſeiſed of this Manor 49 *Edward* III. and *Anne* his Wife had it aſſigned to her as Part of her Dower. *William Beauchamp* Lord *Bergavenny*, died ſeiſed of it 12 *Henry* IV. It was Part of *Herbert* the late Earl of *Orford*'s Eſtate; then of Lord *Sandys*, who married the Heireſs of the ſaid Earl; and it was ſold by him to *George Montgomerie*, Eſq; late one of the Repreſentatives in Parliament of the Borough of *Ipſwich*.

Hundred of Risbridge.

*R*ISBRIDGE Hundred is bounded on the *East* by the Hundreds of *Baberg*, *Thingoe*, and *Lackford*; on the *West* by *Cambridgeshire*; on the *South* by the *Stour*, which parts it from *Essex*; and, on the *North*, by *Lackford*. It contains the following Towns and Parishes.

BARNARDISTON, commonly called *Branson*, gives Name to a Family whose several Branches have had Seats at *Kedington*, *Brightwell*, and *Wyverston*, in this County. The Lordship is still in the Family of *Barnardiston*, of *Kedington*.

Great BRADLEY. *Thomas* Lord *Botetourt* was Lord here 8 *Edward* III. in Right of his Wife *Joan*, one of the Sisters and Coheirs of *John de Someri*, Baron of *Dudley*. Here is a Fair yearly on *Sept*. 29. ——— *Brand*, Esq; is Lord of the Manor, and Patron of the Church.

Little BRADLEY. This Church seemingly belonged to *Stoke* College.

CLARE, a pretty large Town, situated on the *Stour*; it is now of little Note, but formerly was, for its Owners, and the Earls descended from them.

Richard Fitz-Gilbert, a Kinsman of King *William* the Conqueror, was the first Earl of *Clare*; he was also called from the usual Place of his Residence, *Richard de Tunbridge*. The Earldom continued in that Family to the Time of King *Edward* II. when *Gilbert* the Son of *Gilbert* Earl of *Clare*, by *Joan de Acres* Daughter of King *Edward*

HUNDRED *of* RISBRIDGE. 247

Edward I. dying without Iffue Male, the Honour became extinct. Afterwards *Lionel*, third Son of K. *Edward* III. in the 36th Year of his Reign was created Duke of *Clarence:* His Daughter marrying *Edward Mortimer* Earl of *March*, carried this Lordfhip into that Family, who enjoyed it fome Time. The Dukedom was extinct at her Father's Death; but 13 *Henry* IV. *Thomas* his fecond Son was created Duke of *Clarence*, who dying without Iffue Male, the Title of *Clare* lay again dormant, until *George Plantagenet* Brother of King *Edward* IV. was created Duke of *Clarence:* Upon his Attainder and Death, the Title was extinguifhed again; but in 22 *James* I. *John Hollis*, of *Houghton* in *Nottinghamfhire*, was created Earl of *Clare:* In 1688, *John* his great Grandfon fucceeded to his Earldom, who married *Margaret* the third Daughter of *Henry Cavendifh*, Duke of *Newcaftle:* After his Father's Death, he was in 6th King *William* III. created Marquis of *Clare* and Duke of *Newcaftle*. He died without Iffue 17 *July* 1707, and left the Bulk of his Land Eftate to *Thomas Hollis Pelham*, Son of his youngeft Sifter *Grace*, who by King *George* I. was created Earl and Marquis of *Clare*, and afterwards Duke of *Newcaftle*.

South-Eaft of this Town, between it and the River, are ftill the Ruins of a very ftrong Caftle, built by one of the Earls of *Clare*; but it is not certain which of them.

In the Church of St. *John Baptift* in the Caftle, was a very ancient fmall Houfe of *Benedictine* Monks, a Cell to the Abbey of *Bece* in *Normandy*, until the Year 1124, when they were removed to *Stoke*. Here was alfo a Houfe of Friers *Eremites*, of the Order of St. *Auftin*, founded by *Richard de Clare* Earl of *Glocefter*, A.D. 1248; which was given by King *Henry* VIII. to *Richard Friend*. It is now vefted in Mr. *Poulter*.

The Church is a very good Structure, which with the Ruins of the Caftle and Monaftery, are the only Things worth Notice. There is a mean Market on *Fridays*, if it deserves that Name; and one Fair on *Easter-Tuesday*, and another on *July* 25th yearly. Not far from *Clare* is *Honedon*; where, in the Year 1687, the Sexton digging a Grave, found a large Quantity of *Saxon* Coins. See *Phil. Transact.* N°. 189, 203.

CHEDBURGH. This Church is now consolidated with *Ickworth*; the Lordship and Patronage belong to the Right Hon. the Earl of *Bristol*.

CHILTON, rather *Chipley*, is a Hamlet of *Clare*. Here was formerly a small Priory, which was united *A. D.* 1468, to the College of *Stoke*; the Remains of which are now converted into a Dwelling-House.

COOLING, corruptly called *Coolige*. In this Parish is a good Seat, called by the Name of *Branches*; which, with the Manor, was the Estate of *William Long-Espee* Earl of *Salisbury* and *Somerset*, base Son to King *Henry* II. by fair *Rosamond*. They are now vested in *Ambrose Dickins*, Esq; who has a handsome Mansion here. Here was anciently a Free Chapel, dedicated to St. *Margaret*; on whose Feast-day 20 *July*, one of the Fairs is kept; the other is on *October* 6. The Advowson of the Church was granted *A. D.* 1333, by Sir *John* and Sir *Thomas de Shardelowe*, Sons of *John Shardelowe*, Justice of the Common-Pleas to the Custos and Scholars of *Trinity-Hall* in *Cambridge*, to be appropriated to their Use.

DALHAM, anciently the Lordship and Demesne of *William de Ufford*, Earl of *Suffolk*; afterwards it came into the Family of the *Estotevilles*, who sold it to the Right Rev. *Simon Patrick* Bishop of *Ely*, and his Son disposed of it to *Gilbert Affeck*, Esq; Father to *John Affleck*, late one of the Representatives of this County.

DENHAM,

HUNDRED of RISBRIDGE. 249

DENHAM. *Thomas Hethe* was Lord of *Denham*, by *Barrow*, in the latter Part of King *Edward* the Third's Reign; the Lordship, after that, belonged to *Margaret de Say*, then to *Edward Lukemore*, Esq; then to *Horatio* Lord Viscount *Townsend*, who married *Mary*, sole Heiress of *Edward Lukemore*; and is now possessed by that Family.

It was extraparochial until Sir *Edward Lukemore* built a Church or Chapel here, and endowed it with the Tithes.

DENSTON, or DENARDESTON. Here was a College or Chauntry endowed with 22 *l*. 8 *s*. 9 *d*. *per Ann*. and granted with a Manor called *Beaumonds* thereto belonging 17 *June* 2 *Edward* VI. to *Thomas* and *John Smith*. *Thomas Smith* sold it 9 *Elizabeth* to *William* the Son of *William Bird*, Citizen and Mercer of *London*. In this Parish is a beautiful Seat, which now is the Mansion of *John Robinson*, Esq; late Lieutenant-Colonel in the *Coldstream* Regiment of Foot-Guards, who has the Lordship.

DEPDEN. The Hall did formerly belong to the *Jermyns*; afterwards to the *Coels*; from them it became the Seat of *Coel Thornhill*, Esq; who sold it to *Hutch. Mure*, Esq.

GAZELY, or GAIESLY. This Church was given to the College of *Stoke-Clare*, to be the Portion of one of the Prebendaries; and the Rectory was granted 9 *Jac*. I, to *Francis Moore* and *Francis Philips*.

HAVERHILL, is a long Thorough-fare Town; the South-end of the Street is Part in this County, and Part in *Essex*. It has a mean Market on *Wednesdays*, and two Fairs, *i. e.* on 1 *May* and 15 *August*. Here were formerly two Churches, or at least a Church and a Chapel; one of which was called *Le nether Chirche*, in *Haverhill*.

The

The Manors of *Defening* and *Haverhill* were Lord *Stafford's*, 4 *Henry* IV. and *Humphrey* Duke of *Buckingham's* 28 *Henry* VI. *Henry* Lord *Grey* of *Codnoure*, had a Grant of the Manors of *Haverhill* and *Herſham*, 1 *Richard* III. The Church was impropriated to the Priory of *Caſtleacre*, in *Norfolk*; and the Rectory and Advowſon of the Vicarage were granted 29 *Henry* VIII. to *Thomas* Lord *Cromwell*.

HAWKEDON. There are two Manors in this Town; one belongs to *Philip Hammond*, Eſq; who has a Seat here: The other belongs to the Family of *Maltyward*. *Gilbert d'Umfreville* died ſeiſed of the Manor of *Thorſtanton*, or *Thurſtruſton* in *Hawkedon*, 4 *Richard* II. *Robert* Lord *Harington* died ſeiſed of it 7 *Henry* IV. in Right of his Wife, who was Daughter of Sir *Nigel Loryng*, Knight of the Garter. There is alſo a Seat called *Swan-Hall*, which was long in the Family of *Abbot*, and ſince purchaſed by the *Stewarts*; in whoſe Family it now is.

HUNDON. *Lionel* Earl of *Clarence* died ſeiſed of the Manor of *Hundon, Erdbury*, and *Wood-Hall* in *Sudbury*, 43 *Edward* III. The Church was given to the College of *Stoke-Clare*, by *Aloſtan* Prieſt of *Hundon*, and *Edward* his Son; and the Rectory and Advowſon of the Vicarage were granted to Sir *John Cheke*, 5 *Edward* VI. The Manor is now veſted in *Henry Vernon*, Eſq. There was alſo a Manor or reputed Manor in *Hunden*, with the Parks called *Great* Park, *Eſtry* Park, and *Broxley* Park, granted to Sir *John Cheke* 3 *Edward* VI. as Parcel of the Poſſeſſions of *Stoke-Clare*.

KEDINGTON, or as it is written in Domeſday-Book *Kediture*, now corruptly *Ketton*, was then the Lordſhip and Demeſne of *Ralph Barnard*; afterwards it belonged to the Earls of *Clare*; but in late Times to the *Barnardiſtons*, who have been here ever ſince the Year 1500, according

according to *Weaver*, p. 733. Sir *Thomas Barnardiston*, of this Place, Knt. was created a Baronet 7 *April*, 1663. Sir *Samuel Barnardiston* lately resided at *Kedington-Hall*, a beautiful Seat. It was the Jointure of his Lady; but, upon her Death, it came to Sir *John Barnardiston*; who had sold the Reversion to Mr. *Mertins*, Goldsmith and Jeweller in *London*. The Fair is Yearly on *July* 29.

KENTFORD, a Hamlet to *Gazely*.

LIDGATE. Here was a Mount moated round near the Church, on which remain the Ruins of a Castle: But this Parish is more memorable for giving Birth and Name to *John Lidgate*, who was a *Benedictine* Monk of *Bury St. Edmunds*. He died *A. D.* 1440, and was famous for his Learning and his Poetry.

The Lordship of this Town did formerly belong to *John Hastings* Earl of *Pembroke*, 49 *Edward* III. since to the Lord *Jermyn*, late to Sir *Jermyn Davers*, Bart. and then by Sale to his Grace the late Duke of *Somerset*.

MOULTON, is a Peculiar to the Archbishop of *Canterbury*, and under the Jurisdiction of the Dean of *Bocking*. *John Agnerus* had the Grant of a Market here 26 *Edw.* I. Sir *John de Chyvereston* was Lord 25 *Edward* III. but he shortly after sold the Manor to *Elizabeth*, Relict of Sir *Andrew Lutterell*; one of whose Descendants, Sir *Hugh Lutterell*, died seised of it 6 *Henry* VI.

OUSDEN. In this Parish is the Seat of *Richard Moseley*, Esq; who is also Lord of the Manor.

POSLINGFORD, was anciently the Lordship of *Ralph Baynard*. *New-House*, in this Parish, is the Seat of *George Golding*, Esq. The Impropriation and Advowson of the Vicarage belonged to the Priory of *Dunmow*, in *Essex*; and were granted 28 *Henry* VIII. to *Robert* Earl of *Sussex*; and are now vested in *Henry Moore*, Esq.

STANSFIELD. In this Parish is the Seat of *Robert Kedington*, Gent. The Lordship is in the Crown.

STOKE *juxta Clare*, is remarkable for a Priory translated from the Castle of *Clare* thither, by *Richard de Tonebridge* Earl of *Clare:* It was of the *Benedictine* Order. About *A. D.* 1415, *Edmund Mortimer* Earl of *March* augmented its Revenues, and got it changed from a Priory to a Collegiate Church, consisting of a Dean and Secular Canons; the Popes *John* 23d and *Martin* 5th ratifying this Exchange. It was valued at the Dissolution at 324 *l.* 4 *s.* 1¼ *d. per Annum*, and granted to Sir *John Cheke*, and *Walter Mildmay*; from whom it passed to the Family of *Trigg*; then it became the Possession of Sir *Gervaise Elweys*, who married *Amy* the Daughter of Dr. *Trigg*. He was created a Baronet 22 *July*, 1660; whose Successor Sir *Hervey Elweys*, now enjoys the Honour and Estate. He resides in a good old Seat, where the Priory stood. *Stoke* Fair is on the *Monday* in *Whitsun*-Week.

STRADDISHALL.

Great THURLOW. Here was a small Hospital or Free Chapel, of the yearly Value of 3 *l.* which was granted by King *Edward* IV. to the *Maison de Dieu* in *Cambridge*, now Part of *King*'s-College. The Lordship formerly belonged to *John King*, Esq; then to the *Waldegraves*, then to Sir *Cordel Firebrace*, Bart. who sold it to *James Vernon*, Esq; whose Son *Henry* has his Seat at the Hall in this Parish.

Little THURLOW. In this Parish is a noble old Seat, where the Family of *Soame* have long resided. It is now the Seat of *Stephen Soame*, Esq.

WHIXOE.

WICKHAM-*Brook*, now a Parish of large Bounds, to which several Hamlets or Parishes have been annexed: Four of these appear in some old Writings, now in the Custody of *Robert Edgar*, of *Ipswich*, Esq; 1. The Hamlet or Parish of *Clopton*, or *Cloptune*, the Tithes of which did anciently belong to *Stoke* College. 2. *Badmondisfield*-Hall, was formerly the Possession of *Charles Somerset*, Son of Sir *George Somerset*, who was the second Son of *Charles* Earl of *Worcester*; since Sir *Henry North*'s; now of —— *Warner*, Esq. There was a Free Chapel here dedicated to St. *Mary*, of which Sir *John Hastings* Lord *Bergavenny*, and his Descendants, were Patrons; and after them *John Grey*, of *Ruthin*; this Chapel was granted by Queen *Elizabeth* in 1583, to *William Mansey*, Ironmonger of *London*. 3. *Giffords*-Hall, once in Sir *Hugh Francis*; since in *Thomas Heigham*, Esq; afterwards in *John Owers*; now in *George Chinery*, Gent. 4. *Clopton*, or *Wickham*-House, was formerly the Habitation of Major *Robert Sparrow*, and now sometimes the Residence of *Robert Edgar*, Esq.

WETHERSFIELD.

Great WRATTING, and *Little* WRATTING. Lady *Barnardiston* is Lady of the Manor in these Parishes.

HUNDRED of BABERGH.

BABERGH Hundred is parted from *Essex* by the River *Stour*; it is bounded on the *North* by *Thingoe* and *Thedwastre*; and on the *East* by *Cosford*. The Towns and Villages in this Hundred are as followeth, viz.

ACTON, formerly called *Aketon*. The Manor in this Parish in 9 *Edward* I. was the Inheritance of *Robert de Buers*. King *Edward* IV. afterwards gave it to *Henry* Lord *Bouchier*; he left it to *Henry*, his Grandson. Sir *Richard Bacon*, Bart. is now Owner of the Hall, and Lord of the Manor. *Acton-Place*, was formerly the Seat of the *Daniels*; they sold it to *Robert Jennens*, Esq; who began to rebuild the same; it is now finished by *William Jennens* his Son, and is a fine Structure. There was anciently in this Parish a Chauntry, of the yearly Value of 7l. 2s. 8½d. *Ambrose Kedington*, Esq; has a Seat in this Parish, by the Side of *Babergh-Heath*. The Advowson is in Mr. *Jennens*.

ALPHETON, was formerly the Lordship of *John de Welnetham*, who in the Reign of *Edward* III. left a Daughter his Heir, married to *Edmund Brokesborn*, Esq; by whom he had Issue *Eleanor*, who married Sir *William Raynsforth*, Knt. This Manor is now vested in Mrs. *Little*.

ASSINGTON. Sir *Andrew de Nevile* claimed the Patronage and Advowson of this Church, 18 *Edward* I. but he released it to the Prior and Convent of *Hatfield Peverel*; upon the Dissolution of which House the Rectory and Advowson vowfon of the Vicarage were granted 29 *Henry* VIII. to *Giles Leigh*. The Manor belonged to the Family of the *Corbets*, which were feated here; Sir *Piers Corbet* was a Knight Banneret in the Time of *Edw.* I. and Sir *Thomas Corbet* was at a Tournament in *Dunftable*, 2 *Edward* II. This Family continued here until the Reign of *Hen.*VIII. then *Robert Gurdon*, Efq; purchafed the Eftate of the *Corbets*. In the 26th Year of Queen *Elizabeth*, *John Gurdon*, of *Affington*, Efq; was High-Sheriff of this County; and ever fince their firft Settlement here, the *Gurdons* have been Men of Figure and Eftate in this County, as they ftill remain. The prefent Poffeffor is *Nathaniel Gurdon*, Efq.

BOXFORD, fituated in a Bottom between two Brooks, which join each other a little below it. It is a Place of confiderable Trade. Here are two Fairs yearly; one on *Eafter-Monday*, and the other on *December* 21. The Crown prefents to it.

About a Mile South-Eaft of this Village, fituated in the Parifhes of *Boxford*, *Stoke* and *Affington*, is *Peyton*-Hall, granted by *William* the Conqueror to *Robert Mallet*, a *Norman* Baron, and a Progenitor of the ancient Family of *Peyton*, (from which defcended the *Uffords* Earls of *Suffolk*) who being firft feated at *Peyton*-Hall in *Ramfholt*, in *Willford* Hundred, afterwards fettled at *Peyton*-Hall in this Parifh, by Marriage with *Gernoon*. There was a Sir *John Peyton*, of *Suffolk*, in the Time of *Edw.* I. and *John de Peyton* was Knight of this Shire 28, 29 *Ed.* III. This has for fome Time been the Eftate of the *Dafhwoods*, and is now vefted in *George Dafhwood*, Efq; who has a Seat in or near *Sudbury*, called *Wood-Hall*. Here is a Free Grammar-School, founded by Queen *Elizabeth*.

South-Weft of *Boxford* Church, is *Coddenham*-Hall; a very good Seat, formerly the Lordfhip and Demefne of Sir *Jofeph Brand*; now of *Thomas Bennet*, Efq. At the

Eaft-

East-end of *Boxford-street* is another neat Manfion, now the Seat of the Rev. Mr. *Benyon*.

BOXSTEAD, formerly the Lordfhip of the Abbot of *Bury St. Edmund*, 9*Edw*. I. but afterwards, by what means we know not, it was granted to *Robert Harlefton*, Efq; who being attainted in the Reign of *Edw*. IV. it was granted to *Richard* Duke of *Glocefter*, Brother to the faid King. It was afterwards the Seat of the *Pooleys*. This ancient Family of Knights Degree fpread itfelf into feveral flourifhing Branches here, and at *Columbine*-Hall in *Stowmarket*, and *Badley* in *Bofmere* Hundred. Sir *John Pooley*, the laft Knight of this Houfe, was chofen Burgefs for *Sudbury* in the Convention of 1688. It is now the Seat of *George Weller*, Efq.

BURES, or BUERS, is a Village on the *Stour*, over which it has a fair Bridge, leading through *Bures* Hamlet in *Effex*, to *Colchefter*. *Galfridus de Fontibus*, (who wrote about the Year 1156) tells us, that King *Edmund* who was cruelly murdered by the *Danes* at *Hoxne* in this County, was crowned here. His Words are thefe: " Be-
" ing unanimoufly approved they brought him to *Suffolk*,
" and, in the Village called *Burum* made him King ; the
" venerable Prelate *Hunibert* affifting, and anointing and
" confecrating *Edmund* to be King. Now *Burum* is an
" ancient Royal Hill, the known Bound between *Eaft*-
" *Sexe* and *Suffolk*, and fituate upon the *Stour*, a River
" moft rapid both in Summer and Winter." Which Paffage (faith the Author of the Additions to *Cambden*, from whom we have it) is the more obfervable, becaufe it fhews what we are to underftand by *Burva*, in *Afferius*'s Life of *Alfred*; that it is not *Bury*, as the Chronicle under *Brompton*'s Name fuppofes; nor yet *Burne* in *Lincolnfhire*, as hath been afferted; but this *Bures* or *Buers*, as *Matthew Weftminfter* calls it.

The Church and Spire-steeple were great Ornaments to this Village; but in 1733 the Spire was set on fire by Lightning, and burnt down to the Steeple; the Bell-Frames were likewise burnt, the Bells melted, and the Steeple much damaged. In a Tomb on the *North*-side of this Church lieth a Knight cross-legged, his Name is supposed to be *Cornard*, who is said to have sold a Farm in this Parish called *Corn*-Hall, for Four-pence; Temp. *Hen*. III. *Buers* Fair is yearly on *Holy-Thursday*.

Small-Bridge, in this Parish, has been memorable for the *Waldegraves*, an ancient Family, who long resided here; but afterwards removed into *Essex*. Sir *Richard Waldegrave* was Knight of the County of *Suffolk*, 50 *Edward* III.

Gilbert de Clare, who died *A. D.* 1151, gave the Church of *Bures* to the Monks of *Stoke-Clare*. *Hugh* Lord *Bardolf* died 32 *Edward* I. seised of the Manor of *Bures* in *Suffolk*, in the Right of his Wife *Isabel* the Daughter and Heiress of *William Aguillon*. King *Edward* IV. in the 19th Year of his Reign granted unto *Anne* the Wife of *William* Lord *Bouchier*, and Sister to his Queen, the Manor of *Overhall*, as also the Manor of *Netherhall*, otherwise called *Sylvesters*-hall, in St. *Mary Bures*, in *Suffolk* and *Essex*.

BRENT-*Illeigh*, a Village and Manor belonging to the Ancestors of Sir *Henry Shelton*, by Marriage with the Co-heiress of *Illeigh*; who procured a Market for it of *Henry* III. long since discontinued. His Posterity flourished here a long time; but afterwards it descended to the Family of *Colman*, who now enjoy it. Dr. *Colman*, Fellow of *Trinity* College *Cambridge*, built a fine Parochial Library at the End of the Chancel, and well furnished it with Books. Since that *Edward Colman*, Esq; built a neat Alms-house for six poor People, and plentifully endowed it. The last of which Family *Edward Colman*, Esq;

Efq; gave this Eftate to his Kinfman *Edward Goat*, Efq; whofe Son *Edward* is is now poffeffed of it. The Manor and Advowfon of the Vicarage were granted 34 *Hen.*VIII. to *Robert Goodwin*, as Parcel of the Poffeffions of St. *Ofith*'s Abbey, in *Effex*; but the Impropriation was granted 5 *Elizabeth* to *Bartholomew King*, and *Edward Wifeman*.

CAVENDISH, is fituated on the *Stour*, and is memorable for giving Name to the noble Family of *Cavendifh*. Sir *John Cavendifh*, born in this Place, was Lord Chief Juftice of the King's Bench 46 *Edward* III. and continued in that Station until the 5th *Richard* II. when unhappily falling into the Hands of that Rabble affembled under *John Raw* and *Robert Weftbroom*, he was beheaded by them at *Bury*. From this learned Judge defcended *William Cavendifh*, who was created by King *Jac.* I. Baron *Cavendifh* of *Hardwick*, and Earl of *Devonfhire*; his Succeffor is now Duke of *Devonfhire*. *Jefus* College in *Cambridge* hath the Advowfon of the Church.

· CHILTON, is faid to be a Hamlet of *Great Waldingfield*. The Hall appears to be a good old Seat; it formerly belonged to the Knightly Family of *Crane*; for Sir *John Crane*, of this Place, Knt. was created a Baronet 11 *May*, 1627; which Family is now extinct. It is now vefted in Sir *Armine Woodhoufe*, who is Lord of the Manor there, called *Waldingfield*-Hall, *Carbonells* with *Chilton*.

COCKFIED, or *Cokefield*, or *Cookfield*, confifts of the Manors *Cockfield*-Hall, which probably belonged to the Abbey of *Bury St. Edmunds*; but Sir *William Spring*, Knt. died feized of it 42 *Elizabeth*. The other is *Earls*-Hall, fo called from the *Veres*, Earls of *Oxford*. In 24 *Edw.* I. *Robert de Vere* Earl of *Oxford* had it. Afterwards *John* Earl of *Oxford* taking part with the *Lancaftrians* againft *Edward* IV. forfeited his Eftates, and the faid *Edward* gave them to his Brother *Richard* Duke of *York*. But
Henry

Henry VII. restoring him to his Honours and Estates, his Successors enjoyed them till the Death of *Aubrey de Vere*, the last Earl of that Family. These Manors are now vested in *John Moore*, Esq. The Advowson is in St. *John's* College, *Cambridge*.

There is a handsome Mansion in this Parish, which has been for some time, and now is the Seat of the *Herveys*.

CORNARD-*Magna*, formerly the Lordship of the Abbess of *Malling*, in *Kent*; who bought it of *Thomas de Grey*, about *A. D.* 1317. It was granted to the Archbishop of *Canterbury* in Exchange, 32 *Henry* VIII. but resumed by Queen *Elizabeth*.

CORNARD-*Parva*, was the Lordship of *Thomas de Grey*. Sir *Roger de Grey*, of *Merton* in *Norfolk*, Knt. died seised of it 1371; and Sir *William de Grey*, of the same Place, died seised of *Cawstons* Manor in *Little Cornard*, 19 October 1632.

EDWARDSTON, a Village of Note for the Lords formerly inhabiting in it. *Herbert de Montechensy* was here in the Time of the Conqueror, whose Son *Waryne* succeeded him in this Lordship. *Hubert*, Son of *Waryne*, married *Mariel* the Daughter of *Peter de Valoignes*, and had Issue by her *William de Montechensy*, who was a great Soldier, and in high Esteem with *Edward* I. and the whole Kingdom. This *William* married a Daughter of *D'Albany* Earl of *Arundel*, by whom he had *Waryne*, who was so vastly wealthy that he was called the *English Crœsus*, and died worth above 200,000 Marks, according to *Cambden*. The Lordship descended at length to the *Waldgraves*, by a Marriage with *Jane* sole Daughter of Sir *Edward Montechensy*. Sir *William Waldegrave*, about the Year 1598, sold it to *John Brand*, of *Boxford*, Clothier; from which Family it came to the late Sir *Robert Kemp*, Bart. by his

Marriage

Marriage with the sole Daughter of *John Brand*, Esq. Sir *Robert* sold the Manor and Advowson to *William French*, Citizen of *London* and Draper in 1714, who now enjoys it.

St. EDWARD's *Place*, was formerly a Religious House, and a Cell to the Monastery of *Abingdon*, near *Oxford*; but the Monks were removed about the Year 1160 to the Priory of *Colne*, in *Essex*; which got the great Tithes of this Parish appropriated to it. It is now the Estate of the Bishop of *Ely*, to which See it was annexed by Queen *Elizabeth* in 1599, in exchange for some valuable Manors which belonged to that See. The Bishop of *Ely* pays to the Vicar after the Rate of Twelve-pence a Day, or 18 *l.* 5 *s. per Annum*.

A little South of *St. Edward's-Place* is a neat Mansion, which was the Seat of *Joseph Alston*, Esq; and was lately sold by his Heirs to Mr. *Sheldon*, of *London*.

GLEMSFORD, was one of the Manors which *Odo* was possessed of when Domesday-Book was taken. Some Rents are paid out of this Lordship to the Bishop of *Ely*, and the Inhabitants are exempted from serving on any Juries elsewhere but at the Isle of *Ely*. The Church of *Ely* had Possessions here as early as *Edward* the Confessor's Time. It is a very large Parish in Bounds; and if the Houses stood contiguous, it is supposed, there would not be four larger Towns in the County. The Fair is yearly on *June* 24; and the Manor now belongs to *Henry Moore*, Esq.

A Sermon is to be preached at *Glemsford* once a Year, by a Fellow of *Christ*'s College *Cambridge*, according to the Will of Dr. *Hawford* 1580, who charged Lands in *Dullingham* for the Support of it.

GROTON, formerly the Lordship of the Abbot of *Bury*. It was granted at the Dissolution of that Abbey to *Adam Winthorp*,

HUNDRED of BABERGH. 261

Winthorp, Efq; in which Family it continued till about the 4th Year of *Charles* I. when it was purchafed by *Thomas Waring*; and is now the Seat of *Thomas Waring*, Efq.

HARTEST, belonged to the Convent of *Ely*, in King *Edward* the Confeffor's Time; but was afterwards appropriated to the Bifhopric, and alienated from it 4 *Eliz.*

LAVENHAM, ftands on the River *Breton*, and is fituated on a Hill of eafy Afcent, on the Top of which is the Market-place. The Market is on *Tuefdays*; but tho' it was formerly very confiderable, when the Trade for blue Cloth was largely carried on here; fince that was loft, it is almoft reduced to nothing. The Fair is on *Sept.* 29, much frequented for Butter and Cheefe. The Church and Steeple are the chief Things remarkable here, both efteemed as being very fine Buildings, perhaps the beft in the County of their Kind. They were built by the *Veres* Earls of *Oxford*, affifted by the *Springs*; *Thomas Spring*, the rich Clothier, lies buried in the Church; he was a great Benefactor to it. In the Steeple are fix large tuneable Bells, much admired by the curious, particularly the Tenor, which is faid to weigh but 23 C. yet founds like a Bell of 40 C. Weight. The College of *Gonvile* and *Caius*, in *Cambridge*, are Patrons of the Rectory.

Lavenham was one of the Two hundred and Twenty-one Lordfhips in *Suffolk*, that King *William* the Conqueror gave to *Robert Mallet*; but he forfeited by joining *Robert*, eldeft Son to the Conqueror, in the 2d of *Hen.* I. which King gave it to *Aubrey de Vere*; in whofe Pofterity it remained till alienated by *Edward* Earl of *Oxford* in Q. *Elizabeth*'s Time to *Paul D'Ewes*, Efq; and is now vefted in *Henry Moore*, Efq.

There are many good Charities belonging to this Town. The Inhabitants purchafed an Eftate of 80 *l. per Annum* for repairing their Alms-houfes, and maintaining the Poor thereof. Dr. *Coppinger*, formerly Rector, gave 10 *l. per Ann.* for the Maintenance of four poor People. *John Carder* 40 *s. per Ann.* to be given to the Poor in Bread: And *John Cream* 40 *l.* towards the Maintenance of twelve poor Widows. Others have given liberally for the Education of Children here, *viz. Richard Peacock* 23 *Car.* II. gave 5 *l. per Ann.* for educating five poor Boys: *Edward Colman*, of *Furnival*'s-Inn, in 1636, gave 200 *l.* to which other Persons gave such Additions, as purchased a convenient Dwelling-House and School-Room, and an Annuity of 30*l.* for a Master. Mr. *Colman* gave 200 *l.* more to be laid out in Land, the Rent of which is to be applied towards binding out one poor Boy yearly from *Milden, Brent-Illeigh*, or *Lavenham*. And *Robert Rice* gave 5 *l. per Ann.* for binding out two poor Boys from *Preston*, or for want of such there, from *Lavenham*. *Thomas Cook*, Lord-Mayor of *London*, A. D. 1463, was a Native of this Town.

LAWSHALL. *Alfwinus* the Son of *Bricius*, gave this Lordship *A. D.* 1022, to the Abbey of *Ramsey*, in *Huntingdonshire*; at the Dissolution it was granted, with the Patronage of the Rectory, to *John Rither*, 37 *Hen.* VIII. and belongs now to *Baptist Lee*, Esq.

MELLFORD, commonly called *Long-Mellford*, is above a Mile in Length from *South* to *North*; it is a pleasant Village, and perhaps one of the largest in *England*, that is not a Market-Town. *Mellford*-Hall is a noble old Seat: Sir *William Cordell*, Master of the Rolls in Queen *Elizabeth*'s Time, had a great Kindness for this Town, and settled his Family at the aforesaid Hall; but dying without Issue, he made *Jane* the youngest of his two Sisters his sole Heir, who married *Richard Allington*, of *Horseheath*, in *Cambridgeshire*, Esq. Upon this Marriage the Estate was sold to *Savage* Earl *Rivers*, in which Family

HUNDRED *of* BABERGH. 263

mily it continued to the Restoration, when the *Cordels* became Purchasers. *Robert Cordel*, of *Melford*, Esq; was created a Baronet 22 *June*, 1660. From the *Cordels* it descended into the Family of *Firebrace*, and is now the Seat of Lady *Firebrace*, Relict of Sir *Cordel Firebrace*, Bart. late one of the Representatives of this County.

Kentwell-Hall, another good old Seat in this Town, belonged to the ancient Family of the *Cloptons*; they continued here for many Descents, and to their Memory several fair Tombs in the Church are erected. From the *Cloptons* it descended to ———— *Darcy*, Knt. and from him to the *Robinsons*; *Thomas Robinson*, of *Kentwell* Hall, Esq; was created a Baronet 26 *Jan.* 1681; but his Heir, who lived at *Worlingham* near *Beccles*, sold his Estate in these Parts to *John Moore*, Esq; Citizen of *London*, and Uncle to *John Moore*, Esq; the present Possessor.

At the South-end of the Town is an old Seat, where the Family of *Martin* hath long resided. *Roger Martin*, Mercer, Son of *Laurence Martin* of this Town, was Lord-Mayor of *London* in 1567: His Descendant *Roger Martin*, of this Town, Esq; was created a Baronet 28 *March* 1667: It is now the Seat of Sir *Roger Martin*, Bart. The Church is a beautiful and noble Structure, standing at the North-end of the Town: There were two Chauntries in it, one founded by *William Clopton*, of the yearly Value of 6*l*. 6*s*. 8*d*. and the other founded by *John Hill*, of the yearly Value of 7*l*. 5*s*. *Weaver* saith, that on some Part of the Out-side of the Church are these Words: " Pray for the Souls of *John Clopton* and *Richard Boteler*, " of whose Goodys this Chapel was built." The Manor and Advowson of the Rectory belonged formerly to the Abbey of *Bury*, to which it was given by *Alfric* the Son of *Widgar*, a famous Knight. They were granted by Queen *Mary* I. to *William*, afterwards Sir *William Cordel*; who built here an Hospital for the Poor, and plentifully endowed it. The present Bishop of *Worcester* is a

S 4 Native

Native of this Place, and Son to the late Rector. *Mell-ford*-Fair is yearly on the *Tuesday* in *Whitsun* Week; but it was granted to the Abbot of *Bury* 19 *Henry* III. to be held on the Eve, Day, and Morrow of the *Holy Trinity*; with a Market on *Thursdays*.

MILDING, formerly the Lordship and Demesne of *Remigius de Milden*, who took his Name from this Place. Afterwards it descended to the *Allingtons*; from them, by Purchase, to the *Canhams*. It is now vested in *John Canham*, Esq; who has his Seat at the Hall.

In this Parish is also *Wells*-Hall, some time belonging to the Family of *Shoreland*. The Heirs of that Family sold it to *Paul D'Ewes*, Esq; who left it to Sir *Simon D'Ewes*, Knt. his Son. Afterwards it was sold to the *Colmans*; and from them it came, with the Estate at *Brent-Illeigh*, to *Edward Goat*, Esq. See p. 257.

MONKS-*Illeigh*, so called because the Lordship formerly belonged to the Monks of St. *Peter* (now commonly called St. *Austin*'s) in *Canterbury*, to whom it was given with *Hadleigh*, by *Brithnoth*, *Dux* or *Comes* of *Essex*, when he went to fight against the *Danes*, by whom he was killed at the Battle of *Malden*, *Anno* 991. It is a Peculiar of the Archbishop's, who is also Patron of the Church; but the Manor belongs to the Dean and Chapter.

NEWTON, formerly the Lordship of *William Butvillein*.

NEYLAND, a Town situated on the *Stour*, over which it has a fair Bridge leading into *Essex*. The Church and Spire-Steeple, standing in the Middle of the Town, are good Ornaments to it. The Woollen Manufacture has flourished here, but not now so much as formerly; yet the Inhabitants make Bays and Says. Here is a mean Market Weekly on *Fridays*; and one Fair Yearly on 21 *Sept*. The Manor belonged to Lord *Scroope*, of *Masham*, 13 *Edward* III.

POLSTEAD,

POLSTEAD, formerly the Lordship of *James Lamburn*, Esq. It is at present most remarkable for its Cherries. Here is the Seat of *William Beal Brand*, Esq. In this Parish there was anciently a Chauntry of the yearly Value of 6*l.* 6*s.* 0½*d.*

PRESTON, is a Village, which comprehendeth several Manors : The first is called the Priory, as originally belonging to the Priory of the *Holy Trinity* in *Ipswich*, which presented to the Vicarage; but the Advowson of the Vicarage is now in the Master and Fellows of *Emanuel* College, *Cambridge*. The next is the Manor of *Maisters*, as belonging to the *Maisters* at *Batisford*, the Commandery of this County, where the Tenants paid their Rents; and from thence they were paid again to the Prior of St. *John*'s of *Jerusalem*, and his Brethren Knights of the same in *London*. These two Manors were granted by King *Henry* VIII. in the 35th Year of his Reign to *Andrew Judde*. The third was called *Mortimers*, in which Name it long continued, till the Heir-general was married to *Ferrers*, and his Daughter to *Cressener*, who afterwards sold it to other Lords. The fourth is the Manor of *Swifts*, which *Cecily* the Mother of King *Edward* IV. gave to the Guild of *Jesus* College, in *Bury*; and, at the Dissolution, was granted to *Richard Corbett*, 2 *Edw.* VI. There is yet another Manor near the Church, called *Preston*-Hall, which belonged to the Earls of *Oxford*; till *John* the fourteenth Earl, dying without Issue about the 18th of *Henry* VIII. it descended to his Sister (married to Sir *Anthony Wingfield*, Knt.) in which Family it continued three Descents, and was lately purchased by Sir *William Beachcroft*, Knt. and Alderman of *London*. In the Reigns of *James* and *Charles* the First, here lived *Robert Rice*, Esq; an accomplished Gentleman, and a great Preserver of the Antiquities of this County.

SHIMPLING,

SHIMPLING, was in the Conqueror's Time the Lordship of *Odo de Campania*. It afterwards descended to the Lords *Fitz-walter*. *Robert Plampyn*, Esq; has now his Seat here, called *Cheracre*, or *Shadacre*-Hall.

SOMERTON. The Lordship of *Thomas de Burgh*, A.D. 1274. It is at present vested in the Lord *Blundel*, of the Kingdom of *Ireland*.

STANSTEAD. Sir *Robert de Wachesham* had the Advowson *A.D.* 1358.

STOKE *juxta* NEYLAND, called in our Histories *Stoke-Neyland* to distinguish it from *Stoke-Clare*, *Stoke-Ipswich*, &c. Its Church and Steeple are noble Structures: The Steeple lifting up a majestic Head, is seen as far as *Harwich*, near twenty Miles distant. Here was a Monastery of good Note before the Conquest; but we meet with little or nothing of it afterwards. *Stoke* has two Fairs; one on the 24th *Feb.* the other on the 1st of *May*.

Giffards-Hall, in this Parish, hath belonged to the *Mannocks* ever since the Time of King *Henry* IV. and it is now vested in Sir *William Mannock*, Bart.

Tendring-Hall, belonged to a Family of that Name. *William de Tendring* had a Grant of a Market and Fair at *Stoke* at *Neyland*, 31 *Edward* I. Sir *William Tendring*, about the Year 1421, left *Alice* his Daughter and Heiress who married Sir *John Howard*, Knt. direct Ancestor to the Dukes of *Norfolk*. From that Family it came to the Lord *Windsors*. From the Reformation it was the Seat of the *Williams*'s. Sir *John Williams*, Knt. and Lord-Mayor of *London* in 1736, built here a noble Seat, which by Purchase is now become the Property of Admiral Sir *William Rowley*, Knt. of the Bath, and one of the Lords of His Majesty's Board of Admiralty.

HUNDRED of BABERGH. 267

SUDBURY, ſtands upon the *Stour*, which is navigable for Barges from *Maningtree* to this Town. It was anciently called *South-Burgh*, as *Norwich* is ſaid to have been called *North-Burgh*. It is a very ancient Town; and at preſent conſiſts of three Pariſhes, having three beautiful and large Pariſh Churches; St. *Gregory*'s, St. *Peter*'s, and *All Saints*. This Town was one of the firſt Places where King *Edward* III. put the *Dutchmen* whom he brought into *England* from the *Netherlands*, to teach the *Engliſh* to manufacture their own Wool; and the Woollen Trade hath continued here ever ſince.

It is a Town-Corporate, governed by a Mayor, ſix Aldermen, twenty-four capital Burgeſſes, and other Sub-Officers. It has divers Privileges, and ſends two Members to Parliament. His Grace the Duke of *Grafton* takes the Title of Baron from this Place.

Simon Sudbury, who was Archbiſhop of *Canterbury* A. D. 1375, and beheaded by the Rabble in *Wat Tyler*'s Inſurrection, was a Native of this Town: He built the upper End of St. *Gregory*'s Church; he founded a College where his Father's Houſe ſtood, and endowed it ſo well that it was of the Value of 122*l*. 18*s*. *per Ann*. when it was ſuppreſſed. He is alſo ſaid by *Leland* with *John de Chertſey*, to have founded a Priory here of the Order of St. *Auſtin*; tho' *Weaver* aſcribes it to one *Baldwin* of *Shipling* (*Shimpling* perhaps) and *Mabil* his Wife. This Priory was valued at 222*l*. 18*s*. 3*d*. It is now the Manſion of *Denny Cole*, Gent. Town-Clerk of *Sudbury*.

WALDINGFIELD *Magna*, formerly the Lordſhip of *James Butler* Earl of *Wiltſhire*; and afterwards of the Earls of *Eſſex*. Sir *John Carbonwell* had a Manor here, and the Advowſon of the Church about the Year 1300; but the Advowſon is now in the College of *Clare*-Hall, *Cambridge*.

Cambridge. About the Year 1360, *Hawis* the Relict of Sir *Roger de Bavent*, releafed the Manor of *Brandefton-Hall* in *Waldingfield Magna* to the Nunnery of *Dartford* in *Kent*. The Manor of *Moreves* was granted to *Henry* Lord *Bouchier* 14 *Edward* IV. at prefent it belongs to the Family of *Keddington*.

WALDINGFIELD *Parva*, the Lordfhip of *William Beauchamp* and *William Fitz-Ralph* 9 *Edward* I. Sir *Ralph Lutteril* is faid to have died feifed of this Manor 6 *Henry* VI. The Rev. *Dey Syer* hath it now.

WISTON, fometimes called *Wiffington*. The *Cluniac* Monks at *Thetford* had the Advowfon of this Church by the Gift of *Robert* the Son of *Godbold*, and they gave it to their Cell of *Horkefley* in *Effex*, A. D. 1240.

HUNDRED of COSFORD.

COSFORD Hundred joins to the Hundred of *Babergh* before-mentioned towards the *West*; and contains the seventeen following Parishes.

ALDHAM, the Lordship of the second *Robert de Vere* Earl of *Oxford*, 24 *Edward* I. The third *Robert* died seised of it 33 *Ed.* III. as did *Thomas de Vere* 45 *Ed.* III. Sir *John Howard* obtained a Grant of this Manor 15 *Edward* IV. as Part of the Estate of *John* late Earl of *Oxford*, attainted. It belonged lately to the Earl of *Leicester*; now to Sir *Joshua Vanneck*, Bart.

BILDESTON, is a Town in a Bottom, meanly built, and the Streets are dirty; it appears to have been more populous than it is now, which is owing to the Decay of the Woollen Manufacture which formerly flourished here. The Church is a very good Building, standing on a Hill on the *West*-side of the Town, near which is the Mansion of the late *Bartholomew Beal*, Esq; who left two Daughters Heiresses: One married *Jacob Brand*, Esq; of *Polstead*; and the other *William Alston*, Esq; of *Bramford*, descended from the *Alstons* formerly of *Marlsford*, in the Hundred of *Loes*. Here is a mean Market Weekly on *Wednesdays*, and two Fairs Yearly; the one on *Ash-Wednesday*, and the other on *Ascension*-Day. Besides the Parish Churches, there was formerly a Chapel of St. *Leonard*, in which before the Reformation there was a Chauntry, called *Erdington*'s Chauntry; and long after the Reformation there used oftentimes to be Divine Service performed

performed in it, by reason of the Distance of the Church from the Town. *Henry* Lord *Bouchier* died seised of the Manor of *Bildeston*, 23 *Edward* IV. William Lord *Parr* having married *Anne* Daughter and Heiress to *Henry Bouchier* Earl of *Essex*, had Livery of all the Lands of her Inheritance 33 *Henry* VIII. and amongst others of the Manor of *Bildeston* in *Suffolk*, with the Advowson of the Church. They now are both vested in *William Beal Brand*, and *William Alston*, Esqrs. jointly.

BRETTENHAM, a Parish at the Head of the little River *Breton*, supposed to be the *Combretonium* of *Antoninus*; at present of no Remark but for the Family of *Wenyeve*, who have their Seat here, which is now vested in *Edward Wenyeve*, Esq; Son of Sir *George Wenyeve*, by *Christian* Daughter of Sir *Dudley* (afterwards Lord *North*) Temp. *Car.* II. The Earl of *Glocester* was Patron of this Church till 1344; the Earl of *Stafford* till 1432; the Earl of *Buckingham* till after 1504; and the Crown did not present till 1552.

CHELSWORTH. In this Parish the River *Bret* or *Breton*, before-mentioned, receives the Water of two other Rivulets, and becomes more considerable. On a rising Ground near the Church are the Remains of the Foundation of a Stone-Building, which appear to have been very large, and to have been encompassed by the River; and near them is a Field called, *The Park*; and other Fields, called *Park-Fields*; and a small Wood, called, the *Park-Wood*. From which Circumstances it is supposed to have been the Habitation of some Person of great Figure and Consequence; probably, of the Founders of the Church, which formerly belonged to the Duke of *Norfolk*'s Family. Sir *John Howard*, Knt. by Will dated in 1385, gave a Legacy of Twenty Shillings, towards the Repair of his Church of *Chelsworth*. *Æthelfled* the Daughter of *Alfgar* had *Chelsworth* of the Gift of King *Edgar*, and

according

according to her Father's Requeſt gave it to the Abbey of *Bury*; yet *John de St. Philibert* had free Warren in his Demeſne Lands here 10 *Edw.* II. and died ſeiſed of a Manor in *Chelſworth* 7 *Edw.* III. *Richard Plaiz* had a Manor here, 27 *Edw.* III. or 1352 : And *John de Vere* had a Manor here in 1472, in Right of his Wife, whoſe Grandmother, Wife of Sir *John Howard* before-mention'd, was Daughter and Heireſs of Sir *John de Plaiz*. His Son dying without Iſſue, it deſcended to *John Vere* his Nephew, Son of Sir *George Vere*, Knt. This *John* married *Ann* Daughter of *Thomas* Duke of *Norfolk*, and was the fourteenth and laſt Earl of *Oxford*, of that Name and Family. He died without Iſſue in 1526, and all his Eſtates went to his three Siſters : *Dorothy*, married to *John Neville*, Lord of *Latimer* ; *Elizabeth*, married to Sir *Anthony Wingfield*, of *Letheringham*; and *Urſula*, married to Sir *Edward Knightley*. This Manor afterwards became the Property of the Family of *Jenny*; of whom it was purchaſed in the Year 1737, by *Robert Pocklington*, Eſq; who has built a handſome Manſion, and now reſides there.

ELMSETT. This was the Birth-place of that eminent Critic in the *Greek* Tongue *John Bois*, Prebendary of *Ely*. Here is a Fair Yearly on the *Tueſday* in *Whitſun*-Week. The Lordſhip of this Pariſh belongs at preſent to *Richard Gideon Glanville*, Eſq. The Advowſon of the Rectory to *Clare*-Hall, in *Cambridge*.

HADLEIGH, is a large Town on the North-ſide of the River *Breton*. Its Church is a ſumptuous Building, graced with a Spire-ſteeple, which is a great Ornament to it; but our Antiquaries have a greater Reſpect for it, as being the Burial-place of *Guthrum*, or *Gormo* the *Dane*. This *Guthrum* the Pagan King of *Denmark*, being overcome in Battle by King *Alfred*, was by his Perſuaſion baptiſed, who afterwards gave him freely the Country of the *Eaſt-Angles* to govern ; which he did twelve Years, and

and dying in the Year 889, was buried in this Church. However this may be, it is certain *Hadleigh* has since that been remarkable for the Martyrdom of Dr. *Rowland Taylor*, who was Rector of this Church, and burnt *A. D.* 1555, upon the Common in this Parish, tho' commonly, but improperly, called *Aldham* Common. On the Spot where he is said to have been executed, was a Stone with this mis-spelt Inscription:

Anno 1555
Dr. *Taylor* for defending what was god
In this Place shed his Blod.

It has been a Town Corporate, but a *Quo Warranto* being brought against them, they surrendered their Charter, and their Deed of Surrender being enrolled, and Judgment being entered up against them upon Record, they could not be reinstated by the Proclamation of *James* II. of 17 *Oct.* 1688; and no other has been granted since. Here are two Markets Weekly, on *Mondays* and *Saturdays*; the Market on *Monday* for Corn, is very considerable. Here are two Fairs Yearly on the *Tuesday* in *Whitsun*-Week, and on the 29th of *Sept.* The Buildings and the Town in general have of late Years been much improved. *Joseph Beaumont*, D. D. and Regius Professor at *Cambridge*, was a Native of this Town.

Dr. *Wilkins* the late Rector, erected a very handsome Altar-piece in the Chancel; and both the Church and Parsonage-House have been greatly improved and beautified by the present Rector, the Rev. Dr. *Tanner*.

The Manor, which is very extensive, is now vested in *Ebenezer Maurice*, Esq.

The strong Gate-way to the Rectory-House was built by that Dr. *Pykenham*, Chancellor of *Norwich*, who built the Archdeacon's House in *Ipswich*. See p. 43.

Pond-hall in this Parish was formerly the Seat of the *D'Oylys*, before they removed to *Shottisham* in *Norfolk*;
where

where Sir *William D'Oyly* was created a Baronet 29 *July*, 1663. This Honour hath lately defcended to the Rev. Sir *Hadley D'Oyly*, of *Ipfwich*; but this Eftate is come by Purchafe to the Right Hon. the Earl of *Dyfart*.

HITCHAM. The Manor and Advowfon belonged to the Bifhop of *Ely*, till 4 *Elizabeth*. The Crown did not prefent to this Church till 1561.

KETTILBARSTON. *William de la Pole* Marquis of *Suffolk*, obtained a Grant of the Manors of *Kettilberfton* and *Nedding* in *Suffolk*, 23 *Hen.* VI. to hold by the Service of carrying a golden Sceptre with a Dove on the Head of it upon the Coronation-Day of the King's Heirs and Succeffors; and another Sceptre of Ivory, with a golden Dove on the Head of it, upon the Day of the Coronation of the then Queen, and all fucceffive Queens of *England.* It is faid the *Waldegraves* had their Seat at the Hall here; afterwards it defcended to the *Lemans*; from them to the *Beachcrofts*, in which Family it now is.

KERSEY, is memorable only for a Priory of *Benedictine* Monks, as fome fay; but rather of *Auftin* Canons, dedicated to St. *Mary* and St. *Anthony*. It was granted by King *Henry* VI. to *King*'s College in *Cambridge*. Here is a Fair yearly on *Eafter Tuefday*.

Here is a large Manfion called *Sampfons-Hall*, formerly in the Family of the *Sampfons* who gave Name to it. It is now the Property of Sir *Thomas Thorrowgood*, Knt. late High-Sheriff of this County, who refides there.

LEYHAM. *John de Leyham* was found 18 *Edw.* I. to hold the Manor of *Overbury*-Hall in *Leyham* in *Suffolk*, of the Earl-Marfhal. *Edmund Woodftock* Earl of *Kent* died feifed of the Manors of *Kerfey* and *Leyham* in *Suffolk*, 4 *Edward* III. *Edmund* his Son died feifed of the fame Manors without Iffue; and *Joan* his Sifter, then the Wife of Sir *Thomas Holland*, was found to be his next Heir. The said

said *Joan* died seised of these Manors 9 *Richard* II. *Thomas de Holland* her Son, died seised of the same 20 *Ric.* II. whose two Sons dying without Issue, *Edmund Mortimer* Earl of *March*, who married one of their Sisters had this Branch of the Estate, and died without Issue seised of the Manors of *Kersey* and *Leyham*, 3 *Hen.* VI. *Henry Grey* Lord *Powis* died 28 *Hen.* VI. seised of the Manor of *Kersey*, and one third Part of the Manor of *Leyham*. *Richard* his Son died seised 6 *Edw.* IV. yet Sir *John Howard* is said to have a Grant of a Manor in *Leyham* in *Suffolk* 1 *Edward* IV. Perhaps this was only one other third Part; the remaining third Part was in Sir *John Tiptoft*, who died seised of it 22 *Hen.* VI. These Manors and Mansion were sometime vested in the Family of the *Hodges's*, of whom they were purchased by the *D'Oylys*, and are now the Property of *Peregrine D'Oyly*, Gent.

LINDSEY, is an Impropriation belonging to *King's* College, *Cambridge*.

NAUGHTON. The Manor is in the Heirs of the *D'Autreys*; and the Advowson of the Living in the Family of the *Stubbings*.

NEDGING. See KETTILBARSTON.

SEAMERE. This Lordship belonged to the Abbey of *Bury*, and was appropriated to the Use of the *Celarer*. The Manor, Advowson, and a great Part of the Estates in this Parish are vested in the Rev. *Thomas Cooke*, M. A. the present Rector.

THORP-*Morieux*, anciently the Lordship and Demesne of *Hugh de Morieux*, and perhaps from him might derive its Name. The Lordship belongs at present to —— *Risby*, Esq.

WAT-

WATTISHAM. *Giles de Wachesham* held this Manor by the Serjeantry of jumping, belching, and f——g before the King, as appears by the Memorandum in the Exchequer, *Anno* 21 *Edw.* I. In 33 *Edward* III. or *A. D.* 1358; Sir *Robert de Wathesham* had it. The Church was impropriated to the Priory of *Bricet*, and the Impropriation belongs to King's College in *Cambridge*.

WHATFIELD, or WHEATFIELD, has four Manors in it: The Manor of *Cosford*, late Sir *Henry D'Oyly*'s, and now the Right Hon. the Earl of *Dysart's* ; the Manor of *Barrard*'s, late Sir *William Spring*'s, and now in the Heirs of *Thomas Martin*, Gent. the Manor of *Hornham*, late *Robert Barwell*'s, Gent. and now *Robert Pocklington*'s, Esq; and the Manor of *Whatfield*-Hall, late *William Vesey*'s, Gent. (of whom there is a fair Monument of white Marble in the Church) and now *William Mayhew's*, Gent. of *Colchester*, in *Essex*.

This Town is chiefly remarkable for growing the most excellent Seed-Wheat. The Advowson of the Rectory is vested in *Jesus* College in *Cambridge*.

CROSS-ROADS
Not Engraved.

From *Ipswich* to *Catawade* Bridges.

FROM *Bourn*-Bridge go right forward; at 2 Miles 5 Furlongs from the Cross in the Market-square the left goes to *Wherstead* Church, turn on the Right, then on the Left, and avoiding several small Lanes to the Right and Left keep in the principal Road; at 4 m. 5 f. the Left goes to *Tattingston* Church; at 4 m. 7 f. cross *Bently* Brook; at 7 m. 3 f. is *Brantham-street*, where the left Acute backward goes to *Stutton* and *Shotley*; at 7 m. 7 f. turn on the Left, the Right goes to *Eastbergholt*; at 8 m. 1 f. is *Brantham* Church close on the Left; at 8 m. 3 f. turn on the Left, the right Acute backward goes to *Bentley*, the right forward to *Eastbergholt*; at 9 m. 3 f. is *Catawade* first Bridge.

From *Ipswich* to *Shotly-Ferry*.

At *Bourn* Bridge turn to the Left by the Water-side; at 3 m. 4 f. from *Ipswich* Cross the Right goes to *Freston* Church, on the Left you see the Tower; at 3 m. 7 f. the Right goes to *Belstead* and *Copdock*, the forward Road to *Holbrook*, *Stutton*, and *Brantham*, turn to the Left; at 6 m. 2 f. the Left goes to *Chelmondiston* Church, leave the Church about a Furlong on the Left; at 7 m. 4 f. the Left goes to *Shotly* Church; at 8 m. 6 f. is *Arwerton* Park close on the Right, turn on the Left; at 9 m. 6 f. the Left in at a Gate goes to *Shotly* Church; at 10 m. 2 f. is *Shotly-Ferry*.

From *Ipſwich* to *Langer-Fort* and *Felixſtow-Ferry*.

Through St. *Clement*'s-ſtreet and the lower Hamlet, when you are up *Biſhop*'s Hill, keep by the Left-hand Hedge, the Right-hand Road goes to *Nacton*; paſs the Race-ground cloſe on the Right; at 2 m. 5 f. is the Warren-houſe cloſe on the Left; at 4 m. 5 f. are the ſeven Hills, the Right goes paſt the *Houſe of Induſtry* to *Nacton*, the Left thro' *Buckleſham* to *Woodbridge*; keep right on; at 8 m. 6 f. are *Trimly* two Churches; at 10 m. 2 f. is *Walton*-Croſs; at 10 m. 5 f. the forward Road leads to *Felixſtow*-Ferry; turn on the Right, and at 13 m. 1 f. is *Langer-Fort*, and *Orwell-Haven*.

From *Ipſwich* to *Debenham*.

Through *Claydon* Toll-Gate at 4 m. 7 f. turn to the Right, paſt *Shrubland*-Hall and Park, cloſe on the Left; at 6 m. 4 f. the Right goes to *Hemingſton*, turn on the Left over *Coddenham* Brook and paſs the Church, where the Left goes to *Needham*; at 7 m. the Right to *Wickham-Market*; at 7 m. 5 f. turn to the Right, the Left goes to *Crowfield* and *Stonham-Aſpal*; at 9 m. 2 f. the Right goes to *Goſbeck*; at 9 m. 5 f. the Left Acute backward to *Crowfield* Chapel; at 10 m. 3 f. the Right to *Helmingham*; at 10 m. 6 f. is *Pettaugh* Church, a little on the Right; the Right to *Framſden*; at 11 m. 5 f. the Right to *Winſton*, leaving *Winſton* about a Mile on the Right; at 13 m. the Right leads to that Church; at 13 m. 1 f. the Right leads by *Aſhfield*-Swan to *Wickham* Market; at 13 m. 5 f. is *Debenham* Market-Croſs.

From *Ipſwich* to *Bildeſton*.

At the Stones-End in St. *Matthew*'s-ſtreet take into *Claydon* Road, but leave it at the firſt Turning on the Left-hand Acute forward; at 1 m. 3 f. the Left goes to *Sproughton*; at 2 m. 3 f. turn on the Left, the Right to *Whitton*;

Whitton; at 2 m. 5 f. cross the *Gippen*; at 2 m. 6 f. you enter the *London* Road from *Stow* to *Copdock*, turn on the Right through *Bramford*; at 3 m. 3 f. the Right goes to *Claydon*; at 4 m. 4 f. the Right-on Road leads to *Stow* and *Bury*, turn on the Left, leave *Little Blakenham* Church 1 f. on the Right; at 5 m. 7 f. is *Somersham* Church, where the Left goes to *Flowton*; at 6 m. 3 f. is *Somersham* Village, where the Left goes to *Flowton*, the Right to *Nettlestead*; at 7 m. the Left to *Elmsett*; at 7 m. 2 f. the Right-on Road leads to *Barking-Tye*, turn to the Left; at 7 m. 3 f. the Left leads to *Offton* Castle-Hill, turn on the Right; at 7 m. 6 f. the Right to *Barking-Tye*; at 7 m. 7 f. is *Offton* Church on the Left; at 9 m. 4 f. and at 10 m. 2 f. the Right to *Bricet*; at 10 m. 4 f. the Left to *Naughton*; at 10 m. 6 f. the Left to *Naughton* Church, leaving that 2 f. on the Left, cross *Nedging-Tye*, and leaving *Wattisham* Church about 6 f. on the Right; at 12 m. 6 f. is *Bildeston* Market-Cross.

From *Woodbridge* to *Baudsey-Ferry*.

At *Melton* in the engraved Road turn on the Right, and cross the *Deben* over *Willford*-Bridge; at 2 m. take the Right-hand Way up the Hill; at 2 m. 5 f. take the Right which goes to *Sutton* Church, and passing over heathy Land at 3 m. 6 f. the Right goes to *Sutton*, the Left to *Eike*, and avoiding divers Turnings to the Right and Left leave *Shottisham* Church a little on the Right; at 6 m. the Right goes to *Shottisham*, the Left to *Hollesly*; at 8 m. the Right leads to *Ramsholt*, turn on the Left leaving *Alderton* Church a little on the Right; at *Alderton* Village turn on the Right, leaving the Left-hand Way to *Hollesly*; at 9 m. 1 f. is *Baudsey* Church; and at 11 m. 1 f. is *Baudsey-Ferry*.

From *Woodbridge* to *Orford*.

Cross the *Deben* over *Willford*-Bridge, as before; at 2 m. 6 f. is a Sand-pit, avoiding the Left forward to *Eyke*, and

and the Right to *Sutton*, take the middle Way; at 4 m. 2 f. the Right to *Hollefly*, the Left to *Eike*, enter in at a Gate; at 5 m. 5 f. *Staverton* Park on the Left; at 6 m. 4 f. leave it; at 6 m. 7 f. is *Butley* Oifter; the Right, on this Side the Oifter, goes to *Capel*; the Right on the other to *Butley* Abbey, therefore turn on the Left over the River; at 8 m. 1 f. turn to the Right, the Left to *Wantifden*; at 8 m. 2 f. is *Chillesford* Church on the Left; at 8 m. 4 f. the Right to *Chillesford* Mill, the Left to *Tunftal*; pafs on the Side of *Sudbourn* Park; at 10 m. 3 f. turn to the Right, the Left to *Saxmundham*; at 11 m. 4 f. is *Orford* Market-Crofs.

From *Woodbridge* to *Aldborough*.

Crofs the *Deben* over *Willford*-Bridge, and at 2 m. 6 f. by the Sand-pit take the Left-hand Road, and leaving *Bromefwell* Church 2 f. on the Left; at 3 m. 4 f. are two Gates, the Right to *Sutton*, the Left to *Ufford*; at 5 m. is *Eike* Church on the Right, where the Right leads to *Orford*, the Left to *Ufford*; at 5 m. 4 f. the Left leads to *Campfey-Afh*, and paffing by *Rendlefham* Church on the Left; at 6 m. 4 f. the Right to *Hollefly*, the Left to *Wickham*; at 7 m. 2 f. is *Rendlefham* Houfe; at 7 m. 6 f. the Left to *Afh*, the Right to *Butley*; at 8 m. 5 f. the Left to *Blaxhall*, the Road right forward to *Afh*, therefore turn to the Right; at 8 m. 6 f. is *Tunftall* Village, the Right to *Orford*, avoiding divers Turnings to the Right and Left, and leaving the Ruins of *Doningworth* Chapel a little to the Left; at 10 m. 7 f. is *Doningworth*-Hall clofe to the Left; from thence paffing over *Snape* Bridge at 11 m. 5 f. is *Snape* Crown Inn; then leaving *Frifton* Decoy a little on the Right, at 13 m. 3 f. is *Polfborough* Gate, take the Right-hand and fo over *Halefwood* Common; at 15 m. 1 f. is *Aldborough*.

The Back-Road from *Woodbridge* to *Blithborough*, by *Snape* Bridge.

Proceed over *Willford* Bridge in the Road now mentioned to *Aldborough*, crofs the *Ore* at *Snape* Bridge, and proceed to *Polfborough* Gate at about 12m. where the Right to *Aldborough*, the Left to *Benhall*; at 12 m. 2 f. the Right to *Aldborough*, the Left to *Saxmundham*; at 13 m. 1 f. the Right to *Aldborough*, the Left to *Knodifhall*; at 13m. 5f. is *Colt-Fair-Green*; at 14 m. 5 f. is *Leifton* White-Horfe, leave the Abbey a little on the Left; at 15 m. 6f. the Left to *Yoxford*; at 17m 1 f. is *Eaft-Bridge*, and leaving a Wind-mill a little on the Left; at 18m. 4 f. the Right to *Dunwich*, the Left to *Weftleton*; at 18 m. 7 f. the Left to *Weftleton*, the Right to *Dunwich*, leaving it about 2 m. diftant; at 19m. 2 f. the Left to *Darfham*; at 20m. 7f. the Right to *Walderfwick*, the firft Left-hand Road leads to *Darfham*, the fecond to *Halefworth*; at 21 m. 7f. is a Wind-mill clofe on the Left; the Left leads to *Wenhafton*, the Right to *Walderfwick*; at 22m. 3 f. the Right leads to *Weftwood* Lodge; and about 2 f. farther is *Blithborough*.

The exact meafured Diftance from *Woodbridge* to *Blithborough*.

By *Willford* and *Snape* is————22 m. 5¼ f.
Through *Wickham* and *Saxmundham*—21 m. 6½ f.
So the laft-mentioned is the neareft by————6¾ f.

See Plate I.

Crofs-Road from *Wickham-Market* to *Eye*.

From the Crown Inn at 3f. the Left goes to *Needham*; at 5f. crofs the *Deben* at *Glevering* Bridge; at 1 m. 2 f. the Right turns back to *Campfey-Afh*; at 2 m. 3 f. are *Eafton* Church on the Right, and *Eafton* White-Houfe on the Left; here the Right to *Parham*, the Left to *Letheringham*; at 2m. 5 f. is a Pound on the Right, and that Road leads to *Framlingham*; at 3 m. 2f. *Letheringham* is in view; at 3 m. 5f. the Left to *Hoo*, the Right to

CROSS ROADS. 281

to *Framlingham*; at 3 m. 7 f. is *Kettleburgh*, where the Right to *Framlingham*; at 4 m. 5 f. Mr. *Sparrow*'s Houſe cloſe on the Right, then the Left forward to *Debenham*, turn on the Right; at 4 m. 7 f. the Left to *Debenham*, the Right to *Framlingham*; leave *Brandiſton*-Hall about 1 f. on the Left, keep right forward over *Brandiſton*-Green; and at 7 m. is *Earl-Soham*, paſſing over a Brook avoiding the Left-turning to *Aſhfield*; at 8 m. 1 f. the Left to *Ipſwich*; at 10 m. 1 f. the Left to *Debenham*; at 10 m. 3 f. is *Kenton* Church on the Left, the Left-Road leads to *Debenham*; at 11 m. 1 f. the Right to *Worlingworth*; at 11 m. 2 f. the Left forward to *Debenham*, turn on the Right; at 11 m. 7 f. the Right to *Worlingworth*-Green; at 12 m. 1 f. the Left to *Riſhangles*, turn on the Right, and avoiding ſeveral Turnings to the Right and Left, at 13 m. 3 f. is *Occold* Church cloſe on the Right; at 14 m. 5 f. the Left Acute backward to *Thorndon*; at 15 m. the Left to *Thorndon*; at 16 m. the Right to *Framlingham*, turn on the Left over the Bridge; at 16 m. 4 f. is *Eye* Market-Croſs.

Croſs-Road from *Wickham-Market* to *Needham-Market*.

From the Crown-Inn at 3 f. avoid the laſt-mentioned to *Eye*, and go forward over *Potford* Green; at 1 m. 3 f. is *Letheringham*-Park on the Right; at 2 m. leave the Park, where the Right leads to *Letheringham*; at 2 m. 6 f. turn on the Left over a Brook, the Right forward leads to *Charsfield*; at 3 m. 3 f. the Right to *Charsfield* Church; at 4 m. 4 f. the Left to *Woodbridge*; at 5 m. 3 f. the Right to *Hoo*, the Left to *Clopton*; at 6 m. is *Catts-Hill*, the Right backward to *Monewden*; at 6 m. 2 f. turn on the Right, the Left to *Woodbridge*; at 6 m. 7 f. turn on the Left, the Right to *Otley* Church; at 7 m. 7 f. the Right to *Helmingham*, the Left to *Ipſwich*; at 8 m. 3 f. the Right to *Aſhbocking*, the Left to *Ipſwich*; at 8 m. 7 f. turn on the Right, the forward Road leads to *Henley*; at
10 m.

10 m. 4 f. is *Stonewall,* the Right to *Helmingham,* the Left to *Ipswich*; at 10 m. 7 f. the Left to *Hemingston*; at 11 m. 3 f. take the Left, the Right to *Gosbeck*; at 11 m. 5 f. is *Coddenham,* here the Right to *Debenham,* and a little farther the Left over the Brook to *Ipswich*; at 13 m. 1 f. cross the *Pye*-Road near the Brook; at 14 m. 2 f. is *Bosmere* Mill; and 5 f. farther is *Needham* Chapel.

Cross-Road from *Wickham-Market* to *Harleston.*

From the Crown-Inn over the Bridge, at about 5 f. leave the *Yarmouth* Road on the Right, and take the Left-hand Road; at 1 m. the Right to *Aldborough,* the Left to *Easton*; at 1 m. 7 f. is *Hacheston* Church close on the Right, the Left to *Easton*; at 2 m. 1 f. the Right backward is the Road from *Framlingham* to *Orford*; at 2 m. 3 f. is *Hacheston* Village, the Right to *Parham,* the Left to *Easton*; at 4 m. 5 f. the Left in at a Gate to *Easton,* turn on the Right and cross the *Ore* at the broad Water; at 5 m. 3 f. avoid the Left to *Denington*; and at 5 m. 7 f. is *Framlingham* Griffin-Inn; passing the *Ore* at 6 m. 1 f. the Left Acute forward leads to *Saxted*; at 8 m. turn on the Right, the Left forward to *Stradbrook*; at 8 m. 3 f. is *Durrants*-Bridge; at 8 m. 4 f. turn on the Left, the Right forward to *Badingham*; at 9 m. is *Dennington* Parsonage a little on the Left, the Left forward to *Brundish*; turn on the Right at 9 m. 2 f. the Left Acute backward to *Saxted,* and *Dennington* Church is close on the Right; at 10 m. is *Freizly*-Bridge, where the Right to *Badingham,* the Left to *Brundish*; at 12 m. 3 f. the Right to *Laxfield* Church, turn on the Left; at 13 m. 3 f. is *Laxfield* White-Horse, turn on the Left; at 13 m. 4 f. turn on the Right, the Left to *Stradbrook,* leaving Archbishop *Sancroft's* Seat 3 f. on the Left; at 15 m. 1 f. turn on the Left, the Right to *Cratfield*; at 16 m. 6 f. turn on the Right, the Left to *Stradbrook,* the Left forward to *Eye*; at 16 m. 7 f. is *Fresingfield* Church close on the Right, through the Street,

Street, the Right goes to *Cratfield,* therefore turn on the Left, and over a Brick-Bridge, where turn on the Right; at 19 m. 1 f. the Left to *Weybread* Church; a little farther turn on the Right, the Road right forward leads to *Weybread* Mills; at 19 m. 5 f. the Left Acute backward to *Hoxne*; at 19 m. 6 f. the Right to *Wetherſdale*; proceed over *Shottisford* Heath, leaving a Wind-mill a little on the Right; at 20 m. 2 f. the Right to *Haleſworth*; at 20 m. 3 f. is *Shottisford* Bridge; turn on the Left, the Right to *Mendham*; at 20 m. 7 f. the Left Acute backward to *Scole* Inn; and at 21 m. 2 f. is *Harleſton* Chapel.

Croſs-Road from *Wickham-Market* to *Aldborough.*

From the Crown-Inn take the *Saxmundham* Road, and at the five Croſs-ways take the ſecond Turning on the Right; at 1 m. 2 f. the Right to *Campſey-Aſh,* the Left to *Hacheſton*; at 1 m. 6 f. the Right forward to *Tunſtal*; at 2 m. is the Well-houſe, where the Right to *Campſey-Aſh,* the Left to *Marleſford*; at 2 m. 5 f. is *Black-ſtock* Water, the Left Acute backward to *Marleſford*; at 4 m. is *Blaxhall* Church on the Left; at 4 m. 4 f. leave *Blaxhall-lane,* the Left Acute backward to *Little Glemham*; at 4 m. 5 f. the Left to *Langham-*Bridge; at 5 m. 7 f. *Dunningworth-*Hall cloſe on the Left, paſs the *Ore* at *Snape-*Bridge, and ſo on in the Road from *Woodbridge* to *Aldborough*; (p. 759.) and at 11 m. 4 f. is *Aldborough* Market-Croſs.

Road from *Yoxford* to *Haleſworth.*

At 1 m. 1 f. on the Right is a Spur-way leading from *Yoxford* to *Haleſworth,* take the Left-way; and at 2 m. 1 f. from *Yoxford* is *Sibton* Church cloſe on the Left; at 2 m. 3 f. is a Gate leading to *Sibton* Abbey; at 2 m. 5 f. the Left thro' *Peaſenhall* and *Badingham,* to *Framlingham*; at 2 m. 7 f. the Left thro' *Heveningham-Long-lane* to *Ubbeſton*; at 3 m. 7 f. the Left to *Heveningham,* the Right to *Sibton-*Green; at 4 m. 3 f. is *Threadbare-*Hall cloſe on the

the Right; at 5 m. 6 f. the Left thro' *Heveningham* and *Ubbeston* to *Laxfield*; at 5 m. 7 f. is *Walpole* Village, turn on the Right, pafs by *Walpole* Church on the Left; at 6 m. 6 f. the Right Acute forward leads to *Holton*; at 7 m. turn on the Left; at 7 m. 1 f. crofs the River *Blyth*; and at about 8 m. is *Halefworth* Church.

Crofs-Road from *Halefworth* to *Bungay*.

At the End of the Street the Right leads to *Loweftoft*; at 7 f. from the Market-Crofs the Right to *Holton*; at 1 m. 1 f. the Right Acute forward to *Beccles*; at 1 m. 5 f. is *Fairftead*-Gate on the Left; at 3 m. 5 f. the Right to St. *Andrew*'s; at 4 m. 6 f. the Left to St. *Margaret*'s; at 5 m. 7 f. the Right to St. *Laurence*, the Church about 1 f. diftant; then thro' a ftrait Way called *Stone-ftreet* turn on the Left, and at 6 m. 6 f. is St. *John*'s Church clofe on the Right; at 8 m. 2 f. the Left to *Homersfield*, the Right to *Beccles*; at 8 m. 7 f. is *Bungay* Market-Crofs.

Crofs-Road from *Halefworth* to *Southwold*.

From the Market-Crofs avoid the Roads from *Wiffet* to *Bungay*, both going to the Left, keep the Right-hand Way thro' the Street; at 1 m. 2 f. is *Holton*, where the Left goes to *Beccles*; leave the Wind-mill on the Right, pafs *Blythford* Church on the Right; at 2 m. 7 f. the Right goes over *Blythford*-Bridge to *Wenhafton*; a little farther on, the Left goes to *Sotherton*-Moor, avoiding feveral Turns to the Right and Left; at 4 m. 1 f. crofs the great Road from *Ipfwich* to *Beccles*; at 5 m. 7 f. is *Wolfey*-Bridge; and at 8 m. 6 f. is *Southwold* Market-Crofs.

Crofs-Road from *Halefworth* to *Loweftoft*, after crofling the Road from *Ipfwich* to *Beccles*.

From the Market-Crofs, paffing in the Road laft-mentioned, avoid the Road on the Right leading to *Wolfey*-Bridge, and pafs on leaving *Henham*-Park on the Left;

at

CROSS ROADS.

at 6 m. 6 f. is *Wangford* Church clofe on the Right; here the Right thro' *Raydon* to *Southwold*, keep the Road right forward; at 6 m. 7 f. the Right to *Southwold*, the Left to *Uggeſhall*; at 8 m. 2 f. turn on the Right, the Left to *Froſtenden*; at 8 m. 4 f. turn on the Left, the Right to *South-Cove*; at 8 m. 7 f. the Right to *Benacre*; at 9 m. 6 f. is *Wrentham* Church clofe on the Left; leave the Hall a little on the Right, and pafs over *Satterly* Common; at 11 m. 6 f. the Right to *Benacre*, the Left paſt *Henſtead* Church to *Beccles*, leave the Church a little on the Left; at 13 m. 1 f. is *Ruſhmer* Church clofe on the Right; at 14 m. 7 f. is *Carlton-Colvile* Church a little on the Left; at 15 m. are the five Crofs-ways where the Right Acute backward to *Southwold*; the Right to *Pakefield*, the Left to *Beccles*; at 16 m. 6 f. is *Mutford*-Bridge, where the Road right forward to *Yarmouth*; turn on the Right, and at 18 m. 7 f. is *Loweſtoft* Queen's-Head Inn.

Crofs Road from *Haleſworth* to *Beccles*.

From the Market-Crofs in the Road to *Southwold*, at 1 m. 2 f. is *Holton* Blackſmith's Shop; here turn to the Left, leaving the Church about a Furlong to the Left; at 4 m. 4 f. is *Weſthall* Church, clofe on the Left; at 5 m. 1 f. is *Brampton* Church; here you enter the engraved Road from *Ipſwich* to *Beccles*. Plate I.

Crofs-Road from *Haleſworth* to *Harleſton*.

Proceed through *Cheddiſton-ſtreet*, and at 2 m. is the Church clofe on the Right; at 3 m. 3 f. is *Linſtead* Chapel clofe on the Right; at 7 m. 1 f. is *Metfield* Church clofe on the Left; at 8 m. 6 f. is *Wetherſdale*-Crofs, where the Right to *Mendham*, the Left to *Freſſingfield*; at 10 m. 7 f. is *Shottisford*-Bridge; and at 11 m. 6 f. is *Harleſton* Chapel.

Crofs-

Cross-Road from *Stowmarket* to *Botesdale*.

From the Market-Cross proceed in the *Bury* Road; at 1 m. 6 f. leave the *Bury* Road which is right forward, and take the Right-hand Way over the River; at 2 m. 4 f. enter *Haughley-street*, where the Right Acute backward goes to *Newton*; at 2 m. 6 f. is *Haughley* Church on the Left, turn on the Right; at 3 m. the Right to *Newton*, turn on the Left over *Haughley*-Green; at 4 m. 4 f. leave the Green; at 5 m. 6 f. the Left to *Wyverston*; at 6 m. 3 f. the Left to *Wyverston*, the Road right forward to *Westhorpe*; turn on the Right, *Bacton* Church close on the Right; at 7 m. the Road right forward goes through *Cotton* to *Mendlesham*; turn on the Left over a Common; at 7 m. 5 f. the Right to *Mendlesham*; at 8 m. the Right to *Wickham-Skeith*, the Left to *Wyverston*; at 8 m. 1 f. is *Finningham* White-Horse, where the Left through *Pakenham* to *Bury*, the Right through *Thornham* to the *Pye*-Road, pass the Church on the Right; at 8 m. 3 f. the Right to *Gislingham*; at 9 m. 6 f. enter *Alured* Green; at 10 m. 6 f. leave it; at 12 m. 2 f. is the Church of *Rickingale-superior* on the Right, the forward Road leads to *Whattisfield*, turn on the Right; at 12 m. 4 f. is the Road from *Yarmouth* to *Bury*, turn on the Right; and at 13 m. 3 f. is *Botesdale* Crown Inn.

Cross-Road from *Stowmarket* to *Ixworth*, and from *Ixworth* to *Thetford*.

From the Market-Cross at 1 m. 6 f. avoid the last-mentioned Road to *Botesdale*, and keep the *Bury* Road; at 3 m. 3 f. avoid the Left-turning, which leads to *Bury*, and keep the forward Road; at 3 m. 7 f. is *Wetherden-street*, where the Right to *Haughley*-Green; at 5 m. 1 f. the Right to *Elmswell*, the Left to *Woolpit*; at 5 m. 4 f. the Right Acute backward to *Elmswell*-Green, leave the Church close on the Right; at 5 m. 4 f. turn to the Right, the forward Road to *Tostock*; at 7 m. 6 f. the

the Right to *Ashfield*, the Left to *Bury*, *Norton*-Dog close on the Right; at 8 m. 3 f. you see Dr. *Macro*'s Seat on the Left; at 8 m. 7 f. the Right through a Gate to *Stow-Langtoft*; at 9 m. 2 f. cross the Road from *Finningham* to *Bury*; at 9 m. 4 f. cross a Brook, pass over the Fielding; and at 11 m. 2 f. is *Ixworth-street*, where the Right to *Botesdale*, the Left to *Bury*.

From *Ixworth* cross the River, and leave the Mill on the Left; avoid the Left-hand Turning to *Livermere*, and keep the forward Road; at 1 m. 4 f. is *Ixworth-Thorp* Church close on the Left; pass over a Common, and at 2 m. 6 f. comes in on the Left the Road from *Bury* to *Gastrop*-Gate, leave *Hunnington* Church close on the Right; at 2 m. 6 f. the Left to *Livermere*, the Right to *Gastrop*, keep the forward Road; at 4 m. 4 f. the Right Acute backward to *Sapiston*, leave *Fakenham* Church close on the Right, pass over the Champaign Lands, leave *Euston* Church on the Right; at 6 m. the Left to *Barnham*, turn on the Right over *Euston*-Bridge, the Park close on the Right; at 6 m. 1 f. turn on the Left through *Euston* Village; at 6 m. 7 f. enter *Norfolk* at *Carlford*-Bridge, avoid the forward Road, and take that on the Left-hand over the Warrens; at 8 m. 4 f, re-enter *Suffolk* at *Folly*-Bridge; and at 9 m. 3 f. is *Thetford*-Bridge.

	m. f.
The exact Distance from *Stow* to *Ixworth*, is	11 2¾
From *Ixworth* to *Thetford*, is	9 3¼
From *Stow* to *Thetford*, is	20 6

Cross-Road from *Stowmarket* to *Bildeston*, and from *Bildeston* to *Hadleigh*.

Pass over *Combs-Ford* in the *Ipswich* Road, at 4 f. avoid the Left to *Ipswich*, and the Right to *Finborough*, and keep the forward Road, avoiding several Turnings to the Right and Left; at 3 m. 6 f. enter *Battisford-Tye*, where the

the forward Road leads to *Ringſhall*, take the Right-hand Road over the *Tye*; at 4 m. 3 f. leave it; at 6 m. 3 f. is *Wattiſham* Church, cloſe on the Left; at 6 m. 6 f. is a Blackſmith's Shop, cloſe on the Left; at 7 m. 3 f. the Acute backward leads to *Needham*; and at 8 m. 2 f. is *Bildeſton:* Market-Croſs.

From thence at 1 f. avoid the Left-turning to *Ipſwich*; and at 2 f. the Right leading to *Lavenham*; leave *Nedging* Church about 2 f. on the Left, and paſs over *Seamere-*Bridge; at 2 m. 3 f. the Right to *Kerſey*; at 3 m. the Left to *Naughton*; at 3 m. 3 f. the Right to *Kerſey*, the Left to *Cosford-*Bridge; at 3 m. 7 f. comes in the Road from *Sudbury* to *Hadleigh*; and at 5 m. 1 f. is *Hadleigh* George.

	m.	f.
The exact Diſtance from *Stow* to *Bildeſton*, is	8	2¾
From *Bildeſton* to *Hadleigh*, is	5	1¼
From *Stow* to *Hadleigh*	13	4

Croſs-Road from *Hadleigh* to *Stratford*.

Avoid the Right-hand Road leading to *Layham*, and the Left leading to *Ipſwich*, and keep the forward Road; at 4 f. is the End of the Street, leave *Layham* Church 2 f. on the Right; at 1 m. 7 f. croſs a Brook, where the forward Road goes to *Eaſtbergholt*, turn on the Right; at 2 m. 6 f. turn on the Left, the forward Road leads to *Shelly*; leave that Church 2 f. on the Right; at 3 m. paſs a Brook; at 3 m. 1 f. turn on the Right, the Left to *Raydon*; at 4 m. 6 f. the Left to *Holton*; at 4 m. 7 f. is *Higham* Village, where the Right to *Stoke*, the Left to *Ipſwich*; and at 6 m. and half a Furlong is *Stratford* Swan.

The Road from *Bury* to *Gaſtrop-Gate*, being the Road to *Norwich*.

Through the *North-*gate at 1 m, 5 f. leave the engraved Road to *Thetford*, and turn to the Right, leaving *Fornham St.*

St. Martin's Church a little on the Left ; at 3 m. 1 f. the Right to *Barton*, the Left to *Timworth* ; at 3 m. 4 f. the Right to *Ixworth*, the Left to *Timworth*, the Church on the Left 2 f. at 3 m. 6 f. the Right to *Ixworth* ; at 5 m. 2 f. the Right to *Ixworth*, the Left to *Great Livermore*, leaving the Church on the Left near 2 f. at 6 m. 2 f. is *Trofton* Bull-Inn clofe on the Right, where turn on the Right, the Left to *Rhymer*-Houfe ; a little farther the Right to *Ixworth*, the forward Road to *Ixworth-Thorp* ; turn to the Left in at a Gate, *Trofton* Church a little on the Right ; at 7 m. 2 f. the Right to *Bardwell*, the Left to *Thetford* ; at 8 m. the Road comes in from *Ixworth* to *Thetford*, leave *Honington* Church on the Right ; at *Honington-ftreet* turn on the Right over the River, the Left to *Little Livermore*, the forward Road to *Thetford* ; at 8 m. 7 f. is *Sapifton* George-Inn ; at 9 m. the Right to *Sapifton*, the Left to *Pakenham* ; at 9 m. 5 f. a Brick-kiln clofe on the Right, pafs by *Barningham*-Park on the Left ; at 11 m. 4 f. the Right to *Barningham*, the Left to *Thetford* ; at 13 m. 3 f. the Right to *Hopton*, the Left to *Rufhford*, leave *Knottifhal* Church 1 f. on the Right ; at 13 m. 4 f. the Right Acute backward to *Coney-Wefton*, paffing by a Pound on the Right, where the Right to *Hopton*, the Left to *Thetford* ; at 13 m. 5 f. enter *Norfolk* ; and at 13 m. 7¾ f. is *Gaftrop* Gate-Inn.

From *Bury* to *Brandon*.

At 1 m. 5 f. on the Road laft-mentioned, avoid the Right to *Thetford*, and keep the forward Road ; at 2 m. 3 f. the Left Acute forward to *Fornham All-Saints* ; at 2 m. 7 f. leave *Fornham Genoveve* Church 2 f. on the Left; at 4 m. 2 f. is *Culford* Church 2 f. on the Left ; at 4 m. 4 f. the forward Road to *Thetford*, turn on the Left ; at 4 m. 7 f. the Left to *Weftow*, the Right to *Ingham* ; at 5 m. 4 f. is *Wordwell* Church, clofe on the Left ; at 8 m. 5 f. the Right to *Thetford*, the Left to *cklingham* ; at 9 m. 3 f.

Cross Roads.

3 f. the Right Acute forward to *Elvedon*; at 10 m. 2 f. cross the Road from *Newmarket* to *Thetford*; at 15 m. pass the *Maid's-Head* Inn, where the Left to *Mildenhall*; at 15 m. 3 f. is *Brandon*-Bridge.

From *Bury* to *Mildenhall*.

Through *Risby*-Gate at 2 m. leave the engraved *Newmarket* Road, and take the Right-hand Way; at 3 m. 3 f. is *Risby* Church close on the Right; pass *Risby-street*, and at 7 m. 1 f. in an open Country is *Cavenham* Church close on the Right; where the Right to *Lackford*, the Left to *Higham*-Green; at 8 m. 7 f. turn on the Right, the Left Acute backward to *Barrow*; at 8 m. 7 f. *Tuddenham* Church close on the Right; at 9 m. the Right to *Icklingham*, the Left to *Kentford*; at 9 m. 4 f. the Left Acute forward to *Worlington*; at 10 m. 7 f. are *Barton*-Mills, turn on the Right over the River; at 11 m. the forward Road goes from *Newmarket* to *Brandon*, turn on the Left; at 11 m. 6 f. enter *Mildenhall-street*; and at 12 m. 2 f. is *Mildenhall* Market-Cross.

Road from *Bury* to *Finningham*.

Pass out at the East-Gate in the engraved Road to *Yarmouth*, pass *Barton* Church close on the Left; at 3 m. 4 f. leave the engraved Road to *Ixworth*, and take the Right-hand Way; at 4 m. 5 f. the Right leads to *Bradfield-Manger*, the Left to *Ixworth*; at 5 m. the Left goes to *Ixworth*, turn on the Right through *Pakenham* Village; at 5 m. 1 f. is *Pakenham* Bell on the Left, the Road right forward goes to *Norton*, turn on the Left leaving *Pakenham* Church a little on the Right; at 6 m. 6 f. the Right goes through *Norton* to *Stow*, the Left through *Ixworth* to *Thetford*; at 7 m. 1 f. is *Stowlangtoft* Church close on the Left; at 8 m. 1 f. is *Hunsdon* Church a little on the Right; at 8 m. 7 f. is a Wind-mill a little on the Left, where the Right goes through *Ashfield* to *Finningham*, but the Road right forward is the common Coach Road; at

CROSS ROADS. 291

9 m. 2 f. is *Badwell-Ash* Church close on the Left, the Road right forward goes to *Walsham*; turn on the Right leaving *Badwell* Church about 3 f. on the Right; at 10 m. 1 f. the other Road through *Ashfield* comes in on the Right; at 11 m. 5 f. enter in at a Gate by *Cutting*'s Hole; at 12 m. 1 f. the Right leads to *Bacton*, the Left to Mr. *Barnardiston*'s, leave *Wyverston* Pond close on the Left; at 12 m. 7 f. *Wyverston* Church close on the Left; at 13 m. 3 f. a Gate on the Right, which leads to *Bacton*-Hall; at 13 m. 7 f. is *Westhorp*-Hall, a little on the Left; and at 14 m. 6 f. is *Finningham* White-Horse.

From *Bury* to *Clare*.

Through the *West*-Gate at 5 f. is *Stanford*-Bridge; at 6 f. the Left Acute forward to *Hawstead*, a little farther the Right to *Horringer*; at 1 m. 2 f. *Bury* Bounds Post; at 1 m. 4 f. the Right Acute forward to *Horringer*; at 3 m. 3 f. the forward Road to *Brockley*; at 4 m. 1 f. the Left to *Nowton*, turn on the Right, leave *Whepstead* Church 2 f. on the Left; at 4 m. 4 f. the Right to *Chevington*; at 6 m. 5 f. the Right to *Reed* Church, leave it about a Furlong to the Right; at 7 m. 3 f. the Left to *Brockley*; at 8 m. 3 f. is *Hawkedon* Church a little on the Left; at 8 m. 4 f. the Left Acute backward through *Somerton* to *Hartest*, the forward to *Glemsford*, turn on the Right; at 9 m. 2 f. the Right to *Burnt-Ash* Bridge, thro' *Wickham-Brook* to *Newmarket*, leave *Stansfield* Church a little on the Right; at 9 m. 4 f. the Right thro' *Denston* to *Staddishall*, the Left to *Hartest*, cross over the Brook; at 9 m. 3 f. the Left to *Boxted*; at 9 m. 6 f. the Right to *Kedington*; at 12 m. 1 f. the Right to *Hundon*, leave *Poslingford* Church a little on the Right; at 12 m. 2 f. the Left to *Glemsford*; at 13 m. 2 f. the Right through *Chilton-street* to *Kedington*, turn on the Left past *Chilton* Chapel, now a Dwelling-House; and at 14 m. ¼ f. is *Clare* Market-Cross.

From *Bury* to *Lavenham*.

Through the *South*-Gate in the engraved Road to *Sudbury*, at 6 m. avoiding the forward Road, take the Left-hand Way; at 6 m. 7 f. is *Cockfield* Church 2 f. on the Left; at 7 m. 3 f. a Wind-mill, the Left to *Felsham*; at 8 m. 6 f. the Right to *Alpheton*; at 10 m. 6 f. is the End of *Lavenham-street*, where the Left to *Preston*; at 11 m. ½ f. is *Lavenham* Swan-Inn.

Cross-Road from *Lavenham* to *Sudbury*.

From the Swan-Inn avoid the Left-hand Way to *Bildeston*, proceed leaving the Church close on the Right; at 2 f. turn on the Left, the forward Road to *Alpheton*; at 4 f. the Right to *Melford*; at 1 m. enter *Washmore*-Green, the Left thro' *Waldingfield* to *Bury*; at 2 m. 7 f. the Left Acute backward thro' *Little Waldingfield* to *Bildeston*; at 3 m. 2 f. enter *Baberg* Heath, the Right thro' *Acton* to *Melford*, the Left through *Great Waldingfield* to *Hadleigh*, being the nearest Way from *Melford* to *Ipswich*; at 4 m. 1 f. the forward Road to *Colchester*, turn on the Right; at 4 m. 7 f. is a View of *Chilton*-Hall, about a Furlong on the Left; and at 6 m. 2¼ f. is *Sudbury*.

	m.	f.
From *Bury* to *Lavenham*, is	11	0½
From *Lavenham* to *Sudbury*, is	6	2½
From *Bury* to *Sudbury* by way of *Lavenham*	17	3
From *Bury* to ditto by way of *Melford*	16	2½
The Way by *Melford* is nearest by	1	0½

The Cross-Road from *Sudbury* to *Haverhill*.

In the engraved Road from *Bury* to *Sudbury* thro' *Melford*, leave *Melford*-Hall and the *Bury* Road on the Right; and at 3 m. 3 f. is *Melford* Black-Lion, turn on the Left; at 4 m. the Right thro' *Stansfield* and *Wickham*-Brook, to *Newmarket*;

Newmarket; at 4 m. 6 f. is *Glemsford*-Bridge; at 5 m.
1 f. the Right to *Glemsford*; leave *Pentlow* Church in
Essex about 2 f. on the Left; at 6 m. 7 f. the Left to
Foxearth; a little farther cross a Brook at the End of
Cavendish-street, where the Right to *Glemsford*; at 7 m.
1 f. is *Cavendish* Church close on the Right, where the
Right to *Poslingford*, leave a Wind-mill close on the Left;
a little farther cross a Brook at the Entrance of *Clare*,
where the Right to *Chilton*, leave the Ruins of the Castle
on the Left; at 9 m. 5 f. is *Clare* Half-Moon Inn; thro'
Clare-street avoid the Left thro' *Brantree* to *London*; at
11 m. 2 f. the Right to *Hundon*, turn on the Left; at
12 m. 1 f. is *Stoke* Church close on the Left, where the
Left goes over the *Stour* into *Essex*, leave the Priory on the
Left; at 13 m. 1 f. the Right thro' *Kedington* to *Newmarket*, turn to the Left over the *Stour* into *Essex*; at 13 m.
3 f. is *Bathan* Inn close on the Left, where the forward
Road to *Colchester*; turn on the Right, leave *Whixoe*
Church about 3 f. on the same Hand; at 14 m. 1 f. the
Right to *Whixoe* Mill, turn on the Left; at 14 m. 3 f.
the forward Road to *Bumsted*, turn on the Right; at
14 m. 5 f. is *Whatsfar*-Bridge; at 14 m. 7 f. the Right
to *Whixoe*; at 15 m. 4 f. is *Sturmer* Village, where the
Right to *Kedington*, the Left to *Bumsted*; at 16 m. 3 f.
re-enter *Suffolk* at *Haverhill* Bounds; at 16 m. 5 f. the
Right to *Kedington*; and at 17 m. $3\frac{1}{4}$ f. is *Haverhill*
Church.

From *Sudbury* to *Stratford* Swan.

At the *East*-End of the Town avoid the engraved Road
to *Ipswich*; at 4 f. the Left to *Chilton*; at 7 f. is *Great
Cornard* Church close on the Left; at 1 m. 1 f. the Right
to *Cornard*-Mill, the Left to *Cornard-street*; at 1 m. 5 f.
the Right to *Amey* Mill, the Left to *Cornard-street*;
at 2 m. the Left to *Little Cornard*; passing along and a-
voiding several Turnings to the Left, keep the Road
turning to the Right; at 5 m. 1 f. is *Bures-street*; and
at

at 5 m. 3 f. is the Church close on the Right; here the Right to *Colchester*; at 5 m. 5 f. is the Pound close on the Right; at 6 m. 4 f. pass over a Brook; at 7 m. 5 f. the Left to *Newton*, turn on the Right; at 8 m. 1 f. the forward Road to *Assington*, turn on the Right, leave *Wiston* Church 2 f. on the Right; at 8 m. 6 f. turn on the Left; at 8 m. 7 f. the Left to *Assington*; at 9 m. 6 f. enter *Nayland-street*; at 10 m. *Nayland* Cross-street, the Right to *Colchester*, the Left thro' *Stoke* to *Lavenham*; at 11 m. is *Stoke*-Park, cross a Brook, and leave *Stoke* Church on the Left, and Sir *William Rowley*'s Seat on the Right; at 11 m. 6 f. is *Stoke* Village, where the forward Road to *Hadleigh*, the Left thro' *Assington* and *Newton* to *Sudbury*, turn on the Right; leave the Park on the Right; at 13 m. 1 f. the Right to *Boxted*, the Left to *Hadleigh*; pass thro' *Thirteen-street* over a Brook; at 13 m. 7 f. the Right to *Langham*; at 14 m. 5 f. is *Higham*-Bridge; at 14 m. 7 f. the Left to *Hadleigh*, the forward Road to *Ipswich*, turn on the Right past the Church; at 15 m. 4 f. the Left to *Holton*, the forward Road to *Ipswich*, turn on the Right; and at 16 m. 1 f. is *Stratford* Swan-Inn.

	m. f.
From *Sudbury* to *Bures*, is	5 3
From *Bures* to *Nayland*	4 5½
From *Nayland* to *Stratford* Swan	6 0½
	16 1

Cross-Road from *Lavenham* to *Bildeston*.

From the Swan-Inn turn on the Left at the Corner of the House; at the End of the Street the forward Road to *Kettlebarston*, turn on the Right; at 7 f. cross *Brent-Ely* first Bridge; and at 1 m. 3 f. cross the second; at 2 m. the Right to *Little Waldingfield*, turn on the Left, passing by the Church and Hall on the Left; at 2 m. avoid the forward Road to *Preston*, turn on the Right thro' *Brent-Ely* Village; at 2 m. 3 f. the forward Road to *Milden*,

turn

CROSS ROADS. 295

turn on the Left over the River; at 3 m. 3 f. the Right to *Milden*, the Left to *Kettlebarſton*; at 3 m. 7 f. *Monk's-Ely* Church, the Left to *Kettlebarſton*; at 4 m. 2 f. the Right turns over the Bridge to *Hadleigh* and *Ipſwich*, being the common Road from *Lavenham* thither, but keep the forward Road; at 4 m. 6 f. the Left to *Kettlebarſton*; at 4 m. 7 f. *Chelſworth* Church a little on the Right; at 5 m. the Right to *Seamere*; a little farther the Left to *Bildeſton* Church; at 5 m. 1 f. the Right to *Nedging*; at 5 m. 7 f. enter the Road from *Bildeſton* to *Hadleigh*, turn on the Left; and at 6 m. 1¾ f. is *Bildeſton*-Croſs.

Croſs-Road from *Newmarket* to *Sudbury*.

From the Greyhound-Inn paſs in the *Bury* Road; at 1½ f. leave it, and take the Right-hand Way over Champain Plains, avoiding divers Turnings to the Right and Left, leave *Cheevely* Church about a Mile on the Right; at 3 m. 5 f. are the Ruins of a Chapel on the Right; at 4 m. 4 f. are the Ruins of *Silvery* Church, a little on the Left; at 6 m. 3 f. croſs a Brook; at 6 m. 4 f. is *Lidgate* Church, a little on the Left; paſſing thro' *Lidgate* Village at 10 m. is *Wickham-Brook* Church, cloſe on the Right; at 10 m. 4 f. the Right to *Straddiſhall*, the Left thro' *Depden* to *Bury*; at 12 m. 7 f. is *Stanſfield* Church cloſe on the Right, croſs a Brook; at 13 m. 1 f. the *Bury* Road turns on the Right to *Clare*, avoid divers Turnings to Right and Left; at 17 m. 7 f. is *Glemſford* Church cloſe on the Right; at 18 m. 4 f. the Left to *Bury*, leave *Stanſtead* Church 4 f. on the Left; at 20 m. 3 f. enter the Road from *Sudbury* to *Clare*; at 21 m. is *Melford* Black-Lion Inn; paſs thro' *Melford ſtreet* in the Road from *Sudbury* to *Clare* before-mentioned; and at 24 m. 3¾ f. is *Sudbury* Market-Croſs.

Croſs-Road from *Thetford* to *Brandon*, and from thence to *Mildenhall*.

At 1 f. avoid the Road to *Bury* and turn on the Right, and leaving the Ruins of the *Friers* Preachers Houſe on
the

the Right, enter in at a Gate; at 1 m. the forward Road to *Lakenheath*, the Right to *Downham*, take the middle Way directly for the Warrener's Lodge; at 2 m. is the Lodge close on the Right; at 2 m. 7 f. is another Lodge close on the Right; at 5 m. 7 f. is *Brandon* Maid's-Head Inn, where the Left to *Mildenhall*, the Right to *Downham*. Leave *Brandon* Church 6 f. on the Right; at 4 m. 5 f. the Left to *Bury*, the Right to *Lakenheath*, leave *Ereswell* Church about a Mile on the Right; at 8 m. 3 f. the Left Acute backward to *Thetford*; at 8 m. 4 f. the Road comes in on the Left from *Bury*; and at 9 m. is *Mildenhall* Market-Cross.

Cross-Road from *Thetford* to *Gastrop*-Gate.

From the Bridge take the first Right-hand Way, at the East-end of the Town; at 5 f. cross over *Melford*-Bridge, avoiding the Left to *Shadwell*-Lodge, and the Right to *Euston*, take the middle Road; leave a Shepherd's Lodge half a Mile on the Right, going directly for *Rushford*; at 3 m. 5 f. is *Rushford* Church on the Right, the Left to *Shadwell*; at 3 m. 6 f. re-enter *Suffolk* at *Rushford*-Bridge, leave the *Red-House* close on the Left, pass over Champain Lands, having the *Little Ouse* on the Left; at 6 m. 6 f. is a Pound, here the Right goes from *Gastrop*-Gate to *Bury*; turn on the Left over the *Ouse* into *Norfolk*; and at 7 m. 1¼ f. is *Gastrop*-Gate Inn.

F I N I S.

BY the Affiftance of Mr. *Bacon*'s MS. and the Great Court Books of this Borough, we are enabled to carry the Lift of the Reprefentatives of *Ipfwich* almoft one hundred Years higher than that in *Willis's Not. Parl.* goes. Mr. Bacon remarks, that John Smith and Wm. Ridout in 25 *Hen*. VI. were the Firft Burgeffes fent by this Borough to Parliament. This further fhews how much the Town was favoured by that King. For his Charter [which fee p. 54] was granted in the 24th Year of his Reign, and in the following Year, the Borough was permitted to fend Members to Parliament.

Members of Parliament for IPSWICH.

Kings Reigns.	A. D.	Names of the Members.
25 Hen. 6.	1447	John Smith and William Ridout, Burgeffes Refident.
26 Hen. 6.	1448	John Smith and William Wethereld, at Five Marcs each.
27 Hen. 6.	1449	John Andrews and Richard Felaw.
28 Hen. 6.	1450	John Smith and Thomas Duncon.
29 Hen. 6.	1451	Gilbert Debenham and John Smith.
31 Hen. 6.	1453	John Smith and Edm. Winter; the laft without Fee.—This, we think, was the firft Bribe.
33 Hen. 6.	1455	Jn. Timperley & Gilb. Debenham, jun. Efq;
38 Hen. 6.	1460	William Worfop and John River, at 13d. per Day each.
1 Edward 4.	1461	Richard Felaw and William Baldree.
2 Edward 4.	1462	Wm. Worfop and John Lopham.—Worfop to have 20d. a Day at York; at any nearer Place 16d. and at London 12d.—Lopham 12d. a Day every where.
3 Edward 4.	1463	John Lopham and Wm. Worfop.
4 Edward 4.	1464	John Wallworth and Wm. Ridout.
7 Edward 4.	1467	John Wymondham and James Hobart.
9 Edward 4.	1469	John Timperley, junior, and John Alfray of Hendley.—Timperley at 8d. per Day; Alfray ferveth in Confideration of his Admiffion to be a Free Burgefs.
12 Edw. 4.	1472	Wm. Worfop and John Wallworth.—Worfop at 5s. per Week, and if the Parliament be adjourned to have 1s. per Day; Wallworth 3s. 4d. per Week.
17 Edw. 4.	1477	James Hobart and John Timperley, at 26s. and 8d. each, or 2 Marcs.
1 Edward 5.	1483	John Timperley and Roger Wentworth.
1 Richard 3.	1483	Tho. Baldry and John Wallworth. — Baldry at 2s. per Day; Wallworth at 1s.

Members for IPSWICH.

Kings Reigns.	A.D.	Names of the Members.
1 Richard 3.	1483	Benet Caldwell and Thomas Baldry.
1 Henry 7.	1485	Tho. Samson and William Wimbell.
3 Henry 7.	1487	Tho. Fastolf and John Wallworth, at 12 d. per Day each.
7 Henry 7.	1490	John Yaxley & Tho. Baldry.—Their Wages to be at the Order of Great Court.
11 Henry 8.	1494	John Fastolf and Ed. Bocking; at 1l. 6s. 8d. each, if at Westminster; if further off, to be order'd by Great Court. N.B. *The Great Court ordered more to Fastolf, 4l. to Bocking 3l.*
12 Henry 7.	1496	Thomas Alvard and Richard Bailey.
19 Henry 7.	1503	Thomas Baldry and Thomas Alvard. — To serve without Wages, not otherwise.
1 Henry 8.	1509	Wm. Spencer and Thomas Hall. — Spencer to have 40 s. N.B. *He had 6 s. 8 d. more.*
3 Henry 8.	1511	Thomas Baldry and Edmund Daundy.
6 Henry 8.	1514	The same.
14 Henry 8.	1522	Hump. Wingfield and Tho. Rush; and they came into Court, and took their Oaths of Free-Men.
21 Henry 8.	1529	Tho. Rush and Tho. Haward.
31 Henry 8.	1539	William Sabyn and Edmund Daundy.
33 Henry 8.	1541	Ralfe Gooding and John Sparrow.
1 Edward 6.	1547	John Gosnold and John Smith, alias Dyer.
7 Edward 6.	1553	John Smith, alias Dyer, and Richard Bird.
1 Mary.	1553	John Gosnold, Esq; and John Sulyard, Esq;
	1554	Clement Higham, Esq; Privy Counsellor, and Thomas Pooley, Esq;
1 Ph. & M.	1554	Ralfe Gooding and John Smith, alias Dyer.
2 & 3 Ph. & M.	1555	John Sulyard, Esq; and Richard Smart, Esq;
4 & 5 Ph. & M.	1557	Wm. Wheecroft and Philip Williams. —The said Williams remitted to the Town half his Burgess Fee.
1 Elizabeth.	1559	Tho. Seckford, jun. Esq; and Robert Barker.—Barker had 31 l. 4 s.
5 Elizabeth.	1563	Tho. Seckford, Esq; Master of Requests, and Edward Grimeston, Esq;
13 Eliz.	1571	Edw. Grimeston, Esq; and John Moor, Gent.
14 Eliz.	1572	Tho. Seckford, jun. Esq; & Edward Grimeston, Esq;
27 Eliz.	1585	Sir John Higham and John Barker. Esq; — Provided Sir John Higham shall take the Free-Man's Oath.
28 Eliz.	1586	John Lany, Esq; Recorder, and John Barker, Portman.
31 Eliz.	1588	John Barker, Esq; and Wm. Smart, Gent.
35 Eliz.	1592	Rob. Barker & Zac. Lock, Esq;—Lock 5 l.

Members for IPSWICH.   299

Kings Reigns.	A.D.	Names of the Members.
39 Eliz.	1597	Michael Stanhope and Francis Bacon, Esq;
43 Eliz.	1601	The same.
1 James.	1603	Sir Henry Glemham, Sir Francis Bacon.
12 James.	1614	Sir Francis Bacon, Robert Snelling; and afterwards Wm. Cage in the Place of Sir Francis, who was elected by the University of Cambridge.
18 James.	1620	Robert Snelling, Wm. Cage, Gent. — Snelling 50 l. Cage 50 l.
21 James.	1623	Robert Snelling, William Cage, Esq;
1 Charles 1.	1625	The same.
dit. 2d Parl.		Robert Snelling, Sir William Younge.
3 Charles.	1628	Wm. Cage, Esq; Edmund Day, Gent.
15 Charles.	1640	William Cage, John Gurdon, Esq; of Great Wenham. — John Gurdon had 104 Votes, Edmund Day had 95.
16 Charles.	1640	John Gurdon, Wm. Cage, Esq; and in the Place of Cage, deceased, Fra. Bacon, Esq; *N. B.* 18 Car. 1, *Cage had* 100 l. *and Dec.* 5, 1643, *John Gurdon had* 100 l. *and Cage* 50 l. *more, besides the* 100 l. *formerly granted.*
	1654	Nathaniel Bacon and Francis Bacon, Esqrs.
	1656	The same.
	1658-9	The same.
	1660	Sir Frederick Cornwallis in the Place of Nathaniel Bacon, deceased.
13 Cha. 2.	1661	John Sicklemore, William Bloyse, Esqrs. and John Wright in the room of Sicklemore.
	1678	Gilbert Linfield, John Wright.
25 Cha. 2.	1680	John Wright, Gilbert Linfield.—60 l. was order'd for Mr. Wright, 20 l. for Linfield.
	1681	The same.
	1685	John Wright, Sir John Barker, Bart.
	1688	Sir John Barker, Peyton Ventriss; and in the Place of Ventriss (made a Judge) Sir Cha. Bloise.
2 Wm. & M.	1689	Sir John Barker, Sir Charles Bloise.
7 William 3	1695	Sir John Barker, Charles Whitaker.
9 William 3	1698	Samuel Barnardiston, Richard Phillips.
12 Wm. 3.	1700	Joseph Martin, Esq; Sir Charles Duncomb.
13 Wm. 3.	1701	Charles Whitaker, Richard Phillips.
1 Ann.	1702	Charles Whitaker, John Bence.
3 Ann.	1705	Henry Pooley, John Bence; and in the Place of Pooley, Wm. Churchill, Esq;
	1708	John Bence, William Churchill.
	1710	Wm. Churchill, Sir Wm. Barker.
	1713	The same.
	1714	Wm. Churchill, Wm. Thompson.
	1722	Sir Wm. Thompson, Francis Negus, Esq;

X 2

Members for IPSWICH.

Kings Reigns.	A.D.	Names of the Members.
	1727	Sir Wm. Thompson, Francis Negus. In the Place Sir Wm. made a Judge, P. Broke. In the Place of Negus, dead, Wm. Wollaston.
	1734	Wm. Wollaston, Samuel Kent.
	1740	Samuel Kent, Edward Vernon.
	1747	The same.
	1754	The same.—In the Place of Vernon, Thomas Staunton;—In the Place of Kent, Geo. Montgomerie.
	1761	Tho. Staunton, Francis Vernon, (afterwards Lord Orwell.)

KNIGHTS of the SHIRE in Parliament For the County of SUFFOLK.

Kings Reigns.	A.D.	Names of the Members.
33 Henry 8.	1542	Sir Arthur Hopton.
1 Edw. 6.	1547	Sir Ant. Wingfield, Sir Tho. Wentworth.
7 Edw. 6.	1553	Sir Wm. Drury, Sir Tho. Bedingfield.
1 Mary.	1553	Sir Wm. Drury, Sir Henry Jerningham.
	1554	Sir Tho. Jerningham, Sir Wm. Drury.
1 Ph. & M.	1554	Henry Jernegan, Sir Wm. Drury.
2 & 3 P.& M.	1555	Henry Jernegan, Sir Wm. Drury.
4 & 5 P.& M.	1557	Sir T. Cornwallis, W. Cordell, Esq; Speaker.
1 Eliz.	1559	Robert Wingfield, Wm. Walgrave.
5 Eliz.	1563	Wm. Walgrave, Sir Robert Wingfield.
13 Eliz.	1571	Sir Owen Hopton, Tho. Seckford.
14 Eliz.	1572	Nicholas Bacon, Esq; Sir Rob. Wingfield.
27 Eliz.	1585	Sir Wm. Drury, Sir Robert Jermyn.
28 Eliz.	1586	Sir Robert Jermyn, Sir John Higham.
31 Eliz.	1588	Anthony Wingfield, Arthur Hopton, Esqrs.
35 Eliz.	1592	Edward Bacon, Sir Clement Heigham.
39 Eliz.	1597	Sir Wm. Walgrave, Henry Warner, Esq;
43 Eliz.	1601	Sir Henry Glemham, Calthrop Parker.
1 James.	1603	Sir John Higham, Sir Robert Drury.
12 James.	1614	Sir Henry Bedingfield, Sir Robert Drury.
18 James.	1620	Sir Robert Crane, Tho. Clinch, Esq;
21 James.	1623	Sir Wm. Spring, Sir Roger North.
1 Charles.	1625	Sir Edmund Bacon, Bart. Tho. Cornwallis,
dit. 2d Parl.		Sir Robert Naunton, Sir Robert Crane.
3 Charles.	1628	Sir Wm. Spring, Nat. Barnardiston, Esq;
15 Charles.	1640	Sir Nat. Barnardiston, Sir Phil. Parker, Knt.
16 Charles.	1640	Sir Nat. Barnardiston, Sir Philip Parker.
5 July.	1653	Jacob Caley, Francis Brewster, Robert Dunken, John Clark, and Edward Plumstead.

Knights of the Shire for SUFFOLK. 301

Kings Reigns.	A. D.	Names of the Members.
Parliament	1654	Sir Tho. Barnardiston, Sir Wm Spring, Bart. Sir Tho. Bedingfield, Knt. Wm. Bloyse, Esq; John Gurdon, Esq; Wm. Gibbs, Esq; John Brandling, Esq; Alex. Bence, Esq; John Sicklemore, Esq; Tho. Bacon, Esq;
Parliament	1656	Sir Henry Felton, Knt. Sir Tho. Barnardiston. Henry North, Edmund Harvey Edward Wyneive, John Sicklemore. Wm. Bloys, Wm. Gibbs. Robert Brewster, and Daniel Wale, Esqrs.
Parliament	1658-9	Sir Hen. Felton, Sir Tho. Barnardiston, Knt.
	1660	Sir Hen. Felton of Playford, Sir Henry North of Mildenhall, Barts.
	1661	Sir Hen. Felton, Sir Hen. North: And Sir Sam. Barnardiston, in the room of Sir H. North.
	1678	Sir Gervase Elwes, Sir Sam. Barnardiston.
	1679	Sir Wm. Spring, Sir Sam. Barnardiston.
	1681	The same.
	1685	Sir Robert Brook, Sir Henry North.
	1688	Sir John Cordel, Sir John Rous.
	1690	Sir Gervase Elwes, Sir Sam. Barnardiston.
	1695	The same.
	1698	Sir Sam Barnardiston, Sir Lionel Talmach, Earl of Dysert in Scotland.
	1700	Earl of Dysart, Sir Sam. Barnardiston.
	1701	The same.
	1702	Earl of Dysart, Sir Dudley Cullum.
	1705	Earl of Dysart, Sir Rob. Davers.
	1707	Sir Rob. Davers, Henry Martin in the room of the Earl of Dysart, a Peer of Gr. Brit.
	1708	Sir Tho. Hanmer, Sir Rob. Davers.
	1710	The same.
	1713	The same.
	1714	Sir Tho. Hanmer, Speaker, Sir Rob. Davers.
	1722	Sir Tho. Hanmer, Sir Rob. Davers, and Sir Wm Barker in room of Davers, dead.
	1727	Sir Wm. Barker, Sir Jermyn Davers, and Sir Rob. Kemp in the room of Sir Wm. dead.
	1734	Sir R. Kemp, Sir J. Davers.—Sir C. Firebrace in the room of Kemp, dead.
	1740	Sir Jermyn Davers, Sir Cordel Firebrace.
	1747	Sir Cordel Firebrace, John Affleck.
	1754	Sir Cordel Firebrace, John Affleck; and in the room of Firebrace, Rowland Holt.
	1761	Rowland Holt, Tho. Charles Bunbury.

Members for DUNWICH.

Kings Reigns.	A. D.	Names of the Members.
33 Henry 8.	1542	Robert Brown, George Coppyn,
1 Edward 6.	1547	Robert Coppyn, John Harrison.
7 Edward 6.	1553	Francis Yaxley, Robert Copping.
1 Mary.	1553	Robert Coppyn, Nicholas Harborough.
	1554	Robert Browne, George Jerningham, Esqrs.
1 Ph. & M.	1554	Robert Browne.
2 & 3 P.&M.	1555	George Saxmundham, Andrew Greave.
4 & 5 P.&M.	1557	Tho. Peyton, Gent. John Browne, Gent.
1 Elizabeth.	1559	John Mulwick, John Browne.
5 Elizabeth.	1563	Robert Hare, Esq; Robert Coppyn, Gent.
13 Eliz.	1571	Wm. Humberston, Arthur Hopton.
14 Eliz.	1572	Robert Coppyn, Richard Lane.
27 Eliz.	1585	Walter Dunch, Esq; Anth. Wingfield, Esq;
28 Eliz.	1586	Anthony Wingfield, Esq; Arthur Miller, Gent.
31 Eliz.	1588	Edward Honnings, Walter Dunch, Esqrs.
35 Eliz.	1592	Henry Savill, Thomas Corbett, Esqrs.
39 Eliz.	1597	Arthur Atyte, Clipseus Gawdy, Esqrs.
43 Eliz.	1601	John Suckling, Francis Mingay, Esqrs.
1 James.	1603	Valent. Knightley, Philip Gawdy, Esqrs.
12 James.	1614	Sir Robert Yaxley, Edmund Doubleday.
18 James.	1620	Clement Coke, Thomas Bedingfield.
21 James.	1623	Sir John Rouse, Sir Robert Brooke.
1 Charles.	1625	Sir Robert Rouse, Sir Robert Broke.
ditto 2d Parl.		Sir ——— Rouse, Thomas Bedingfield, Esq;
3 Charles.	1628	Sir Robert Broke, Francis Winterton, Gent.
15 Charles.	1640	Henry Coke, Anthony Bedingfield, Esqrs.
16 Charles.	1640	Henry Cooke, Esq; Anthony Bedingfield, and in his Place Robert Brewster, Esq;
Parliament	1654	Robert Brewster of Wrentham, Esq;
Parliament	1656	Francis Brewster, Esq;
Parliament	1658-9	Robert Brewster, John Barrington, Esqrs.
	1660	John Rous, Henry Bedingfield.
	1661	Sir John Rous, Richard Cook; and in their room Sir John Pettus, William Wood.
	1678	Sir Philip Skippon, Thomas Allen.
	1679	Sir Robert Kemp, Sir Philip Skippon.
	1681	The same.
	1685	Roger North, Thomas Knivet.
	1688	Sir Philip Skippon, Sir Robert Rich.
	1690	Sir Robert Rich, Sir Philip Skippon; & John Bence in the room of Sir Philip dead.
	1695	Sir Robert Rich, Henry Heveningham.
	1698	The same, and Sir Charles Blois in the room of Sir Robert Rich, dead.
	1700	Sir Charles Blois, Robert Kemp.
	1701	The same.

Members for DUNWICH.

Kings Reigns.	A. D.	Names of the Members.
	1702	Sir Charles Blois, Robert Kemp.
	1705	Sir Charles Blois, John Rous.
	1708	Sir Richard Allen, Daniel Harvey.
	1710	Sir Geo. Downing, Rd. Richardson, Serjeant at Law.
	1713	Sir Robert Kemp, Sir George Downing.
	1714	Sir Robert Rich, Charles Long.
	1722	Sir George Downing, Edw. Vernon, wav'd; Sir John Ward in his room, and Jn. Sambrook in the room of Sir John, dead.
	1727	Sir George Downing, Thomas Windham.
	1734	Sir Geo. Downing, Sir Orlando Bridgman.
	1740	Sir Geo. Downing, Jacob Garrard Downing.
	1747	Sir Geo. Downing, Miles Barnes.
	1754	Sir Jac. Gar. Downing, Alex. Forrester.
	1761	Henry Fox, Sir Jac. Garard Downing. — In the Place of Fox, now Lord Holland, Eliab Harvey.

Members of Parliament for the Borough of ORFORD.

Kings Reigns.	A. D.	Names of the Members.
33 Henry 8.	1542	John Cook, Esq;
1 Edward 6	1547	John Hare, Thomas Godsalve.
7 Edward 6.	1553	William Honing, Henry Cornwallis, Esqrs.
1 Mary.	1553	George Jerningham, Thomas Hervey.
1 Ph. & M.	1554	Thomas Seckford.
2 & 3 P.&M.	1555	Thomas Seckford, Thomas Spicer.
4 & 5 P.&M.	1557	Francis Stone, Thomas Seckford, Esqrs.
1 Elizabeth.	1559	Thomas Seckford, William Yaxley.
5 Elizabeth.	1563	Laurence Meres, William Yaxley, Esqrs.
13 Eliz.	1571	Anthony Wingfield, Anthony Rushe, Esqrs.
14 Eliz.	1572	The same.
27 Eliz.	1585	Henry Wingfield, Esq; John Cutting, Gent.
28 Eliz.	1586	Rich. Wingfield, Esq; Wm. Downing, Gent.
31 Eliz.	1588	Rich. Wingfield, Esq; Geo. Chilting, Gent.
35 Eliz.	1592	Edw. Grimston, sen. John North, Esqrs.
39 Eliz.	1597	Thomas River, William Forth.
43 Eliz.	1601	Sir John Townsend, Sir Richard Knightley.
1 James.	1603	Sir Michael Stanhope, Sir W. Cornwallis.
12 James.	1614	Sir Wm. Cornwallis, Sir Robert Gardiner.
18 James.	1620	Sir Lionel Talmache, Sir Robert Townsend.
21 James.	1623	Sir Robert Hitcham, William Glover, Esq;
1 Charles.	1625	Sir Robert Hitcham, Sir Wm. Whitepole.
ditto 2d Parl.		Sir Robert Hitcham, Charles Croft, Esq;
3 Charles.	1628	Sir Cha. Le Grofs, Sir Lion. Talmache, Bart.
15 Charles.	1840	Sir Charles Le Grofs, Edward Duke, Esq;
16 Charles.	1640	Sir W. Playters, Bart. Sir Ch. Le Grofs, Knt.

Members for ORFORD.

Kings Reigns.	A. D	Names of the Members.
Parliament	1658-9	Thomas Edgar, Efq; Jeremy Cepping, Gent.
	1660	Walter Devereux, Sir Alan Broderick.
	1661	The same.
	1678	Lionel Lord Huntingtower, Sir Jn.Duke, Bt.
	1679	Sir John Duke, Henry Parker.
	1681	Sir John Duke, Thomas Glemham.
	1685	Lionel Lord Huntingtower, Tho. Glemham.
	1688	Sir John Duke, Thomas Glemham.
	1690	Thomas Glemham, Thomas Felton.
	1695	Sir Adam Felton, Bart. Sir John Duke, Bart. Sir T.Felton in the room of Sir Adam, dead.
	1698	Sir Edm. Bacon, Bart. Sir John Duke, Bart.
	1700	Sir Edmund Bacon, Sir Edward Turner.
	1701	The same.
	1702	The same.
	1705	The same.
	1707	The same.
	1708	Clement Corrance, William Thompson.
	1710	Sir Edward Turner, Clement Corrance.
	1713	The same.
	1714	The same.
	1722	Dudley North, William Acton.
	1727	Price Devereux, wav'd; Dudley North, dead. William Acton, Robert Kemp.
	1734	Richard Powis, Lewis Barlow.
	1740	Lord Glenorchy, Henry Bilson Legge.
	1747	Henry Bilson Legge, John Walgrave.
	1754	Henry Bilson Legge, John Offley.
	1761	John Offley, Thomas Worsley.

Members for the Borough of SUDBURY.

(The Borough of SUDBURY did not send Members to Parliament before 1 Eliz.)

Kings Reigns.	A. D.	Names of the Members.
1 Elizabeth.	1559	Clement Throgmorton, Hen.Fortefcue,Efqrs.
5 Elizabeth.	1563	John Heigham, Thomas Andrews, Efq;
13 Eliz.	1571	John Hunt, Gent. John Gurdon.
14 Eliz.	1572	Richard Eden, Gent. Martin Cole, Gen.
27 Eliz.	1585	Edward Walgrave, Henry Blagge, Efqrs.
28 Eliz.	1586	Thomas Eden, Thomas Jermyn, Efqrs.
31 Eliz.	1588	Henry Blagge, Efq; Geffry Rusham, Gent.
35 Eliz.	1592	William Fortefcue, Dudley Fortefcue, Efqrs.
39 Eliz.	1597	William Walgrave, Efq; John Clapham.
43 Eliz.	1601	Philip Gawdy, Edward Glaffcock, Efqrs.
1 James.	1603	Sir Thomas Beckingham, Henry Eden.

Members for SUDBURY.

Kings Reigns.	A.D.	Names of the Members.
12 James.	1614	Charles Cibborne, William Towse.
18 James.	1620	Edward Osborne, Brampton Gurdon, Esq;
21 James.	1623	Sir Robert Crane, Sir William Pooley.
1 Charles.	1625	Sir Robert Crane, Sir Nath. Barnardiston.
dit. 2d Parl.	——	Sir Nath. Barnardiston, Tho. Smith, Gent.
3 Charles.	1628	Sir Rob. Crane, Bart. Sir Wm. Pooley, Knt.
15 Charles.	1640	Sir Rob. Crane, Bart. Richard Pepys, Esq;
16 Charles.	1640	Sir Simmons D'Ewes, Bart. Sir Rob. Crane.
Parliament	1654	John Fothergill, Esq;
	1656	John Fothergill, Esq;
	1658-9	Samuel Hasel, John Fothergill, Esqrs.
	1660	John Gurdon, Joseph Proud.
	1661	Sir Robert Cordel, Sir Gervase Elwes, Barts.
	1678	Sir Robert Cordel, Bart. Gervase Elwes.
	1679	Sir Gervase Elwes, Bart. Gervase Elwes.
	1681	The same.
	1685	Sir John Cordel, Bart. Sir Geo. Weneive, Knt.
	1688	Sir John Poley, Knt. Philip Gurdon.
	1690.	Philip Gurdon, John Robinson. — Sir Tho. Barnardiston in the room of Gurdon, dead.
	1695	Sir T. Barnardiston, Bt. Sir J. Robinson, Knt.
	1698	Sir Tho. Barnardiston, Sam. Kekewich, both dead. — John Gurdon, Sir Gervase Elwes.
	1700	Sir Gervase Elwes, Sir John Cordel.
	1701	Sir Gervase Elwes, George Dashwood.
	1702	Sir Gerv. Elwes, Philip Skippon. — Sir Harvey Elwes in the room of Sir Gervase, dead.
	1705	Sir Harvey Elwes, Philip Skippon.
	1707	The same.
	1708	Philip Skippon, Sir Harvey Elwes.
	1710	John Mead, Robert Echlin.
	1713	Sir Harvey Elwes, Robert Echlin.
	1714	Sir Harvey Elwes, Thomas Weston.
	1722	John Knight, William Windham.
	1727	John Knight, Carteret Leathes; and in the room of Knight, dead, Richard Jackson.
	1734	Richard Price, Edward Stephenson.
	1740	Carteret Leathes, Thomas Fonnereau.
	1747	Thomas Fonnereau, Richard Rigby.
	1754	Thomas Fonnereau, Thomas Walpole.
	1761	Tho. Fonnereau, John Henniker.

Members for the Borough of ALDBOROUGH.

(ALDBOROUGH did not send Members to Parliament before 13 Queen Elizabeth.

Kings Reigns.	A. D.	Names of the Members.
13 Eliz.	1571	Roger Woodhouse, Tho. Highford, Esqrs.
14 Eliz.	1572	Francis Beaumond, Charles Seckford.
27 Eliz.	1585	Peter Osborne, John Fox, Merchant.
28 Eliz.	1586	Peter Osborne, Edmund Bell, Esqrs.
31 Eliz.	1588	Edward Cook, Esq; William Bence.
35 Eliz.	1592	Thomas Knevet, William Bence.
39 Eliz.	1597	Francis Haton, Francis Johnson.
43 Eliz.	1601	Martin Statevill, Francis Corbet, Esqrs.
1 James.	1603	Sir William Woodhouse, Thomas Revet, Esq;
12 James.	1614	Sir Henry Glemham, Sir John Samms.
18 James.	1620	Sir Henry Glemham, Charles Glemham, Esq:
21 James.	1623	Nich. Ryvet, Esq; John Bence, Gent.
1 Charles.	1625	Sir Tho. Glemham, Charles Glemham, Esq;
ditto 2d Parl.	——	Sir Tho. Glemham, Wm. Mason, Esq;
3 Charles.	1628	Sir Simeon Steward, Knt. Marm. Rawden.
15 Charles.	1640	Wm. Rainborough, Esq; Squire Bence.
16 Charles.	1640	Squire Bence, Esq; Alex. Bence, Esq;
Parliament	1658-9	Laur. Oxburgh, Esq; John Bence, Merchant.
	1660	Robert Brooke, Thomas Bacon.
	1661	The same.
		John Holland Bar, John Bence.
	1678	Sir Richard Haddock, Knt. Henry Johnson.
	1679	John Bence, John Corrance.
	1681	John Bence, John Corrance.
	1685	Henry Bedingfield, King's Serjeant, Jn. Bence.
	1688	Sir Henry Johnson, William Johnson.
	1690	Sir Henry Johnson, Wm. Johnson.
	1695	The same.
	1698	The same.
	1700	The same.
	1701	The same.
	1702	The same.
	1705	The same.
	1707	The same.
	1708	The same.
	1710	The same.
	1713	The same.
	1714	The same, both dead.—In their room Sam. Lowe, Walter Plummer.
	1722	Samuel Lowe, Walter Plummer.
	1727	Wm. Wyndham, Sam. Lowe, both dead.—In their room Sir Jn. Williams, Geo. Purvis.

Members for ALDBOROUGH.

Kings Reigns.	A. D.	Names of the Members.
	1734	William Conolly, George Purvis.
	1740	William Conolly, Richard Plummer.
	1747	Wm. Wyndham Aſhe, Zach. Phil. Fonnereau.
	1754	Wm. Wyndham Aſhe, Zach. Phil. Fonnereau.
	1761	Zach. Philip Fonnereau, Philip Fonnereau.

Members for the Borough of EYE.

(EYE did not ſend Members to Parliament before 13 Q. Eliz.)

Kings Reigns.	A. D.	Names of the Members.
13 Eliz.	1571	Richard Beddal, Charles Cutber, Eſqrs.
14 Eliz.	1572	Charles Calthorpe, Charles Cutber.
27 Eliz.	1585	——— Baſingborne, George Broke, Eſqrs.
28 Eliz.	1586	Bartholomew Kemp, Tho. Bedingfield, Eſqrs.
31 Eliz.	1588	Edward Grimſton, Edmund Bacon, Eſqrs.
35 Eliz.	1592	Edward Honing, Philip Gawdy, Eſqrs.
39 Eliz.	1597	Anthony Gawdy, John Honing, Eſqrs.
43 Eliz.	1601	Edward Hunnings, Ant. Gawdy, Eſqrs.
1 James.	1603	Edward Honing, Eſq; Sir Henry Bockenham.
12 James.	1614	Sir John Crompton, Sir William Croft.
18 James.	1620	Sir Roger North, Sir John Crompton.
21 James.	1623	Sir Henry Crofts, Francis Finch, Eſq;
1 Charles.	1625	Sir Roger North, Francis Finch, Eſq;
dit. 2d Parl.		Sir Roger North, Francis North, Eſq;
3 Charles.	1628	Sir Roger North, Francis Finch, Eſq;
15 Charles.	1640	Sir Fred. Cornwallis, Bart. Sir Roger North.
16 Charles.	1640	Sir Fred Cornwallis, Bart., Sir Roger North, and in his Place Morris Barrow.
Parliament	1658-9	Edward Dendy, Joſeph Bliſſet, Eſqrs.
	1660	Charles Cornwallis, George Reeve.
	1661	Charles Cornwallis, George Reeve. Sir Robert Reeve, Knt. only.
	1678	Sir Charles Gawdy, Sir Robert Reeve, Bart.
	1679	Sir Charles Gaudy, Sir Robert Reeve, Cha. Fox, Geo. Walch.
	1681	Sir Charles Gaudy, Sir Robert Reeve.
	1685	Sir Charles Gaudy, Sir John Rous.
	1688	Thomas Knyvitt, Henry Poley.
	1690	Henry Poley, Thomas Davenant.
	1695	Charles Cornwallis, Tho. Davenant.—Cornwallis made a Peer, Sir Joſeph Jekyl.
	1698	Spencer Compton, Sir Joſ. Jekyll.
	1700	The ſame.
	1701	The ſame.
	1702	The ſame.

Members for EYE.

Kings Reigns.	A. D.	Names of the Members.
	1705	The same.
	1707	The same.
	1708	The same.
	1710	Sir Jos. Jekyll, Thomas Maynard.
	1713	Thomas Maynard, Edward Hopkins.
	1714	Edw. Hopkins, Tho. Smith.
	1722	Edward Hopkins, James Cornwallis.
	1727	Stephen Cornwallis, John Cornwallis.
	1734	Stephen Cornwallis, John Cornwallis.
	1740	Stephen Cornwallis, John Cornwallis.
	1747	Edward Cornwallis, Roger Townshend.
	1754	Courthorpe Clayton, Nicholas Harding.
	1761	Joshua Lord Viscount Allen, Richard Burton.

Members for the Borough of ST. EDMOND'S BURY.

(ST. EDMOND'S BURY did not send Members to Parliament before 12 James I.

Kings Reigns.	A. D.	Names of the Members.
12 James.	1614	Sir Thomas Jermyn, Robert Crane.
18 James.	1620	Sir Thomas Jermyn, John Woodford.
21 James.	1623	Sir Thomas Jermyn, Anthony Crofts, Esq;
1 Charles.	1625	Sir Thomas Jermyn, Sir Wm. Spring.
ditto 2d Parl.	—	Sir Thomas Jermyn, Emanuel Gifford.
3 Charles.	1628	Sir Thomas Jermyn, Sir William Hervey.
15 Charles.	1640	Sir Thomas Jermyn, John Godbold.
16 Charles.	1640	Thomas Jermyn, Esq; Sir W. Spring, and in his Place Sir Tho. Barnardiston.
Parliament	1654	Samuel Moody, John Clark, Esqrs.
	1656	Samuel Moody, John Clark, Esqrs.
	1658-9	John Clark, Tho. Chaplin, Esq;
	1660	Sir Henry Crofts, Sir John Duncombe.
	1661	Sir Henry Pooley, Sir John Duncombe. — In the Place of Pooley, Sir John Duncombe; and of Sir John, Sir William Duncombe.
	1678	Sir Thomas Hervey, Thomas Jermyn.
	1679	Sir Thomas Hervey, Thomas Jermyn.
	1681	Sir Thomas Hervey, Thomas Jermyn.
	1685	Sir Thomas Hervey, William Crofts.
	1688	Sir Rob. Davers, Bart. Sir Tho. Hervey, Knt.
	1690	Sir Rob. Davers, Henry Goldwell.—In the Place of Goldwell, dead, John Hervey.
	1695	Sir Robert Davers, John Hervey.
	1698	Sir Robert Davers, John Hervey.
	1700	Sir Robert Davers, John Hervey.

Members for ST. EDMOND'S BURY.

Kings Reigns.	A.D.	Names of the Members.
	1701	John Hervey, Sir Thomas Felton, Bart.
	1702	John Hervey, Sir Tho. Felton.—In the room of Hervey, made a Peer, Sir Rob. Davers.
	1705	Sir Tho. Felton, Sir Rob. Davers.—In room of Davers, who wav'd, Awberry Porter.
	1707	Sir Thomas Felton, Awberry Porter.
	1708	Awberry Porter, Sir Tho. Felton. —In room of Felton, dead, Joseph Weld, Serjeant at Law.
	1710	Joseph Weld, Awberry Porter.—In the room of Weld, dead, Samuel Batteley.
	1713	Carr Harvey, Awberry Porter.
	1714	Carr Hervey, Awberry Porter.—In the room of Porter, dead, J. Reynolds, Serj. at Law.
	1722	James Reynolds, Sir Jermyn Davers, Bart.—In the room of Reynolds, made a Judge, John Lord Hervey.
	1727	John Lord Hervey, Thomas Norton.—In the room of Lord Hervey, become a Peer, Th. Hervey.
	1734	Tho. Hervey, Thomas Norton.
	1740	Tho. Hervey, Thomas Norton.
	1747	Lord Petersham, Felton Hervey.
	1754	Lord Petersham, Felton Hervey.
	1761	Charles Fitzroy, William Hervey.

The VALUATION of the Parishes in Suffolk.

Parishes.	King's Books.			Value certified.		
	l.	s.	d.	l.	s.	d.
Acton All Saints,	9	6	8	—	—	—
Akenham St. Mary,	9	11	5¼	45	0	0
Aldborough St. Peter and Paul,	33	6	8	41	3	0
Alderton St. Bartholomew,	14	18	4	—	—	—
Aldham,	10	13	4	—	—	—
Aldringham St. Andrew,	—	—	—	6	15	0
All Saints, South Elmham,	8	0	0	41	10	0
Alpheton,	10	1	8	—	—	—
Ampton St. Peter,	5	2	1	29	12	8
Arwerton St. Andrew,	10	13	4	—	—	—
Ashbocking All Saints,	0	19	10¼	43	17	5½
Ashby,	—	—	—	—	—	—
Ash, by Campsey, St. Jn. Bapt.	14	5	0	—	—	—
Ashfield All Saints,	—	—	—	6	0	0
Ashfield St. Mary,	—	—	—	—	—	—
Ashfield in Blackbourn,	—	—	—	—	—	—
Aspal,	—	—	—	—	—	—
Assington St. Edmund,	10	0	0	47	10	0½
Athelington St. Peter,	4	14	2	29	9	8
Bacton,	19	12	3½	—	—	—
Baddingham,	22	16	8	—	—	—
Badley St. Mary,	—	—	—	—	—	—
Badwell Ash St. Mary,	—	—	—	13	0	0
Bailham St. Peter,	12	4	9	—	—	—
Bardwell,	7	17	1	—	—	—
Barham St. Mary,	12	10	5	—	—	—
Barking St. Mary,	27	10	7½	—	—	—
Barnardiston All Saints,	7	10	5	39	0	0
Barnby,	—	—	—	—	—	—
Barnham St. Gregory,	7	11	10½	—	—	—
Barnham St. Martin,	8	5	5	—	—	—
Barningham St. Andrew,	13	9	2	44	10	4
Barrow,	23	9	9¼	—	—	—
Barsham Holy Trinity,	15	6	8	—	—	—
Barton Great,	10	15	7½	39	10	11
Barton Little,	14	15	10	—	—	—
Battisford St. Mary,	8	0	7¼	45	0	0
Bawdsey St. Mary,	6	13	4	43	4	8
Bealings Great, St. Mary,	10	4	7	41	12	0
Bealings Little, All Saints,	6	7	3½	32	16	10
Beccles St. Michael,	21	12	3¼	—	—	—
Beddingfield St. Mary,	4	14	2	49	5	8
Bedfield St. Nicholas,	8	0	0	48	10	4

Beigh-

Valuation of the Parishes in Suffolk.

Parishes.	King's Books.			Value certified.		
	l.	s.	d.	l.	s.	d.
Beighton,	4	3	9	29	10	11
Belstead Little, St. Mary,	7	6	0½	49	14	11
Belton, All Saints,	17	15	0	31	16	1
Benacre St. Michael,	18	0	0	—	—	—
Benhall St. Mary,	9	1	5	28	16	0
Bentley St. Mary,	6	3	11	45	18	0½
Bildeston,	12	16	10½	—	—	—
Bing,	—	—	—	—	—	—
Blakenham Great, St. Mary,	6	16	0½	30	12	0
Blakenham Little, St. Mary,	10	3	4	—	—	—
Blaxhall St. Peter,	20	0	0	—	—	—
Blundeston St. Mary,	13	6	8	46	4	8
Blyborough Holy Trinity,	—	—	—	—	—	—
Blyford All Saints,	—	—	—	16	0	0
Boulge St. Michael,	3	12	1	28	1	10
Botesdale,	—	—	—	—	—	—
Boxford St. Mary,	20	0	0	—	—	—
Boxted, (consolidated with Hartest)	—	—	—	—	—	—
Boyton St. Andrew,	5	12	1	43	19	1½
Bradfield St. George,	11	17	3½	—	—	—
Bradfield St. Clare,	7	4	7	—	—	—
Bradfield-Combust,	4	19	7	29	12	7
Bradley Great,	17	1	5½	—	—	—
Bradley Little,	5	0	10	44	19	8
Bradwell St. Nicholas,	28	0	0	—	—	—
Braiesworth,	4	8	1½	42	13	4
Bramfield St. Andrew,	6	7	6	40	5	0
Bramford St. Mary,	13	3	9	—	—	—
Brampton St. Peter,	20	0	0	45	2	10
Brandilton All Saints,	9	16	8	41	19	7
Brandon St. Peter and Paul,	20	18	1⅐	—	—	—
Brantham St. Michael,	25	10	0	—	—	—
Bredfield St. Andrew,	4	4	2	46	1	6
Brent-Illeigh St. Mary,	8	0	0	—	—	—
Bretenham St. Mary,	11	3	11½	—	—	—
Bricet St. Mary,	—	—	—	—	—	—
Bricet St. Laurence,	—	—	—	—	—	—
Brightwell St. John Baptist,	—	—	—	—	—	—
Brockford,	—	—	—	—	—	—
Brockley St. Andrew,	10	4	2	—	—	—
Bromswell St. Edmund,	4	15	7½	26	0	0
Broom St. Mary,	10	0	2½	—	—	—
Brundish,	—	—	—	—	—	—
Brusyard St. Peter,	—	—	—	6	13	4
Bulchamp,	—	—	—	—	—	—
Bucklesham St. Mary,	9	1	8	44	11	0
Bungay Holy Trinity,	8	0	0	21	15	0

Bungay

Valuation of the Parishes in Suffolk.

Parishes.	King's Books.			Value certified.		
	l.	s.	d.	l.	s.	d.
Bungay St. Mary,				15	0	0
Bures St. Mary,	12	16	0½			
Burgate St. Mary,	13	10	10			
Burgh St. Botolph,	8	3	4	43	16	10
Burgh-Castle St. Peter,	6	13	4	44	6	1
Burstal,						
Butley St. John Baptist,						
Buxhall St. Mary,	20	0	5			
Buxlow,						
Campsey-Ash,						
Capel St. Mary,	13	18	4			
Capel St. Andrew,						
Carlton-Colvile St. Peter,	3	11	3	20	0	0
Carlton in Hoxne,						
Cavendish St. Mary,	26	0	0			
Cavenham St. Andrew,	5	5	10	30	0	0
Charsfield St. Peter,				8	0	0
Chattisham St. Mary,	4	13	4	24	7	8
Chedburgh,	4	3	1½	46	0	0
Cheddiston St. Mary,	6	7	6	21	12	7
Chelsworth All Saints,	8	8	9			
Chelmondiston St. Andrew,	8	10	0	46	2	8
Chevington,	16	3	9			
Chelsford St. Michael,	5	3	4	33	2	6
Chilton,	5	6	5½	48	12	8
Chilton by Stow,						
Clare St. Peter and Paul,	4	18	9	37	10	0½
Claydon St. Peter,	10	0	0			
Clement, (St.) Ipswich,						
Clopton St. Mary,	16	13	4			
Copdock St. Peter,	9	12	8¼	41	14	0
Cockfield,	30	0	0			
Coddenham St. Mary,	12	5	0			
Combs,						
Cony-Weston,	13	0	5	44	11	4
Cookley St. Michael,	6	13	4	29	3	4
Cooling, or Coolige,						
Cornard St. Andrew,						
Cornard All Saints,						
Corton St. Bartholomew,				10	0	0
Cotton St. Andrew,						
Covehithe,						
Cransford St. Peter,	6	13	4	44	18	0
Cratfield St. Mary,	5	7	11	36	0	0
Creeting St. Mary,	7	14	2	46	14	0
Creeting St. Peter,						
Creeting All Saints,						

Valuation of the Parishes in Suffolk.

Parishes.	King's Books.			Value certified.		
	l.	s.	d.	l.	s.	d.
Creeting St. Olave,	4	17	7½	22	4	0
Cretingham St. Andrew,	9	10	10	42	9	5
Crowfield,	—	—	—	—	—	—
Culford,	8	0	0	44	11	0
Culpho St. Botolph,	5	8	1	7	0	0
Dagworth,	—	—	—	—	—	—
Dalham St. Mary,	15	10	5	—	—	—
Dalinghoe St. Mary,	13	6	8	40	11	0
Darmsden,	—	—	—	—	—	—
Darsham All Saints,	4	10	10	26	2	7
Debach All Saints,	—	—	—	—	—	—
Debenham St. Mary,	15	2	6	—	—	—
Denham,	—	—	—	—	—	—
Denham St. John the Baptist,	5	0	10	39	9	8
Dennington St. Mary,	36	3	4	—	—	—
Denston,	—	—	—	—	—	—
Depden St. Mary,	10	11	5¼	—	—	—
Downham St. Mary,	—	—	—	11	11	6
Drinkeston,	16	17	1	—	—	—
Dunwich All Saints,	—	—	—	13	0	0
Dunningworth,	—	—	—	—	—	—
Earl-Soham,	—	—	—	—	—	—
East-Bergholt Chap. (See Brantham)	—	—	—	—	—	—
Easton-Bevint St. Nicholas,	12	0	0	—	—	—
Easton All Saints,	10	18	6½	45	12	9
St. Edmondsbury St. Mary,	—	—	—	—	—	—
St. Edmondsbury St. James,	—	—	—	—	—	—
Edwardston St. Mary,	4	13	4	39	11	0
Eike All Saints,	15	0	0	41	2	0
Ellough,	—	—	—	—	—	—
Elmset St. Peter,	13	7	11	—	—	—
Elmswell,	11	7	11	—	—	—
Elvedon St. Andrew,	12	17	6	—	—	—
Endgate St. Mary,	7	6	8	6	1	4
Eriswell St. Lawrence,	16	6	8	—	—	—
Erwarton (See Arwarton)	—	—	—	—	—	—
Euston,	13	7	11	—	—	—
Exning,	—	—	—	—	—	—
Eye St. Peter and Paul,	11	14	7	—	—	—
Eyke, (See Eike)	—	—	—	—	—	—
Fakenham St. Peter,	11	10	5	45	10	8½
Fakenham St. Andrew,	—	—	—	—	—	—
Fakenham St. Ethelbert,	7	11	0½	45	11	6
Farnham St. Mary,	—	—	—	15	0	0
Felixstow St. Peter and Paul,	5	9	7	29	12	6

Valuation of the Parishes in Suffolk.

Parishes.	King's Books.			Value certified		
	l.	s.	d.	l.	s.	d.
Felsham St. Peter,	8	4	7			
Finborough Magna,	5	1	3	37	10	0¾
Finborough Parva,	6	13	4	8	0	0
Finningham,	10	10	2½	48	11	5
Flemton St. Cath. with } Hengrave R. annexed,	5 9	0 7	0 1			
Flixton St. Mary,	6	0	0	27	5	11
Flixton St. Andrew,	14	0	0			
Flowton St. Mary,	3	9	2½	26	14	0
Fordley with Middleton, Holy Trin.	5	0	0	36	10	0
Fornham All Saints,	19	10	5			
Fornham St. Genoveve,	8	4	7			
Fornham St. Martin,	7	1	0¼	35	10	11¼
Foxhall,						
Framlingham St. Michael,	43	6	8			
Framsden St. Mary,	10	0	2¾			---
Freckingham St. Andrew,	3	15	2½	25	0	0
Fressingfield St. Peter,	17	17	1			
Friston St. Mary,	5	0	0	14	0	6
Fritton St. Peter,	6	7	8	47	0	0
Fritton St. Edmund,	6	13	4	39	17	9
Frostenden All Saints, .	12	0	0	45	16	0
Gazely All Saints, with Kenford Chapel,	7	3	4	46	16	6
Gedding,	4	13	4	23	13	7½
Gedgrave,						
Gisleham Holy Trinity,	13	6	8	42	9	7½
Gislingham St. Mary,	26	1	5½			
Glemham All Saints, } Glemham St. Andrew,				20	0	0
Glemsford St. Mary,	30	0	0			
Gorleston St. Andrew,	11	0	0	46	16	9
Gosbeck St. Mary,	8	5	5	38	11	4
Groton St. Bartholomew,	8	1	8			
Grundisburgh St. Mary,	17	11	3			
Gunton St. Peter,	5	6	8	20	10	0
Hacheston All Saints,	6	1	10½	22	18	3¼
Hadleigh St. Mary,	45	2	1			
Halesworth St. Mary,	20	0	0	38	0	0
Hardwick-House,						
Hargrave,	4	11	8			
Harkstead St. Mary,	11	3	9			
Harleston,	7	0	0	27	14	8
Hartest All Saints, with Boxsted ann.	29	14	2			
Hasketon St. Andrew,	13	6	8	49	6	8
Haslewood,						

Haver-

Valuation of the Parishes in Suffolk. 315

Parishes.	King's Books.			Value certified.		
	l.	s.	d.	l.	s.	d.
Haverhill St. Mary,	6	5	0	38	10	0¼
Hawkedon,	7	10	0	—	—	—
Haughley St. Mary,	7	19	2½	44	10	0½
Hawsted All Saints,	11	16	10½	—	—	—
Hedgsett,	12	17	11	—	—	—
Helmingham St. Mary,	18	0	0	—	—	—
Helens (St.) Ipswich,	8	3	9	33	13	8
Hemingston St. Gregory,	8	11	5½	—	—	—
Helmly All Saints,	4	19	4	25	14	0
Hengrave, (See Flempton)	—	—	—	—	—	—
Henham,	—	—	—	—	—	—
Henley St. Peter,	10	0	10	32	13	8
Henstead St. Mary,	12	0	0	—	—	—
Hepworth St. Peter,	13	17	3¾	49	10	4½
Heringfleet,	—	—	—	—	—	—
Heringswell St. Ethelbert,	9	9	4½	49	9	4½
Heveningham St. Margaret,	12	6	8	45	10	0
Higham St. Mary,	5	6	8	47	13	10
Higham Green,	—	—	—	—	—	—
Hinderclay St. Mary,	9	19	4½	47	11	3
Hintlesham St. Nicholas,	33	9	7	—	—	—
Hinton,	—	—	—	—	—	—
Hitcham,	26	13	4	—	—	—
Hollesley All Saints,	12	16	8	—	—	—
Holton St. Peter,	10	1⅓	4	39	0	0
Holton St Mary,	7	14	7	49	11	0
Holbrook All Saints,	11	11	3	—	—	—
Homersfield St. Mary,	5	6	8	29	10	0
Honington All Saints,	7	13	4	39	13	2
Hoo St. Andrew,	8	0	0	—	—	—
Hopton,	13	4	2	48	1	4
Hopton St. Margaret,	—	—	—	—	—	—
Horham St. Mary,	12	7	1	—	—	—
Horningherth,	10	17	8½	—	—	—
Horningsherth,	2	16	0	—	—	—
Horsecroft,	—	—	—	—	—	—
Hoxne St. Peter and Paul,	12	3	9	—	—	—
Hulverstreet,	—	—	—	—	—	—
Hundon All Saints,	7	13	4	42	10	0¼
Hunston,	—	—	—	—	—	—
Huntingfield St. Mary,	13	6	8	—	—	—
James (St.) South Elmham,	—	—	—	—	—	—
Icklingham All Saints,	12	17	6	—	—	—
Icklingham St. James,	11	11	5½	44	11	6
Ickworth,	7	11	5½	34	11	0
Iken St Botolph,	6	13	4	41	17	4
Ilketshall St. Andrew,	6	13	4	36	12	0

Ilket-

Valuation of the Parishes in Suffolk.

Parishes.	King's Books.			Value certified.		
	l.	s.	d.	l.	s.	d.
Ilketshall St. John,	8	13	4			
Ilketshall St. Lawrence,	—	—	—	5	12	4
Ilketshall St. Margaret,	8	13	9	27	11	4
Ingham St. Bartholomew,	12	16	0½			
Ixning, or Exning,	13	7	6			
Ixworth St. Mary,						
Ixworth, Thorp,						
Kedington St. Peter and Paul,	16	8	6½			
Kelsale, with Carlton St. Peter	20	0	5			
Kentford,						
Kennet St. Nicholas,	11	10	10			
Kenton All Saints,	8	0	0			
Kersey St. Mary,						
Kesgrave,						
Kettlebaston,	13	6	8	49	11	9
Kettleborough St. Andrew,	10	0	0			
Kessingland St. Edmund,	10	0	0	42	10	0
Kirkley All Saints,	5	16	10½	15	0	0
Kirkton St. Martin,	10	13	4	41	12	4
Knattishall All Saints,	6	7	11	29	11	8
Knodishall St. Lawr. with Buxlow,	11	0	0	32	0	0
Lackford St. Lawrence,	19	10	5			
Lakenheath St. Mary,	4	18	11½			
Langham St. Mary,	5	16	10½	44	9	4¾
Lavenham St. Peter and Paul,	20	2	11			
Lawrence (St.) Ipswich,				6	0	0
Lawshall All Saints,	20	2	8½			
Leyham,	16	0	7½			
Leiston St. Margaret,						
Laxfield All Saints,	9	13	4	44	9	10
Letheringham St. Mary,						
Levington St. Peter,	6	1	8	18	10	0
Lidgate,	15	10	5			
Lindsey,						
Linstead St. Peter,						
Linstead St. Margaret,						
Livermore St. Peter,	15	8	11¼			
Livermore St. Peter and Paul,	6	12	2	34	11	4
Lound St. John Baptist,	8	0	0	40	10	3
Lowestoft St. Margaret,	10	1	0½	43	16	6
Loudham,						
Margaret (St.) Ipswich,				10	0	0
Margaret (St.) South Elmham,	8	8	7¼	41	12	6
Marlsford,						
Martlesham St. Mary,	10	18	6½	47	10	0

Mary

Valuation of the Parishes in Suffolk. 317.

Parishes.	King's Books.			Value certified.		
	l.	s.	d.	l.	s.	d.
Mary (St.) at Elms, Ipswich,				9	0	0
Mary (St.) at Key, Ipswich,				25	0	0
Mary (St.) at Stoke, Ipswich,	12	0	0			
Mary (St.) at Tower, Ipswich,				60	0	0
Matthew (St.) Ipswich,	5	0	0	19	19	0
Melford Holy Trinity,	28	2	6			
Mellis St. Mary,	9	15	0			
Mells,						
Melton St. Andrew,	9	6	8	47	19	8
Mendham All Saints,	5	5	2½			
Mendlesham St. Mary,	14	9	2			
Metfield,						
Metingham All Saints,	6	16	10¼	29	11	4
Michael (St.) South Elmham,	4	17	11	19	10	0
Mickfield St. Andrew,	9	11	0½			
Middleton,						
Milding,	10	13	4			
Mildenhall St. Mary,	22	8	1½			
Monewden,						
Monks-Illeigh,	13	18	11½			
Monk-Soham, (See Soham-Monk)						
Moulton, {	13	6	8			
{	4	7	8			
Mutford St. Andrew, with Barnby,	7	17	1			
Nacton St. Martin,	8	7	1	29	11	0
Naughton,	10	15	0	44	11	0
Needham,						
Newbourn St. Mary,	7	4	2	20	14	8
Nedging,	8	12	11	44	11	0
Nettlestead St. Mary,	8	11	10½	27	11	10
Newton St. Mary,	7	15	5	48	0	0
Newton All-Saints,	17	3	9			
Newmarket St. Mary,	4	15	2½	33	9	0
Newmarket All Saints, Chapel				6	0	0
Nicholas, (St.) Ipswich,				10	0	0
Nicholas South-Elmham,	6	0	0			
Northcove St. Botolph,	10	0	0	48	8	10
Northales St. Andrew,	5	6	8	8	0	0
Norton St. Andrew,	14	3	9			
Nowton,	5	19	4½			
Oakley St. Nicholas,	9	4	9½			
Occold St. Michael,	19	1	5½			
Offley St. Mary,	16	6	5			
Offton St. Mary,	7	18	0½	29	10	11¼
Onehouse St. John Baptist,	7	2	6			

Orford

Valuation of the Parishes in Suffolk.

Parishes.	King's Books.			Value certified.		
	l.	s.	d.	l.	s.	d.
Orford, (Chapel to Sudbourn)						
Oulton St. Michael,	14	13	4			
Ousden.	10	3	9			
Pakefield All Saints,	14	0	0	29	1	1
Pakenham,	10	3	9	41	10	11
Palgrave St. Peter,	19	11	3			
Parham St. Mary,				20	0	0
Peasenhall, (consol. to Sibton)						
Peter, Ipswich,				30	0	0
Peter, South Elmham,	8	0	0	32	10	4
Pettaugh St. Catherine,	9	11	10¼	45	10	3¼
Pettistree St. Peter and Paul,				23	0	0
Playford St. Mary,						
Polstead St. Mary,	22	0	0			
Poslingford,	6	10	0	41	11	0
Preston St. Mary,	5	6	0¼			
Ramsholt All Saints,						
Rattlesden St. Nicholas,	20	0	2¼			
Raydon St. Marg. with Southwold,	13	6	8	28	0	0
Raydon St. Mary,	14	0	0			
Reed,	2	18	1	44	11	0
Redgrave St. Mary, with Botesdale,	25	7	1	48	10	8
Redisham St. Peter,				8	0	0
Redlingfield,						
Rendham St Michael,				36	0	0
Rendlesham St. Gregory,	24	13	4			
Rickengale superior St. Mary,	9	13	11½	43	11	4
Rickengale inferior St. Mary,	16	5	2⅓	37	10	7¼
Ringsfield All Saints,	12	0	0			
Ringshall,	11	18	1½			
Risby St. Giles,	19	10	5			
Rishangles St. Margaret's,	7	13	1½			
Rougham St. Mary,	23	18	6¼			
Roydon, (Church down)						
Rushbrook,	8	1	5½	39	10	11
Rushmere St. Andrew,	4	6	8	37	11	4
Rushmere St. Michael,	9	6	8	25	0	0
Rumburgh St. Michael,				25	0	0
Sancroft St. George,	10	0	0	40	10	0
Sapeston St. Andrew,				10	0	0
Satterly St. Margaret,	10	0	0	44	10	5
Saxham,	11	13	11½			
Saxham St. Nicholas,	8	11	5			
Saxmundham St. John Baptist,	8	15	10	48	13	8

Saxstead

Valuation of the Parishes in Suffolk.

Parishes.	King's Books.			Value certified.		
	l.	s.	d.	l.	s.	d.
Saxstead All Saints,						
Seamere All Saints,	11	7	1			
Shadingfield St. John Baptist,	12	0	0	38	17	6
Shelland,						
Shelly All Saints,						
Shimplingthorn St. George,	16	17	1			
Shipmeadow St. Bartholomew,	10	0	0	36	0	0
Shotley St. Mary,	20	0	0			
Shottisham St. Margaret,	4	17	2½	22	12	8
Sibton St. Peter,				45	0	0
Sizewell,						
Snape St. John Baptist,	5	5	7½	19	8	0
Soham-Monks St. Peter,	19	5	2½			
Soham-Earl St. Andrew,	10	0	0			
Somersham St. Mary,	8	0	0			
Somerliton St. Mary, with Heringfleet St. Margaret,	12	0	0			
Somerton,	6	16	8			
Sotherton St. Andrew,	5	6	8	43	1	7
Southcove St. Laurence,	6	2	11	26	0	0
South-Park,						
Southwold,						
Southolt,						
Spreksall St. Peter,	14	0	0			
Sproughton All Saints,	20	18	10			
Staningfield St. Nicholas,	8	0	2½			
Stanstead St. James,						
Stanton All Saints,	9	6	0½	34	9	9¼
Stanton St. John,	9	0	9½	39	10	8
Stansfield,	11	9	4¼			
Stephen (St.) Ipswich,	4	12	8½	5	2	0
Sternfield St. Mary Magdalen,	8	14	4½			
Stoke by Clare,						
Stoke-Ash All Saints,	11	1	3			
Stoke-Nayland St. Mary,	19	10	0			
Stonham-Aspal St. Mary,	19	10	2½			
Stonham-Earl St. Mary,	17	2	6			
Stonham Little St. Mary,	9	17	8½	49	10	8
Stoven St. Margaret,				6	10	0
Stradbrook All Saints,	9	19	4½	33	9	10
Stradishall St. Margaret,	9	11	0½			
Stratford St. Mary,	13	0	0	49	11	2
Stratford St. Andrew,	5	0	0	25	12	6
Stow-Langtoft St. George,	8	7	8¼			
Stow St. Peter, Stow St. Mary.	16	15	0	46	1	0¼
Sturston,	6	16	8	31	13	4

Stutton

Valuation of the Parishes in Suffolk.

Parishes.	King's Books.			Value certified.		
	l.	s.	d.	l.	s.	d.
Stutton St. Peter, —	12	17	6	—	—	—
Sudbourn All Saints with Orford,	33	6	8	—	—	—
Sudbury All Saints, —	4	11	5½	20	11	0
Sudbury St. Gregory with St. Peter,	—	—	—	—	—	—
Sutton All Saints, —	8	1	10½	24	5	0
Sweffling St. Mary, —	9	2	8½	—	—	—
Swilland St. Mary, —	7	9	4¾	49	6	3¾
Syleham, —						
Tannington St. Mary, —	12	10	2½	45	10	0
Tattingston St. Mary, —	.6	13	4	—	—	—
Theberton St. Peter, —	26	13	4	31	13	4
Thelnetham St. Nicholas, —	16	18	4	49	10	0¼
Thetford, —	—	—	—	—	—	—
Thorndon All Saints, —	24	11	10½	—	—	—
Thornham Great, —	7	11	3	47	10	0½
Thornham Little, —	4	14	4¼	28	13	3
Thorp-Ixworth All Saints, —	—	—	—	—	—	—
Thorp-Morieux, —	18	14	6¼	—	—	—
Thorp by Debenham, —						
Thorp in Blything, —						
Thorington St. Peter,	7	0	0	30	0	0
Thrandiston, —	13	6	8			
Thurleston St. Mary,						
Thurlow Great, —	10	11	5¼			
Thurlow Little, —	7	10	5			
Thwaite St. George, —	6	3	1¼	34	11	9
Thurston St. Peter, —	6	13	4	39	10	0
Tinworth St. Andrew, —	9	17	11			
Tostock, —	6	8	6½	39	10	11
Trimley St. Martin, —	12	0	5	43	10	6
Trimley St. Mary, —	15	13	4	43	10	6
Troston St. Mary, —	10	4	7	44	10	4¼
Tuddenham St. Martin, —	10	13	4	23	0	6
Tuddenham St. Mary,						
Tunstal St. Mich. w. Dunningworth,	21	0	2½	35	17	4
Ubbeston St. Peter, —	6	13	4	35	0	0
Ufford St. Mary, —	8	5	0	48	3	8
Uggeshall St Mary, —	13	6	8			
Walderswick. —						
Waldingfield St. Laurence, —	21	6	8			
Waldingfield Little, —	4	18	11¼	29	11	0
Waldringfield All Saints, —	4	17	11	21	4	0
Walsham le Willows, —				12	0	0
Walpole St. Mary, —				11	0	0

Walton

Valuation of the Parishes in Suffolk.

Parishes.	King's Books.			Value certified.		
	l.	s.	d.	l.	s.	d.
Walton St. Mary,	4	6	8	41	12	6
Wangford St. Dennis,	9	12	0½	39	11	0
Wangford St. Peter and Paul,	—	—	—	—	—	—
Wantesden St. John Baptist,	—	—	—	10	0	0
Washbrook St. Mary,	8	6	8	44	8	6
Watfield,	15	0	5	—	—	—
Wattisfield St. Margaret,	8	11	8	45	11	0
Wattisham,	—	—	—	—	—	—
Welnetham,	9	15	7½	—	—	—
Welnetham St. Mary Magdalen,	4	13	4	35	10	11
Wenham St. John,	7	13	4	45	12	0
Wenham Little,	5	8	11½	45	12	0
Wenhaston St. Peter,	6	0	10	30	0	0
Westhall St. Andrew,	10	2	3½	40	0	0
Westhorp St. Margaret,	4	18	1½	43	11	3
Westley St. Thomas Becket,	9	15	5	—	—	—
Westleton St. Peter,	8	0	0	33	0	6
Westerfield St. Mary Magdalen,	11	10	7½	47	16	10
Weston-Market St. Mary,	8	19	7	44	11	8
Weston-Coney St. Peter,	3	6	8	46	8	7
Weston in Wangford,	—	—	—	—	—	—
Westow,	9	17	3½	39	10	11
Westwood-Lodge,	—	—	—	—	—	—
Wetherden,	6	13	4	49	10	0½
Wetheringsett All Sts. w. Brockford.	33	9	2	—	—	—
Wethersdale St. Mary Magdalen,	6	16	8	41	14	4
Wethersfield St. Mary,	9	17	1	—	—	—
Weybread St. Mary,	5	0	0	26	9	2
Whepstead,	14	4	2	—	—	—
Wherstead St. Mary,	5	6	8	44	10	2
Whitton St. Botolph,	6	11	5½	—	—	—
Whixoe,	5	13	1½	44	12	8
Wickham-Market All Saints,	6	16	8	22	0	0
Wickham-Skeith St. Andrew,	5	8	1½	40	10	1
Wickham-Brook All Saints,	8	6	10½	—	—	—
Wilby St. Mary,	26	6	10½	—	—	—
Willingham All Saints,	10	10	0	35	1	10
Willingham St. Mary and St. Peter,	6	13	4	23	0	0
Willisham St. Mary,	—	—	—	—	—	—
Wingfield St. Andrew,	—	—	—	—	—	—
Winston St. Andrew,	9	3	9	—	—	—
Wisset St. Andrew,	—	—	—	20	0	0
Wissington St. Mary,	4	19	4½	—	—	—
Witnesham St. Mary,	18	13	4	—	—	—
Wiverstone,	8	14	9½	31	11	0
Woodbridge St. Mary,	—	—	—	45	0	0
Woolpit St. Mary,	6	18	9	—	—	—

Valuation of the Parishes in Suffolk.

Parishes.	King's Books.			Value certified.		
	l.	s.	d.	l.	s.	d.
Woolverston St. Mary,	5	8	6¼	34	13	0
Wordwell,	7	7	3½	32	10	0½
Worlingham All Saints,	12	0	0	—	—	—
Worlington,	19	6	8	—	—	—
Worlingworth St. Mary, with Southolt St. Margaret,	19	12	3½	—	—	—
Wortham Eastgate St. Mary,	13	1	0	—	—	—
Wortham Everard,	13	2	8½	—	—	—
Wratting Great,	8	0	0	—	—	—
Wratting Little,	4	19	9½	—	—	—
Wrentham St. Nicholas,	21	6	8	—	—	—
Yaxley St. Mary,	6	6	5½	—	—	—
Yoxford St. Peter,	5	10	2	37	15	0

A List of the PATRONS *of the several Parishes in* Suffolk, *with a Reference to the Page where they are to be found.*

Parishes.		Patrons.	Pag.
Acton All Saints,	V.	Mr. Jennens,	254
Akenham St. Mary,	R.	Mr. Drury,	199
Aldborough St. Peter and Paul,	V.	E. of Strafford,	118
Alderton St. Bartholomew,	R.	Bishop of Norwich, &c.	109
Aldham,	R.	Sir Joshua Vanneck,	269
Aldringham St. Andrew,	C.	Mr. Hervey's Heirs,	128
All Saints, South Elmham,	R.	Mr. Adair,	155
Alpheton,	R.	Mr. Martin,	254
Ampton St. Peter,	R.	Mr. Calthrop,	222
Arwerton St. Andrew,	R.	Sir P. Parker's Heirs,	61
Ashbocking All Saints,	V.	The Crown,	199
Ashby,			151
Ash, by Campsey, St. Jn. Bapt.	R.	Mrs. Braham,	95
Ashfield All Saints,	C.	Mr. Bridges,	184
Ashfield in Blackbourn,			230
Aspal,	C.	Mr. Chevalier,	172
Assington St. Edmund,	V.	Mr. Gurdon,	254
Athelington St. Peter,	R.	The Crown,	164
Bacton,	R.	Mr. Barker,	172
Baddingham,	R.	Mr. Syer,	164
Badley St. Mary,	C.	Mr. Crowley's Heirs,	200
Badwell Ash St. Mary,	C.	Mr. Clough,	230

Bailham

Patrons of the Parishes, &c.

Parishes.		Patrons.	Page.
Bailham St. Peter, —	— R.	Mr. Acton, ———	201
Bardwell, —	— R.	St. John's Coll. Oxford,	230
Barham St. Mary, —	— R.	Mr Bacon, ———	200
Barking St. Mary, —	— R.	Mr. Crowley's Heirs,—	200
Barnardiston All Saints, ——	R.	Mr. Unwin, ———	246
Barnby, ——			149
Barnham St. Gregory, ——{	R.	Duke of Grafton,———	231
Barnham St. Martin, ——			
Barningham St. Andrew, ——	R.	Mr. Evans, ———	231
Barrow, ———	R.	St. John's Col. Camb.	216
Barsham Holy Trinity, ———	R.	Mr. Missenden, ———	159
Barton Great, ——— —	V.	Sir Wm. Bunbury,———	222
Barton Little, ——— —	R.	The Crown, ———	238
Battisford St. Mary, ———	V.	Mr. Watson, ———	200
Bawdsey St. Mary, ———	V.	The Crown, ———	109
Bealings Great, St. Mary,———	R.	Mr. Bridges, ———	72
Bealings Little, All Saints, —	R.	Mr. Atkinson, ———	73
Beccles St. Michael, — —	R.	Mr. Bence's Heirs,———	159
Beddingfield St. Mary, ———	V.	Mr. Bedingfield,———	164
Bedfield St. Nicholas,———	R.	Sir John Rous, ———	165
Beighton, ——— —	R.	The Crown, ———	223
Bellstead Little, St. Mary, ———	R.	Captain Harland, ———	61
Belton, All Saints, ———	R.	Bishop of Norwich, —	151
Benacre St. Michael, ———	R.	Sir Thomas Gooch, —	128
Benhall St. Mary, ——— —	V.	Mr. Rush, ———	119
Bentley St. Mary, ———	V.	Mr. Dean, ———	61
Bildeston, ———		Mr. Beale's Heirs, ———	269
Bing, ———			110
Blakenham Great, St. Mary,—	R.	Eaton College, ———	201
Blakenham Little, St. Mary,—	R.	Lord Orwell, ———	201
Blaxhall St. Peter, ———	R.	Mr. Jackson, ———	119
Blundeston St. Mary, ———	R.	Sir Thomas Allen,———	151
Blyborough Holy Trinity, ———	C.	Sir John Blois, ———	128
Blyford All Saints, ——— —	C.	Mr. Chapman, ———	130
Boulge St. Michael, ———	R.	Sir Wm. Bunbury,———	110
Botesdale, ——— —			173
Boxford St. Mary, ——— —	R.	The Crown, ———	255
Boxted, (consol. with Harteft)			256
Boyton St. Andrew, ——— —	R.	Mrs. Warner's Trustees,	110
Bradfield St. George, ———	R.	Sir C. Davers, ———	223
Bradfield St. Clare, ———	R.	} Mr. Young,——— {	223
Bradfield-Combust, ———	R.		223
Bradley Great, ———	R.	Mr. Brand, ———	246
Bradley Little, ——	R.	Mr. Dickens, ———	246
Bradwell St. Nicholas, ———	R.	Sir Thomas Allen,———	151
Braiesworth, ———	R.	Earl Cornwallis, ———	173
Bramfield St. Andrew, ———	V.	The Crown, — —	130
Bramford St. Mary, ———	V.	Chapter of Canterbury,	201

Parishes.		Patrons.	Page.
Brampton St. Peter,	R.	Mr. Leman,	130
Brandiston All Saints,	V.	Trustees for a Charity,	95
Brandon St. Peter and Paul,	R.	Mr. Holt,	238
Brantham St. Michael,	R.	Sir Jof. Hankey,	62
Bredfield St. Andrew,	V.	The Crown,	111
Brent-Illeigh St. Mary,	V.	Mr. Goat,	257
Bretenham St. Mary,	R.	The Crown,	270
Bricet St. Mary,	C.	King's College, Camb.	202
Bricet St. Laurence,		(See Offton)	202
Brightwell St. John Baptist,	C.	Mr. Barnardiston's Heirs	73
Brockford,			174
Brockley St. Andrew,	R.	Mr. Grigby,	217
Bromswell St. Edmund,	R.		173
Broom St. Mary,	R.	Earl Cornwallis,	112
Brundish,		Mr. Major,	165
Brusyard St. Peter,	C.	Sir John Rous,	120
Bulchamp,			131
Bucklesham St. Mary,	R.	Mr. Broke,	73
Bungay Holy Trinity,	V.	Bishop of Ely,	157
Bungay St. Mary,	C.	Duke of Norfolk,	157
Bures St. Mary,	V.	Mr. Benyon,	256
Burgate St. Mary,	R.	Mr. Holt,	175
Burgh St. Botolph,	R.	Mr. Barnes,	73
Burgh-Castle St. Peter,	R.	The Crown,	151
Burstal,	C.	(See Bramford)	62
Butley St. John Baptist,	C.	Mr. Howard, [95 &	120
Buxhall St. Mary,	R.	Dr. Hill,	186
Buxlow,		Consol. with Knodishall,	131
Campsey-Ash,			95
Capel St. Mary,	R.	Mr. Hingeston,	62
Capel St. Andrew,	C.	(See Butley)	112
Carlton-Colvile St. Peter,	R. & V.]	Sir Tho. Allen,	149
Carlton in Hoxne,			165
Cavendish St. Mary,	R.	Jesus College, Camb.	258
Cavenham St. Andrew,	V.	The Crown,	239
Charsfield St. Peter,	C.	Mr. Leman,	97
Chattisham St. Mary,	V.	Eaton College,	63
Chedburgh,	R.	Earl of Bristol,	248
Cheddiston St. Mary,	V.	Mr. Plummer,	131
Chelsworth All Saints,	R.	The Crown,	270
Chelmondiston St. Andrew,	R.	The Crown,	63
Chevington,	R.	Mr. Turner,	217
Chilesford St. Michael,	R.	Mr. North,	120
Chilton,	R.	Sir Armine Woodhouse,	248
Chilton by Stow,			187
Clare St. Peter and Paul,	V.	The Crown,	246
Claydon St. Peter,	R.	Mr. Drury,	202

Clement

PATRONS of the Parishes, &c.

Parishes.		Patrons.	Page.
Clement, (St.) Ipswich,	R.	Mr. Adkin,	32
Clopton St. Mary,	R.	Mr. Couperthwaite,	74
Copdock St. Peter,	R.	Mr. De Grey,	63
Cockfield,	R.	St. John's Coll. Camb.	258
Coddenham St. Mary,	V.	Mr. Bacon,	203
Combs,	R.	Mr. Crowley's Heirs,	186
Cony-Weston,	R.	Mr. Lewis,	231
Cookley St. Michael,	R.	Sir Jof. Vanneck,	132
Cooling, or Coolige,	C.	Trinity Hall, Cambr.	248
Cornard St. Andrew,	R.	} Mr. Eldred, {	259
Cornard All Saints,	R.		
Corton St. Bartholomew,	V.	The Crown,	152
Cotton St. Andrew,	R.	Mr. Pretyman,	175
Covehithe,			132
Cransford St. Peter,	V.	Mr. Syer,	121
Cratfield St. Mary,	R.	Earl of Leicester,	132
Creeting St. Mary,	R.	Eaton College,	204
Creeting St. Peter,	R.	Mr. W. Bacon,	187
Creeting All Saints,	R.	Mr. Crespigny,	203
Creeting St. Olave,			
Cretingham St. Andrew,	V.	The Crown,	97
Crowfield,		Consol. to Coddenham,	204
Culford,	R.	Earl Cornwallis,	231
Culpho St. Botolph,	C.	Sir John Blois,	74
Dagworth,			187
Dalham St. Mary,	R.	Mr. Affleck,	248
Dalinghoe St. Mary,	R.	Earl of Rochford,	97
Darmsden,			204
Darsham All Saints,	V.	Sir John Rous,	133
Debach All Saints,	R.	Sir William Bunbury,	112
Debenham St. Mary,	V.	Mr. Bridges,	184
Denham,	C.	Lord Townshend,	249
Denham St. John the Baptist,	V.	Lord Maynard,	165
Dennington St. Mary,	R.	Sir John Rous,	165
Denston,	C.	Mr. Robinson,	249
Depden St. Mary,	R.	Mr. Mure,	249
Downham St. Mary,	C.	Mrs. Wright,	239
Drinkeston,	R.	Mr. Moseley,	213
Dunwich All Saints,	C.	Sir Jacob Downing,	133
Dunningworth,			121
Earl-Soham,		(See Soham-Earl)	98
East-Bergholt Chapel,		(See Brantham)	63
Easton-Bavent St. Nicholas,	R.	Sir Thomas Gooch,	137
Easton All Saints,	R.	Mr. Nassau,	98
St. Edmondsbury St. Mary,	C.	} The Corporation, {	211
St. Edmondsbury St. James,	C.		

Edward-

Patrons of the Parishes, &c.

Parishes.		Patrons.	Page.
Edwardston St. Mary,	V.	Mr. Sheldon,	259
Eike All Saints,	R.	Mr. Howard,	99
Ellough,		Sir John Playters,	161
Elmsct St. Peter,	R.	Clare Hall, Cambridge,	271
Elmswell,	R.	Mr. Chapman,	231
Elvedon St. Andrew,	R.	Sir John Tyrrell,	243
Endgate St. Mary,	R.	The Crown,	161
Eriswell St. Lawrence,	R.	Mr. Evans,	242
Erwarton (See Arwarton)			61
Euston,	R.	Duke of Grafton,	231
Exning,			187
Eye St. Peter and Paul,	V.	Earl Cornwallis,	175
Eyke, (See Eike)			99
Fakenham St. Peter,	R.	Duke of Grafton,	232
Fakenham St. Andrew,	R.	Duke of Grafton,	232
Falkenham St. Ethelbert,	V.	The Crown,	74
Farnham St. Mary,	C.	Mr. North,	121
Felixtow St. Peter and Paul,	V.	Mr. Atkinson,	75
Felsham St. Peter,	R.	Dr. Scot,	223
Finborough Magna,	V.	Bishop of Ely,	188
Finborough Parva,	V.	King's Coll. Cambridge,	188
Finningham,	R.	Mr. Frere,	177
Flemton St. Cath. with Hengrave R. annexed,	R. R.	} Sir Wm. Gage, {	217
Flixton St. Mary,	V.	Mr. Adair,	155
Flixton St. Andrew,	R.	Sir Tho. Allen,	152
Flowton St. Mary,	R.	Mr. Sherwood,	205
Fordley with Middleton, H.Tr.		Mrs. Freake,	137
Fornham All Saints,	R.	Clare Hall, Cambridge,	217
Fornham St. Genoveve,	R.	Mr. Hill,	224
Fornham St. Martin,	R.	Mr. Kent,	224
Foxhall,			75
Framlingham St. Michael,	R.	Pembroke Hall, Camb.	99
Framsden St. Mary,	V.	Earl of Dysert,	185
Freckingham St. Andrew, [R.&	V.	St. Peter's Coll. Camb.	243
Fressingfield St. Peter,	V.	Emanuel Coll. Camb.	166
Friston St. Mary,	V.	Earl of Strafford,	121
Freston St. Peter,	R.	Mr. Staunton,	64
Fritton St. Edmund,	R.	Earl of Strafford,	152
Frostenden All Saints,	R.	Mr. Glover's Heirs,	138
Gazely All Saints, with Kenford Chapel,	V.	} Trinity Hall, Camb.	249
Gedding,	R.	Corporation of Ipswich,	224
Gedgrave,			122
Gisleham Holy Trinity,	R.	The Crown,	149
Gislingham St. Mary,	R.	Mrs. Bedingfield,	177

Glem-

PATRONS of the Parishes, &c.

Parishes.		Patrons.	Page.
Glemham All Saints,	C.	Mr. North,	122
Glemham St. Andrew,	R.		122
Glemsford St. Mary,	R.	Bishop of Ely,	260
Gorleston St. Andrew,	V.	Sir John Kemp,	152
Gosbeck St. Mary,	R.	Lord Orwell,	205
Groton St. Bartholomew,	R.	Mr. Waring,	260
Grundisburgh St. Mary,	R.	Trinity Coll. Camb.	75
Gunton St. Peter,	R.	Sir Cha. Saunders,	153
Hacheston All Saints,	V.	Mr. Corance's Heirs,	102
Hadleigh St. Mary,	R.	Archbp. of Canterbury,	261
Halesworth St. Mary,	R.	Mr. Plummer,	138
Hardwick-House,			217
Hargrave,	R.		218
Harkstead St. Mary,	R.	Mr. Canning,	65
Harleston,	R.	Sir Wm. Gage,	188
Hartest All Sts. w. Boxsted ann.	R.	The Crown,	261
Hasketon St. Andrew,	R.	Mr. Stebbing,	76
Haslewood,			123
Haverhill St. Mary,	V.	Mr. Coldham,	249
Hawkedon,	R.	Mr. Gilly,	250
Haughley St. Mary,	V.	Mr. Turner,	188
Hawsted All Saints,	R.	Sir John Cullum,	218
Hedgsett,	R.	Mr. Le Heup,	225
Helmingham St. Mary,	R.	The Crown,	205
Helens (St.) Ipswich,	R.	Consol. to St. Clement,	35
Hemingston St. Gregory,	R.	Mr. Nunn,	205
Helmly All Saints,	R.	The Crown,	76
Hengrave, (See Flempton)			218
Henham,			139
Henley St. Peter,	V.	D. and Ch. of Norwich,	206
Henstead St. Mary,	R.	Mr. Holoway's Heirs,	139
Hepworth St. Peter,	R.	Messrs. Rye and Nunn,	232
Heringfleet,			153
Heringswell St. Ethelbert,	R.	Mr. Holden,	243
Heveningham St. Margaret,	R.	The Crown,	139
Higham St. Mary,	V.	In Trustees,	66
Higham Green,			243
Hinderclay St. Mary,	R.	Mr. Holt,	232
Hintlesham St. Nicholas,	R.	Mr. Adkin,	66
Hinton,			139
Hitcham,	R.	The Crown,	273
Hollesley All Saints,	R.	Mr. Chapman,	112
Holton St. Peter,	R.	The Crown,	139
Holton St. Mary,	R.	Sir Wm. Mannock,	67
Holbrook All Saints,	R.	Mr. Nunn,	66
Homersfield St. Mary,	R.	Mr. Adair,	156
Honington All Saints,	R.	The Crown,	233
Hoo St. Andrew,	C.	Mr. Leman,	103

PATRONS of the Parishes, &c.

Parishes.		Patrons.	Page.
Hopton,	R.	The Crown,	233
Hopton St. Margaret,	C.	D. and Ch. of Norwich,	153
Horham St. Mary,	R.	Earl of Leicester,	167
Horningsherth, Horningsherth,	R.	} Sir Rob. Davers, {	219
Horsecroft,			219
Hoxne St. Peter and Paul,	V.	Lord Maynard,	167
Hulverstreet,			161
Hundon All Saints,	V.	Jesus Coll. Cambridge,	250
Hunston,	C.	Mr. Symonds,	233
Huntingfield St. Mary,	R.	Sir Jos. Vanneck,	140
James (St.) South Elmham,		Mr. Adair,	156
Icklingham All Saints,	R.	Earl of Essex,	243
Icklingham St. James,	R.	Mr. Gwilt,	243
Ickworth,	R.	Earl of Bristol,	219
Iken St Botolph,	R.	Mr. Jeffreson,	123
Ilketshall St. Andrew,	V.	Mr. Adair,	156
Ilketshall St. John,	R.	The Crown,	158
Ilketshall St. Lawrence,	C.	Mr. Strange,	158
Ilketshall St. Margaret,	V.	Eman. Coll. Cambridge,	158
Ingham St. Bartholomew,	R.	Earl Cornwallis,	233
Ixning, or Exning,	V.	Chapter of Canterbury,	187
Ixworth St. Mary,	C.	Mr. Norton,	233
Ixworth, Thorp,			234
Kedington St. Peter and Paul,	R.	Mr. Chevalier,	250
Kelsale, with Carlton St. Peter	R.	Mrs. Bence,	167
Kentford,		Consol. with Gazely,	251
Kennet St. Nicholas,	R.	Mr. Barnardiston's Heirs,	
Kenton All Saints,	V.	Mr. Bridges,	103
Kersey St. Mary,	C.	King's Coll. Camb.	273
Kesgrave,	C.	Mr Barnardiston's Heirs,	76
Kettlebaston,	R.	Mr. Leman,	273
Kettleborough St. Andrew,	R.	Mr. Sparrow,	103
Kessingland St. Edmund,	V.	Bishop of Norwich,	149
Kirkley All Saints,	R.	Mr. Willson,	149
Kirkton St. Martin,	R.	The Crown,	77
Knattishall All Saints,	R.	Mr. Crofts Read,	234
Knodishall St. Lawr. w. Buxlow,	R.	Lord Orwell,	140
Lackford St. Lawrence,	R.	Mr. Kent,	219
Lakenheath St. Mary,	V.	Dean and Ch. of Ely,	243
Langham St. Mary,	R.	The Crown,	234
Lavenham St. Peter and Paul,	R.	Caius Coll. Cambridge,	261
Lawrence (St.) Ipswich,	C.	The Parishioners,	36
Lawshall All Saints,	R.	Mr. Lee,	262
Leyham,	R.	St. John's Coll. Camb.	273
Leiston St. Margaret,	C.	Haberdashers Co. &c.	140

Laxfield

PATRONS of the Parishes, &c.

Parishes.		Patrons.	Page.
Laxfield All Saints,	V.	Sir Jof. Vanneck,	168
Letheringham St. Mary,	C.	Mr. Naunton,	104
Levington St. Peter,	R.	Confol. to Nacton,	77
Lidgate,	R.	Lord Granby,	251
Lindfey,	C.	King's Coll. Camb.	274
Linftead St. Peter,	C.	Sir Jof. Vanneck,	141
Linftead St. Margaret,	C.	Sir Jof. Vanneck,	141
Livermore St. Peter,	R.	Mr. Lee,	225
Livermore St. Peter and Paul,	R.	Mr. Lee,	234
Lound St. John Baptift,	R.	Sir Thomas Allen,	153
Loweftoft St. Margaret,	V.	Bifhop of Norwich,	153
Loudham,			112
Margaret (St.) Ipfwich,	C.	Mr. Fonnereau,	38
Margaret (St.) South Elmham,	R.	Mr. Adair,	156
Marlsford,		Mr. Williams,	105
Martlefham St. Mary,	R.	Mr. Gooding,	78
Mary (St.) at Elms, Ipfwich,	C	The Parifhioners,	39
Mary (St.) at Key, Ipfwich,	C.	The Parifhioners,	40
Mary (St.) at Stoke, Ipfwich,	R.	Dean and Ch. of Ely,	41
Mary (St.) at Tower, Ipfwich,	C.	The Parifhioners,	42
Matthew (St.) Ipfwich,	R.	The Crown,	43
Melford Holy Trinity,	R.	Lady Firebrace,	262
Mellis St. Mary,	R.	The Crown,	177
Mells,			141
Melton St. Andrew,	R.	Dean & Ch. of Ely,	113
Mendham All Saints,	V.	Mr. Whitaker,	168
Mendlefham St. Mary,	V	Mr. Chilton,	177
Metfield,		The Parifhioners,	169
Metingham All Saints,	V.	Mr. Hunt,	158
Michael (St.) South Elmham,	R.	Mr. Adair,	156
Mickfield St. Andrew,	R.	Mr. W. Ray,	207
Middleton,			141
Milding,	R.	Mr. Gurdon,	264
Mildenhall St. Mary,	V.	Sir Wm. Bunbury,	244
Monewden,		Mr. Lumpkin,	105
Monks-Illeigh,	R.	Archbp. of Canterbury,	264
Monk-Soham,		(see Soham-Monk)	
Moulton, } [R.&	V.	Chrift's Coll. Camb.	251
Mutford St. Andrew, w. Barnby,	V.	Caius Coll. Cambridge,	150
Nacton St. Martin,	R.	Lord Orwell,	78
Naughton,	R.	Mr. Stubbing,	274
Needham,			206
Newbourn St. Mary,	R	Mr. Weftern,	81
Nedging,	R.	Mr. Colman,	274
Nettleftead St. Mary,	R.	Mr. Leake,	206
Newton St. Mary,	V.	Mr. Unwin,	191

Patrons of the Parishes, &c.

Parishes.		Patrons.	Page.
Newton All Saints, ———	R.	St. Peter's Coll. Camb.—	91
Newmarket St. Mary, ———	R.	Marquis of Granby, Chapel to Newmarket	190
Newmarket All Saints, ———			
Nicholas, (St.) Ipswich, ———	C.	The Parishioners, ———	45
Nicholas S uth-Elmham, —-	R.	Mr. Adair, ———	156
Northcove St. Botolph, ———	R.	The Crown, ———	161
Northales St. Andrew, ———	V.	Sir Thomas Gooch, —	141
Norton St. Andrew, ———	R	St. Peter's Coll. Camb.	234
Nowton, ——— ———	R.	Sir Charles Davers,—	220
Oakley St. Nicholas, ———	R.	Earl Cornwallis, ———	178
Occold St. Michael, ———	R.	Mr. Malyn, ———	178
Offley St. Mary, ———	R.	Lord Abergavenny, —	81
Offton St. Mary, ——— —	R.	Mr. Leake, ———	208
Onehouse St John Baptist, —	R.	Dr. Pettyward, ———	191
Orford, (Chapel to Sudbourn)			123
Oulton St. Michael, ———	R	Mr. Vanhuythusen, —	154
Ousden. ——— —	R.	Mr. Moseley, ———	251
Pakefield All Saints, ———	R.	Mr. North, ———	150
Pakenham, ———	V.	Miss Discipline, ———	225
Palgrave St. Peter, ———	R.	Earl Cornwallis, ———	178
Parham St. Mary, ———	V.	Heirs of Mr. Corrance,	125
Peasenhall, (consol. to Sibton)			142
Peter, (St.) Ipswich, ———	C.	Mr. Fonnereau, ———	47
Peter, South Elmham, ———	R.	Mr. Adair, ———	156
Pettaugh St. Catherine, ———	R.	Earl of Dysart, ———	185
Pettistree St. Peter and Paul, —	V.	The Crown, ———	113
Playford St. Mary, ———	C.	Earl of Bristol, ———	81
Politead St. Mary, ——— —	R.	Mr. Alston, ———	265
Poslingford, ——— ———	V.	Mr. Golding,———	251
Preston St. Mary, ———	V.	Eman. Col. Camb. —	265
Ramsholt All Saints, ———	C.	Mr. Martin, ———	113
Rattlesden St. Nicholas, ———	R.	Mr. Moseley,———	220
Raydon St Marg. w. Southwold,	V.	Sir John Rous, ———	142
Raydon St. Mary, ———	R.	Mr. Lord, ———	67
Reed, ——— ———	R.	The Crown, ———	220
Redgrave St. Mary, w. Botesdale,	R.	Mr. Holt, ———	178
Redisham St. Peter, ———	C.	Consol. to Ringsfield,—	102
Redlingfield, —- ———	C.	Mr. Willis, ———	178
Rendham St Michael, ———	R.	Mr. Powel, ———	125
Rendlesham St. Gregory, ———	R.	The Crown, ——— —	105
Rickengale superior, St. Mary,	R.	Mr. Holt, ———	179
Rickengale inferior, St. Mary,	R.	Mr. Holt, ———	235
Ringsfield All Saints, ———	R.	Mr. Dawson, ———	162
Ringshall, ——— ———	R.	Mr. Peppen, ——— —	207
Risby St. Giles, ———	R	Mr. Hill, ——— ———	220
Rishangles St. Margaret's,——	R.	Lord Orwell,——— ———	179

Rougham

PATRONS of the Parishes, &c.

Parishes.		Patrons.	Page.
Rougham St. Mary,	R.	Sir Charles Davers,	226
Roydon,	C.	(Church down)	67
Rushbrook,	R	Sir Charles Davers,	227
Rushmere St. Andrew,	V.	Mr. Barnardiston's Heirs,	82
Rushmere St. Michael,	R	Mr. Garneys,	150
Rumburgh St. Michael,	C.	Mr. Elmy,	142
Sancroft St. George,	R.	Mr. Adair,	156
Sapeston St. Andrew,	V.	Duke of Grafton,	235
Satterly St. Margaret,	R.	Mr. Barnes,	162
Saxham,	R.	Mr Mure,	220
Saxham St. Nicholas,	R.	Mr. Crofts,	220
Suxmundham St. John Baptist,	R.	Mr. Long,	126
Saxtead All Saints,		Conf. to Framlingham,	169
Seamere All Saints,	R.	Mr. Cook,	274
Shadingfield St. John Baptist,	R.	Earl of Bristol, &c.	162
Shelland,	C	Mr. Ray,	191
Shelly Al' Saints,	C.	Mr. Samuel Rush,	67
Shimplingthorn St. George,	R.	Mr. Fiske,	266
Shipmeadow St. Bartholomew,	R.	Mr. Suckling,	162
Shotley St. Mary,	R.	Earl of Bristol,	67
Shottisham St. Margaret,	R.	Heirs of Mr. Kell,	114
Sibton St. Peter,	V.	Mr. Edgar,	142
Sizewell,			143
Snape St. John Baptist,	V.	Earl of Strafford,	126
Soham-Monks St Peter,	R.	Mr. Capper,	169
Soham-Earl St. Andrew,	R.	Mr Capper,	98
Somersham St. Mary,	R.	Mr. Heckford,	208
Somerliton St. Mary, with Heringfleet St. Margaret,	C.	Sir Thomas Allen,	154
Somerton,	R.	Lord Blundel,	266
Sotherton St. Andrew,	R.	Sir John Rous,	143
Southcove St. Laurence,	R.	The Crown,	144
South Park,			221
Southwold,			143
Southolt,			170
Spekfall St. Peter,	R.	The Crown,	144
Sproughton All Saints,	R.	Earl of Bristo',	67
Staningfield St. Nicholas,	R.	Sir Charles Davers,	
Stanstead St. James,	R.	Mr. Lloyd,	266
Stanton All Saints,	R.	Mr. Capel,	235
Stanton St. John,			235
Stansfield,	R.	The Crown,	252
Stephen (St.) Ipswich,	R.	Mr. Fonnereau,	49
Sternfield St. Mary Magdalen,	R.	Mr. North,	126
Stoke by Clare,	C.	Sir Harvey Elwes,	252
Stoke-Ash All Saints,	R.	Mr. Tyrrel,	170
Stoke-Nayland St. Mary,	V.	Sir Wm. Rowley,	266

332 PATRONS of the Parishes, &c.

Parishes.		Patrons.	Page.
Stonham-Aspal St. Mary,	R.	Mr. Middleton,	208
Stonham-Earl St. Mary,	R.	Pemb. Hall, Cambridge,	209
Stonham Little St. Mary,	R.	Mr. Alexander,	209
Stoven St. Margaret,	C.	Mr. Payne,	144
Stradbrook All Saints,	V.	Bishop of Ely,	170
Stradishall St. Margaret,	R.	Duke of Devonshire,	252
Stratford St. Mary,	R.	The Crown,	68
Stratford St. Andrew,	R.	The Crown,	127
Stow-Langtoft St. George,	R.	Mrs. Smith,	235
Stow St. Peter, } Stow St. Mary. }	V.	Mr. Aldrich,	192
Sturston,	R.	Earl Cornwallis,	180
Stutton St. Peter,	R.	Mr. Rustat,	68
Sudbourn All Sts. with Orford,	R.	The Crown,	127
Sudbury All Saints,	V.	Mr. Little,	267
Sudbury St. Greg. w. St. Peter,	C.	Mr. Sands,	267
Sutton All Saints,	V.	Sir John Rous,	114
Sweffling St. Mary,	R.	Mr. Dove,	127
Swilland St. Mary,	V.	The Crown,	209
Syleham,			169
Tannington St. Mary,	R.	Bishop of Rochester,	170
Tattingston St. Mary,	R.	Mr. Stebbing,	69
Theberton St. Peter,	R.	The Crown,	144
Thelnetham St. Nicholas,	R.	Mr. Tyrell,	236
Thetford,			244
Thorndon All Saints,	R.	Mr. Howe,	180
Thornham Great, } Thornham Little, }	R.	Heirs of Mr. Killigrew,	180 180
Thorp-Ixworth All Saints,	C.	Mr. Norton,	234
Thorp-Morieux,	R.	Mr. Fiske,	274
Thorp by Debenham,		Mr. Bridges,	185
Thorp in Blything,			145
Thorington St. Peter,	R.	Mrs. Bence,	144
Thrandiston,	R.	Earl Cornwallis,	180
Thurleston St. Mary,	V.	Bishop of Ely,	50
Thurlow Great,	R.	The Crown,	252
Thurlow Little,	R.	Mr. Soame,	252
Thwaite St. George,	R.	Mr. Williams,	181
Thurston St. Peter,	V.	Mr. Tyrel,	228
Timworth St. Andrew,	R.	Earl Cornwallis,	228
Tostock,	V.	Mr. Moseley,	228
Trimley St. Martin,	R.	Sir John Fytch Barker,	83
Trimley St. Mary,	R.	The Crown,	88
Troston St. Mary,	R.	The Crown,	236
Tuddenham St. Martin,	V.	Mr. Fonnereau,	88
Tuddenham St. Mary,	R.	Earl of Bristol,	245

Tunstal

Valuation of the Parishes in Suffolk.

Parishes.		Patrons.	Page.
Tunstal St. Michael, with Dunningworth,	R.	Mr. Jeffreson,	127
Ubbeston St Peter,	V.	Sir John Kemp,	145
Ufford St. Mary,	R.	Mr. Chapman,	114
Uggeshall St Mary,	R.	Sir John Rous,	146
Walderswick,		Sir John Blois,	146
Waldingfield St. Laurence,	R.	Clare Hall, Cambridge,	267
Waldingfield Little,	V.	Mrs. Syer,	268
Waldringfield All Saints,	R.	Mr. Barnardiston's Heirs,	88
Walsham le Willows,	C.	Mr. Hunt's Heirs,	236
Walpole St. Mary,	C.	Mrs. Forward,	146
Walton St. Mary,	V.	Mr. Atkinson,	88
Wangford St. Dennis,	R.	Mr. Holt,	245
Wangford St. Peter and Paul,	C.	Sir John Rous,	146
Wantesden St. John Baptist,	C.	Mr. Chapman,	127
Washbrook St. Mary,	R.	Consol. to Copdock,	69
Watfield,	R.	Jesus College, Camb.	275
Wattisfield St. Margaret,	R.	Mr. Settle,	236
Wattisham,	C.	King's College, Camb.	275
Welnetham,	R.	Sir Wm. Bunbury,	228
Welnetham St. Mary Magdalen,	R.	Sir Charles Davers,	229
Wenham St. John,	R.	Sir P. Parker's Heirs,	70
Wenham Little,	R.	Mr. Hingeston,	70
Wenhaston St. Peter,	C.	Mr. Sparrow,	146
Westhall St. Andrew,	V.	D. and Ch. of Norwich,	147
Westhorp St. Margaret,	R.	Mr. Reilley,	181
Westley St. Thomas Becket,	R.	Clare Hall, Cambridge,	221
Westleton St. Peter,	V.		147
Westerfield St. Mary Magdalen,	R.	Bishop of Ely,	51
Weston-Market St. Mary,	R.	Mr. Tyrel,	237
Weston-Coney St. Peter,	R.	The Crown,	231
Weston in Wangford,			162
Westow,	R.	Mr. Edwards,	237
Westwood-Lodge,			147
Wetherden,	R.	The Crown,	192
Wetheringsett All Saints, with Brockford,	R.	Mrs. Close,	181
Wethersdale St. Mary Magdalen,	R.	Consol. to Fressingfield,	170
Wethersfield St. Mary,	R.	Marquis of Granby,	253
Weybread St. Mary,	V.	Mr. Clubbe,	170
Whepstead,	R.	Mrs. Horrex,	221
Wherstead St Mary,	V.	The Crown,	70
Whitton St. Botolph,	R.	Bishop of Ely,	51
Whixoe,	R.	Mr. Berkley,	252
Wickham-Market All Saints,	V.	The Crown,	116
Wickham-Skeith St. Andrew,	V.	Sir Armine Woodhouse,	182

Wickham-

PATRONS of the Parishes, &c.

Parishes.		Patrons.	Page.
Wickham-Brook All Saints,	V.	The Crown, ———	253
Wilby St. Mary, ———	R.	Earl of Rochford, ———	171
Willingham All Saints, ———	R.	(See Ellough)	161
Willingham St. Mary and St. P.	R.	The Crown, ———	162
Willisham St. Mary, ———	C.	Mr Leak, ———	210
Wingfield St. Andrew, ———	C.	Bishop of Norwich, —	171
Winston St. Andrew, — —	V.	D. and Chapter of Ely,	185
Wisset St. Andrew, ———	C.		147
Wissington St. Mary, ———	V.	The Crown, ———	268
Witneiham St. Mary, — —	R.	St. Peter's Coll. Camb.	93
Wiverstone, ———	R	Dr. Ewer, Bp of Landaff,	182
Woodbridge St. Mary, — —	C	Mr. Carthew, ———	106
Woolpit St. Mary, ———	R.	Mr. Chapman, ———	229
Woolverston St. Mary, — —	R.	Heirs of Mr. Tyson, —	70
Wordwell, —	R.	Earl of Bristol, ———	237
Worlingham All Saints, ———	R	The Crown, ———	162
Worlington, — —	R.	Mr. Montgomerie, ———	245
Worlingworth St. Mary, with ⎱ Southolt St Margaret, — ⎰	V.	Mr. Ransom, ———	171
Wortham Estgate St. Mary, ⎱ Wortham Everard, ——— ⎰	R R.	Mr. Holt, ——— Mr. Holt, ———	182
Wratting Great, ——— — —	R.	Mr. Chevalier, ———	253
Wratting Little, — —	R.	Mr Syer, ——— —	253
Wrentham St. Nicholas, ———	R.	Mr. Brewster, ———	148
Yaxley St. Mary, ———	R.	Dr. Thruston, ———	183
Yoxford St. Peter, ———	V.	Sir John Rous, ———	148

BEFORE the Counties of *Suffolk* and *Norfolk* had each of them a separate Sheriff of their own, the Usage was for the Crown to appoint a Sheriff, one Year out of the Gentlemen of *Suffolk*, and the next, out of the Gentlemen of *Norfolk*; and so on alternately, as the Custom still is in the neighbouring Counties of *Cambridge* and *Huntingdon*. This appears from the following List, and therefore we begin it before the Separation of the two Counties.

HIGH SHERIFFS of Suffolk and Norfolk.

Reign.	Year.	SHERIFFS.
1 Eliz.	1559	Sir Ambrose Jermin, of Rushbrook, Knight.
	1560	Jo. Appleyard, Esq;
	1561	Sir Robert Wingfield, of Letheringham, Knt.
	1562	Sir Thomas Tindall, Knt.
	1563	Sir William Butts, of Redgrave, Knt.

Sir

High Sheriffs of Suffolk and Norfolk.

Reign.	Year.	Sheriffs.
6 Eliz.	1564	Sir Thomas Woodhouse, Knt.
	1565	Sir Owen Hopton, of Yoxforth, Knt.
	1566	Wm. Paston, Esq;
	1567	Lionel Talmach, of Helmingham, Esq;
	1568	Edward Cleere, Esq;
	1569	William Walgrave, of Smalbridge, Esq;
	1570	Sir Christopher Heydon, Knt.
	1571	Edmund Wethypol, of Ipswich, Esq;
	1572	Radolph Shelton, Esq;
	1573	Sir Ambrose Jermin, of Rushbrook, Knt.
	1574	Henry Doyly, Esq;
	1575	Thomas Felton, of Playford, Esq;

Sheriffs of Suffolk singly.

18 Eliz.	1576	Robert Ashfield, of Stowlangtoft, Esq;
	1577	John Higham, of Barow, Esq;
	1578	Sir William Spring, of Pakenham, Knt.
	1579	Sir Robert Jermin, of Rushbrook, Knt.
	1580	Sir Philip Parker, of Arwerton, Knt.
	1581	Sir Thomas Barnardiston, of Kedington, Knt.
	1582	Sir Nicholas Bacon, of Redgrave, Knt.
	1583	Sir William Drurye, of Halsted, Knt.
	1584	Sir Charles Framlingham, of Debenham, Knt,
	1585	John Gurdon, of Assington, Esq;
	1586	George Colt, of Candish, Esq;
	1587	Wm. Clopton, of Kentwell in Long-Melford, Esq;
	1588	Francis Jermye, of Brightwell, Esq;
	1589	Philip Tilney, of Shelly, Esq;
	1590	Sir Wm. Waldegrave, of Smallbridge, Knt.
	1591	Thomas Rowse, of Henham, Esq;
	1592	Nicob. Garnish, of Kenton, Esq;
	1593	Lionell Tallemach, of Helmingham, Esq;
	1594	Robert Ford, of Butley, Esq;
	1595	Thomas Crofts, of Saxham, Esq;
	1596	Sir William Spring, of Pakenham, Knt.
	1597	Thomas Edon, of Sudbury, Esq;
	1598	Sir Anthony Wingfield, of Letheringham, Knt.
	1599	Henry Warner, of Mildenhall, Esq;
	1600	Anthony Felton, of Playford, Esq;
	1601	Edward Bacon, of Bergham, Esq;
	1602	Sir Edmund Wethipoll, of Ipswich, Knt.
	1603	Thomas Estotevill, of Dalham, Esq;
James.	1604	Sir Nicholas Bacon, of Redgrave, Knt.
	1605	Edmund Bokenham, of Great Thornham, Esq;
	1606	Sir Thomas Playters, of Soterly, Knt.
	1607	Anthony Penning, of Ipswich, Esq;
	1608	Jo. Wentworth, of Somerlyton, Esq;

Lionel

336 HIGH SHERIFFS of Suffolk and Norfolk.

Reign	Year	SHERIFFS
James.	1609	Lionel Talmach, of Helmingham, Esq;
	1610	Sir Thomas Wingfield, of Letheringham, Knt. / Sir George Le Hunt, of Bredfield, Knt.
	1611	Thomas Tilney, of Shelly, Esq;
	1612	Sir Calthrop Parker, of Arwerton, Knt.
	1613	Sir Martin Eltoteville, of Dalham, Knt.
	1614	Sir Robert Brook, of Yoxforth, Knt.
	1615	Sir Rob. Barker, of Trimley, Knt. of the Bath.
	1616	Thomas Clench, of Holbrook, Esq;
	1617	Sir Lio. Talmach, of Helmingham, Knt. and Bart.
	1618	Sir Edward Lewknor, of Denham, Knt. / Sir Charles Gawdy, of Debenham, Knt.
	1619	Jo. Wentworth, of Somerlyton.
	1620	Sir Henry North, of Wickham-Brook, Knt.
	1621	Sir William Spring, of Pakenham, Knt.
	1622	William Whettel, of Ampton, Esq;
	1623	Robert Brook, of Nacton, Esq;
	1624	Sir Nath. Barnardiston, of Kediton, Knt.
	1625	Galfridus Pitman, of Woodbridge, Esq;
Charles	1626	Samuel Aylmer, of Akenham, Esq;
	1627	Sir John Prescot, of Hoxon, Knt.
	1628	Mauritius Barrow, of Bermingham, Esq;
	1629	Brampton Gourdon, of Affington, Esq;
	1630	Sir Henry Buckenham, of Thornham, Knt.
	1631	John Acton, of Bramford, Esq;
	1632	Sir Robert Crane, of Chilton, Knt. and Bart.
	1633	Sir William Soame, of Thirlow, Knt.
	1634	Sir Edmund Bacon, of Redgrave, Knt. and Bart.
	1635	Sir John Barker, of Trimly, Bart.
	1636	Sir John Rous, of Henham, Knt.
	1637	Sir Philip Parker, of Arwerton, Knt.
	1638	Sir Ant. Wingfield, of Letheringham, Bart. and / Edward Duke, of Benhall, Esq;
	1639	John Clenche, of Creeting, Esq;
	1640	Sir Simons Dewes, of Stowlangtoft, Knt.
	1641	Sir William Spring, of Pakenham, Knt.
	1642	Sir Wm. Castleton of Bury, Knt. and Bart.]
	1643	Maurice Barrow, of Bermingham, Esq;
	1644	Jo. Cotton, of Earl-Soham, Esq;
	1645	Sir Arthur Jenney, of Knodishall, Knt.
	1646	Thomas Bloss, of Belstead, Esq;
	1647	Thomas Kerridge, of Shelley, Esq;
	1648	Robert Wright, of Wangford, Esq;
———	1649	Sir Wm. Wiseman Bokenham, of Thornham, Knt.
	1650	Sir William Hervey, of Hengrave, Knt.
	1651	Edward Clarke, of East Bergholt, Esq;
	1652	Sir Robert Coke, of Huntingfield, Knt. / Edward Wennieve, of Bretenham, Esq;

Robert

High Sheriffs of Suffolk.

Reign.	Year.	Sheriffs.
	1653	Robert Cordel, of Long-Melford, Esq;
	1654	Sir John Barker, of Trimley, Bart.
	1655	Martin Salter, of Battisford, Esq;
	1656	James Calthrop, of Ampton, Esq;
	1657	Thomas Baker, of Fressingfield, Esq;
	1658	John Wyard, of Brundish.
	1659	The same.
Cha. II.	1660	Sir John Castleton, of Bury, Bart.
	1661	Renold Williams, of Stoke, Esq;
	1662	Joseph Brand, of Edwardston, Esq;
	1663	Francis Thebald, of Barking, Esq;
	1664	
	1665	John Bence, of Ringsfield, Esq;
	1666	Sir Edmund Bacon, of Redgrave, Bart.
	1667	Jeffery Howland, of Covehithe, Esq;
	1668	Samuel Blackaby, of Stowmarket, Esq;
	1669	Sir Robert Diver, of Ipswich, Bart.
	1670	John Clarke, of Bury, Esq;
	1672	John Risby, of Thorp-Morieux, Esq;
	1673	William Soame, of Haly, Esq;

It was *very lately*, and *by Accident*, that we were favour'd with a Copy of the foregoing List. We wish this Chasm could be filled up, but that could not be done without searching the publick Offices in London; and such a Search would greatly delay the Publication of the Book; which, we fear, our Subscribers think, has been already in hand too long. It is, therefore, thought proper to give the List imperfect as it is, altho' the best Information we can procure here in the Country, reaches no further back than the Year 1724.

Geo. I.	1724	Gregory Coppinger, Esq;
	1725	Hustings Wilkinson, Esq;
	1726	Thomas Driver, of Earl-Stonham, Esq;
	1727	Robert Goodrich, Esq;
Geo. II.	1728	Sir John Playter, of Satterley, Bart.
	1729	Tobias Bloss, of Belsted, Esq;
	1730	Sir Thomas Allen, of Somerliton, Bart.
	1731	Nath. Acton, of Hemingston, Esq;
	1732	George Dashwood, Esq;
	1733	Alexander Bence, of Thorington, Esq;
	1734	John Eldred, Esq;
	1735	John Reynolds, Esq;
	1736	John Corrance, of Rougham, Esq;
	1737	Reginald Rabbit, of Bramfield, Esq;
	1738	Sir William Barker, of Ipswich, Bart.
	1739	William Acton, of Bramford, Esq;
	1740	Edmund Jenney, of Bredfield, Esq;
	1741	Samuel Lucas, of Chelmondiston, Esq;

High Sheriffs of Suffolk.

Reign	Year	Sheriffs
Geo. II.	1742	Baron Prettyman, of Bacton, Esq;
	1743	Sir John Barker, of Sproughton, Bart.
	1744	Robert Leman, of Wickham-Market, Esq;
	1745	Charles Scrivener, of Sibton, Esq;
	1746	Philips Colman, of Ipswich, Esq;
	1747	Robert Edgar, of Ipswich, Esq;
	1748	Lamb Barry, of Syleham, Esq;
	1749	Thomas White, of Tattingston, Esq;
	1750	Robert Oneby, of Loudham, Esq;
	1751	George Gooday, of Fornham, Esq;
	1752	William Naunton, of Letheringham, Esq;
	1753	Robert Sparrow, of Brandiston, Esq;
	1754	William Jennings, of Acton, Esq;
	1755	Cooke Freeston, of Metingham, Esq;
	1756	John Canham, of Milden, Esq;
	1757	Henry Moore, of Melford, Esq;
	1758	Robert May, of Sutton, Esq;
	1759	Sir John Rous, of Henham, Bart.
	1760	Thomas Thorowgood, of Kersey, Esq;
Geo. III	1761	Thomas Mosely, of Ousden, Esq;
	1762	Shadrach Brice, of Clare.
	1763	Ezekiel Sparke, of Walsham in the Willows,
	1764	Sir John Blois, of Yoxford, Bart.

INDEX to find the HUNDREDS.

	Page.		Page.
Babergh,	254	Lothing,	150
Blackbourn,	230	Mutford,	149
Blithing,	128	Plomesgate,	118
Bosmere and Claydon,	199	Risbridge,	246
Carlford and Colneis,	72	Samford,	61
Cosford,	269	Stow,	186
Hartismere,	172	Thedwastre,	222
Hoxne,	164	Thingoe,	211
Ipswich,	7	Thredling,	184
Lackford,	238	Wangford,	155
Loes,	95	Willford,	109

INDEX to find the ROADS.

Page,

The great Road from Stratford upon Stour, through Ipswich, Woodbridge, Wickham Market, Saxmundham, Yoxford and Beccles, to Yarmouth in Norfolk, *See Plate* 1.— 61

The great Road from Beccles, thro' Bungay, Harleston, Scole, Botesdale, Ixworth and Bury, to Newmarket. *See Plate* 2. 155

The great Road from Ipswich through Needham, Stowmarket and Bury, to Thetford, and from Thetford to Newmarket. *See Plate* 3. 199

The great Road from Ipswich to Scole, and from Bury St. Edmund's through Melford, Sudbury, Boxford and Hadleigh, to Ipswich. *See Plate* 4. 211

The CROSS-ROADS.

From Ipswich to Catawade Bridge,	276
Ipswich to Shotley-Ferry,	276
Ipswich to Langer-Fort and Felixstow,	277
Ipswich to Debenham,	277
Ipswich to Bildeston,	277
Woodbridge to Baudsey-Ferry,	278
Woodbridge to Orford,	278
Woodbridge to Aldborough,	279
Woodbridge to Blithborough, by Snape Bridge,	280
Wickham-Market to Eye,	280
Wickham-Market to Needham-Market,	281
Wickham-Market to Harleston,	282

From

Index to the Cross-Roads.

	Page.
From Wickham-Market to Aldborough,	283
Yoxford to Halesworth,	283
Halesworth to Bungay,	284
Halesworth to Southwold,	284
Halesworth to Lowestoft,	284
Halesworth to Beccles,	285
Halesworth to Harleston,	285
Stowmarket to Botesdale,	286
Stowmarket to Ixworth and Thetford,	286
Stowmarket to Bildeston and Hadleigh,	287
Hadleigh to Stratford,	288
Bury to Gastrop-Gate,	288
Bury to Brandon,	289
Bury to Mildenhall,	290
Bury to Finningham,	290
Bury to Clare,	291
Bury to Lavenham,	292
Lavenham to Sudbury,	292
Sudbury to Haverhill,	292
Sudbury to Stratford-Swan,	293
Lavenham to Bildeston,	294
Newmarket to Sudbury,	295
Thetford to Brandon and Mildenhall,	295
Thetford to Gastrop-Gate,	296

The Reader is desired to correct the following Errors.

Page 5, Line 28, for *Edward* r. *Henry*. P. 11, l. 12, for *Walk* r *Wa'l*. P. 17. Read the latter Part of the first Paragraph thus; *Duties and Imposts*. *many of which there were: Under the Norman Kings, these Officers*, &c. P. 32, in the Note, for 40 *l*. r. 40 *Shillings*. P. 35, l. 12. r. instituted into *as* a Rectory. P. 50, l. 19, for *as* r. *if*. P. 65, l. 18, for *Hall, House*, r. *Hall-House*. P. 91, l. sixth from the Bottom, for *certainly* r. *commonly*. P. 227, l. 1 and last, and elsewhere, for *Robert* Davers, r. *Charles* Davers. P. 243, after Freckingham, insert, *or* FREKENHAM. P. 336, in the Running-Title, dele *and Norfolk*. P. 324, r. Broomswell, p. 112, and Broom, p. 173. P. 337, Hadleigh, r. p. 271. P. 330, Newton, r. p. 264. And P. 317 & 330, for *Offley*, r. *Ottley*.

F I N I S.

www.ingramcontent.com/pod-product-compliance
Lightning Source LLC
Chambersburg PA
CBHW020318240426
43673CB00039B/847